EASTERN EUROPE SINCE 1945

THIRD EDITION

Geoffrey Swain

and

Nigel Swain

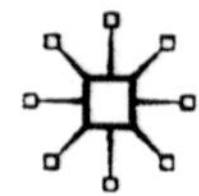

First edition published 1993
Second edition published 1998
Third edition published 2003 by
PALGRAVE MACMILLAN
Houndmills, Basingstoke, Hampshire RG21 6XS and
175 Fifth Avenue, New York, N.Y. 10010
Companies and representatives throughout the world

PALGRAVE MACMILLAN is the global academic imprint of the Palgrave Macmillan division of St. Martin's Press, LLC and of Palgrave Macmillan Ltd. Macmillan® is a registered trademark in the United States, United Kingdom and other countries. Palgrave is a registered trademark in the European Union and other countries.

ISBN-10: 1–4039–0304–2 hardback
ISBN-10: 1–4039–0417–0 paperback
ISBN-13: 978-1-4039-0304-4 hardback
ISBN-13: 978-1-4039-0417-1 paperback

This book is printed on paper suitable for recycling and made from fully managed and sustained forest sources. Logging, pulping and manufacturing processes are expected to conform to the environmental regulations of the country of origin.

A catalogue record for this book is available from the British Library.

Library of Congress Cataloging-in-Publication Data
Swain, Geoff.
Eastern Europe since 1945 / Geoffrey Swain and Nigel Swain.–3rd ed.
p. cm.–(Making of the modern world)
Includes bibliographical references and index.
ISBN 1–4039–0417–0 (pbk.)
1. Communism–Europe, Eastern–History. 2. Europe, Eastern–Politics and government–1945–1989. I. Swain, N. (Nigel) II. Title. III. Series.

HX240.7.A6S93 2003
335.43'0947–dc21 2003041021

Printed and bound in Great Britain by Biddles Ltd., King's Lynn, Norfolk

To our parents

I believed in communism. For me, communism was freedom. That was my mistake. Absolute freedom doesn't exist, especially not in communism, but if I hadn't believed this I wouldn't have become a communist. Of course the quest for such freedom leads to revolution, violence, overthrowing the ruling classes, the long transformation of society by education. But I was convinced that in the end this process was moving towards more and more freedom, no end to this freedom.

Milovan Djilas, January 1992

Contents

List of Tables

CHRONOLOGY

1 April 1939	Final defeat of the Republican Government during the Spanish Civil War.
23 August 1939	Nazi–Soviet Pact: East European Communist Parties adopt new revolutionary programme.
3 September 1939	Start of Second World War.
22 June 1941	Nazis invade Soviet Union: Balkan Communist Parties start insurrections.
May 1943	Dissolution of the Comintern.
June 1944	British Government recognises Tito's Communist government.
July 1944	Red Army crosses into Poland: National Liberation Committee established.
23 August 1944	King Michael's coup in Romania: formation of coalition government.
end August 1944	Stalin's decision to support Bulgarian insurrection.
5 September 1944	Soviet Union declares war on Bulgaria.
9 September 1944	Communist coup in Bulgaria.
1 October 1944	Red Army crosses into Hungary.
November 1944	Start of civil war in Poland lasting until summer 1945.
December 1944	British suppress communist insurrection in Greece.
5 January 1945	Stalin recognises Communist government in Poland.
February 1945	Yalta Conference: decision to form National Unity Government in Poland.
end February 1945	Stalin supports Communist coup in Romania.
March 1945	Stalin shelves plans for Balkan Federation after Allied protests.

April 1945	Liberation of Czechoslovakia.
8 May 1945	End of Second World War.
August 1945	Potsdam Conference: agreement on conditions for signing peace treaties with Hungary, Bulgaria and Romania.
4 November 1945	Hungarian elections.
11 November 1945	Yugoslav elections.
18 November 1945	Bulgarian elections (boycotted by opposition candidates).
2 December 1945	Albanian elections.
26 May 1946	Elections in Czechoslovakia.
30 June 1946	Polish referendum.
27 October 1946	Bulgarian elections in which opposition takes part.
19 November 1946	Romanian elections.
19 January 1947	Polish elections.
February 1947	Truman doctrine; American commitment to anti-communist cause in Greece.
March 1947	Stalin's support for Yugoslavia's role in Greece.
May 1947	Communists excluded from government in France and Italy.
June 1947	Marshall Plan announced.
10 July 1947	Stalin instructs Czechoslovak government to reject Marshall Aid.
30 August 1947	Hungarian elections.
end September 1947	Foundation of Cominform.
27 November 1947	New revolutionary stance adopted by Czechoslovak communists.
December 1947	Diplomatic offensive launched by Yugoslavia. Increased aid for Greek communists.
end February 1948	Communist coup in Czechoslovakia. Start of Stalin–Tito dispute.
1 March 1948	Yugoslavs decide to resist Stalin's demand that they join a Balkan Federation dominated by Bulgaria and Albania.
July 1948	Yugoslavia expelled from the Cominform. Cominform countries adopt 'soviet' model of industrial planning and collectivised agriculture.

May 1949	Trial of Koçi Xoxe.
September 1949	Trial of László Rajk.
November 1949	Cominform denounces Yugoslav regime: diplomatic relations broken off.
December 1949	Trial of Traicho Kostov.
June 1950	Yugoslavs establish workers' self-management.
November 1952	Trial of Rudolf Slánský. Yugoslav Communist Party renamed League of Communists.
6 March 1953	Death of Stalin.
15 June 1953	Restoration of diplomatic relations between Soviet Union and Yugoslavia.
end June 1953	Brioni plenum of Yugoslav Party ends reform programme. New Hungarian Prime Minister Imre Nagy introduces 'new course'.
16 January 1954	Milovan Djilas disciplined for writing that the Leninist Party was obsolete.
23 October 1954	Patriotic People's Front founded in Hungary.
February 1955	Khrushchev replaces Malenkov in Soviet Union.
March 1955	Nagy deposed in Hungary.
26 May 1955	Khrushchev's rapprochement with Tito: interstate relations restored.
February 1956	Khrushchev denounces Stalin at XXth Party Congress.
April 1956	New leadership in Poland and other East European states.
18 April 1956	Cominform abolished.
20 June 1955	Khrushchev's rapprochement with Tito: party relations restored.
end June 1956	Riots in Poznan.
18 July 1956	Rákosi dismissed at Soviet request. Poles cautioned not to relax discipline.
19 September 1956	Start of over three weeks of talks between Khrushchev and Tito.
19 October 1956	Polish Party Plenum restores Gomulka to leadership: mobilised working class frustrates plans for Soviet armed intervention.

23 October 1956	Demonstrations mark start of Hungarian revolution.
24 October 1956	Soviet troops intervene in Hungary.
30 October 1956	Nagy forms multiparty government: the next day opens talks seeking the withdrawal of Hungary from the Warsaw Pact.
2 November 1956	Khrushchev and Tito agree to intervene in Hungary.
4 November 1956	Soviet intervention resumes.
15 November 1956	Soviet–Polish agreement on the stationing of Soviet troops in Poland.
November 1957	Conference of Ruling Communist Parties fails to restore unity to communist movement.
April 1958	Yugoslav League of Communists adopts a programme asserting its unique road to socialism.
May 1958	Meeting of the Political Consultative Committee of the Warsaw Pact Announcement that Soviet troops will withdraw from Romania.
Late 1958	Renewed collectivisation drive.
January 1959	XXIst Congress of the Soviet Party.
April 1961	Soviet Union cancels aid to Albania.
13 August 1961	Building of Berlin Wall.
October 1961	XXIInd Congress of the Soviet Party. Second de-Stalinisation campaign. Beginnings of Sino-Soviet split. New emphasis on economic development and catching up with the West.
August 1962	Kádár: 'Those who are not against us are with us' in Hungary.
Early 1963	'Revolt of the intellectuals' in Czechoslovakia.
July 1963	Plans for a greater degree of Comecon integration abandoned because of Romanian opposition.
September 1963	GDR decides to implement the New Economic System throughout the economy.
July 1964	Hungarian Central Committee accepts the principles of the New Economic Mechanism.

October 1964	Khrushchev replaced by Brezhnev.
July 1965	Yugoslavia's second economic reform.
July 1966	Reformists secure the dismissal of Ranković in Yugoslavia.
March 1968	Student demonstrations in Poland.
January 1968	Dubček replaces Novotný as Czechoslovak Party leader.
June 1968	Student demonstrations in Yugoslavia.
20–1 August 1968	Soviet invasion of Czechoslovakia.
1970–1	Croat nationalist unrest in Yugoslavia.
December 1970	Price increases in Poland lead to 'Baltic Crisis'.
May 1971	Honecker replaces Ulbricht in GDR.
September 1971	Four Power Agreement on Berlin.
November 1972	Measures partially recentralising the economy approved by Central Committee in Hungary.
December 1972	Basic Treaty between GDR and German Federal Republic.
August 1975	Helsinki Final Act.
June 1976	Price increases in Poland result in strikes and demonstrations.
September 1976	Foundation in Poland of the Committee for the Defence of Workers (KOR).
January 1977	Foundation of Charter 77 in Czechoslovakia.
July 1978	China suspends foreign aid to Albania.
July 1980	Price increases in Poland.
August 1980	Solidarity free trade union founded in Poland.
13 December 1980	Martial law declared in Poland.
March–April 1981	Ethnic disturbances in Kosovo.
1982	Debt crisis in Yugoslavia. 'Small business reform' in Hungary.
July 1983	Martial law lifted in Poland.
March 1985	Gorbachev becomes General Secretary of Central Committee of CPSU.
October 1987	Slobodan Milošević becomes leader of Serbian League of Communists.
August 1988	Polish government decides to negotiate with Solidarity.
June 1989	Elections in Poland. Solidarity wins vast majority of seats available to it.

August 1989	Solidarity-led government formed in Poland.
September 1989	Hungary allows GDR citizens to emigrate via Austria. Government and Opposition Round Table Talks concluded.
9 November 1989	Berlin Wall breached.
November 1989	Demonstrations in Prague. Zhivkov resigns in Bulgaria.
December 1989	Government of National Understanding formed in Czechoslovakia.
21 December 1989	Ceausescu rally disrupted. Fighting between demonstrators and security police.
25 December 1989	Nicolae and Elena Ceausescu executed.
January 1990	Poland implements Balcerowicz 'shock therapy' programme.
March–April 1990	Elections in Hungary. Right-of-centre coalition government led by Hungarian Democratic Forum.
April 1990	Elections in Slovenia (won by DEMOS coalition).
April–May 1990	Elections in Croatia (won by nationalistic Croatian Democratic Union).
May 1990	Elections in Romania (won by National Salvation Front which is dominated by former communists).
June 1990	Elections in Czechoslovakia (won by Civic Forum and Public Against Violence). Elections in Bulgaria (won by the former communist party). Miners break up opposition demonstration in Romania.
1 July 1990	German currency union.
3 October 1990	Germany reunified.
November–December 1990	Presidential elections in Poland (Wałęsa elected). Communist-led government in Bulgaria resigns following strike wave. Elections in Macedonia, Bosnia-Hercegovina, Serbia and Montenegro. Former communists win in Serbia and Montenegro. Weak

	coalition government in Bosnia and Hercegovina. Nationalist coalition in Macedonia.
December 1990–January 1991	Anti-government demonstrations in Albania.
April 1991	Elections in Albania (won by former communists).
June 1991	Albanian communist-led government resigns after strike wave.
28 June 1991	Comecon formally dissolved.
1 July 1991	Warsaw Pact formally dissolved.
June–July 1991	Slovenia established *de facto* independence after brief hostilities. Relations between Croatia and Serbia degenerate to fighting. UN imposes peace of sorts.
September 1991	Romanian government resigns after demonstrations led by miners. Broad-based interim government formed.
October 1991	Elections in Poland (no clear winner). Elections in Bulgaria (won by Union of Democratic Forces with small majority).
December 1991	Albanian Democratic Party withdraws support from coalition government.
26 December 1991	Soviet Union formally dissolved, following Gorbachev's resignation on Christmas Day.
15 January 1992	The European Community recognises the independence of Slovenia and Croatia and hence the break-up of Yugoslavia.
March 1992	Bosnian War starts. Elections in Albania bring Democratic Party to power. Romanian elections give victory to anti-reform President Iliescu.
June 1992	Elections in Czechoslovakia result in decision to dissolve state into Czech Republic and Slovakia.
October 1992	Fall of UDF government in Bulgaria.
May 1993	Former communists and allies return to power in Poland.

March 1994	Prime Minister Mečiar temporarily loses power in Slovakia, returns to power in December after October elections.
May 1994	Former communists return to power in Hungary.
September 1994	Socialists return to power in Bulgaria.
November 1995	Walesa replaced as Polish president by former communist.
	Dayton Accord ends the Bosnian War.
June 1996	Conservative government in Czechoslovakia loses overall majority, banking crisis follows. Disputed election in Albania returns Democratic party to power.
November 1996	Reformists win Romanian elections.
December 1996	Widespread demonstrations in Serbia against President Milošević.
Spring 1997	Collapse of socialist government in Bulgaria and return of the UDF to power.
	Albania descends into anarchy after pyramid selling crisis, foreign troops restore order.
May 1997	Demonstrations in Slovakia after collapse of presidential referendum.
June 1997	Czech Republic faces financial crisis.
	Socialists win Albanian election.
September 1997	Former communists lose power in Polish elections.
October 1997	Anti-Milošević candidate wins Montenegrin presidential elections.
December 1997	High Representative in Bosnia and Hercegovina empowered to overrule local politicians and promulgate decrees.
November 1998	Klaus's government falls in Czech Republic. Replaced by interim government headed by governor of National Bank.
March 1998	'Elections' to Kosovo shadow government.
	Serbian police launch operation to destroy Kosovo Liberation Army.
May 1998	Hungarian former communists lose elections to coalition of right wing FIDESZ and Smallholders' parties.

June 1998	Inconclusive elections in Czech Republic. Social Democrats form minority government.
September 1998	Mečiar's party loses parliamentary elections in Slovakia. Replaced by coalition of Right, Left and Hungarian minority parties.
November 1998	Nationalist parties win Macedonian elections.
March 1999	Czech Republic, Hungary and Poland join NATO. NATO bombing of Yugoslavia begins. Mass expulsion of Albanians from Kosovo.
June 1999	NATO Kosovo campaign ends. Return of Albanians to Kosovo. Non-Albanians begin to flee.
December 1999	Death of Franjo Tudjman in Croatia. European Union changes policy on enlargement, opening way for Slovakia to join Czech Republic, Hungary, Poland, Slovenia and Estonia on course for membership in 2004.
March 2000	Croats in Bosnia and Hercegovina announce a short-lived 'third entity', the Croatian National Council, which withers because of support from Croatia.
October 2000	Milošević concedes defeat after demonstrations and general strike. Koštunica appointed president of Yugoslavia (Serbia and Montenegro) Polish presidential elections. Former communist Kwaśniecki re-elected, Wałęsa receives just over one per cent of vote.
November 2000	Illiescu's party wins Romanian parliamentary elections. Nevertheless governs in cooperation with ethnic Hungarian party.
December 2000	Illiescu wins Romanian presidential elections.
February 2001	Ethnic Albanian insurgency begins in Macedonia
June 2001	Socialists win absolute majority in Albanian elections.

	Party of former King Simeon II wins Bulgarian elections.
August 2001	Ohrid agreement ends ethnic Albanian insurgency in Macedonia
September 2001	Victory for former communists in Polish parliamentary elections.
November 2001	Socialist wins Bulgarian presidential elections.
March 2002	EU-sponsored deal for a new, looser federation, 'Serbia and Montenegro', to replace Yugoslavia agreed but not ratified.
April 2002	Former communists and liberal allies win Hungarian elections.
June 2002	Social Democrats re-elected in Czech Republic. Compromise candidate, Alfred Moisiu, wins Albanian presidential elections.
September 2002	Former communists win Macedonian elections. Radical ethnic Albanian party also does well. Centre–Right coalition beats Mečiar in Slovak elections.

Introduction

BACKGROUND AND SUMMARY

What do the countries of Eastern Europe have in common for them to be the subject of a composite history of this type? The land mass given that name comprises Poland, Czechoslovakia, Hungary, Romania, Albania, Yugoslavia and Bulgaria – and at certain times East Germany as well – some seven or eight countries each with very different cultural traditions and backgrounds. Yet, throughout this century, historians have consistently written about them as a single unit, as if they did, after all, have a great deal in common. Why?

There was a certain logic to treating Eastern Europe as a whole in the interwar period. From 1919 to 1939, these were the 'successor states': Poland, Czechoslovakia, Hungary, Romania, Albania, Yugoslavia and Bulgaria were the nation states carved out of the wreckage of the German, Russian, Austrian and Turkish empires. While for some of these states formal political independence had come before 1919, in the years leading up to the outbreak of the Second World War, all the 'successor states', despite their manifest differences, faced similar social, economic and political problems.

The only 'successor state' to have anything like a developed industrial base was Czechoslovakia, and there most of this wealth was concentrated in the Czech lands rather than in Slovakia. The Slovaks were predominantly a peasant people, and the same could be said for the Poles, Hungarians, Romanians, Albanians, Yugoslavs and Bulgarians as well. Peasants formed 80 per cent of the population in Bulgaria, 78 per cent of the population in Romania, 75 per cent of the population in Yugoslavia, 63 per cent of the population in Poland and 55 per cent of the population in Hungary. To quote Robin Okey: 'peasant Eastern Europe was a hopelessly under-capitalised, over-populated bottom-rung of the European economy'.[1]

The industrial development which did occur in interwar Eastern Europe was largely the product of foreign investment. While in the 1920s such investment tended to come from Britain and France, in the 1930s it was more likely to have come from Germany. Wherever it came from, however, it was from abroad: in Poland 60 per cent of capital was foreign owned; in Hungary 50 per cent of capital was foreign owned; and in the Balkans between 50 and 70 per cent of the economy was foreign financed. And, as Hugh Seton-Watson noted, most foreign capital was invested in Hungary, the least egalitarian of East European societies; least foreign capital was invested in Bulgaria, the most egalitarian of the countries.[2]

This link between social inequality and the failure to resolve economic problems was a product of the political system that dominated Eastern Europe in the interwar period. These were peasant societies that were crying out for land reform and economic investment. Despite being universally promised in 1919, progress on implementing land reform remained stalled throughout the region; it remained stalled because the democratic regimes that made the dramatic promises of reform in 1919 soon found themselves replaced by right-wing dictatorships. Only in Czechoslovakia did multiparty democracy become established in the Westminster sense, and only in Czechoslovakia did the land reform make steady progress; in Bulgaria it was the successful implementation of land reform which prompted the 1923 counter-revolutionary coup against the democratically elected government, a parallel that would be followed throughout the region until, by the early 1930s, the whole of Eastern Europe barring Czechoslovakia was ruled by dictatorships of one kind or another.

Such a combination of circumstances was bound to provide a good breeding ground for communism among East European intellectuals. The region was backward, prey to the whims of foreign capitalists when it came to investment decisions, and ruled by self-interested cliques: what Lenin's followers seemed to be achieving in peasant Russia in the interwar years, spectacular economic growth on the basis of peasant cooperative farms, was bound to be attractive. A generation of young people grew up in interwar Eastern Europe convinced that Lenin's message had meaning for them.

This shared Leninist ideology was what enabled historians to consider the varied states of Eastern Europe as a composite whole after the Second World War. The logic for treating the countries of Eastern Europe as a single unit remained, although the justification was now very different: after the Second World War, the states of Eastern Europe were no longer the 'successor states' but the states which 'went communist'.

Between 1945 and 1989 the countries of Eastern Europe were governed by communist parties proud of the fact that they were following in the footsteps of Lenin. Back in October 1917, when Lenin's Bolshevik Party had seized power in Russia in a revolutionary coup, it had been confidently assumed that this would be the start of a world communist revolution. That was not to be. Although the old autocratic order in Germany and Central Europe was overthrown, communists won only transient victories. By 1923 the revolutionary wave accompanying the end of the First World War had ended and communists were everywhere on the defensive.

The interwar period was a paradox for communists. Everywhere they were seen as a growing danger – the threat of Bolshevism was the rallying cry of demagogue and democrat alike – and yet nowhere did they make any progress. In Germany, Europe's largest communist party crumbled before Hitler's onslaught, while in Spain, despite the governmental power they exercised within the Republic, they were unable, or unwilling, to consolidate their position; for a second time they were defeated by a fascist regime. The defeat of fascism by the wartime Allies, Britain, the United States and the Soviet Union, provided communists throughout Europe with a new opportunity to see if Lenin's prediction of world revolution would come true.

Between 1945 and 1948 the whole of continental Europe experienced a dramatic increase in communist activity. Even in the 'West', communists were members of the coalition governments in France and Italy, and only the prompt deployment of British troops prevented a successful communist insurrection in Greece at the start of 1945. Not since 1919 had the prospects of world revolution looked so good, and in the 'East' the chances for communist revolution looked even better. With the exception of the Czechoslovak Communist Party, all the East European communist parties had been illegal during the interwar years, and the young idealists who made up their ranks had found it almost impossible to make contact with the mass of workers and peasants in whose interests they always claimed to act. Participation in the resistance to Hitler and his allies changed all that: communists suddenly found themselves popular in a way they had never been before, the masses were no longer an abstract force about which communist students debated in smoke-filled rooms, but people that they led.

However, what really strengthened the position of communists in postwar Eastern Europe was the presence of the Red Army. At the end of the Second World War the Soviet Red Army had played an important role in liberating every East European state except Albania from fascist rule. In Yugoslavia its presence had been transitory, and in Czechoslovakia only short-term; these states were, after all, closely linked to the wartime Allies. In Bulgaria, Romania and Hungary the Red Army stayed on until 1947 while peace treaties were negotiated with Hitler's former satellites; thereafter it left Bulgaria, but remained in Hungary and Romania to secure communication lines with its occupation forces in Austria. For the similar purpose of maintaining contact with occupation forces in East Germany, the Red Army remained in Poland despite that country's status as a nominal wartime Ally. Throughout Eastern Europe, the presence of the Red Army meant that local communists had a powerful and sympathetic friend by their side.

It was this duality, of local communists and the Soviet Red Army, that was to characterise the East European revolution. By the 1960s it was easy to look back at the East European revolution and deny that any such thing had occurred: the Red Army had simply imposed Stalin's rule on all the countries it had marched through. It was not as simple as this. The Red Army was the key factor in Poland, and scarcely less important in Romania; but the Balkan revolutions were carried out largely without the support of the Red Army, and in Czechoslovakia the Red Army withdrew leaving the local communists to seek power through the ballot box. Commentators in the late 1940s were happy to use the term 'East European revolution' to describe the years 1945–7 when it looked as if the states of Eastern Europe were planning to address the legacy of peasant backwardness in a variety of different ways.

After 1947, the history of Eastern Europe was increasingly dominated by the Soviet Union. As the Cold War between Britain and the United States on the one hand, and the Soviet Union on the other, became more and more intense, Stalin determined to consolidate his hold on Eastern Europe. By the winter of 1946–7 it looked as if the successful socialist revolutions in the Balkans might spill over into Greece and even Turkey; the American President Truman responded by announcing his 'doctrine' in February 1947, that everywhere free peoples would be defended, and backed this up with the offer of Marshall Aid in July 1947, which attempted to kill communism with kindness by dramatically raising the standard of living in those countries that came under the American umbrella; the first triumph of this policy was the ousting of the French and Italian communists from government in May 1947.

Stalin's response was to establish the Cominform in September 1947 and bring all of Eastern Europe under his direct control, a tactic which succeeded brilliantly in Czechoslovakia with the coup of February 1948, but which backfired disastrously when in the same month the Yugoslav leader, Tito, refused to submit to Stalin's demands. Until Stalin's death, the Cominform served both as a vehicle for disciplining Eastern Europe and a propaganda machine to blacken the name of the one communist who dared to stand up to Stalin.

After Stalin's death in March 1953, the degree of Soviet control over Eastern Europe fluctuated considerably. In the years between Stalin's death and the Soviet invasion of Hungary in November 1956 there were moments, particularly during the autumn of 1956, when it looked as if Soviet dominance might come to an end. Yugoslavia had remained free from Stalin's control, and when Stalin's successor Khrushchev began the process of de-Stalinisation, it appeared for a while as if the two leaders might be going to establish a more relaxed order in Eastern Europe, allowing the communist regimes to adopt aspects of both the Soviet and the Yugoslav experiences.

The crushing of the Hungarian revolution by Soviet troops in November 1956 brought this period of relaxation to a dramatic end. For the next 33 years of their rule, East European communists were firmly under Moscow's thumb, kept in check by the formation of the Political Committee of the Warsaw Pact. This did not mean that there had been no change since the Cominform years, but the limits of what was and what was not possible had been clearly set out after 1956. When in Czechoslovakia in 1968 or in Poland in 1980–1 attempts were made to revive political pluralism, the Soviet Union made clear it would and could intervene: in Czechoslovakia, foreign armies were used to restore order, while in Poland, Soviet pressure prompted the local military to declare martial law. On both occasions the key decisions were taken by the Warsaw Pact.

Increasingly, by the end of the 1960s, the history of Eastern Europe became a history of economic reform, or rather the failure of economic reform. Despite the success of the economic reform in Hungary in 1968, it was built on neither by the Hungarians themselves nor any other of the East European states. Instead, all the countries of the region entered a period of prolonged economic crisis. The planning system that had achieved some success in dragging the East European economies out of their peasant backwardness, proved incapable of adapting to the demands of an urban consumer society. As a result both economy and society stagnated, since those who administered the existing planning system had no incentive to bring to an end a system in which they had a significant personal stake.

Under close Soviet tutelage, prevented from embarking on political reform and hampered in the extent to which they could reform their economies, East European communists steadily shed the ideology that had once inspired them; more dramatically, during the 33 years from 1956 to 1989 a whole generation grew up to whom communism did not mean the struggle against fascism and the vagaries of the free market, but economic stagnation and political oppression. The gulf between leaders and the led meant that the ruling communists were quite incapable of responding effectively when a new Soviet leader, Mikhail Gorbachev, told them history had come full circle and Soviet control over Eastern Europe was a thing of the past. They were again free to pursue their own roads to socialism, but those plans had been abandoned so long ago that they proved impossible to revive.

Even before Soviet control over Eastern Europe ended in 1989, it was clear that Eastern Europe as a concept was no longer adequate to describe events in Poland, Czechoslovakia, Hungary, Romania, Albania, Yugoslavia and Bulgaria. Increasingly in the last two decades of Soviet control, two Eastern Europes had emerged, Central Europe comprising Poland, Czechoslovakia and Hungary, where force had been used to retain Soviet influence, and the Balkans, comprising Romania, Albania, Yugoslavia and Bulgaria where the communist revolutions had had more legitimacy. The experience of Stalinism and neo-Stalinism had produced different degrees of industrialisation, urbanisation and cultural development, despite all the attempts by communists to achieve economic integration and uniformity.

As a consequence, this should be the last history of Eastern Europe ever written, for the concepts of 'successor states' and 'communist satellites' which once justified such an approach are now themselves part of history: when a successor volume is planned some years hence about the region's history since 1989, it is certain the potential authors will insist on writing two volumes, one for Central Europe and one for the Balkans, and start by commenting on how both these regions emerged from the years of Soviet control in a very different shape and with very different prospects for the new era of political pluralism.

This is the approach adopted in the final chapter that assesses how the countries of Eastern Europe adapted to capitalism.

Our Approach

The history of Eastern Europe since 1945 is essentially the history of a socialist experiment which failed. It is impossible in the space of one volume to chronicle all that happened in Eastern Europe during forty years of communist rule, and no attempt has been made to write a comprehensive history of each of the countries that go to make up Eastern Europe. Rather our focus will shift from country to country as the issues of socialist construction and collapse evolve. Some of these issues are essentially ideological and a little obscure, but that is the nature of communism; the rulers of Eastern Europe did worry about the nature of popular front politics, the leading role of the Party, the labour theory of value, the 'law of value' and commodity production, and so on. However, the main themes addressed are fairly clear cut, corresponding roughly to the chapter headings: the road to power, diverse paths to socialism, Stalinist uniformity, the impossibility of democratised communism, the attempt at economic reform, bureaucratic resistance, and economic and social collapse.

Such an approach has resulted in what might appear an unbalanced treatment of certain countries. The Yugoslav question dominated the first four of these themes. As only the second country in the world to experience a successful communist insurrection, the Yugoslav experience is central to a discussion of the road to power; during the period of diversity, Yugoslavia was the most Stalinist state in Eastern Europe, the model Stalin hoped the rest of Eastern Europe would follow; in the period of sovietisation, Yugoslavia refused to give in to Stalin and established its own rival version of communism; and so, in the period of de-Stalinisation, Yugoslavia was inevitably to the fore in the arguments about the future form communism should take. Then, after Yugoslav support for the Soviet invasion of Hungary in November 1956, East European communists lost interest in Yugoslavia. This reality is reflected in our study.

For similar reasons, coverage of East Germany is unbalanced. Just as Yugoslavia hardly merits a mention after Chapter 4 after having dominated the first few chapters of the book, East Germany is mentioned infrequently in the first half of the book, but features extensively thereafter. This, again, simply mirrors reality. Until the mid-1950s a question mark hung over the future of East Germany; thereafter, it developed one of the most successful economies of Eastern Europe and is given extensive coverage on those grounds.

Although a one-volume history offers little scope for innovation, there are two elements to this study that could claim to have altered traditional interpretations. First, Chapters 1–3 go a long way to challenging some of the assumptions of Hugh Seton-Watson's *The East European Revolution*. In this and other works Seton-Watson developed a theory of the pattern of Soviet domination of Eastern Europe: genuine coalition, false coalition, followed by total Soviet control.

This approach is challenged in two ways: first, Seton-Watson's approach implies 'sovietisation' was always Stalin's goal in Eastern Europe, and second, he assumes that the same pattern can be discerned in all East European countries, though occurring at different times. Because we argue the Balkan revolutions were carried out by the Balkan communists themselves, Stalin's desire to sovietise them or not was neither here nor there; they were keen to follow the Soviet path but their model was Yugoslavia and genuine coalition was never on their political agenda. Elsewhere in Eastern Europe, Seton-Watson's pattern is similarly open to challenge. A clear distinction can be drawn between Poland and Romania, where Stalin ruthlessly 'sovietised' from the moment the Red Army crossed into those countries and where genuine coalition was never seriously attempted, and Czechoslovakia and Hungary where Stalin was initially happy for the communists to have influence but not power in coalition governments. Sovietisation of Czechoslovakia and Hungary began in earnest only after the formation of the Cominform in autumn 1947, and was part of Stalin's response to the American Marshall Plan; there transition, it is suggested, was straight from genuine coalition to Soviet control, without the intermediary stage of false coalition.

The second area of innovation comes in Chapter 6. Here we address the complex question of economic reform in Eastern Europe. We not only chart clearly the limits to reform under neo-Stalinism, but also identify four stages of economic reform. These are categorised as the simple restructuring of priorities associated with the period immediately after Stalin's death; the removal of one whole layer of the economic planning pyramid, a feature of the 1960s; using the market for current distribution but relying on planning for decisions concerning the future; and, finally, radical market socialism where even decisions about the future are left to the market.

While writing the first edition of this book, the postwar political structure of Eastern Europe progressively unravelled until, on Christmas Day 1991, Mikhail Gorbachev resigned as President of the Soviet Union; on Boxing Day a rump of the Soviet parliament voted the state out of existence. Such dramatic developments might have tempted us to adopt a more radical restructuring than the addition of an extra chapter. Four chapters are still devoted to the formation of the political system which operated in Eastern Europe, for it is central to our argument that Soviet control was not simply established by right of conquest in 1945; the politics of Eastern Europe remained dynamic, even volatile, until 1956 if not later. Chapter 5, which fully describes the political system of Eastern Europe, is more necessary than ever in a world in which the mechanics of communist politics have almost been forgotten.

Two other points explain the wealth of material devoted to the first decade after 1945. First, for many members of a generation now departed, communism was a liberating ideology, it signified idealism rather than corruption, and the attempt to build an East European version of Soviet socialism deserves to be recorded in terms other than those of post-Cold-War triumphalism. Even Stalinist bureaucrats such as Erich Honecker and Gustáv Husák, who resisted reform to the end, had revolutionary pasts. Honecker spent much of the 1930s in Nazi prisons; and Husák participated in the Slovak National Uprising in 1944. In the 1990s, when privatisation of the economy is widely accepted as a cure for all economic ills, it is important to remember that for an earlier generation, whose only experience of the free market was the economic failure of the 1930s, the communist ideal of a planned economy offered much that was attractive.

The second reason for devoting so much space to the first post-war decade is that, as political pluralism has come to Eastern Europe, the new politics has revived many of the issues current then, at least in the initial phase of the revolution against communist rule. The nature of this revolution was characterised in part by the degree of legitimacy the communists had achieved in the first post-war years, and the degree of their conflict with pre-existing social democratic parties.

On the other hand, historical perspective has lessened the significance of the Brezhnev years: the period from 1968 to the early 1980s was a 'long decade' during which East European society was held in aspic and change seemed inconceivable; although, as the Polish experience showed, force could always be used to maintain the *status quo.*

Yet, 'all that is solid melts into air', as Marx wrote in the *Communist Manifesto*, and a single chapter has proved sufficient to cover an era that seemed as if it would go on forever.

Conventions Used

In writing this book we have adopted a number of conventions that require explanation. We use the conventional terms 'Comecon' and 'Warsaw Pact' since these less than accurate terms have entered everyday speech. Likewise, the term 'communist party' is used for the ruling parties between 1948 and 1989, even though most parties were differently named. The full official names of the ruling parties are given in Table 5.9 in Chapter 5. 'Party' with an upper case initial invariably refers to these communist parties. For similar reasons of clarity, all socialist and social democratic parties in the pre-1948 period are termed socialist.

For the sake of brevity, the term 'countries of the region' refers to all eight countries including Yugoslavia and Albania; 'Comecon countries' refers to the countries of the region excluding Yugoslavia; and 'Warsaw Pact countries' refers to the countries of the region excluding Yugoslavia and Albania.

Wherever possible we have cited readily accessible sources. This has not always been possible since for many historians Eastern Europe remains a collection of states 'about which we know little'. However, every effort has been made to refer the reader to English language sources and standard reference works.

1

Revolution in Eastern Europe

THE COMMUNISTS AND INTERWAR EASTERN EUROPE

Life in interwar Eastern Europe was unpleasant. Czechoslovakia was a democracy, but all the other states of Eastern Europe were governed by authoritarian regimes: Poland was a 'directed democracy'; Albania, Bulgaria, Romania and Yugoslavia were monarchical dictatorships; and Hungary was a monarchical dictatorship with a Regent rather than a King. As Hugh Seton-Watson, Britain's leading interwar authority on Eastern Europe, commented, the 'strong governments' there were 'no more than greedy, corrupt and brutal class regimes'.[1]

interwar governments

Popular opposition to those regimes, which Seton-Watson averred was widespread, was only patchily channelled into support for the communist parties. In Hungary the experience of the 1919 Soviet Revolution and its brutal suppression had marginalised the illegal communist party. In Poland and Romania support for the communists was severely hampered by the so-called anti-national stance of those parties: after the First World War both countries had acquired territory once part of the Tsarist Russian Empire and the Soviet Union insisted on the return of these territories throughout the interwar period, successfully recovering its Polish claim in September 1939 and its claim on Romania in June 1940; since the Polish and Romanian Communist Parties consistently argued in favour of the Soviet claims, it was easy for their political opponents to describe them as enemies of the existing nation state.

Elsewhere in Eastern Europe the communists fared better. In Czechoslovakia, where they operated legally, they consistently won

10 per cent of the vote, polling well not only in industrial parts of the country but in rural Slovakia and Ruthenia as well. In Yugoslavia and Bulgaria, when the communists were allowed to operate freely, they also did well: in Bulgaria in 1919 they came second in the elections and in 1920 in Yugoslavia they came third; later, as the Labour Party, the communists won the Sofia municipal elections of 1932, while Yugoslav communists won trade union elections in 1938. However, for most of the interwar period the Yugoslav and Bulgarian Communist Parties were forced to operate illegally. In Albania the Communist Party was only formed during the Second World War.

The illegality of the majority of East European Communist Parties during the interwar period left them even more subject to the whims of Moscow than the large legal parties of Western Europe. With each successive change in the political 'line' dictated by the Communist International (Comintern) during the 1920s and 1930s, the East European Communist Parties split into smaller and smaller factions, squabbling for control of the pot of gold Moscow made available to its most loyal disciples. In 1938 Moscow interference of this type culminated in the closure of the Polish Communist Party and the suspension of the Yugoslav Communist Party; Stalin feared their reluctance to obey instructions was proof they had been infiltrated by spies.

The first years of Hitler's New Order in Europe, the period before his invasion of the Soviet Union in June 1941, put the communists of Eastern Europe under even more pressure. There was practically no chance of communist activity taking place in those parts of Eastern Europe under direct German administration, that is, Poland and the Czech parts of Czechoslovakia. On the other hand, there was some chance of sustaining illegal operations in those East European states allied to Hitler, especially where communist traditions were strong: thus activity in Hungary and Romania was low, but in Bulgaria communist activity was tangible, as it was in Slovakia, a Hitlerite creation Stalin was prepared to recognise by establishing a separate Slovak Communist Party in 1939.

However, the country offering the best prospects for communist activity under Hitler's New Order was Yugoslavia: it had a tradition of communist activity, and the monarchical dictatorship there was by 1939 in a state of advanced decay, with popular pressure preventing the country's rulers siding openly with Hitler. With hindsight it is not surprising that it was from Yugoslavia that the communist revival was to come, and from there that communists were to launch a revolutionary insurrection that would spread throughout the Balkans and establish the essentials of a communist revolution in Albania, Bulgaria and Yugoslavia before the arrival of the Red Army on the scene in the autumn of 1944.

Rejuvenated Communism

The rejuvenation of the communist movement in Eastern Europe began on the eve of the Second World War as a consequence of Stalin's confused intervention in the affairs of the Yugoslav Communist Party. Between 1938 and 1939, when the leadership of the Party was officially suspended, Josip Broz Tito was appointed caretaker leader. Unwilling to await the restoration of funds from Moscow and its endorsement of a new Central Committee, he virtually relaunched the Party on a new financial and organisational footing, loyal to but not dependent on Moscow.[2] Thus, just as the first cracks were appearing in the authoritarian facade of Yugoslav political life – in November 1939 the King granted limited autonomy to the Croats – the Communist Party began to pose a serious challenge to the government.

Between 1939 and 1941 the Yugoslav Communist Party made steady progress, successfully exploiting the contradictions of a weakening regime, and Tito's obvious success in running an underground party earned him growing respect in Moscow, reflected in reports from Comintern emissaries who visited Yugoslavia at the end of 1939 and again in the summer of 1940. During the autumn of 1940, two large strikes in the industrial town of Split were enough to prompt the government to close down the communist controlled trade union organisation, while between 19 and 23 October 1940 Tito brushed aside warnings from Moscow about the impossibility of such a task and organised, under the very noses of the Yugoslav authorities, the Fifth Party Conference attended by over 100 delegates.

At this time the Yugoslav Communist Party became for Moscow the first party among equals. The great legal communist parties of Germany, Spain and France, on which Moscow had relied so heavily in the interwar years, had all disappeared and of all the illegal communist parties the Yugoslav Party seemed to be the most viable, and the Yugoslav government the least pro-German and hence the most benign. Strategically, Yugoslavia was the key to the Balkans, and the Balkans were an area where Stalin believed the Soviet Union had legitimate interests recognised by Hitler in the Nazi–Soviet Pact. Yugoslavia's neutrality, and its willingness to establish diplomatic relations with the Soviet Union in

June 1940 both suggested that skilful diplomacy might keep the country outside the Nazi camp. It was hardly surprising, therefore, that the Comintern saw Yugoslavia as a relatively safe haven, and in January 1940 established a radio transmitter in Zagreb from which to maintain contact with the Italian, Swiss, Austrian, Hungarian, Bulgarian, Greek, Slovak and Yugoslav Parties. The transmitter was fully operational by June 1940.[3]

During this 'Yugoslav' period, the Comintern line turned sharply to the Left, from reformism to revolution. Up until the Nazi–Soviet Pact, the premise of Soviet foreign policy, which the communist parties were duty bound to support, was that the Soviet Union would form some kind of anti-German alliance with Britain and France; in other words the proletarian state, Soviet Russia, would form an alliance with two bourgeois states, Britain and France, against a fascist one, Germany. The Communist International's support for a popular front between communist parties, socialist parties and bourgeois parties against the fascist threat mirrored this foreign policy stance of the Soviet state.

After the Nazi–Soviet Pact Stalin asserted that Britain and France were not genuine bourgeois democratic states at all but actually imperialist powers, as hostile to the Soviet Union as Nazi Germany. What the Soviet Union faced was not one hostile state, Nazi Germany, with potentially friendly allies to the west, but two hostile imperial blocs. Britain and France, traditional imperial powers with sea-based empires, and Nazi Germany, a modernist, fascist imperial power intent on creating a land-based empire in the east as the Kaiser had once done. Stalin justified his pact with Hitler using the same arguments with which Lenin had justified his 1918 pact with the Kaiser at Brest Litovsk: it was necessary to play the two imperial blocs off against each other and keep Russia out of the war.

The suggestion that the Second World War was simply a replay of the First World War, an imperialist skirmish of no interest to the workers, split the British and French Communist Parties and marginalised them from national life. For Eastern European communists the change in line was far easier to accept, largely as a result of their experiences during the Spanish Civil War. Communists felt the defeat of the Republican Government in Spain had been brought about not only by fascist intervention from Hitler and Mussolini, but also by the Anglo-French policy of non-intervention which had evolved from benign sympathy towards the Republic, aimed at localising the conflict, to a blockade of Republican ports, aimed primarily at preventing the delivery of Soviet arms shipments. Communists felt betrayed by Britain and France, and East European communists felt this particularly acutely since one in five of the European volunteers fighting in Spain came from Eastern Europe and at the end of the war, unable to return home, they found themselves interned in camps, not in fascist Germany but democratic France.[4]

In accordance with the Comintern's new revolutionary line, its official explanation for the causes of the Spanish defeat, published in February 1940, was highly critical not only of Britain and France but also of the Spanish socialist and liberal parties associated with them. The communists' mistake had been to trust these other parties, fellow members of the Popular Front Government: they had formed a coalition government, a popular front 'from above'; they should have formed a popular front 'from below'. A popular front 'from below' meant building up a powerful mass movement, via such organisations as the trade unions, through which communists could counterbalance their weakness at government level. Thus, while communists might only have one seat in government, control over the trade unions could enable them to dictate terms to other ministers and acquire *de facto* control of the government. Spanish communists, the Comintern concluded, should have 'broken with the old state apparatus which served reaction and replaced it with a new apparatus which served the working class'. Thus two lessons from the Spanish Civil War stood out: the need to break with the old order, and to build a popular front 'from below'.[5]

This revolutionary analysis was not only shared by those East European communists trapped in internment camps in Southern France, but was also fully endorsed by Tito and the Yugoslav communists, as the decisions of their Fifth Conference made clear. The Conference endorsed the view that the only solution to Yugoslavia's ills was a 'people's government', and precisely what this meant was spelled out in the Party's New Year message of 1941: drawing on the lessons of the Spanish Civil War, the Party pointed out that a 'genuine people's government' was only possible if it was formed 'not between leaders but from below, among the depths of the working masses'. No clearer statement on Tito's determination not to play second fiddle in any revolutionary crisis to bourgeois politicians is needed. And, Tito expected such a crisis to develop soon: in March 1941 a party school heard a report on The Strategy and Tactics of the Armed Uprising which suggested such a rising was imminent. Tito believed that if the

Second World War really was a rerun of the First World War, there was no reason why it should not end, as the First World War had done, in a new era of socialist revolutions.[6]

Partisan Insurrection and Communist Resistance to Fascism

In March 1941 German, Italian and Bulgarian troops divided Yugoslavia between them. In June 1941 Germany and her allies invaded the Soviet Union. After some hesitations and false starts over the summer, the Yugoslav communists began their insurrectionary partisan war against the occupying forces in the autumn of 1941 and from then until the arrival of the Red Army in October 1944 succeeded in liberating large areas of Yugoslav territory and resisting five German offensives. From September 1941 onwards, the leading organisation in the Party was not the Central Committee, which was evacuated that month from Belgrade in disarray, but the partisan General Staff, formally established two months earlier; it commanded partisan units soon numerous enough to comprise divisions and brigades, all wearing the communist red star and all assigned political commissars to carry out ideological training. By November 1942 the partisans had been transformed into the People's Liberation Army controlling a 'state' larger than Switzerland.[7]

The nature and extent of the liberated territory changed frequently, but everywhere Tito implemented the ideas he had argued for since 1940. The old order was overthrown and a new popular administration constructed around 'liberation committees'. Sometimes these would control a single village, sometimes a hierarchy of committees would control a whole town or territory, complete with postal service, health service and publicly controlled industry. In November 1942 elections were held from these liberation committees to a national parliament, the National Anti-Fascist Liberation Council, which comprised representatives not only from all liberated territories but also underground groups operating in occupied territory.

Communist control over this new political system was total. Although prominent liberal figures were persuaded to join liberation committees, and even allowed to play prominent public roles, they were never more than figureheads. Although at local level, liberation committees were allowed a large degree of freedom to take their own initiatives, and used that freedom to win genuine popularity, higher up the pyramid of committees communist control was total, often exercised through so-called narrow committees that would fix the agendas of meetings in advance. When in the summer of 1944 communist control began to be extended into large new liberated areas, Tito warned his staff that there should be no lessening of communist control.[8]

The revolutionary nature of Tito's struggle was made quite clear in his dealings with the Serbian Nationalist leader Draža Mihailović. In the first phase of the liberation war, in the autumn of 1941, the two men tried to reach an understanding, but the one sought the restoration of the old order and the other a new revolutionary regime. Tito's proposed compromise, that Mihailović become joint commander of the partisans in return for liberation committees being extended into Mihailović's territory, was a classic manoeuvre of the popular front 'from below' and was rejected as such by Mihailović. Consequently, during 1942 and 1943 Tito's partisans not only fought a liberation war against the occupiers, but also a civil war against representatives of the old Yugoslavia.[9]

The Communist International was enthusiastic in its support for Tito and the Yugoslav partisans. Its journal *The Communist International* published fulsome reports on Tito's partisans throughout the autumn of 1941, and through the spring and autumn of 1942. Furthermore, the journal instructed all communist parties to follow the Yugoslav lead, spelling out in detail the steps which needed to be taken, and confronting one by one the possible objections to following the Yugoslav lead: the Yugoslavs and Yugoslavia were not exceptional, the journal argued, every country and every communist party could start a partisan insurrection. By May Day 1942 the Comintern claimed, with some exaggeration, partisan insurrections were underway in Yugoslavia, Bulgaria, Albania, Greece and Slovakia.

In organising this warfare, the Yugoslav Communist Party continued to play an important coordinating role. It did much to help the return of battle hardened Spanish Civil War veterans from their internment in France. Although overall responsibility for this was given to the Migrant Workers' Section of the French Communist Party headed by the Czech communist Artur London, because of the sheer number of Yugoslavs involved (the Yugoslavs sent more volunteers to Spain than any other East European country), and the prominence of the Yugoslav Communist Party in the Comintern, the Yugoslavs were active in this operation from the very beginning: since the summer of 1940 London and the Yugoslavs had cooperated in the task of either smuggling the internees out of the country or obtaining false visas for them.[10]

Equally, through its Comintern transmitter in Zagreb, and later through transmitters based at partisan headquarters, Tito remained in regular contact with the Comintern, evacuated from Moscow to far off Siberia. It was the Yugoslav Party which arranged the travel plans of emissaries sent to Bulgaria, Greece, Albania, Italy, Austria and Hungary, to mention only recorded incidents in operations which were by their very nature secret. Given this coordinating role, it is not surprising that communists fighting in the partisan resistance adopted strategies and tactics in common with those adopted by the Yugoslavs.[11]

The Yugoslav Communist Party, learning the lesson of the Spanish Civil War, insisted that in forming a new people's government the old order had to be completely overthrown and a popular front built up 'from below'. In much of Yugoslavia Tito had been helped by the fact that during the war most political parties had collapsed. In Slovenia, however, he did have to take other parties into consideration. In its original form the Slovene Liberation Front was based on classic principles of a 'bourgeois' coalition government; each party to the coalition being represented in equal numbers or in numbers proportionate to their strength. Tito steadily undermined this arrangement by making the lower level committees of the Liberation Front open to mass membership.

'Below', in the local committees, there were no reserved places on local executives for representatives of the socialists or any other party involved in the coalition and control over local committees could be captured by the most active political party. By February 1943 the communists had won control of sufficient local committees in the Slovene Liberation Front to force the National Committee to abandon the principle of equal or 'parity' representation and accept the leading role of the Communist Party. This Slovene model was the one successfully 'exported' via Yugoslavia to resistance movements in Albania, Bulgaria, Northern Italy and Greece where the method by which communists ensured their control over the other parties within the popular front was simple: the 'parity' principle was weakened by insisting that votes in the popular front were given to the communist controlled mass organisations.[12]

Realpolitik in the Balkans

By the last year of the war armed communist partisans, in control of new popular front political movements formed 'from below', seemed to be capable of bringing Europe, both East and West, to the verge of revolution. To a greater or lesser extent communist partisans were fighting in France, North Italy, Albania, Yugoslavia, Greece, Bulgaria and Slovakia. The possible international repercussions of this were first addressed by the Great Powers as soon as victory over Nazi Germany seemed certain. In August 1942 Churchill and Stalin met, and immediately afterwards the Comintern watered down its revolutionary rhetoric and launched a campaign against 'sectarianism', implicitly criticising the Yugoslav model of the popular front 'from below' and urging communists to cooperate with all anti-Nazi groups, even those which represented the 'bourgeoisie'. In May 1943, Stalin decided that the only way to impress the Allies that the Second World War was not going to usher in a new revolutionary era was to dissolve the Comintern completely.[13]

Stalin had decided to control international communism not by relying on the Comintern, but by his dominance over the individual leaders of the communist parties. Each would be instructed to return home with a set of policies specifically designed for the role Stalin saw their country playing in the postwar world. Thus in both France and Italy, countries clearly in the West's sphere of influence, the returning Moscow leaders told dismayed comrades that there was to be no bid for power and they were to accept seats in a coalition government. Stalin's message was that they should drop talk about the popular front 'from below', and see the popular front simply as a coalition government in which they would be partners, even junior partners.[14]

In Yugoslavia the revolution had gone too far for Stalin or anyone else to stop. Stalin's concern, therefore, was to persuade Tito to act cautiously and not to antagonise the Western Allies, in particular the British who had given sanctuary to the Yugoslav Government-in-Exile. Thus in November 1943, when the Yugoslavs wanted to turn their National Anti-Fascist Committee into a Provisional Government, Stalin advised them not to. Although Tito rejected this advice, to Stalin's fury, and put himself at the head of a Provisional Government, he had already begun the process of winning British support for a communist revolution. Abandoning his earlier policy of caution towards British military missions sent to contact him, Tito had since May 1943 been busy convincing them that he, rather than Mihailović, by then the Government-in-Exile's Minister of War, was killing more Germans and therefore the more worthy of support. Once Churchill had been persuaded of this, after a personal meeting with Tito, there was nothing to stop the signing in June 1944 of a negotiated merger between Tito's government and the Government-in-Exile. When in mid-September 1944 Tito flew secretly to Moscow to prepare for the arrival of the Red Army, he could tell a still sceptical Stalin that there would be no Great Power complications following his assumption of power in Belgrade.[15]

Where Yugoslav influence was uncontested, in Albania, all attempts to limit the revolutionary nature of the partisan movement were frustrated. Acting first as agents for the Comintern, and later on their own initiative, the Yugoslav communists had taken the lead, in the autumn of 1941, in pulling together the various communist groups of Albania into a proper Albanian Communist Party; had insisted, in June 1942, in expelling from it all those opposed to the strategy of partisan insurrection; had encouraged the Albanian communists to form, by the summer of 1943, a National Liberation Movement (later Front) and an Army of National Liberation on the Yugoslav model. And then, in August 1943, they had instructed them to tear up a British-brokered agreement with the rival nationalist National Front resistance group, before establishing in September 1943 a National Liberation Council which in May 1944 declared itself to be the 'supreme executive and legislative organ'. In October 1944 Enver Hoxha formed his Provisional Democratic Government. The Soviet Military Mission, which arrived in August 1944, arrived too late to check the Yugoslav determination to push through an Albanian Revolution.[16]

In Greece, however, a country Stalin always accepted as a British sphere of influence, the revolution would have to be stopped, something that proved easier said than done. The strongest resistance movement there was the communist-controlled National People's Liberation Army (ELAS) which had been strongly supported by the Yugoslavs and whose tactics were closely modelled on those of the Yugoslavs. Over the summer of 1944 the Greek Communists had been on the point of forming a Yugoslav style National Liberation Government, responsible to a network of liberation committees, when messages began to arrive from Moscow that they should behave like their Italian comrades and join a coalition government. Obediently they did so, but when it became clear this would involve disarming their resistance army they decided to reverse the policy and resume the path of insurrection. In December 1944, encouraged by the Yugoslavs, their armed uprising began, but Stalin did nothing to help them and watched impassively as the British forces in Greece firmly restored order. In January 1945 Stalin told Tito bluntly to concentrate on the internal politics of Yugoslavia and leave international affairs to him. In March 1945 this was formalised into a Yugoslav acceptance that Stalin had a veto over foreign policy, and no initiatives could be taken without seeking prior clearance from Moscow.[17]

The Greek affair contrasted starkly to the very different message Stalin sent the Bulgarian communists during the summer of 1944. The partisan communist insurrection that swept through Yugoslavia and Albania was also felt in Bulgaria. There, however, its success was limited first by Bulgaria's position as a Nazi ally and subsequently as a consequence of Bulgaria being an occupied enemy state. Nevertheless, the communists in Bulgaria were part of the same rejuvenated communist movement seen in Yugoslavia, they sought to imitate their Yugoslav mentors and largely succeeded in doing so, although domestic and international circumstances made their path to socialist revolution a more tortuous one.

As in Yugoslavia, in June 1941 the Bulgarian communists responded to the Nazi invasion of the Soviet Union by establishing a Military Commission alongside the Central Committee. However, unlike in Yugoslavia, the continued existence of the Bulgarian state, and in particular the ever vigilant political police, meant that most of the leaders of this original Military Commission were soon under arrest; a series of trials held during the summer of 1942 brought this first attempt at insurrection to an end. However, during the spring of 1943 veterans of the Spanish Civil War returned to the country and the partisan operation was put on a new footing, with the scattered partisan groups being gathered together into the People's Liberation Insurgent Army.[18]

Direct radio contact had been lost with Moscow in September 1941, so these changes were carried out with the active support of the Yugoslavs. In September 1943 Shteryu Atanasov, a Bulgarian Comintern official who had met Tito in Moscow at the end of 1939, was parachuted into Yugoslavia to join Tito's staff and oversee links with the Bulgarian partisans. Thereafter the importance of the Yugoslav link was evident in almost every proclamation issued by the partisans: in these, potential recruits were always reminded that they would not be fighting alone but in the company of the Yugoslav Liberation Army and the Red Army, listed in that order. Copying the Yugoslav experience the reformed Military Commission was renamed the General Staff of the Resistance and, at the end of 1943, the Central Committee decided to abandon its headquarters based in Sofia and move its centre of operations to be with the partisans. Despite erratic communications with both Tito and Moscow, by May 1944 five partisan brigades had been formed.[19]

The scale of these partisan operations was never to reach Yugoslav proportions. With the exception of the area bordering Yugoslavia no free territories were ever established, despite serious attempts to do so in the spring of 1944. Most of the partisan units remained small, only 10–12 poorly armed men; before September 1944 the partisans only had 2000 rifles, and despite the existence of the general staff, few operations were coordinated with the centre. However, despite this limited military potential, the partisans succeeded in tying down enormous numbers of Bulgarian troops in counter-insurgency operations, something recognised by the British who sent a Military Mission to them in December 1943.[20]

The reasons for this limited success were, first, the fact that, although German forces were stationed in Bulgaria, the country was never occupied: the Bulgarian government stayed in power, albeit on German terms, which meant that the partisans mostly fought fellow Bulgarians in a struggle to replace a reactionary government with an overtly revolutionary one. Second, the Bulgarian government's pacification policy towards the guerrillas was ruthless. A massive counter-insurgency operation took place in spring 1943, while a special counter-insurgency gendarmerie was established in March 1944. The tactics were brutal: a reward of 50,000 leva was paid for each partisan body handed to the authorities; it would then be put on public display to discourage potential recruits.[21]

Despite the government's policy of repression, by the summer of 1944 the limiting factor on the growth of the partisan movement was no longer manpower but simply the supply of arms, for there were twice as many men in loosely formed sabotage units as there were in regular partisan formations. When seeking explanations for their shortage of arms the partisans became more and more convinced they were being used as pawns in a political game, for although early in 1944 an agreement had been reached with the British Military Mission to supply arms, little had been received. By the summer of 1944 the communist partisans were convinced that the British did not want to see a communist revolution in a country so near to Greece and would prefer some sort of negotiated end to the pro-German Bulgarian regime. In frustration the partisans turned to the Soviet Union, whose air drop organised at the end of August 1944 quadrupled the number of properly armed partisans by September 1944.[22]

This was a dramatic message from Moscow, the very reverse of Stalin's intervention in Greece, and came after talks between Stalin and the Bulgarian former head of the Comintern, Georgi Dimitrov.[23] It marked the end of a zig-zag policy in Moscow towards the future of the communist insurrection in Bulgaria. In July 1942 the communists had established the Fatherland Front and invited other parties to join this Bulgarian version of the popular front. Most of the traditional opposition parties had ignored the call, with support only coming from some socialists, the so-called 'Pladne' group within the Agrarian Party led by Nikola Petkov, and adherents to the 'Zveno' Military League (*zvenari*) led by Kimon Georgiev. Although the partisans nominally fought in the name of the Fatherland Front, the only party to establish partisan units was the communists, so communist control over the Fatherland Front remained secure. When a constitutional crisis developed in August 1943 the communists firmed up their control of the Fatherland Front by establishing a National Committee.

Then, in March 1944, messages from Dimitrov in Moscow suggested communists should show more flexibility and try to broaden the front to involve the traditional parties. In May 1944, when another government crisis developed, the Party followed this advice, and took the opportunity presented by the formation of a more liberal government to open up talks not only with the opposition but with the government as well. To the Party leaders' surprise Dimitrov did not welcome this initiative. By June 1944 he had changed his mind and firmly rejected the idea of a coalition with any representatives of the old order. He was determined to follow Tito in overthrowing the old regime through a popular insurrection and by August had won Stalin's approval.

The Party responded enthusiastically to this call to arms. On 26 August the Central Committee issued 'Circular 4' which called on local Fatherland Front committees to be transformed into organs of popular power. Then, on 29 August the Fatherland Front's National Committee was reorganised: initially there had been one representative for the four constituent groups plus one independent, now the partisan leadership was brought onto the committee which comprised five communists, three representatives of the Pladne agrarians and the *zvenari*, two socialists, and three independents; mass organisations were given nonvoting representation. On 2 September the Party gave the signal for partisan units to start attacking towns, and began preparations for a coup against the government, details of which were finalised on the 5th.[24]

That was the day the Soviet Union declared war on Bulgaria. On 6–7 September the country was shaken by a series of strikes, demonstrations and riots organised by the communists. At the same time partisan forces advanced towards the towns, although, having liberated them they were not always able to hold them. On 8 September the Red Army crossed the border and, in the small hours of the 9th, junior officers loyal to Zveno seized the Ministry of War, where the Government was based, and allowed representatives of the Resistance General Staff to take over. By the evening of the same day a cease-fire had been agreed with the Red Army and a new Fatherland Front Government formed.[25]

BUILDING SOCIALISM IN THE BALKANS

In Albania, Bulgaria and Yugoslavia the communists had fought their way to power, and with Stalin's blessing immediately began to construct socialism.

Yugoslavia

In Yugoslavia there was nothing to slow this process down. At the Yalta Conference in February 1945, Tito's agreement on merging his government with the Government-in-Exile was endorsed, and on 7 March 1945 the Allies recognised a government in which, although the former Croat leader Ivan Šubašić would be foreign minister and the former Serbian Democrat politician Milan Grol Deputy Premier, only one-third of the seats went to non-communist groups.[26]

These concessions were never seen by Tito as anything other than a manoeuvre: his was always a popular front 'from below'; his liberation committees dominated the situation on the ground and his partisan army was the only effective armed force. Although his government was provisional in the sense that its decisions would have to be endorsed by a Constituent Assembly, there was never any doubt the communists would win any elections held. Although members of parties such as the Socialists, Republicans, Serbian Democrats or the Croatian Peasant Party were allowed to join liberation committees as individuals, the only party allowed to retain a separate organisation within them was the Communist Party.

Communist dominance of the National Liberation Committee, renamed the People's Front in August 1945, was confirmed by events surrounding the elections of 11 November 1945 to a Constituent Assembly. Tito restricted any political activity outside that of the People's Front by harassing their activists and suppressing their publications.

Justification for this was given in terms of the regulations disenfranchising those who had collaborated with the enemy and in protest the non-communist ministers resigned and boycotted the election. However, with 90 per cent of votes going to the People's Front in an 88.7 per cent turn-out, the communists had no qualms about advancing smartly towards socialism, proud that they were only the second country in the world to take that path.[27]

Not surprisingly Yugoslavia modelled itself closely on the experience of the first socialist state, the Soviet Union. The People's Front programme made clear that socialism would be achieved by means of nationalisation and land reform: both had been embarked on before the elections took place. In August 1945 an Agrarian Reform Law limited landholdings to a range of 25–45 hectares and thereby allocated 80 per cent of the country's land to landless peasants and war veterans, while the wartime policy of expropriating the property of all collaborators meant that at the end of the fighting something like 54 per cent of the country's industry was already socially owned. In April 1945 a currency reform effectively deprived the urban middle class and richer peasantry of any savings accumulated during the war.

The full paraphernalia of Soviet style communism soon followed. In July 1946 a Basic Law on Co-operatives was passed, the first step towards socialised agriculture. Thereafter peasants had to face fixed low prices, compulsory deliveries, high taxes, credit restrictions and bans on hired labour unless they joined a cooperative where new machinery would be made available to them. Progress was also soon made in the other area of the economy where Soviet experience could be drawn on, industrialisation. By the end of 1946, at the cost of tremendous self-sacrifice, the country had recovered from its wartime devastation and the government was determined to launch an ambitious programme of economic development. In April 1947 the First Five Year Plan was announced.[28]

The new regime dealt harshly with its political opponents, arresting many thousands under the broadly defined charge of collaboration. In March 1946 the Serbian nationalist Mihailović was captured and later executed, charged with fighting alongside the Germans. His trial was followed in the autumn of 1946 by that of the Catholic Cardinal Stepinac whose ministry to his Croatian Church had brought him close to the leaders of the Independent Croat State established during the war by the Italians. That same summer also saw moves against the former leaders of Serbian and Croatian peasant organisations.[29]

Albania

The revolution in Albania inevitably took the same course, since it was the product of Yugoslav action. With the liberation of Tiranë in November 1944 the front was renamed the Democratic Front, in August 1945, and Hoxha's government recognised by the Allies in November 1945. Elections were held on 2 December 1945, when no groups opposed to the Democratic Front were allowed to stand. Some 93 per cent of those who voted supported the Democratic Front with only 7 per cent registering their disagreement by voting in the 'No' box: this was identical to the system operated in Yugoslavia. In fact, Albania was little more than a Yugoslav client state at this time, the operation to mine the Corfu Channel and sink two British destroyers in October 1946 being an operation closely coordinated with the Yugoslavs.[30]

Bulgaria

In Bulgaria the new communist administration at first acted as decisively as the Yugoslavs and Albanians in its mission to construct socialism. However, as a defeated Axis power Bulgaria's sovereignty was limited by the right of the wartime Allies to supervise its political and economic reconstruction. Therefore, after an initial hectic and bloody revolution, the pressure of international events forced the communists to slow the pace of change and adapt their tactics to those more acceptable to the West. With the signing of the Bulgarian Peace Treaty in February 1947 and the end of any external limitation on their ambitions, the Bulgarian communists resumed their socialist offensive.

Formally, the Fatherland Front government established on 9 September 1944 was a coalition of four communists, four agrarians, four *zvenari*, two socialists and two independents; the reality was very different, since only the communists had formed partisan units and only the communists had been in any way serious about establishing Fatherland Front committees. A lack of weaponry had been the only thing holding the Bulgarian partisans back, and with the arrival of the Red Army this was no longer a problem. Within a matter of days after the 9 September coup the communists had achieved the revolution they had been working towards for the previous two years.

Soviet involvement in this revolution was minimal: there were occasions when, on 7 and 8 September, advancing partisan units found themselves outgunned and had to call on Red Army support; in areas bordering Romania, where partisan activity had hardly existed, the Red Army helped the Party form and supply partisan units; but that was about all. The Bulgarian Communist Party had achieved more than any other communist party in an Axis state by offering sustained armed resistance for a period of two years, and had successfully carried out an insurrection against an unpopular government. It was determined to consolidate this triumph and showed few scruples when it came to coping with enemies, both real and imagined.

At the time of the September coup there were 700 Fatherland Front committees in Bulgaria: by November there were 7000 with a total membership of 25 000 in which the communists outnumbered the agrarians by two to one and the *zvenari* by thirty to one. Local government was in communist hands. The subsequent bloodletting was horrific: at least 30 000 representatives of the old regime were put on trial and in February 1945, 100 leading figures of the old regime were shot in batches of twenty during the space of one night, a purge more thoroughgoing than any other in Eastern Europe; memories of the publicly displayed naked corpses of captured partisans no doubt justified such vengefulness for some.[31]

In quick succession a number of radical reforms were implemented. The establishment of workers' councils after September 1944 led to a campaign against alleged 'bourgeois' profiteers, and later to the formation in March 1945 of a new Trade Union Federation dominated by the communists. Land reform was quickly implemented, involving the seizure of all holdings of 25 hectares or more and the property of collaborators, and the first of new socialist inspired cooperatives launched to replace the pre-war ones that favoured the better-off peasant. At the same time the general staff of the resistance was transformed into the new People's Militia.

Those politicians not prepared to accept these rapid moves towards socialism were treated as badly as their counterparts in Yugoslavia. While the Pladne agrarians had joined the Fatherland Front, other agrarians had refused to do so and during the autumn of 1944 these were led by G. M. Dimitrov (Gemeto). The communists forced him to resign as leader in January 1945 after seizing on some incautious remarks about the country's need for peace at a time when all out support for the war effort was the touchstone of loyalty to the new regime. The communists then turned their fire on opponents within the Fatherland Front. As the party leadership informed Moscow, the arrival of an Allied Control

Commission (ACC) persuaded some fellow members of the Fatherland Front to stand up for their rights. In a mirror image of the situation in postwar Italy, the dominant role in the ACC would be played by the Soviet representative, but British and American representatives would also have a voice. Backed by the British and the Americans the non-communist members of the Fatherland Front focused their criticisms on the work of the communist controlled militia; they may even have wanted to destabilise the country to the point of inviting British troops to restore order. The communists responded by attacking Nikola Petkov, who as a founder of the Fatherland Front was still a government minister. He had criticised communist manipulation of the Fatherland Front and was successfully ousted as Party leader in May 1945. The same month the communists neutralised opposition within the Socialist Party when the Left won control, although this was not formally endorsed until later in the year.[32]

Building on this social transformation of the country, it was quite logical that discussions should begin with the Yugoslavs about the rapid formation of a Balkan Federation comprising Albania, Bulgaria and Yugoslavia. This had first been raised when Atanasov had arrived at Tito's headquarters in autumn 1943; Stalin and Tito had again raised the issue in September 1944, and it was then that the Bulgarian former leader of the Comintern, Georgi Dimitrov, was brought into the discussions. Dimitrov noted in his diary that despite the 'complete mutual understanding' between the two men, there could well be problems putting future plans into effect. He was not sure if the future would be 'an alliance between Bulgaria and Yugoslavia' or 'a federation of the south Slavs' to comprise Bulgarians, Macedonians. Serbs, Croats, Montenegrins and Slovenes'. This was precisely the issue that led to problems when serious bilateral talks got underway under Soviet chairmanship in Moscow in December 1944. The Yugoslav side had a draft treaty on the formation of 'a south Slav federation' ready to sign on 31 December with a public announcement planned for 1 January 1945, when the Bulgarian side suddenly pulled out. An amended draft was similarly rejected shortly afterwards, and Stalin himself had to explain to the Yugoslavs on the 9th that the Bulgarians saw a 'federation of south Slavs' as a means 'to swallow them up'; a confederation of the two existing states had to be the starting point. The talks reconvened at the end of January, but had effectively stalled in February 1945 when the British, ever mindful of their position in Greece, objected to the idea pointing out that, until Bulgaria had signed a peace treaty it did not have the sovereignty to enter into such negotiations and the idea of a Balkan Federation was shelved. With the end of hostilities in sight Stalin could not ignore the wishes of his wartime Allies.[33]

Once the war in Europe was over, the British and American members of the ACC began to assert themselves more forcefully in overseeing Bulgarian postwar reconstruction. Bulgaria became just one of the many problems confronting Stalin as he prepared for the Potsdam Conference. Despite evidence provided by Bulgarian communists that Petkov was planning a coup, Stalin made clear early in July that the time was no longer right for such a campaign; the pace of the revolution in Bulgaria would have to be slowed. The elections planned for August 1945 had envisaged only parties loyal to the Fatherland Front participating: after protests from Britain and the United States, the Soviet representative, who chaired the ACC, ruled that the elections would have to be postponed; they were held in November under a new electoral law allowing a separate opposition electoral list.

In this way Allied pressure, brought to bear because of Bulgaria's position as a defeated power, was seen to work. An opposition movement headed by Petkov, and operating outside the Fatherland Front, had been officially sanctioned and as the elections approached Petkov again played the Western card. At the Potsdam Conference of the Great Powers in August 1945 it had been decided that peace treaties with defeated powers could only be signed when recognised governments had been established. Petkov withdrew his candidates from the autumn 1945 election and then called on the West not to recognise the government formed after them. The strategy worked: the elections were held, but the government was not recognised and between November 1945 and March 1946 Bulgaria was the subject of much high-level diplomacy, with Stalin prepared to ask the Bulgarian communists to include token opposition politicians in their government, but not prepared to allow those politicians to exercise any real power.[34]

The failure of these internationally sponsored moves to form a united government of the Fatherland Front and Petkov's opposition meant that an electoral contest was inevitable. The communists spent the summer of 1946 reinforcing their position in the Fatherland Front by bringing the *zvenari* still further under their sway. The Allies had demanded reductions in the size of the Bulgarian Army and when the *zvenari* War Minister General Damian Velchev tried to use the occasion to sack former partisan commanders he suspected of disloyalty, the communists responded by accusing him of friendship with Mihailović and other actions against the people; the cabinet as a whole was made responsible for defence matters and Velchev was persuaded to become ambassador to Switzerland.[35]

The electoral clash with Petkov came at the end of October 1946 when elections were held to elect a new assembly empowered to endorse a new constitution. In these elections, accompanied by allegations of ballot rigging and frequent complaints to the ACC, Petkov secured 22 per cent of the vote, winning the votes of many who had once supported the Fatherland Front. The net effect of this, however, was to entrench the communists still more firmly in control of the Fatherland Front: over three-quarters of the votes went to the Fatherland Front and over three-quarters of those votes went to the communists, giving them over 50 per cent of the vote.[36]

Nevertheless, Petkov had won nearly a quarter of the votes and, more worryingly, he did have significant support within the youth and women's organisations affiliated to the Fatherland Front. He still represented a threat and as soon as the Peace Treaty with the Allies had been signed in February 1947 and Bulgaria was no longer an enemy power subject to Allied supervision, the communists began a campaign against him that culminated in his arrest and execution. Dimitrov's revolution might have been slowed by foreign supervision, but it was no less far-reaching or brutal than Tito's. As if to signify the resumption of the revolutionary course, in April 1947 Stalin suggested the idea of a Balkan Federation be put back on the agenda.[37]

In Albania, Bulgaria and Yugoslavia the communists were aggressive and enthusiastic in their desire to mimic the Soviet Union. They had won a revolution through war and were simply disdainful of the need to legitimise their regimes through the procedures of 'bourgeois' democracy. Democracy expressed through a popular front formed 'from below' was, they believed, a fairer way of gauging popular support. Ironically there seems little doubt that the communists in all three countries could have won Western style elections in 1945 had they chosen to do so, but that was alien to the Leninist culture in which they had been trained.

2

Different Roads to Socialism

STALIN AND LIBERATED EASTERN EUROPE

If in the Balkans communists came to power at the head of their own revolutions and, as it were 'sovietised' themselves, elsewhere in Eastern Europe the role played by the Soviet Union in shaping the nature of postwar politics was far more important. However, prior to 1947 Stalin had no overall blueprint for expansion, nor a single uniform policy to be applied throughout the area. He operated, as before, via messages from Moscow and, having endorsed revolution in the Balkans, retained two policy options for the rest of Eastern Europe.

In Poland and Romania Stalin intervened decisively to ensure the establishment of sympathetic regimes: these, after all, were the countries which had had territorial disputes with the Soviet Union throughout the interwar period, disputes which Stalin had solved in 1939 and 1940 and whose resolution he sought to make permanent. Here there was to be no pretence about coalition governments and communists not being interested in power; the communists were to have power and would if necessary be kept in power by the Red Army.

In both countries Stalin followed what could be termed a dual strategy: communists would be encouraged to attain power through a popular front formed 'from below', but, as a back-up in case that failed, Stalin built up within the Soviet Union parallel Communist Party organisations which could intervene decisively with the support of the Red Army. These organisations were less active in Romania, where the revolutionary ferment of the Balkans spilled over into support for the communist-led democratic front, but played a crucial role in Poland where the communists' popular mandate scarcely existed.

Stalin had no immediate interest in supporting revolution in Czechoslovakia and Hungary, and the messages the communists in these two countries received from Moscow reflected this: communists should not try to enforce their will by imposing a popular front 'from below', but should observe the parity principle and take part in coalition governments, making no overt bids for power; the two parties were sent what amounted to the same message as those sent to the French and Italian communists.

However, in one crucial respect Moscow's guidance differed to that given to communists in the West's sphere of influence. Whereas in Italy, France and Greece communists had been advised to disarm their communist dominated militias and put them at the disposal of 'bourgeois' politicians – in Greece it had been this request which sparked off the ill-fated communist insurrection – in Czechoslovakia and Hungary the communist militias were not disbanded, and soon became the basis of a new army and security service. While this did not of itself give the communists power, it did make it difficult for other parties to ignore them.

Romania

As in Bulgaria, the first attempts by Romanian communists to construct a popular front had been confused. Initially, from the summer of 1943, they had followed a Leftist policy and concentrated on winning over only those groups ideologically close to them, the Ploughmen's Front, the Hungarian Minority Organisation (MADOSZ), and small left-wing groups that together formed the Anti-Hitlerite Patriotic Front. The base of this organisation was broadened significantly in April 1944 when a Moscow representative deposed the then Party leader and prepared the way for the emergence of the future Party leader, the well-known working class communist Gheorghe Gheorghiu-Dej. The Party was instructed to open talks with the socialists and the 'traditional parties', the National Liberal Party and the National Peasant Party. Another leading communist, Lucreţiu Pătrăşcanu, handled these talks and although he succeeded in winning over the socialists in April and formed with them a United Workers' Front, his talks with the traditional parties soon ran into trouble.

Although they agreed in June 1944 to form a National Democratic Bloc, the programme of the Bloc foundered on the question of Moldavia. The traditional parties wanted to return to the pre-1939 borders of Romania which would have involved the Soviet Union returning Moldavia, annexed in 1940. This the communists would not accept and, aware of the likely breakdown in these talks, Gheorghiu-Dej concentrated his efforts on securing communist influence over the Ploughmen's Front and establishing partisan units.[1]

No agreement had been reached between the communists, their allies and the traditional parties when these talks were overtaken by events. On 23 August 1944 King Michael staged a coup against the pro-Nazi dictator Antonescu and pre-empted the plans for a politicians' coup to be carried out by the four leading anti-fascist parties, the National Peasant Party, the National Liberal Party, the Socialist Party and the Communist Party, plans still hampered by the lack of agreement on national boundaries. Presented with the King's action, the parties responded in very different ways.

The traditional parties rallied to support the King and clearly hoped to repeat what might be termed the Italian experience. In Italy Mussolini had been deposed, the Allies had agreed to an armistice, and a coalition administration had been formed which kept the communists firmly in a minority. The same could be done for Romania, they felt, especially as British landings in the Balkans were expected at any moment. From their perspective there was absolutely no need to rush into an alliance with the communists, although the communists were probably less of a danger inside government rather than outside.

The communists responded to the King's coup by resolving to make a bid for power: how, rather than if they should bid for power became the major issue within the Romanian Communist Party, for Stalin held in reserve a Moscow-based communist organisation, to be used in conjunction with the Red Army if the Romanian leadership proved unequal to the task. The Soviet Union had long encouraged Romanian prisoners of war to join the so-called Tudor Vladimirescu Battalion and fight with the Red Army. Alongside this, Moscow-based communist leaders such as Ana Pauker and Vasile Luca had established a Communist Party 'Bureau'. The policy of the Bureau was quite clear and simple: there was no need to worry too much about broad popular fronts, about traditional parties and parliamentary games, even about partisan operations, as the Red Army advanced into Romania and existing order collapsed, the Communist Party should simply seize power with the support of the Red Army. Stalin could afford the luxury of relying either on domestic communists like Gheorghiu-Dej or Moscow communists such as Ana Pauker, and it seems clear he thought the Pauker option the more likely. When in September 1944 Pătrăşcanu visited Moscow, he was told that the action by the domestic communists had 'upset all our plans'.[2]

The National Democratic Bloc Government of the four main parties – the National Liberal Party, the National Peasants Party, the Socialist Party and the Communist Party – formed after the King's coup and headed by General Constantin Sănătescu, was not agreed about the most basic of issues. By October 1944 the communists and socialists, supported by the Ploughmen's Front, had formed a National Democratic Front with its own programme of agrarian reform, the energetic pursuit of the war, workers' rights in industry, and democratisation and defascistisation. The traditional parties in the government, without developing an alternative policy of their own, insisted that all such issues be shelved until after the war.

Campaigning on their radical programme won the communists much popular support. Farm-workers and peasants, sometimes spontaneously but often at the instigation of the communists and socialists, began to seize land, unwilling to wait for the end of the war as the government advised. The communists and socialists launched a joint campaign for the breaking up of all estates over 50 hectares and the annulment of all peasant debts.[3] Equally effective was the campaign to produce 'everything for the front', which enabled the communists and socialists to establish production committees within enterprises, and use the trade unions to force the employers to sign collective contracts. On 1 September 1944 the two parties jointly established an organising commission for a new trade union federation.[4]

Confident in its popular support, the National Democratic Front, immediately after its formation on 12 October, asked the King to form a new government led by Petru Groza, the leader of the Ploughmen's Front. When he refused, the two workers' parties left the government in protest, only to find that in their absence the government was proposing to put severe restrictions on the activities of the new trade unions. Thus in the second half of October almost continuous talks took place between the political parties about how a united government might be restructured.

On 2 November Stalin gave the communists a little help. As in Bulgaria, Romania – a defeated Axis power – was subject to the authority of an Allied Control Commission under Soviet chairmanship. This then now asked the government to act more vigorously against former fascists, for it was a condition of the armistice Romania had signed with the Soviet Union that all fascist organisations be dissolved and all war criminals put on trial. Then, on 3 November, the National Democratic Front organised a 100 000 strong demonstration against the government, followed by the threat on the 4th that it would resort to 'direct action' if the government were not restructured.

On 5 November Sănătescu resigned and formed a new broader government, giving the National Democratic Front a larger role and introducing legislation to arrest members of the Romanian fascist militia, the Iron Guard, and to abolish all anti-semitic legislation. But as social polarisation continued to grow apace, later in November the National Peasant Party Minister of the Interior used military force to disperse a pro-communist demonstration. This provoked another government crisis which resulted in the resignation of Sănătescu and the formation of a new administration on 2 December 1944 under Prime Minister Nicolae Radescu, which strengthened the influence of the communists still further. Although Radescu made himself the nominal Minister of the Interior, he brought in a communist as his deputy who refused point-blank to dissolve the Party's partisan units that had renamed themselves patriotic guards and were steadily usurping the powers of the police.[5]

After the British had exercised their rights in Greece in December 1944 by crushing the communist insurrection, Stalin decided to exercise his rights in Romania which, by agreement with Churchill, was within his sphere of influence. In January 1945 Gheorghiu-Dej and Pauker were summoned to Moscow and asked whether the Communist Party felt strong enough to act on its own to form a new government under its control, or whether the time had not come to operate the Pauker strategy of active Red Army support for a government formed by the Communist Party alone. Gheorghiu-Dej convinced Stalin that the Party was strong enough to dominate any future government.[6] On his return, the Romanian Communist Party dropped all talk of coalition government and launched an aggressive campaign for a new National Democratic Front Government. The campaign began on 27 January 1945 and, after a month of rallies, a massive demonstration was planned for 24 February, to gather outside the Ministry of the Interior.

The traditional parties responded to events in Greece quite differently. The British action there persuaded them that a firm stance against the communists might win Allied favour, even support, especially since at that very moment British pressure had persuaded Stalin to drop talk of a Balkan Federation. Thus when the communist demonstration gathered outside the Ministry of the Interior on 24 February 1945 the King feared the country was on the brink of civil war. Right-wing army units attacked communist party buildings, Ana Pauker fled to the protection of the Soviet embassy, some 600 000 National Democratic Front demonstrators took to the streets; some were armed and in several exchanges of fire three people were killed. To restore order Prime Minister Radescu instructed troops to open fire and then, in justification of his actions, roundly abused Ana Pauker and Vasile Luca in almost fascist terms, accusing them of not being real Romanians at all because they belonged to the Jewish and Ukrainian minority communities respectively.

Fearing that the communists might not be as on top of the situation as Gheorghiu-Dej had maintained when they met in January, Stalin used his military option and intervened to help the National Democratic Front into power. The Red Army occupied the Romanian Army Headquarters, disarmed all troops in the capital, and the Soviet chairman of the ACC ordered the King to appoint a new government. Despite the arrival of more and more Soviet troops, the King spun out the negotiations for as long as possible, unwilling to see the demise of the traditional parties and urging London to come out more clearly in his support. But it was all to no avail, and the crisis ended with the formation of a National Democratic Front Government on 6 March 1945, headed by the leader of the Ploughmen's Front; it included representatives of the socialists, the communists and those so-called 'Tartarascu' Liberals prepared to cooperate with them. Although only two communists were ministers, Pătrăşcanu and Gheorghiu-Dej, there was never any question that this was anything other than a government dominated by the communists; those socialists not prepared to support the communists closely were simply forced out of the party.[7]

Further consolidation of the communist regime was hampered, as it had been in Bulgaria, by Romania's position as a defeated power. After the Potsdam Conference in July 1945 the King urged the British and American Governments not to follow the Soviet lead in recognising the Groza Government, but to call on Groza to resign; he then went 'on strike' and refused to sign any bills until Groza resigned. The Western Allies agreed to do as the King requested and it was not until December 1945, when Stalin called on Groza to include one member of both the National Peasant Party and the National Liberal Party in his

Government, that the King stopped his strike and the West recognised Groza's Government.[8]

Stalin's intervention was timely. By early December 1945 the Soviet representative on the ACC was worried that Groza was himself tiring of Moscow's tutelage and preparing to do a deal with the traditional parties. The need to pay reparations to both the Soviet Union and Yugoslavia, as well as the actions of some communist party cells in taking over local branches of the Ploughmen's Front, had pushed him close to the opposition camp. This potential reverse was counterbalanced by the communists' success in cementing their alliance with the socialists. In December 1945 the socialists had decided to put up separate candidates in future elections, but after an intense campaign in the trade unions and local party cells the communists were able to get this decision reversed. When the Socialist Party held its Congress in March 1946 it not only decided to put forward a joint list of candidates with the other National Democratic Front parties, but also voted by a large majority for a merger with the Communist Party. The defeated minority had no choice but to form their own Independent Socialist Party.

In a similar way, the pro-communist parties were able first to seek allies within, and then divide, the traditional parties. By May 1946 the National Democratic Front had been extended to include the National Popular Party, the Alecsandrescu National Peasant Party, plus representatives from the trade unions, the youth organisations and the democratic women's organisations, the usual trappings of a popular front formed 'from below'. The Front went to the polls on 19 November 1946 and won 80 per cent of the vote. While the published results were not accurate, and there were certainly abuses during these elections (including the closure of newspapers and the mysterious deaths of leading figures), the opposition came nowhere near a victory.[9]

With considerably more Soviet help than elsewhere in the Balkans, the communists had succeeded in putting themselves at the head of popular opposition to the old regime, and implementing a social revolution as far-reaching as those in Albania, Bulgaria and Yugoslavia. The association in the popular mind of the traditional parties with the old regime meant that revolutionary change in Romania was inevitable; Soviet involvement ensured that it was the communists who dominated the revolutionary forces within the National Democratic Front, communists prepared to put on one side the thorny question of Moldavia. By the end of 1946 Stalin had helped make the whole of the Balkans socialist.

Poland

As in Romania, Stalin was to follow a dual strategy in Poland: while serious attempts were made to develop a native Communist Party that would evolve a popular front strategy, a parallel 'Russian Bureau' of the Party was built up in Moscow. As in Romania, the question of territory hampered the prospects for talks between the domestic political parties, pushing the communists away from coalition towards the tactic of the popular front 'from below'. There were important differences, however. Romania had become an Axis power, and its liberal and conservative parties were hopelessly compromised by vacillating relations with the fascist Antonescu regime. In Poland no pro-fascist or quisling administration had been formed. Poland was an honorary ally in the struggle against fascism, and its liberal and conservative groups were untainted with any hint of collaboration.

This resulted in serious differences within the Communist Party when it came to how best to deal with the traditional parties. While in Romania there may have been some tension between Pătrăşcanu and Gheorghiu-Dej over the question of how important the talks were with the traditional parties there, in Poland a clear rift developed between Wladslaw Gomułka and Bolesław Bierut on this very issue.

The pattern of events surrounding the formation of a popular front in Poland was similar to that in Romania, except that in Poland the Party had to be rebuilt from scratch. From the beginning these attempts to revive a Polish Workers (Communist) Party were characterised by isolationism. The Initiative Group which arrived in Warsaw in January 1942 was soon calling for a 'popular front without traitors or capitulators' and insisting on close party control over its People's Guard: both moves made it unlikely any agreement could be reached with parties loyal to the London based Government-in-Exile or units belonging to the existing pro-London Home Army.[10]

However, in 1943 the communists' line softened and in accordance with the Comintern's campaign against 'sectarianism' the Party instructed its deputy leader, Gomułka, to offer talks to the Warsaw representatives of the Government-in-Exile. The offer was made in January 1943; the talks began in February and continued into April; but they soon ran into difficulty over the question of the 1939 borders. The discovery of the Katyn massacre on 13 April 1943 put a further question mark over them, and arrests among the Home Army leadership in June 1943, followed by the death of the head of the Government-in-Exile in July meant that they were not resumed.[11]

However, even in this unpromising climate the coalition tactic was taken up again by Gomułka in the autumn of 1943 after he had become Party leader. If agreement with the Government-in-Exile was impossible, a new understanding with the socialists was on the cards, for in April 1943 those socialists dissatisfied with the London Government had split away to form the Polish Socialist Workers' Party. Although in September 1943 the First Conference of this party had rejected links with the Polish Workers' Party, the margin had been narrow. So, in November 1943, Gomułka proposed forming a broadly based popular front around a so-called Homeland National Council. Talks with the socialists began in December 1943, but were immediately put in jeopardy by two new developments.

Poor communications between Warsaw and Moscow meant that the details of these events were not known in Moscow. There, since early in 1943, Stalin had been building up the Union of Polish Patriots as a focus for all Poles living in the Soviet Union. After its congress in June 1943, the Union of Polish Patriots was granted permission to form its own Tadeusz Kosciuszko Division in the Red Army. Party members within this organisation had soon established their authority over the 30 000 men who had joined the Polish Division by the end of 1943; with 100 000 men under arms by the middle of 1944 the Union of Polish Patriots was potentially far stronger than the Polish Workers' Party. To strengthen the political role of this organisation, at the very same time as the Homeland National Council was being formed in Warsaw, a 'Central Bureau' of Polish Communists was established in Moscow.[12] Stalin had an alternative source of support should the Polish Workers' Party let him down.

The other threat to Gomułka's talks with the socialists came from within the Party. During the summer of 1943 Stalin sent one of his most trusted representatives, the former Comintern official Bolesław Bierut, to join Gomułka. Bierut's successive interventions in the Party's affairs during the spring of 1944 were all designed to prevent too many concessions being made to the socialists or to any other party. Bierut insisted that communist control over the Homeland National Council was more important than whether or not the socialists joined it. Largely as a result of his actions, communist hegemony over the Homeland National Council was accomplished so blatantly that only a socialist splinter group agreed to join; Gomułka pointedly boycotted its first session.

During the spring of 1944 a power struggle developed between Gomułka and Bierut. Despite Bierut's attitude, and the opposition of the Central Bureau of Polish Communists in Moscow, Gomułka succeeded in reviving talks with the majority of socialists in May 1944 and proposed that the Homeland National Council should be merged with the so-called Central People's Committee that the socialists planned to set up. On 23 May Gomułka proposed to the Party Central Committee that both these organisations should then merge with the Council of National Unity being proposed in London. These initiatives were fiercely denounced by Bierut. In a letter to the Comintern leader Dimitrov, Bierut accused Gomułka of 'stitching up' leadership meetings and forcing through a policy which meant 'following at the tail' of 'London reactionaries'. Bierut won Stalin's support: Moscow endorsed the Homeland National Council and all discussion of its merger ceased.

Stalin sided with Bierut because he had decided to use the military option in Poland. In July 1944 the Red Army crossed the River Bug and with it the Curzon Line: it then entered what all three Allied powers recognised as Poland. This offered the Party the opportunity of taking power not in alliance with a broad national front but on the back of the Red Army within the narrow framework of the Homeland National Council, a policy supported by the Central Bureau of Polish Communists and by Stalin. In Poland revolution would occur at the point of Soviet bayonets. At the end of July the Homeland National Council announced it had assumed control over the Union of Polish Patriots and its military forces and renamed itself the Polish Committee for National Liberation; the reality was, however, that the Union of Polish Patriots had swallowed up the Homeland National Council. Showing his mistrust for Gomułka, Stalin ensured that both the Party's new Politburo and the Polish Committee for National Liberation were dominated by Moscow communists.[13]

This revolution at the point of Soviet bayonets began on 21 September 1944 when Bierut, President of the Polish Committee for National Liberation, announced that the Committee was assuming the prerogatives of the pre-war parliament, the Sejm, and basing its authority on a new hierarchy of people's councils. He urged other parties to rally to the Committee, but only the socialists did so wholeheartedly. In September they ended the divisions between their pro- and anti-London factions and reformed the pre-war Polish Socialist Party; its leader Edward Osobka-Morawski became the Premier of the Polish Committee for National Liberation. The Peasant Party decided not to recognise the Committee, but nevertheless one of its pre-war leaders did agree to become Deputy Premier in charge of agrarian reform. With Socialist and Peasant Party support radical social changes were enacted in quick succession: land reform was implemented and all factories employing over 20 workers instructed to establish factory committees which had direct representation on the management board and the right to be consulted on wages, hiring and firing and other matters.[14]

With only the Socialist Party ready to collaborate wholeheartedly with the communists, Stalin believed it was essential they should not be unduly offended. They were allowed to re-establish their pre-war cooperative network and played an important role in reconstructing the trade unions: Osobka-Morawski had some 30 meetings with Stalin during the second half of 1944 to settle disputes between the socialists and the communists. Such indulgence was essential, for from October 1944, backed openly by the Red Army, the communists had to fight a virtual civil war against the pro-London Home Army: in October 1944 Stalin's security chief Lavrentii Beria sent in 100 members of the elite SMERSH forces, who helped arrest more than 2500 former members of the Home Army; in the last four months of 1944, 300 Red Army officers were killed in clashes with the Home Army, before it formally ceased operations in December 1944.[15]

By 5 January 1945 Stalin felt confident enough to recognise the Polish Committee for National Liberation as the country's Provisional Government, with Bierut as President and Osobka-Morawski as Prime Minister. Britain and the United States did not recognise this regime and raised the issue of Poland at the Great Powers' Yalta Conference in February 1945. Yalta favoured Stalin by recognising Poland's new eastern frontiers but called for the Provisional Government to be broadened by including in it other domestic and émigré groups. The Allied Foreign Ministers would oversee this process.

Up until the Yalta Conference the Government-in-Exile had not only insisted on returning to the pre-1939 boundaries, but also wanted to retain the authoritarian 1935 constitution; it had therefore been easy for Stalin to denounce them as 'reactionaries'. However, on 24 November 1944 the Peasant Party leader Stanisław Mikołajczyk had resigned as Prime Minister of the Government-in-Exile, and in December he had called on his Peasant Battalions to cooperate with Bierut's forces, leaving only right-wing Nationalist guerrillas in the field against the communists. Then, in February 1945, the Council of National Unity, once loyal to London, cut its links with the Government-in-Exile, recognised the Yalta agreement and began talks about cooperating in the formation of a Unity Government. This was a significant step forward; suddenly the vista of a genuine Government of National Unity stared Stalin in the face and he panicked. As the talks were taking place, on 27 March 1945, the Soviet Security Service intervened and the representatives of the Council of National Unity were spirited away to Moscow. On 3 April Gomułka informed the Soviet Foreign Minister Vyacheslav Molotov of his fears. Various leaders of the now underground Home Army were trying to open talks with the government. They clearly wanted some sort of coalition that would weaken the government by inviting western troops to Poland to oversee any future elections. In this damaging situation, at separate talks amongst the Allied Foreign Ministers about the future membership of a National Unity Government, and in exchanges between the three allied leaders, Moscow stalled to prevent any progress from being made until the end of May 1945.[16]

Between April 1945 and June 1945 an even more desperate civil war was fought in Poland, with pitched battles occurring between the Home Army and the security forces. In mid-May Beria agreed to increase the number of Soviet security troops operating in Poland because reports made clear that in some areas the Home Army 'completely controlled the situation'. As late as June 1945 the head of the Soviet military mission to Poland had to report 300 casualties in the previous month. Gomułka had little choice but to confess to the May Central Committee Plenum that without the Red Army's support they would have been unable to 'fight reaction'. Only after this bloodletting did Stalin feel secure enough to let the Provisional Government take up once again the proposal for a National Unity Government. Meaningful consultations began in June and it was announced on the 23rd that a Polish Provisional Government of National Unity had been formed: the Peasant, Socialist and Communist Parties would have six seats each, with three further seats going to the Catholic Labour Party. As if to stress the real source of power, however, at the very same time Muscovites saw the trial open of the leaders of the Council of National Unity charged with secretly preparing an underground war against the Red Army.[17]

The Government of National Unity did not stay united for long. It endorsed all the legislation of the previous Provisional Government, it was recognised by Britain and the United States, and it implemented the Potsdam Conference decision that gave it 'temporary administration of the territory up to the Oder-Neisse line until a peace conference'. These major decisions made, it rapidly fell apart. The socialists and communists in the government pushed on with their programme of social reform: all factories employing more than 40 workers were nationalised; the land reform was extended to the new western territories; and all industries there were rapidly brought under state control. But in August 1945 Mikołajczyk left the government to launch the new Polish Peasant Party, leaving behind a rump of the old Peasant Party still in government. Mikołajczyk believed he could use peasant support to make Poland ungovernable by the communists: this was a high-risk strategy, for he recognised that if Poland became ungovernable the Soviet Union would intervene; however, at that point he argued the West would express its displeasure and Stalin could be persuaded to accept the 'Finlandisation' of Poland.[18]

Stalin was determined Poland should be tied far more firmly to the Soviet Union than that. According to Jakub Berman, Poland's security chief during the 1940s, 'Stalin's one overriding aim in all this was, of course, to ensure that Poland would be bound to the Soviet Union by firm ties of loyalty'. So the civil war continued. Reports on the activity of what were now termed 'nationalist bandits' showed that as soon as the authorities relaxed, as they did near Lublin in February 1946, bandit activity revived. March 1946 saw nearly 500 bandit attacks, a worrying increase. At the end of May Gomułka told Stalin in person of the increasing number of acts of individual terror. It was not until autumn 1946 that the security forces felt on top of the situation, but even in the last three months of 1946, when the police carried out 2000 operations and made 4000 arrests, there were still over 3000 'bandit acts' recorded and 600 communist killed. Only the amnesty of February 1947 brought this civil war to an end.[19]

However, Stalin did not operate through repression alone and continued his policy of wooing the socialists, for, while the socialist–communist alliance stood firm, Mikołajczyk's threat could be contained; only if the socialists deserted the communists for Mikołajczyk would the regime truly be in danger. So Stalin continued to indulge the socialists, still siding with them rather than the communists when disputes blew up. For example, after February 1946 the communists argued that it was no longer worth trying to persuade Mikołajczyk to rejoin the Unity Government, they were convinced a clash with him was inevitable; the socialists, on the other hand, believed a deal could still be done. The crux of the matter was this: if Mikołajczyk rejoined the government, elections could be held on a single government ticket, with the parties dividing the seats amongst themselves according to an agreed percentage. The socialists believed Mikołajczyk's insistence on

75 per cent of the seats was idle rhetoric and that he could be persuaded to reduce this substantially. Under pressure from Stalin the communists agreed to renew talks with Mikołajczyk.

These got underway in May 1946, but were immediately complicated by the results of a referendum held in June that showed significant support for Mikołajczyk's party. As a consequence, the socialists were prepared to offer Mikołajczyk not 33 per cent but 40 per cent of the seats in a future parliament. When the communists protested at such generosity, and complained to Moscow that the socialists had become increasingly troublesome and were demanding an equal say in government, particularly in the army and the security services, they were outflanked by Osobka-Morawski who flew to Moscow in August at the head of a joint delegation of the two workers' parties. After detailed discussion he again persuaded Stalin to intervene on the socialists' behalf. Stalin's response to his complaint that the communists had accumulated 80 per cent of government power was to lecture the communists that political power in Poland could not be the monopoly of one party. Stalin also criticised the communist-controlled security forces for falsifying the results of the referendum.

In the end it was clear even to the socialists that Mikołajczyk was not prepared to accept a deal and it was announced in September that the elections would be contested rather than fought on a common ticket. Stalin's interventions had ensured that the socialists felt they had bent over backwards to accommodate an intransigent Mikołajczyk. His victory, the socialists concluded, would mean a new 'reactionary' insurrection and civil war, putting all the gains of the social revolution in jeopardy. In November they agreed on an electoral pact with the communists, which envisaged the two parties' eventual merger and their short-term collaboration in falsifying the election results of January 1947.[20]

Czechoslovakia

At the end of the war the communists dominated the resistance movement in Czechoslovakia. That movement had developed rather differently in the nominally independent Slovak state than it had in the Czech lands, formally incorporated into the German Reich. In those areas under direct German occupation, little in the way of armed resistance had proved possible until April 1945 when the German Army started to withdraw. As this happened, however, it was the communists who organised and soon dominated the 'revolutionary national committees', set up as a new system of local government built from the bottom up. These soon became the only nucleus of power, but restricted their activities to the local level: the communists made no attempt to dominate the Czech National Council on which they sat alongside representatives of the other political parties.[21]

The potential for communist dominance was even greater in Slovakia. There, as in Bulgaria, the communists had set themselves the task of establishing a partisan movement strong enough to head a popular insurrection against the pro-German government. The tactics they used were similar to those used in Yugoslavia or Bulgaria, and the result was the creation in summer 1943 of a Slovak National Council nominally based around parity of representation between communist and non-communist groups, but in practice under communist control, the popular front 'from below'; echoing the experience of Tito's partisans, the Slovak National Council had refused to recognise the émigré Czechoslovak government based in London. By August 1944 the communist partisans felt strong enough to stage the Slovak National Uprising, which, led by people like Rudolf Slánský and Gustáv Husák, continued throughout September before being overwhelmed by government forces. However, despite experiencing defeat, the communists were in a strong position to dominate the new 'national committees' when the Red Army crossed the Slovak border at the end of October 1944, especially since, moved by the spirit of the popular front 'from below', the Slovak socialists had agreed to merge with the communists in September 1944.[22]

Thus, given the experience of the Slovak National Uprising, where the concept of the popular front 'from below' clearly ruled supreme, and the communists' hegemony over the 'revolutionary national committees' at local level, it is clear the Communist Party could have seized complete power in 1945 had it so wished. It deliberately chose not to do so, and responsibility for that lay with Party leader Klement Gottwald who stuck loyally to the message he received from Stalin that there should be no attempt by the communists to break up the coalition government agreed in principle in Moscow in 1943. His government gave equal representation to the main political parties: the Communist Party, the Socialist Party, the National Socialist Party, the People's Party and the Democratic Party. The communists controlled important ministries, the Ministry of the Interior, Ministry of Education, Ministry of Agriculture and Ministry of Information, but were in a minority.[23]

Far from immediately asserting their hegemony over the 'national revolutionary committees', communists sought to broaden them and involve the other parties in their work. That they did so unwillingly and not always effectively was hardly surprising, opening up committees they already controlled to representatives of other parties must have seemed an unnecessary retreat to many communists, but it was attempted, although by October 1945 nearly all the chairmen of national committees were still communists or Left socialists, and the parity principle, while strictly observed at district level, was frequently ignored lower down the committee hierarchy. However, in a more effective move against the radical communists, the communist partisans of Slovakia found themselves firmly elbowed out of the limelight.[24]

The communists were not even in the forefront of the moves to nationalise industry. Since nearly 70 per cent of the country's economic wealth had been taken over by the Nazis, the expropriation of much of this industry by the new Czechoslovak state was not a particularly controversial act. Extending nationalisation to all firms employing over 150 workers, and implementing this in October 1945 by decree, caused more of a stir, but pressure for this came from the trade unions, and Left socialists within the trade unions rather than the Communist Party leadership. The area where the Communist Party was radical was land reform, enacted by the communist Minister of Agriculture in June 1945.

Quite when, if ever, the Czechoslovak communists saw themselves coming to power was far from clear. In the summer of 1945 Gottwald mapped out a decidedly unexciting road to power: he spoke of consolidating the Party's dominant position in the national councils, retaining their influence over important government ministries, building up the state security apparatus, and working within the trade union movement. It was to be the gradualist revolution *par excellence*, revolution by winning the directorships of nationalised industries and manipulating the chiefs of police. For in Czechoslovakia, more than any other East European country, the revolution had been the joint work of socialists, communists and others working under the guiding hand of President Beneš. In many ways it simply was enough for the communists to strengthen their position within this new state structure.[25]

At the elections of May 1946 the communists won 38 per cent of the vote and with their Socialist Party allies these 'working class parties' had a total of 51 per cent. Although their vote in Slovakia (30 per cent) was less than their showing in the Czech lands (40 per cent), their position was secure. In the subsequent reapportioning of seats in the local and district national committees, the communists were allocated 44 per cent of the seats; 37.5 per cent of local national committees were led by communists. Some 35 per cent of the directors of nationalised factories were communists, and the army and police hierarchies were firmly under their control. Yet the Party did not push for power, content that the major social revolution of nationalisation plus land reform had been achieved. While opposition within the Communist Party to this gradualist approach existed, it was kept firmly in check. At the March 1946 Party Congress, held during the election campaign, there was no trace of opposition to Gottwald's line, although discussions within party cells before the Congress suggested a widespread desire to speed up the revolutionary process.[26]

During 1946 Gottwald began to develop a theoretical model around this form of inertia politics. At the Party Congress in March 1946 he talked vaguely of the present system continuing almost indefinitely: with a working-class majority after the elections, none of the revolutionary changes so far introduced could be reversed. Then, after August 1946 when Stalin told a visiting delegation from the British Labour Party that there were different roads to socialism, and that the electoral road chosen by the Labour Party could, in certain circumstances, lead to socialism, Gottwald began to explore the implications of this for Czechoslovakia. In September 1946 the Central Committee debated Stalin's comments, and Gottwald suggested that his Party was already well along its own road to socialism. Just by being there, the Communist Party was edging Czechoslovakia towards socialism.

There were of course divisions between the parties that went to make up the National Front. The National Socialist Minister of Justice angered the communists by allegedly showing leniency towards war criminals, particularly the members of the former Protectorate Government that had ruled the Czech lands for the Nazis, and with his attitude to the nationalisation of small firms. For Gottwald, such issues were essentially minor niggling ones within the parties adhering to the National Front: at worst 'reaction' was fighting a rearguard action, there was simply no chance of the Communist Party ceasing to dominate the coalition.

These policies continued to be met with some scepticism by the rank and file. During the autumn of 1946 the message coming up from roughly half the party districts was that the other parties in the National

Front were forming a bloc against the communists and, if they succeeded, 'reaction' really could triumph. During the spring of 1947 the Party's Presidium regularly discussed whether the Party was on the right road, whether the forces of 'reaction' were a thing of the past or an immediate threat; but its conclusion, to campaign in the elections of 1948 for an overall majority, hardly suggested any imminent plans to seize power.[27]

Hungary

In Hungary too, the communists were instructed by Stalin not to bid for power but to settle for a role in a coalition government. Of course, unlike in Czechoslovakia where the pre-war Communist Party had been legal and influential, the Communist Party in Hungary was weak, and occasionally needed the support of Stalin to retain even a coalition stake in the government of postwar Hungary. Like Romania, Hungary was a defeated Axis power and the mechanism for Soviet intervention was the Allied Control Commission under its Soviet chairman.

The first anti-Nazi moves in Hungary had taken place within the Hungarian parliament towards the end of 1942, when an alliance had been formed between the Socialist Party and the 'Peasant Alliance' set up by the Smallholders' Party led by Ferenc Nagy; since the Communist Party was illegal, it was not involved in this essentially parliamentary alliance. It was only when the Germans occupied Hungary on 19 March 1944 and suppressed the Peasant Alliance and the Socialist Party that the Communist Party came into its own. With all three parties on the same illegal footing the communists, led by László Rajk, were able to put themselves forward as equals for the first time and an alliance of communists, socialists and smallholders was formed.[28]

The Red Army reached the Hungarian border at the end of September and Debrecen, the first major regional centre, in mid-October 1944; and, while the Hungarian Government remained loyal to Hitler to the end, increasing numbers of anti-fascists rallied to the territory brought under Soviet control. During the autumn of 1944 the Hungarian communists sought to dominate their alliance with the socialists and smallholders by some of the classic manoeuvres of the popular front 'from below'. Thus the 10 October 1944 agreement signed between the communists and socialists, which envisaged the eventual merger of the two parties, was reminiscent of a similar agreement signed during the Slovak National Uprising; the decision to allow trade union representatives on the planned national committees suggested a clear intention of outvoting the smallholders, while on many of the factory committees established in newly liberated areas communists spoke openly of establishing the 'dictatorship of the proletariat'.[29]

The communist leadership that returned from Moscow with the Red Army made clear that this revolutionary behaviour had to stop. Ernő Gerő, one of the first Moscow leaders to return, said as much in an address to party activists on 9 November; however, the fact that Hungary's popular front, the National Independence Front, was only formed on 2 December 1944, and that there were still trade union representatives on it, although balanced by representatives of the Democratic Party, suggested the issue had not yet been settled. Indeed, even Gerő got swept along by events and in January 1945 wrote to Mátyás Rákosi, the Party's leading figure still then resident in Moscow, asking permission to launch a party offensive. It was only when Rákosi himself returned towards the end of February and was elected general secretary that Stalin's line was adopted unequivocally.[30]

Thereafter Rákosi stamped his authority on the Party. In May 1945 the National Party Conference passed a resolution strongly condemning the 'Left sectarian veterans of 1919' who had dreamt of seizing power, and committed the Party to coalition politics, a line to which it remained committed until the autumn of 1947. It built up its alliance with the socialists, won extensive control over the trade union movement, but, like its Czechoslovak counterpart, made no bid for power. Indeed, until 1947 the actions of the Communist Party were essentially defensive rather than offensive, for the possibility always existed of the smallholders and the socialists reforming their 1942 alliance to the exclusion of the communists.

This danger first became apparent when elections were held in the autumn of 1945. Local elections in October, in particular the voting in Budapest, was a disaster for the communists. They were confident the bloc of communists and socialists would win, and Rákosi had guaranteed as much to the Soviet member of the ACC Kliment Voroshilov; but victory went to the smallholders.[31] When the nervous communists launched a press campaign against the smallholders, Voroshilov intervened to try and re-establish a working relationship between Rákosi and the leader of the smallholders, Zoltán Tildy before the national elections at the start of November. Tildy was genuinely worried that his party had become a rallying point for anti-Soviet elements and proposed agreeing on the composition of the government in advance of the elections.

This was a novel notion, yet it contradicted the express instructions Voroshilov had received from Moscow to encourage the formation of a single electoral list for all three major parties, the communists, socialists and smallholders. Voroshilov asked Moscow for guidance, but as it was slow in coming, and as the socialists as well as the smallholders had now decided to fight the national elections separately from the communists, Voroshilov decided to endorse Tildy's proposal, only to earn an angry rebuke from the Soviet Politburo. Tildy, who became Prime Minister, stuck to the agreement he had reached about sharing power, but that did not prevent wrangling over the allocation of posts. Stalin instructed Voroshilov that the communists had to be awarded the Ministry of Internal Affairs. It took Voroshilov ten days to achieve this, in the course of which he spoke of resignation, asked for permission to make concessions and moaned that 'intervention here means organising a series of meetings'. At the lowest ebb in these negotiations he asked Moscow if Béla Kovács, general secretary of the Smallholders' Party, could be made Minister of the Interior since 'we can work with Kovács'. In the end the smallholder leadership decided to acquiesce. It wanted to keep the coalition government alive until the Peace Treaty had been signed; then the communists could be quietly excluded from government. This, at any rate, was the substance of Molotov's interpretation of events.[32]

In such circumstances there was no love lost between the communists and the smallholders. Communist tactics were simple, to build up an alliance with the socialists and the small National Peasant Party to the point where this 'Left Bloc', rather than the smallholders, had more than 50 per cent of the vote: since the smallholders had won 57 per cent of the vote in the November 1945 elections and the votes of the putative Left Bloc totalled the other 43 per cent, this was not such an impossible task, and could easily be done by exploiting the natural inclination of the smallholders to bully their junior coalition partners. Most of the government crises of 1946 and 1947 were initiated by the Right; those that were initiated by the Left ended with the Left backing down.

In January 1946 the monarchy was abolished and a republic proclaimed. Tildy was appointed President and replaced as Prime Minister by the fellow smallholder Ferenc Nagy. With the establishment of the republic it was not unreasonable for the Left Bloc to propose a bill for the Defence of the Republic that would make plotting the overthrow of the republic a criminal offence. It was the Right-wing of the Smallholders' Party which used this proposal to launch a vitriolic campaign against the Red Army, their coalition partners the Communist Party, the terms of the armistice and, for good measure, made chauvinistic statements about the alleged victimisation of the Hungarian minority in Slovakia. In response to this outburst, it was not difficult for the Left Bloc to appear pillars of moderation and organise 100 000 strong protest demonstrations demanding that the smallholders expel these right-wing leaders; they were, of course, also echoing the concerns of the Soviet representative on the ACC. Embarrassed by his own supporters, Ferenc Nagy, the Smallholders' Party leader and Prime Minister, agreed and 20 smallholder MPs were expelled from the party on 12 March 1946.[33]

The May crisis in 1946 was similarly provoked by the Smallholders' Party. General Secretary Béla Kovács asked the Left Bloc to agree to make a number of concessions: provincial elections should be held at once, half the jobs in the police force should be allocated to smallholders, and 'arbitrary action' by the police should cease. As Tildy explained to the Soviet representative on the ACC, it had been agreed in the autumn that jobs in local government and the police and security services would be allocated according to the percentage of votes received in the parliamentary elections, but this had never been done. After intensive negotiations between the parties and the ACC, the Left Bloc agreed to most of these requests: the provincial political police was wound up, a number of important police jobs were allocated to smallholders, and it was agreed provincial elections would be held in the autumn; it was Ferenc Nagy who decided not to hold the elections until after the Peace Treaty had been signed.[34] Over the summer the ACC became increasingly concerned at what it saw as the growing activity of 'the reactionary wing' of the smallholders. The banning of the Boy Scouts and Catholic Youth was the result of right-wing provocation, after Red Army soldiers had been killed by youths linked to the Smallholders' Party and Catholic Church.[35]

On the other hand, initiatives taken by the Left Bloc were only partly successful. When in September 1946 the Soviet controlled ACC tried to ban the Freedom Party, formed by those right-wing smallholders expelled from the party in March, Ferenc Nagy persuaded them to back down. In October 1946 the Left Bloc put forward a series of demands: Nagy agreed to introduce state supervision of the banks, but refused to appoint Left Bloc supporters to government posts which had fallen vacant; ignoring vociferous street demonstrations, Nagy insisted on appointing smallholders to all the empty jobs.[36]

Even the spring crisis of 1947, which culminated in the resignation of Nagy and the collapse of the Smallholders' Party, was the responsibility of the smallholders themselves. On New Year's Eve, the communist controlled Ministry of the Interior announced that a widespread anti-republican conspiracy had been uncovered, implicating many important officials in the Smallholders' Party; for several weeks the security service had been tapping the Prime Minister's phone, while the communists had blackmailed informers in the leadership of all their rival parties. For the Left Bloc things could hardly have turned out better, they could now legitimately demand that the parliamentary immunity of these officials be lifted, and Ferenc Nagy could scarcely reject such demands since there was incontrovertible evidence that leading members of his party were plotting to restore the pre-war Regency.

When on 24 January 1947 Ferenc Nagy had lunch with the Soviet representative on the ACC, he accepted the reality of the plot and the existence of 'reactionary elements' within his parliamentary party; but he complained that the communists were making use of the plot to split his party in two. This was indeed the Soviet tactic, and as part of that campaign the party's General Secretary Béla Kovács was accused of participation in the conspiracy. When news of his involvement broke in February 1947 he was persuaded to resign his post, but the party would not agree to lift his parliamentary immunity. Unfortunately for the smallholders this attempt at damage limitation did not work. The Soviet authorities had evidence that Kovács' plans had involved plotting against the occupation forces and, faced with Ferenc Nagy's refusal to arrest him on charges of anti-republican activity, promptly arrested him for crimes against the Red Army and took him to Moscow. Voroshilov's earlier judgement that 'we can work with Kovács' was forgotten.[37]

With the reputation of the Smallholders' Party severely damaged, the Left Bloc was able to demand more say in government. After talks early in March 1947 the smallholders, socialists and communists agreed that anti-communist smallholder ministers should be replaced by smallholders prepared to work with the Left Bloc and representatives of the pro-Communist National Peasant Party. The Left Bloc had achieved its basic objective, the Smallholders' Party had been so battered by the aftermath of the conspiracy that it could not claim superior status within the coalition; it was no longer a coalition of one party plus two others, but of three equal parties. That there could be no return to the past was ensured when, at the end of May, Ferenc Nagy was persuaded to resign as Prime Minister after it was put to him that Kovács might be about to implicate him in his anti-Soviet activities. The veracity of this is hard to judge. On 29 April Rákosi met Molotov in Moscow and asked, since the Soviet interrogation of Kovács had suggested that Ferenc Nagy and even Tildy were implicated in the conspiracy, if Kovács could not be returned to Hungary and appear before a Hungarian court; Molotov refused, adding the enigmatic comment 'who knows what he might tell a Hungarian court'.[38]

The communists were quick to push home their advantage and consolidate the gains made in discrediting the smallholders by holding fresh elections. Given that the Left Bloc had achieved 43 per cent of the vote in 1945, and since then the Smallholders' Party had collapsed, the Left Bloc was optimistic it would achieve more than 50 per cent of the vote. In the event, the elections held on 30 August saw the Left Bloc vote increase only by 2 per cent to 45 per cent: victory was assured only by the fragmentation of the Right into the Independence (Freedom) Party, Democratic Party and Radical Party, all competing for votes with the smallholders. Within the Left Bloc a certain amount of gerrymandering ensured that the Communist Party emerged with more seats than the Socialist Party, but the Smallholders' Party was still needed for stable government.

Thus the new administration gave five seats to the Communist Party, two to the National Peasant Party, four to the Socialist Party and four to the Smallholders' Party. The communists could claim to be the leading force in the coalition, but could still be outvoted if the smallholders and socialists voted together. In September 1947 the Hungarian communists were no more securely entrenched than their Czechoslovak counterparts, and the British Labour Government, whose Foreign Minister Ernest Bevin was vociferously anti-communist, was optimistic that the socialists could still marginalise communist influence within the Left Bloc.[39]

The evidence clearly suggests, then, that between 1945 and 1947 Stalin had no overall blueprint for Eastern Europe. He was determined to win friendly governments in Poland and Romania; that is, governments which would recognise the territorial adjustments made in 1939 and 1940. As to Czechoslovakia and Hungary, he was content to see the communists exercising influence: in Czechoslovakia this came naturally to them, while in Hungary Stalin had occasionally to intervene to support the communists there.

3

AN END TO DIVERSITY

In the spring of 1947 diversity rather than uniformity characterised Eastern Europe. The Balkan revolutions were an accomplished fact: Yugoslavia and Albania were further along the socialist road than Bulgaria, but that was largely because Bulgaria had been subject to Allied scrutiny. Romania and Poland had experienced revolutions at Soviet prompting, the Romanians responding with more enthusiasm to embarking on the road that their Balkan fellows were already following, while the Poles had, literally, experienced revolution at Soviet bayonet point. As to Czechoslovakia and Hungary, the one an honorary ally with a large communist party, the other a defeated power with a tiny communist party, Stalin seemed to have satisfied himself with influence rather than control: communist influence in the security services meant the communists there had more say than the communists in the French and Italian postwar governments. This situation was to change as the Cold War developed.

COLD WAR POLITICS

As early as autumn 1945 Stalin had doubts about how much longer the wartime alliance with Britain and America could last; his correspondence with Molotov and other Politburo members shows his determination to prevent the smallest concessions being made to his former allies. By spring 1946 Stalin was convinced that the era of wartime cooperation with Britain and the United States was over for good and that the newly formed United Nations would become a forum for confrontation rather than cooperation as its leading members, Britain, America and France increasingly 'ganged up' against the Soviet Union. At the start of the year Stalin established a foreign policy commission within the Politburo which paved the way for the creation in April of a new Foreign Policy Department headed by Andrei Zhdanov, one of Stalin's most rigid disciples. Yet Stalin was always cautious, and his recognition that the wartime alliance was over did not mean he wanted direct conflict with his former allies. Thus in September 1946 he asked the Yugoslavs to act as his proxy and step up support for the Greek communists in their nascent civil war against the British supported Greek government; but he was still unwilling to commit himself fully to such confrontation, and by December 1946 Soviet aid to the Greek communists, though promised, had still not come.[1] As his comments to the British Labour Party in August 1946 had shown, Stalin had at this time no interest in seizing those countries of Eastern Europe not already in his orbit.

Stalin's support for the Greek communists, however limited, was seized on by the Americans. Thus the fate of Eastern Europe began to change with the announcement of the Truman doctrine in February 1947, the first move towards the adoption of the Marshall Plan, and the exclusion of the communists from the postwar coalition governments of France and Italy in May. This latter development was of particular significance for Czechoslovakia and Hungary. Put crudely, in France and Italy the socialist parties decided they had more in common with their countries' liberal and conservative parties than with their 'working class allies' the communists. If the socialists in Czechoslovakia and Hungary came to the same decision, the communists could similarly be excluded from government, possibly with difficulty in Czechoslovakia, where the communists were strong, but with no difficulty at all in Hungary.

Indeed, in Hungary steps towards this end were already well under way. Although the general secretary of the British Labour Party had visited Hungary twice in 1946 as the guest of the Hungarian Social Democratic Party, contacts between the two parties only took on political significance later. Denis Healey, the Labour Party's International Secretary, paid two visits to Hungary in the first half of 1947 for talks with social democrat leaders. On the first occasion, to attend the 35th Congress of the Hungarian Social Democratic Party in January 1947, he brought with him the clear message that all talk of fusion with Rákosi's communists should be resisted. On his second visit three months later Healey repeated essentially the same message, this time at the International Congress of Danube Valley Socialist Parties held in Budapest.

However, on this second occasion Healey had been closely briefed by the British Foreign Office, which, after the demise of the Smallholders' Party, saw the social democrats as the only force capable of resisting the communist advance. After Healey's second visit the number of contacts between the social democrats and British diplomats steadily increased and the Labour Party actively courted its Hungarian comrades at such gatherings as the International Socialist Conference in Zurich; they even identified an alternative party leader in the event of a complete break with the communists. With the elections set for 30 August, the Foreign Office was delighted that the pressure exerted through the Labour Party seemed to be paying off. The social democrats, while happy to fight the elections in alliance with the communists, refused point-blank to put up a joint electoral list; they anticipated an increase in their vote of between eight and ten per cent and had no intention of putting this in jeopardy. Despite pressure from Soviet diplomats, the social democrats stood firm and relations between them and the communists turned sour as the elections approached. In response to a communist assertion that the merger of the two parties was just a matter of time, the social democrat leader said 'if the question of a merger of the two working class parties is levelled at us, our reply is – never'. When gerrymandering of the election results allowed the communists to claim more votes than the social democrats, the alliance between the two parties stood in tatters. In mid-September a special emissary was sent for talks with the British Foreign Secretary Ernest Bevin.[2]

To a Marxist like Stalin, who believed in the power of the economic base over the political superstructure, it was not accidental that the exclusion of the communists from the governments of France and Italy and the British Labour Party's interest in the future of the Hungarian Socialist Party, coincided with the American proposals for Marshall Aid: the socialists of Western Europe had been bought off, bribed even, to desert their communist comrades by the promise of dollars and American investment, and the same could happen in Eastern Europe. In the circumstances Stalin believed it was crucial that Marshall Aid be rejected and to help him in this resolve he turned to Tito, whose opposition to all things American was, if anything, even more outspoken than his own.

The Communist Information Bureau (Cominform)

In June 1947 the Soviet Foreign Minister Vyacheslav Molotov suggested to the leading Yugoslav communist Milovan Djilas that, in order to rally the communist parties of Europe against the offer of Marshall Aid, the time had come to reform some sort of Communist International. The need for such an international body had long been accepted by the Yugoslavs and they therefore accepted with alacrity the initial proposal for some sort of new journal, with a clear ideological line, which would bind the communist parties more firmly together.[3] Stalin's worst fears were confirmed when Molotov concluded at the meeting held in Paris on 26 June–3 July that Marshall Aid not only meant the consolidation of western Europe into an anti-communist bloc but also constituted an attempt to undermine Soviet influence in Eastern Europe. However, Stalin's handling of the Marshall Aid proposals had been too subtle for other East European communist leaders. Stalin had encouraged participation in the Paris meeting in order to discover, or unmask, the true ambitions of the West; but he had expected his allies to act in unison once Molotov's negative verdict had been given. The Czechoslovak government failed to do this and on 4 July 1947 made clear it was willing to accept Marshall Aid. Stalin intervened dramatically, summoned Gottwald and his key ministers to Moscow on 9 July and told them bluntly that 'for us this question is one of friendship between the Soviet Union and Czechoslovakia', any possible economic advantages offered by Marshall Aid would be matched by Soviet purchases. The next day the Czechoslovak government reversed its decision. Thereafter none of the countries of Eastern Europe accepted Marshall Aid, but Stalin's intervention had been essentially stopgap; a more permanent solution had to be found, and that was the Communist Information Bureau or Cominform. After consultation on a preparatory agenda produced on 15 August, the East European leaders gathered at Szklarska Poręba in Poland on 22–27 September 1947.[4]

At that gathering of nine leading communist parties (the Soviet, Polish, Czechoslovak, Hungarian, Bulgarian, Romanian, Yugoslav, French and Italian), the Yugoslavs took centre stage. Their delegates, Djilas and Foreign Minister Edward Kardelj, severely criticised the French and Italian communists for allowing themselves to be ousted from government, and argued further that they understood why and how the Italian and French communists had been so easily duped;

it was because they had not strengthened the popular front 'from below'. Because the French and Italian communists had accepted parity in coalition governments, they had been forced to agree to the disbanding of their resistance militias and had been unable to counter their weakness at the zenith of government by strength in grass root councils. The implication of the Yugoslav argument was clear, unless the communist parties in Eastern Europe acted quickly, they too might find themselves being edged out of government, and to stop this happening they needed to make radical changes in the nature of their popular front organization.

Stalin readily endorsed the Yugoslav line. At his insistence Belgrade was made the headquarters of the Cominform, and the publishing centre for the journal *For a Lasting Peace, for a People's Democracy*. The Yugoslavs were understandably flattered by Stalin's apparent favour, particularly the way in which the Soviet delegate to the Founding Conference simply endorsed their speeches and made plain to all other delegates that a dramatic change of policy was needed. The nature of those changes was repeated once more by Tito in a keynote speech to the Second Congress of the Yugoslav People's Front held almost contemporaneously. Like Kardelj and Djilas, he too lambasted those who had constructed popular fronts 'only from above'; he praised the achievements of the Yugoslav popular front built 'from below'; and he insisted that this Yugoslav pattern could be followed by all parties: popular front organisations had to be transformed from all-party coalitions into 'single, united, all-peoples organisations'. This became the constant refrain of the journal *For a Lasting Peace, for a People's Democracy*.[5]

The Czechoslovak Coup, February 1948

Perhaps not surprisingly, given Stalin's concern with Czechoslovak affairs at this time, the other person favoured by Moscow at the Founding Conference was the Czechoslovak delegate Rudolf Slánský. Slánský had been a participant in the partisan Slovak National Uprising, suggesting a certain affinity for the Yugoslav road to socialism, and both in his speech to the Founding Conference and immediately on his return to Czechoslovakia, he took up the theme of the need to change the nature of the Czechoslovak National Front. His proposal, the classic tactic of the popular front 'from below', was to highlight the absence of mass organisations such as the trade unions and women's organisations and demand that in the future such organisations should play a far greater role in the affairs of the National Front.

Slánský needed some time to win Gottwald over to this new strategy, for it contradicted everything he had stood for since 1945,[6] but at the end of November the Central Committee decided to follow those policies outlined at the Founding Meeting of the Cominform.[7] For the first time, Gottwald dropped the parliamentary conception of the National Front and highlighted instead the role of the (communist controlled) mass organisations, which he too now argued had to be brought back into the National Front. This policy, a direct echo of Tito's speech to the Second Congress of the People's Front, was formulated with utter clarity in the Communist Party's New Year message to the Czechoslovak people in January 1948: 'the communists do not see the National Front as a coalition of political parties ... [or] a gathering of the leaders of political parties, it is an alliance of workers, peasants, handicraftsmen and intellectuals, an alliance which must become firmer every day'.[8]

By February 1948 the need to do something about the National Front was acute, for the communists could no longer guarantee control over it. In November 1947 the socialists had deposed their Leftist leader and replaced him with a man hostile to the Communist Party. The significance of this move, the possible start of a repetition of the French and Italian scenarios, became clear in January 1948 during the so-called police affair. When the communist-controlled Ministry of the Interior sacked several police officials who were not Communist Party members, the socialists joined with the other coalition parties in calling for a cabinet committee to investigate the circumstances surrounding these personnel changes. Then, on 10 February 1948, the socialist minister for the Civil Service won government support for a pay deal opposed by the communists and the trade unions.

This defeat for the trade unions provided the perfect opportunity for communists to raise once again the issue of replacing 'reactionary' groups within the National Front by representatives from the trade unions. Fortuitously, a Congress of Workers' Councils was already planned for 22 February, and this provided the perfect backdrop for a vociferous campaign aimed at ousting from the National Front those 'reactionaries' opposed to the workers. With factory councils working overtime to whip up working-class anger, the dispute at cabinet level continued to be about police personnel: on 13 February the cabinet united against the communists and called for the personnel changes to be rescinded. For the next week Gottwald used every imaginable excuse to prevent the cabinet returning to the issue until on 20 February, exasperated, the National Socialist ministers, People's Party ministers and Slovak Democratic Party ministers all resigned.

This played into the communists' hands. The resignation could be interpreted as an 'attempted reactionary coup' which deemed them unworthy of membership of the National Front; with these 'bourgeois' parties out of the National Front, the front itself could be reformed 'from below'. On 21 February the communists called for revolutionary 'action committees' to be formed to rejuvenate the National Front by bringing in the mass organisations, and on 23 February the first meeting of the Central Action Committee of the National Front met at the instigation of the trade unions and called a token one hour general strike on the 24th. This show of working-class militancy was all-important, for it persuaded the socialists that, if they wanted to retain their industrial base, they would have to remain in alliance with the communists.

This working-class pressure 'from below', which persuaded the socialists to restore their alliance with the communists at the height of the political crisis, meant there was no way in which the communists' coup could be prevented constitutionally; since the two parties controlled over half the seats in parliament, there were no grounds on which the president could refuse their request to reform the government. The communists had broken some unwritten parliamentary procedures, and the 'action committees' had clearly operated outside the law when purging opponents, but the constitution had not been violated. Nor, indeed, had public opinion been violated, for the coup was not the act of a few individuals but the result of mass action on a wide scale. It had public support, probably more support than the communists themselves realised, since it resulted in a government dominated by both communists and socialists which was committed to a programme of further progress along the Czechoslovak road to socialism; that it opened the way for perpetual one-party rule was known only to those most privy to the inner workings of the Cominform, but within weeks the first signs of just such a development were clear. On 9 April Gottwald announced that the 30 May elections would be on the basis of a single National Front list; and the following day the socialists agreed to merge their party with the communists, a merger formalised on 17 June. In the new parliament the newly merged Communist Party awarded itself over 75 per cent of the seats.[9]

Hungary and the Formation of the German Democratic Republic (GDR)

In Czechoslovakia the transformation of the National Front occurred with the active participation of many rank and file trade unionists; outside Czechoslovakia 'pressure from below' was a total fiction. In Hungary and in the Soviet Zone of Germany 1948 saw the same reconstruction of Anti-Fascist Fronts as had been seen in Czechoslovakia, but with Soviet pressure substituting for the pressure of the masses.

In Hungary the process began towards the end of 1947 when the communists launched a campaign to bring about the merger of the communist and socialist parties. Many leading socialists were unhappy with this idea, but they were expelled from the party in February 1948. That cleared the way for a congress held on 8 March 1948 that voted for merger with the communists. Unity was formalised at the First Congress of the new Party that opened on 12 June 1948. The common programme of Hungary's socialists and communists, issued on 9 March 1948, had criticised the existing coalition government as weak and advocated in its place 'an Independence Front similar to the regimes in other East European Countries'. Other party leaders were not enthusiastic, but after a series of arrests and expulsions in autumn 1948 the ground had been prepared for the official founding of the Hungarian People's Independence Front on 1 February 1949, made up of all Hungary's political parties, the trade unions, the youth movement, the women's movement and other mass organisations. When fresh elections were held on 15 May 1949, only candidates from the People's Independence Front could stand.[10]

The same pattern of events was evident in the Soviet Occupation Zone of Germany, where until the Cominform meeting there had been no serious discussion of constructing a separate socialist state in Eastern Germany. Back in July 1945 the Communist Party, the Social Democratic Party, the Liberal Party, and the conservative Christian Democratic Union had issued a joint five-point programme to restore democracy and had established a permanent committee to run the affairs of the Anti-Fascist Front they established. The committee operated on the parity principle, took no votes, and made all decisions unanimously; and on this basis agreed on a radical land reform and the sorts of social policies seen throughout Eastern Europe at this time. This basic working arrangement was unaffected by the merger which took place between the socialist and communist parties in April 1946. That merger was largely the result of pressure from the communists who thought it would help distance the party from the Soviet occupation authorities. Initially, in spring 1945, it had been the socialists who had wanted a merger: the communists only took up the idea once it became clear how unpopular association with the Soviet occupying forces had made them. From the very start, the brief of those communists who had returned to Germany had been to help the Soviet occupation authorities, but by autumn 1945, when several large factories had been dismantled brick by brick for reconstruction in the Soviet Union and a quarter of the zone's productive capacity had been taken over by Soviet companies, the communists could feel support ebbing away; merger with the socialists offered the opportunity for survival.

By December 1945 the communists had coaxed and cajoled the socialists to agree to the principle of merger, and, after campaigns in all the localities in the spring the Socialist Unity Party (SED) was founded in April 1946. The Party, with slightly more former socialists than former communists, formed an executive composed of representatives drawn in equal numbers from both former parties, and committed itself to implementing the heritage of Marx rather than Lenin by following a German road to socialism. The merger meant that when elections to regional assemblies were held in October 1946 the SED won just over half the votes; but as had been the case in Czechoslovakia and Hungary, this did not lead to any change in the functioning of the Anti-Fascist Front. It continued to work on the basis of parity; indeed there were occasions on which the SED had to restrain some of its activists for fear of antagonising the other two parties. Thus in Dresden in January 1947 the SED stopped trade union militants organising protests against a law allowing the return of certain factories to their previous owners. Equally, in some parts of the country the Christian Democratic Union (CDU) and the Liberal Democratic Party of Germany (LDPD), could successfully frustrate the SED controlled higher authorities.[11]

Up until the March 1947 meeting of the foreign ministers of Britain, the USA, France and the Soviet Union, the reunification of Germany seemed a shared goal. Thereafter, as 1947 developed, with the disagreement over Marshall Aid and the formation of the Cominform, reunification seemed less and less likely; no progress was made when the four foreign ministers met again from 25 November until 15 December. Although the SED was not a participant in the founding of the Cominform in September 1947, the Party was not immune to its decisions.

The leader, Walter Ulbricht, informed delegates to the Second SED Congress on 21 September that the Party was becoming 'a Party of a new type', this phrase, with all its Leninist associations, showed that the tradition of Marx and a German road to socialism, so recently adopted, was about to be abandoned. At the same time as the Cominform meeting, the first hints were dropped to political leaders in the Soviet Occupation Zone that a separate East German State might be formed.[12]

As moves towards statehood gathered pace, Ulbricht and his associates operated increasingly on the basis of a 'popular front from below'. The first move in this direction was not entirely successful. On 6–7 December 1947 the First People's Congress was held, attended not only by representatives of the Soviet Zone's political parties but also by mass organisations such as the trade unions and youth movement; however, the CDU did not send any official representatives, allowing members to participate only as individuals. Ten days later the Soviet Military Government called on the CDU to elect new leaders; the party's refusal to send an official delegation to the People's Congress was frustrating the credibility of the 'popular front from below'. There was no such problem when a Second People's Congress was formed on the same basis in March 1948, and this body went on to elect a so-called People's Council to represent the German people.

Statehood became even more likely when Stalin decided to confront the West over Berlin. On 20 March 1948 the Soviet representative walked out of the Allied Control Council for Germany and on 31 March the Soviet Military Government announced restrictions on transit routes to Berlin. Tension mounted as the Western Allies prepared to introduce a new currency for the three Western zones, and reached boiling point when the West insisted its currency, introduced on 18 June, should circulate in Berlin. Stalin insisted that Berlin, while politically divided, was economically part of the Soviet Zone and the restrictions on travel to Berlin became a blockade. The Berlin Blockade lasted from 24 June 1948 to 12 May 1949 and was aimed at securing Berlin as a capital for an east German state; during the blockade further steps were made to establish a secure 'popular front from below' on which to build the new state. At meetings held between June and September 1948 the SED leadership took a series of decisions that transformed the Party into a Leninist Party. Then in Berlin at the end of November 1948, when the West insisted on going ahead with elections in Berlin, the pro-Soviet parties and sympathetic mass organisations formed a 'Berlin democratic bloc' which organised a series of rallies, declared the existing elected administration deposed, and boycotted the elections; while there was little genuine mass pressure from below in these events, the participation of Fritz Ebert, younger son of the former President of Weimar Germany Friedrich Ebert, gave the affair a certain credibility.

By 19 March 1949, when it was clear both that the division of Germany was inevitable and that Stalin would back down over Berlin, the People's Council agreed a constitution for the proposed German Democratic Republic and organised elections to a Third People's Congress: these elections were held on 15–16 May 1949 and produced an assembly which on 30 May endorsed the proposed constitution; the elections were again held on a single list and showed clearly how important 'pressure from below' was in establishing communist control. As a result of the elections the SED had only 90 seats, the same number as the liberal and conservative parties put together; but they also controlled the 30 seats allocated to the trade unions, the ten seats allocated to the youth organisation, the ten seats allocated to the women's organisation – in all there were 75 seats allocated to various mass organisations. When the GDR was created on 7 October 1949 the government's first act was to endorse the manifesto of the National Front of Democratic Germany. Only the careful observer noticed how near the rank and file of the CDU and LDPD came on 10 October to passing votes of no confidence in their leaders who had agreed to serve in a government formed in this way.[13]

The Stalin–Tito Dispute

To the Yugoslavs, the Prague events, if not their imitation in Hungary and East Germany, were a text-book example of what the popular front 'from below' could achieve. Stalin, too, personally endorsed the Czechoslovak 'constitutional coup', offering support from Soviet troops should that prove necessary.[14] Yet, it was at the very moment when, steeled in the new Cominform line, the Czechoslovak communists took power, that the twin originators of that line, Tito and Stalin, fell out.

Tito completely misinterpreted Stalin's flattery in making Belgrade the headquarters of the Cominform and in endorsing the strategy of the popular front 'from below'. Tito assumed he was being given *carte blanche* to take the lead in responding to United States' 'dollar imperialism' with a revolutionary counter-offensive. In Tito's view, the wily Stalin had backed down from a confrontation with the wartime Allies for the sake of the common struggle against fascism, but now recognised that the time for compromise and conciliation was over; resistance to United States imperialism could create the same revolutionary ferment as resistance to Nazi imperialism had so recently done.

Two things had happened which reinforced Tito's view that there had been a radical change of mind on Stalin's part. With the signing of the Bulgarian Peace Treaty in February 1947, Stalin had endorsed reviving moves towards establishing a Balkan Federation, and in March 1947 he let it be known that he would welcome an increase in the hitherto rather cautious support given by the Yugoslavs to the Greek communists in their civil war. Two years earlier these very same issues had prompted Stalin to place a veto on all Yugoslavia's foreign policy initiatives. By changing his policy on Greece and the Balkan Federation Stalin seemed to be implying that the March 1945 injunction on foreign policy initiatives had been lifted. That, certainly, is how Tito interpreted matters.[15]

In the immediate aftermath of the Cominform Founding Conference, Tito launched a diplomatic offensive, parts of which he had not cleared with Stalin in advance. In a whirlwind tour of neighbouring states Tito visited Bulgaria at the end of November 1947, then Hungary in the first week of December, and finally Romania in the middle of December. Immediately after these visits changes took place in the countries' popular fronts, bringing them closer to the Yugoslav model. In Bulgaria and Romania, where Tito's public reception was ecstatic,[16] the popular fronts were immediately adapted to the new Yugoslav style: thus on 2–3 February 1948, to chants of Stalin–Tito–Dimitrov, delegates to the Second Congress of the Fatherland Front heard Dimitrov announce that the Front was being transformed from below into a disciplined, mass organisation with an elected leadership; similarly on 23 February 1948 the Congress of the Romanian Workers' Party, again to chants of Tito, heard Gheorghiu-Dej announce that similar changes would be made to the country's popular front.[17]

In Hungary, Tito met with opposition. In both Bulgaria and Romania, communist domination of the postwar coalition governments had been a reality since the end of 1944 and adopting Tito's model simply involved dropping a pretence introduced under international pressure; in Hungary Tito's policy required that Rákosi introduce a radical change of strategy. Immediately after the Cominform's

Founding Conference, in November 1947, the Independence (Freedom) Party was forced to dissolve itself, and after expelling leading Rightists, the socialists voted in favour of fusion with the communists at their March 1948 Congress. However, despite these changes, Rákosi opposed the idea of a new popular front and a Hungarian delegation was in Belgrade in March 1948 putting its case against the Cominform line when news of the Stalin–Tito dispute broke. When at the end of 1948 the National Independence Front (from February 1949 the People's Independence Front) was established in Hungary, Tito's inspiration was a thing of the past.[18]

Rákosi's opposition did not upset Tito too much. The purpose of his whirlwind diplomacy was not simply to see the victory of his favoured tactic of the popular front 'from below'. All these visits were followed up with mutually advantageous treaties which, by the end of 1947, had created a customs union comprising Albania, Bulgaria, Romania and Yugoslavia.[19] A Balkan Federation was clearly in the process of formation and the idea had long been acceptable to Stalin. What was not acceptable to him was a Balkan Federation pursuing an independent foreign policy and, when addressing a press conference on 22 January 1948, Dimitrov had referred to Greece being included among the future members of the Balkan Federation.[20] In the autumn of 1947 military aid to the Greek partisans from the Balkan communist states had increased considerably and, using the Cominform journal as a launch pad, the Yugoslav Party had begun an active campaign to establish an international aid network for Greece. Indeed as the crisis reached its height, a joint Greek–Yugoslav delegation was touring Eastern Europe seeking military support, while Tito was encouraging the notion that the Cominform should hold a special meeting to support the Greek communists. On 26 January 1948 Tito raised the stakes in Yugoslavia's commitment to Greece by stationing Yugoslav troops in Albania to help defend Greek communist bases; but he did so without consulting either Stalin or the Albanian leader Enver Hoxha. Hoxha assumed Tito must have been acting with Stalin's blessing.[21]

This was, for Stalin, the final straw: a Balkan Federation headed by Tito might get up to all sorts of foreign policy adventures. Stalin had promised Churchill that Greece would not go communist, and the Americans, with their atomic arsenal, were increasingly committed to the Greek nationalist cause; caution rather than adventurism was the order of the day. Stalin had supported Tito's revolutionism in order to consolidate his control over Czechoslovakia and Hungary, not to spread revolution in Greece; there was to be no counter-offensive in the face of United States imperialism. Yugoslav and Bulgarian delegations were summoned to Moscow on 10 February and the Yugoslavs again instructed not to take any foreign policy initiatives without Moscow's agreement. As an insurance policy, to guarantee no repetition of Tito's adventurism, Stalin insisted that the Balkan Federation should be formed at once in a way that he could control. The Yugoslavs were prepared to accept the reimposition of the Soviet veto on their foreign policy, but were not prepared to play a captive role in Stalin's Balkan Federation. The Central Committee rejected Stalin's proposal on 1 March 1948. Thereafter things deteriorated rapidly: the Soviet Union delayed ratifying its annual trade agreement with Yugoslavia; the Yugoslavs refused to supply any new economic information to the Soviet Union; and on 18 March all Soviet specialists were withdrawn.[22]

The extraordinary content of the letters exchanged between the Soviet and the Yugoslav Communist Parties during the spring and summer of 1948 gave only a hint of what the argument came to be about.[23] As far as the Yugoslavs were concerned, Stalin was not only asserting his sole right to control the foreign policy of communist states, something the Yugoslavs were grudgingly prepared to accept, but sacrificing the Greek revolution on the altar of a wartime agreement with Churchill: it was parliamentary coalition politics on an international scale and the Yugoslavs wanted nothing to do with it. Yugoslavia saw its adventurous foreign policy simply as a commitment to revolution, a commitment to revolution characterised by the Party's strategy and tactics ever since 1941.

To Stalin, or more accurately to Molotov reviewing events in 1955, the Soviet case was equally clear. The Yugoslavs had adopted a nationalist stance and had fostered division within the socialist camp. Instead of accepting comradely criticism, they had insisted in their reply of 18 April that, for them, concern for the Soviet Union had to be a lesser matter than concern for Yugoslavia itself; thus they questioned what was fundamental to Soviet self-belief, that the Soviet Union had a historic responsibility for the construction of worldwide socialism. As the first country to embark on 'building socialism' the Soviet Union had the right to expect support from all communists, no matter what their nationality. It was this leading role of the Soviet Union in the socialist world that Tito dared to question. This could not be stated openly, and so Stalin and his immediate entourage settled down to think up a list of other ideological crimes committed by Tito.

Although Stalin's attack on Tito included allegations of Berns Bukharinism, and other alleged political deviations, he maαe four specific criticisms of the Yugoslav Communist Party: it had operated semi-legally; it had not collectivised agriculture; it had exaggerated the importance of guerrilla warfare; and it had submerged the Party within the People's Front. As the dispute developed, the Yugoslavs took immediate action to rectify three of these criticisms. Addressing the question of legality, it held its Fifth Congress in July 1948 at which elections were held to all the Party's executive bodies; in 1949 a drive to complete the collectivisation of agriculture was launched; and the question of partisan warfare was blurred into a rather arid dispute on a different topic, the respective roles of the Red Army and the Yugoslav Army in liberating Belgrade, something which occurred after the Yugoslav partisans had already begun to operate as regular military formations.

However, the strange accusation that the Yugoslav Party had submerged itself in the People's Front was never conceded by Tito. Encapsulated in this allegation was a rejection of the whole strategy of the popular front 'from below'. The Yugoslav Communist Party only appeared 'submerged' in the popular front because it had achieved such a dominant position within it that no other party was able to operate within it. As Tito had made clear in his speech to the Second Congress of the People's Front, the Yugoslavs' 'correct' attitude to the popular front 'from below' had not only led to their victory in Yugoslavia, but was the key to the revolutionary transformation of Europe; he could compromise on this only by abandoning his revolutionary heritage. Stalin realised this too, and henceforth any communist associated with those wartime policies of the popular front 'from below' would be suspected of Titoism.[24]

THE PURGES

Poland and Romania

When organising the July 1948 Conference to expel the Yugoslavs from the Cominform, Stalin was faced with an acute dilemma: on which of the East European leaders could he most rely. The Bulgarians and the Albanians had been hopelessly compromised in the Balkan Federation affair and the Czechoslovaks and Hungarians had only been brought fully into the fold after the founding of the Cominform nine months earlier. The choice clearly lay between Poland and Romania, the two countries that had been 'sovietised' from the very start. Of the two, however, it was only from Romania that Stalin could expect complete loyalty, for in Poland the Party leadership was hopelessly split.

Gomułka had had reservations about joining the Cominform from the start and, when during the Founding Conference it had become clear that the Cominform would be something more than a consultative body, he had instructed the Polish delegation not to join. It was only after the delegation in Szklarszka Poręba had insisted on calling a full Politburo meeting and that meeting had voted in favour of Poland joining that Gomułka had lifted his opposition.[25] These tensions within the leadership continued for the next year and became intermingled with the on–off process of merger between the Polish Workers' Party and the Polish Socialist Party; Gomułka, as was the case back in May 1944, did not want to dictate terms to the socialists, nor expel any of their members. In April 1948 the Soviet Communist Party wrote a detailed report on the Polish Party which was extremely critical of the way Gomułka was playing the nationalist card, by talking of a specific 'Polish Marxism', as distinct from Marxism–Leninism, around which the Polish communists and socialists could coalesce.[26]

By June 1948 a third issue divided the leadership. Stalin had identified the failure to collectivise agriculture as one of the principal sins of the Yugoslav Communist Party and the Soviet Communist Party's report had identified Gomułka's lack of an agricultural programme as a major failing. It was therefore clear that the proposed Cominform Conference in July would endorse the policy of collectivisation as the touchstone of orthodoxy. Gomułka, however, was opposed to collectivisation and insisted that he would make his dissenting views known when the Party held a Central Committee Plenum in June. He also called on the Polish delegation to the July Cominform Conference to make their opposition to collectivisation clear. Things came to a head at the Ninth Plenum of the Central Committee on 9 June when, without clearing his text in advance with the Politburo, Gomułka used ideological code (an attack on Rosa Luxemburg and the soviets of 1919) to denounce those who slavishly followed the Soviet model. Thus the Polish Party was in disarray over the summer of 1948, the crisis only ending in September with the removal of Gomułka from power and his replacement by Bierut. Merger with the socialists was then forced through by December on the basis of the expulsion of that party's right wing.[27]

So it was that at the two full conferences of the Cominform, in July 1948 and November 1949, it fell to the Romanian Communist Party leader Gheorghiu-Dej to denounce the Yugoslavs. He had, with none of the problems faced by the Poles, swiftly engineered a merger with the independent socialists and, with no major opposition within his party, launched the collectivisation of agriculture. Of the two communist parties on which Stalin felt he could rely, the Romanians stood head and shoulders above the Poles, and it was to Bucharest that the Cominform headquarters was moved.

It was not accidental that the wave of purges which swept through the communist parties as Stalin imposed his orthodoxy on Eastern Europe largely passed Romania and Poland by. That is not to say that there were no trials in Poland and Romania, but that their nature and extent was different. In Poland Stalin seems to have wanted to avoid trials altogether. In December 1948 he saw Gomułka in person and tried, unsuccessfully, to persuade him to accept a token post in the newly formed Polish United Workers' Party (PZPR). Thereafter, despite regular Polish promises to take security seriously, followed by inaction, the Soviets seem to have been content to let Gomułka work on his memoirs in silence, whilst 'spies' were removed from their posts without public trials. Stalin vetoed Gomułka's arrest in September 1949, but agreed to it in August 1951.[28]

In Romania, the trials that took place followed a Romanian agenda connected to Gheorghiu-Dej's strengthening dictatorship rather than the dictates of Soviet policy. The purge of Pătrăşcanu, the 'Romanian Gomułka' who in 1944 had favoured collaboration with the traditional parties, was already well advanced by the end of 1947 and therefore had no connection with the Yugoslav events. Its origin lay in the general survey of the health of the Romanian Party carried out for the Cominform after its first conference. Thus in January 1948 Pătrăşcanu complained to the Soviet ambassador that he was being isolated within the leadership and criticised for his policies in 1944, unaware that the Soviet ambassador had already advised Gheorghiu-Dej and Pauker that Pătrăşcanu 'had adopted an anti-party and anti-Soviet position and had links to foreign-based groups of reactionary émigrés'.

The long-running conflict between Gheorghiu-Dej, on the one hand, and Ana Pauker and Vasile Luca on the other, was based on personal enmity and anti-Semitism. It also long predated the break with Yugoslavia.

In February 1947 Stalin summoned both Gheorghiu-Dej and Pauker to Moscow to warn of growing racism in the Romanian Party and explained to Gheorghiu-Dej that Pauker could not be excluded from the leadership just because she was Jewish. However, a report at the end of August 1947 showed that the relationship between the two leaders had become even worse, with Gheorghiu-Dej refusing to discuss issues with the full Politburo; a Soviet diplomat had tried and failed to bring about a reconciliation. In autumn 1949 Gheorghiu-Dej clearly thought the other East European trials had given him the opportunity to move against his opponents and he wrote asking for advice in preparing public trials; his request went unanswered. Finally when the atmosphere in Moscow made a move against the Jews Pauker and Luca possible in May 1952, Soviet diplomats dismissed it as 'a factional struggle'.[29]

In Poland and Romania purge trials were not needed to secure Soviet domination, for Soviet control had been a reality since early 1945. Elsewhere in Eastern Europe Stalin could not be so confident. The Balkan revolutions had been consolidated, or were well on the way to consolidation, before the arrival of the Red Army, and between 1945 and 1947 the communists of Hungary and Czechoslovakia had been largely left to their own devices.

Albania and Bulgaria

The hunt to unearth Titoites was obviously easiest where Titoites actually existed, in the Balkans. The first trial in Eastern Europe took place in May 1949 and involved Koçi Xoxe the former Albanian Minister of the Interior. There is little doubt that he had been prominent among those Albanian communists who favoured political union with Yugoslavia and the Stalin–Tito break enabled the Albanian leader Enver Hoxha to play the Soviet card and stop this process in its tracks. If death was a just punishment for supporting close Albanian–Yugoslav relations, Xoxe was justly punished. During the trial Xoxe made a dramatic admission, telling the court he had been informed in 1943 by the head of the British Military Mission to Albania that Tito was a British agent.[30]

The trial victim in Bulgaria was also easy to identify. Before Dimitrov's return the Party had been led by Traicho Kostov; he had organised the wartime partisan operations and, as a consequence, had been in contact with the Yugoslavs. Although these contacts had turned him into a sceptic about the prospects for a Balkan Federation, he was an obvious target, all the more so because his firm stance in trade negotiations with the Soviet Union in February 1948 had not endeared him to Stalin. In May 1948 Soviet representatives picked up reports that Kostov had been telling military recruits that the Bulgarians had done much to liberate themselves, and that it had not all been the work of the Red Army; Tito had said the same thing. In January 1949 Kostov was accused of a 'nationalist deviation' and removed from his posts: his arrest, delayed by the intervention of Dimitrov who was terminally ill in Moscow, took place at the end of June and the trial opened on 7 December 1949. To the embarrassment of all, at the trial he retracted his confession and admitted only to a nationalistic attitude towards the Soviet Union in trade relations, not to links with Tito and the British; he was executed on 16 December 1949.[31]

Hungary

It was not difficult to establish wartime links between Albanian and Bulgarian communists, the Yugoslav partisans, and British Military Missions. Such links, however, were far more difficult to establish in Hungary and Czechoslovakia, and it was precisely there that a widespread purge might prove necessary, given that both countries had only recently been incorporated into the Cominform orbit. Although links between Hungarian communists and the British proved impossible to establish, there were other links with 'imperialism' to be found. The Yugoslav Communist Party had played a prominent role in helping the return of Spanish Civil War veterans interned in France, and investigations on this front led to the discovery not of a British connection, but an American connection; his name was Noel Field.

Field had been an idealistic employee of the American State Department who from 1935 to 1937 passed information to the Soviet Union. He then worked as a diplomat attached to the League of Nations which, after the withdrawal of the International Brigades from Spain in autumn 1938, had been instructed to work to ensure their safe return home. This task inevitably meant Field developed good contacts with the Communist International. In 1940, disillusioned with US diplomacy and the League of Nations, he took up a job with the religious charity, the Unitarian Service Committee (USC), running its Marseilles office. When the Nazis occupied Vichy France in November 1942, Field moved to Geneva to become the European Director of the USC.

Field had always been an anti-fascist, and soon established a network between Marseilles and Geneva which, among other things, smuggled former International Brigaders across the Swiss frontier. Since no other organisation had much interest in the internment camps, and Field had a strong personal interest, the USC undertook to help feed the internees and was given open access to the camps. In these circumstances it was not difficult for the French Communist Party's Migrant Workers' Office, headed by the Czechoslovak communist Artur London, to organise the escape of internees and their concealment in one of the USC's nursing homes near Toulouse, before making the journey to Marseilles and then Geneva, where, after further recuperation with the USC, they could make their way home. Involvement with their onward journey meant that Field had good contacts with various communist organisations, but in particular with the German, Austrian and Hungarian communists in emigration. No doubt on the basis of these contacts, in 1943 he was approached by Soviet intelligence to resume acting as an informer, but refused.[32]

It was his communist contacts which, towards the end of the Second World War, aroused the interest of the American undercover organisation, the Office of Strategic Services (OSS), in Field. Alan Dulles, the Head of OSS and brother of John Foster Dulles future United States Secretary of State, contacted Field to help organise the return of émigré groups of German and Hungarian communists to their respective countries. It was this Hungarian operation that was to be so controversial: in December 1944 money provided by Dulles was used by Field to organise the return to Hungary of a small émigré group headed by Tibor Szőnyi. Field obtained surplus Yugoslav partisan uniforms and planned a return route via France, Italy and Yugoslavia, a partisan route run by the Yugoslavs. A Hungarian link between Tito and American imperialism had been established.[33]

Apart from Szőnyi himself, the obvious target for suspicion was László Rajk. He had served in Spain, had been interned in France for three years, and he had returned to Hungary in 1941 to head the underground Central Committee of the Communist Party. While under his leadership the Party had operated the 'Titoist', '1919', popular front 'from below' strategy aimed at limiting the number of concessions made to 'bourgeois' parties, the policy that the returning Rákosi had confronted on his arrival from Moscow. To make matters worse, after

1945 Rajk had often asked Szőnyi, who became head of the Party's Cadre Department, to find jobs for various veterans of the Spanish Civil War. At the same time, at least this was the complaint of the Soviet representative on the ACC, he had systematically removed from positions of authority in the police service those officers who had spent the war years in the Soviet Union.

In reality Rajk had simply become too outspoken. He upset Rákosi because the two men clashed over which of them the political police should report to. He clashed with Hungary's security chief over how much independence the security services should have within the Ministry of the Interior. And he clashed with the Soviet Union because, once the ACC had been wound up, he refused to have Soviet advisors in the Ministry of Internal Affairs and persistently requested to be informed of the names of all Soviet agents working in Hungary. In September 1948 Rajk was moved from the Ministry of the Interior, responsible for security, to become foreign minister. At the same time Rákosi asked Soviet security officials to help uncover the extent of the alleged conspiracy.

By April 1949 a full list of Rajk's crimes had been compiled, starting with his suspension from the Spanish Communist Party on suspicion of Trotskyist leanings and ending with the bourgeois connections of his wife's family and his brother's service as a police officer under Horthy. However, Rákosi only acted after an interview with the Soviet ambassador in May and the contemporaneous report from his security chief that Szőnyi had confessed that his 'controller' was indeed Rajk; Rákosi realised at this point that in Moscow Stalin's security chief Lavrentii Beria was heading the case. Arrested on 19 June, Rajk at first admitted only to making a few political mistakes; by mid-July he had confessed to spying. Rajk's trial began on 16 September 1949 according to an indictment agreed in person by Rákosi and Stalin. During the trial he duly explained in detail how in the French internment camps the Yugoslavs had committed every imaginable sin, from recruiting agents to both the Gestapo and the French Secret Service, to holding 'Trotskyist' conversations; at one point Rajk agreed with the prosecutor's suggestion that the majority of Spanish Civil War veterans were under the 'Trotskyite' influence of the Yugoslavs. However, as a furious Soviet investigator noted, Rajk had turned the tables on the court: the inexperienced Hungarian officials had allowed him to sow doubts as to the veracity of the proceedings by claiming to have met people in Spain and France who simply had not been there; and he had also been allowed to use the dock to give 'a Marxist analysis of events'. Perhaps it was for this reason that Stalin insisted on the death penalty, having first allowed Rákosi to believe that the ultimate penalty would not be necessary.

The verdict was announced on 24 September 1949, and Rajk and his co-defendants executed on 15 October 1949. Shortly after the trial, the Cominform met in Budapest at the end of November 1949 and heard Gheorghiu-Dej introduce a resolution which denounced the Yugoslav leadership as 'spies and murderers' and ruling that they no longer deserved the name communist; it became the duty of all communists to attempt to overthrow them.[34] Thus the Rajk trial verdict was used to justify the Soviet Union and all the other East European states breaking off diplomatic relations with Yugoslavia, and offering support to a pro-Cominform Yugoslav Government-in-Exile and the terrorist groups operated by it.

Czechoslovakia

Stalin's attempt to spread the hunt for Titoite agents to Czechoslovakia proved even more problematic than had been the case in Hungary. The Czechoslovak authorities did not at first take seriously the suggestion that their nationals had been involved in the Field conspiracy. It was only after the verdict of the Rajk trial that, at the end of September 1949, Gottwald was persuaded there might be more to the affair and agreed Soviet security advisers would have to be brought in.[35] One obvious target was Artur London. Not only had he run the French Communist Party's Migrant Workers' Office during the War, and thus organised much of the repatriation of Spanish Civil War veterans, but in 1947, when suffering from tuberculosis, had gone to recuperate in a Swiss sanitorium run by Field. Another early target was Eugene Loebl, Deputy Minister for Foreign Trade, responsible for negotiating a trade deal with Yugoslavia over the winter of 1947–8.

Both men noticed changes in their pattern of interrogation early in 1950. On his arrest London was bombarded with accusations concerning his activities in Spain and the 'Trotskyist' activities in the French internment camps: later, contacts with International Zionism were to feature prominently.[36] Stalin, who prided himself on not being anti-Semitic and who in 1947 had upbraided Gheorghiu-Dej for his anti-Semitism, had invested a good deal in the Israeli cause in 1947 during the last days of the British Mandate, even to the extent of providing Israeli terrorists with arms; his reward had been to find the new state of Israel siding openly with the Americans. By September 1948 his attitude to Israel and the Jewish question had hardened, and by November he had decided to act.[37] On 20 November the Soviet Union's Jewish Anti-Fascist Committee was closed down and a steady purge of all Jewish cultural organisations began. Central to this investigation was Stalin's realisation that during the war not only had the communist parties of Eastern Europe been susceptible to 'imperialist' pressure, but also his own Soviet Communist Party had been contaminated by the West.

In 1943 the Jewish Anti-Fascist Committee had visited New York. Then, in autumn 1944, as the Crimean Tartars were being driven out of their land for alleged collaboration with the Nazis, the Jewish Anti-Fascist Committee had revived the idea of turning the Crimea into a homeland for Soviet Jews.[38] This long-forgotten episode came back to Stalin at the end of 1948 and, to his paranoid mind, became the first stage in a well-planned imperialist conspiracy, which was somehow linked to Israel. In March 1949 Molotov was dismissed as foreign minister; his wife, a prominent member of the Jewish Anti-Fascist Committee, was arrested as were all its leading members. As the net was spread further, the Czechoslovak Communist Party clearly became implicated, for it had been via Czechoslovakia that arms had been supplied to Israel in 1948.

Gottwald was extremely unwilling to become involved in the purge trials taking place in Hungary; critics blamed his wife who was 'far from the party'. In spring 1949 Czechoslovakia remained a fairly relaxed country. Soviet advisers were horrified that the press rarely criticised Yugoslavia, that Tito was secretly regarded as hero by many, and that the Yugoslav bookshop was still trading freely as late as December of that year. In June 1949 Rákosi visited Prague and told Gottwald that the Rajk investigations had identified 65 Anglo-American spies in the Czechoslovak Communist Party, two in its leadership; Gottwald's response was to say that the necessary measures had already been taken. In September Rákosi sent Gottwald a personal emissary, who urged the Czechoslovaks to bring in Soviet specialist advisers and who pointed out that Hungary could hardly hold trade talks with Czechoslovak ministers known to be spies. Trapped, Gottwald agreed to bring in Soviet specialists and widespread arrests began in spring 1951.

By then the Soviet security advisers had identified their perfect victim, Party General Secretary Rudolf Slánský. His partisan past leant a hint of Titoism, as did his behaviour at the Founding Conference of the Cominform; and his Jewish descent fitted perfectly with the new requirements. As with the other purge trials, Stalin himself was closely involved. On 24 June 1951 he rejected the first indictment against Slánský, insisting to Gottwald it was not convincing enough. Gottwald felt he could get away with removing Slánský from the post of general secretary and making him deputy prime minister. For a while Slánský remained in the leadership and, at least according to his critics, made only the most perfunctory statement of self-criticism. However, Stalin appointed a new specialist adviser who submitted his report on 19 November. On 22 November Anastasii Mikoyan brought Stalin's verdict in person and Slánský was arrested on the 23rd. His trial was delayed until after the secret trial of the Jewish Anti-Fascist Committee 'conspirators' in the Soviet Union in July 1952; it began on 20 November 1952 and inevitably resulted in Slánský's execution.[39]

East Germany

The German Communist Party was not immune to contacts with Noel Field. Many exiled German communists spent the war years in Switzerland and became a crucial link in Field's contacts with communist resisters in Vichy France; Field's twin bases were Geneva and Marseilles, while French internment camps contained many German veterans of the Spanish Civil War. At the end of August 1950 six leading party officials were expelled from the Party because of their contacts with Field and other activities including links to the resistance movement in France.

Paul Merker, who had been on the Politburo since 1926, had never denied his contacts with Field, nor did Willi Kreikmeyer, the Director of East German railways: both had been in contact with Field as early as 1941, but denied the interpretation put on these contacts. One accused, another Field contact Bruno Goldhammer, was alleged to have sabotaged the work of the communist resistance movement in France, while also amongst those expelled was Lex Ende, a former editor of the party daily *Neues Deutschland*. Finally Franz Dahlem, one of the longest serving Party members and another veteran of the fighting in

Spain, was caught up in the second round of purges. An investigation began into his case in December 1952 and he was expelled from the Politburo and Central Committee on 14 May 1953. The death of Stalin in March 1953 did not help him; he appealed to the Soviet Presidium on 1 April 1953, but Stalin's heirs refused to intervene.[40]

At the end of July 1949 Stalin received the Bulgarian Prime Minister Vulko Chervenkov and explained to him why the Kostov trial was so necessary. He drew on the Soviet experience. In the Soviet secret police, he said, 'there were many foreign agents, sent from abroad, who, quite possibly did not want to harm us, but did so because they had been recruited by foreign intelligence'. The situation was now the same for Eastern Europe: 'in Yugoslavia there are currently many American and English agents, from whom information and services are demanded; whether they want to harm the country, or do not want to, is immaterial – things are demanded of them and they must fulfil those demands; it is the law.' Rajk had been in contact with Dulles, and no matter how honest a communist he claimed to be, that contact could not be cast off. That was Stalin's logic. Even the 'doctors plot', the last and most bizarre of Stalin's purges, which was brought to an end by the dictator's death in March 1953, followed the same basic logic: the leading doctor indicted was Professor M. Vovsi, a close relative of the head of the Jewish Anti-Fascist Committee.[41]

Other Trials

These set-piece political trials were just the tip of the iceberg. Stalin did intervene to stop a second round of trials in Bulgaria in 1951, but in Hungary and Czechoslovakia each trial led to a further trial. Nor, of course, was it just communists who suffered in these years. Repression and persecution occurred at every level. In December 1948 the Catholic Primate of Hungary, Cardinal Mindszenty, was arrested and, after a trial in February 1949, sentenced to life imprisonment. In 1949 the trial took place in Bulgaria of 15 pastors from the United Evangelical Church; in September 1952 in the same country, 27 Catholic priests were put on trial. During 1949 there was a sustained attack on the Catholic Church in Czechoslovakia, which continued in later years. In September 1951 the Bishop of Timişoara in Romania was put on trial for espionage. In July 1950 former leaders of the

Hungarian Socialist Party were arrested, while those socialists who had cooperated with the communists, and even become government ministers, were also put on trial. In June 1951, in Poland, the trials took place of army generals linked to the wartime pro-London Home Army.

Nor should it be forgotten that despite the prominence given to the trials of political activists, the prison population was made up mostly of workers, blue- and white-collar, detained for essentially minor infringements of labour discipline. Through the Cominform Stalin not only imposed Soviet style collectivisation of agriculture on the states of Eastern Europe, but the Soviet model of industrialisation through five-year plans. After 1948 the countries of Eastern Europe all adopted Soviet style economic plans and, as the drive for industrial growth developed, made worse in 1950 by the need to build an arms industry during the Korean War, labour production targets were regularly raised upwards reaching quite unrealistic levels. This ruthless exploitation of labour was hardly compensated for by such bizarre experiments in social engineering as the transportation of the 'bourgeois' population of cities such as Budapest and Prague to the countryside to make housing available for the new working-class aristocracy.[42]

YUGOSLAV REVISIONISM

It was against this background that the Yugoslav Party leadership began to reassess what it thought was meant by socialism. Although at the time of the July 1948 Cominform Conference the Yugoslavs had sought to portray themselves as much misunderstood and thoroughly loyal to Moscow, long before the next conference in November 1949 and their anathemisation as 'murderers', the Yugoslav Party had begun to reconsider its principles. The Central Committee Plenum of January 1949, while insisting on the commitment to collectivisation of agriculture, reinterpreted the Party's stance towards Stalin: the break with Stalin was not the result of a 'misunderstanding' but of Stalin's abandonment of Marxism–Leninism; the Yugoslavs, the Plenum concluded, were the true Marxist–Leninists. As the spring of 1949 progressed, the process of defining the true, Marxist–Leninist, Yugoslav road to socialism got underway: it was then that the idea of workers' self-management was first put to Tito, and it was then that the Yugoslavs revived the notion that under socialism the state might 'wither away'.[43]

Workers' Self-Management

Mass involvement, less bureaucracy, popular participation – these were to be the themes gradually developed by the Yugoslav leadership during 1949. In May Kardelj first proposed that workers' representatives might be given some degree of representation at production conferences, suggesting that this could develop into a continuous form of direct workers' cooperation in the management of enterprises. In December 1949, without any publicity, the Politburo ordered the establishment, as an experiment, of advisory workers' councils at 215 large enterprises. Sometime during the spring of 1950 Tito was convinced of the success of this experiment, which by the summer had been extended to a further 300 enterprises; on 26 June 1950 Tito presented to parliament the bill establishing workers' councils through which the 'self-management' of enterprises would be achieved.[44] Workers' self-management contrasted sharply with the Stalinist system of one-man management supported by draconian labour legislation.

At the same time, Yugoslav leaders developed a critique of the Soviet bureaucracy. In March 1950 Djilas argued that the bureaucratic stratum created during Russia's Civil War, which had been essential for victory in that war, had thereafter cut itself off from the masses and placed itself above society: in November 1950 he was even more specific about the nature of that bureaucratic caste, it had actually carried out a counter-revolution and was governing the Soviet Union according to the laws of monopoly capitalism. In advancing the theory that there had been a 'counter-revolution' in the Soviet Union, Djilas went further than other Yugoslav leaders. Kardelj spoke of 'deformed socialism', of 'bureaucratic–despotic' forms hampering socialist construction, of 'state capitalist elements' but not 'state capitalism': for him the bureaucracy was capable of taking the first steps towards socialism, but then became 'the most dangerous obstacle to the further development of socialism'. Tito was even more cautious. He told the Second Trade Union Congress in 1951: 'we cannot quite say that the Soviet Union is in general not a socialist country, that is, that all the achievements of the revolution have been destroyed; rather the leaders and responsible figures are not socialists'.[45]

These hints of a disagreement among Yugoslavia's leaders about the nature of the Soviet Union had no impact on domestic reforms that continued apace. In line with the attack on 'bureaucracy' and the new stress on local initiative, April 1951 saw the abolition of the old centralised planning body and the progressive decentralisation of planning, and in 1952 the workers' councils, which had at first been fairly limited in their real powers, were granted control of enterprise funds and investment decisions, while a whole new hierarchy of elected Chambers of Production was introduced to give workers a democratic voice.[46]

These reforms were endorsed by the Sixth Congress of the Yugoslav Communist Party that met in November 1952 and adopted a resolution singling out self-management as Yugoslavia's contribution to the theory and practice of socialist construction. Not only did this Congress endorse the workers' councils and other reforms, it changed the name of the Party. Henceforth, drawing on Marx's own proposals, the Party would be called the League of Communists. According to the Sixth Congress resolution, this name change had a profound meaning, for the role of the Party would change: in the Soviet Union the Party had become virtually inseparable from the economic apparatus; in the new Yugoslavia this would not happen. The Congress resolution stated: 'the Yugoslav League of Communists is not and cannot be the direct operative manager and commander in economic, state, or social life'.[47]

The Leading Role of the Party

Precisely what was meant by this new role for the Communist Party soon came to divide Djilas from Kardelj and Tito. Although both Kardelj and Tito believed Lenin's concept of the 'leading role of the Party' did not mean the Party being responsible for everything, they did accept that the leading role of the Party should continue in some form for the foreseeable future. Indeed, at the Sixth Congress Tito had been forthright in his defence of the Party: 'the League of Communists not only does not reduce its role in and its responsibility for the successful development of socialism, but further increases its role and responsibility.... [It] correctly guides and organises our entire social life.... When I said that in future the most important role of the Party will be of an ideological–educational character, I did not mean by that all its other leading functions would end. No!'[48]

The future role of the Communist Party was again debated at the Fourth Congress of the People's Front in February 1953, which renamed that body the Socialist Alliance of Working People. Kardelj hoped the newly named Alliance might become the body through which the Party's new 'ideological–educational' guidance could be executed; the Socialist Alliance would carry out most of the administrative roles which the Party currently played, while the Party would offer guidance in this process. Djilas, however, had already gone one step further, believing that unless the reform process was pushed through into the heart of the Party, any reform of the Socialist Alliance would fail. He wanted 'the whole system of our party work to change' and his attacks on bureaucracy, thus far limited to the Soviet Union, began to be targeted on developments within Yugoslavia itself.[49]

Although Kardelj and Djilas both theorised about the nature of bureaucratic deformation within the Soviet Union, Tito stated simply that while the Soviet Union was a socialist state its rulers were not socialists. Stalin died in March 1953 and on 15 June 1953 the Soviet Union proposed the restoration of diplomatic relations with Yugoslavia. This acted as a catalyst, prompting Tito to put clear limits on the extent of reform within his country. By 1953 he was concerned at some of the consequences of those reforms; even workers' control was causing problems since enterprise-level decision-making made coherent planning impossible.[50] In June 1953 he called a Central Committee Plenum at Brioni, his holiday residence, and made clear that to counter disintegrative forces the leading role of the Party was to be reasserted in the traditional way.[51]

Djilas was not prepared to accept this about-turn. In the autumn and winter of 1953–4, he wrote a series of articles in the newspaper *Borba* attacking the Yugoslav bureaucracy and making clear that the Party itself had to go. It was impossible, he argued, for the revolution to be saved by recreating what had worked in the past, that is, the Party. 'The revolution must find new ideas, new forms... [and] transform itself into democracy and socialism, into new human relations.' No theory could protect a society from despotism, no appeals to the good of the cause replace socialist legality. The idea that only communists were 'conscious forces of socialism' simply cut them off from the masses and gave them privileges. In future the Party should allow itself to wither away and its members be ready to discuss current policies within the Socialist Alliance, ultimately merging with the Alliance. He concluded his last article with the clear words: 'the Leninist form of the Party and state has become obsolete'.[52]

True to his Leninist understanding of the Party, Tito summoned a special session of the Central Committee on 16 January 1954 to deal with Djilas. Tito was clear and to the point: 'I first talked about the withering away of the Party, of the League, but I did not say that it should be in six months, a year or two years, but as part of a long drawn-out process. Until the last class enemy has been disarmed, until the broadest masses have been educated to socialism, there can be no withering away, no liquidation of the League, for it is responsible for implementing this present revolution, just as it was responsible during the earlier revolution and its victory'.[53]

With Djilas expelled, Tito wrote to all party organisations making clear that they knew what their roles were relating to workers' councils. They were not, as they once had, to interfere in the technical management of the enterprise, 'but communists in the enterprise cannot limit themselves to education and raising the consciousness of the unconscious or weakly conscious workers to a higher level. That is insufficient. They must see what general policies are pursued in the enterprises and how the workers' council functions. They give the tone to the work of the workers' councils.' The Party was actively returning to control areas it had recently announced it was abandoning.[54]

4

1956: COMMUNISM RENEWED?

Between 1953 and 1956 the twin processes of de-Stalinisation and Soviet–Yugoslav rapprochement opened up the possibility of renewal for the communist states of Eastern Europe. With Khrushchev pressing the East European leaders to undo the injustices of the purge trials, and Tito urging them to adopt the Yugoslav system of workers' councils, there were moments when it looked as if a very different style of communism might emerge.

After Stalin's Cominform purges, genuine reform in the political system of Eastern Europe was unlikely to occur, as it were, from within: it was the existence 'outside' of an alternative socialist system, coupled with the genuine desire of Khrushchev to bring Yugoslavia back into the family of socialist states, that made the prospect of renewal genuine. So long as Khrushchev wanted to bring Tito back into the fold, he was prepared to negotiate with him about the nature of socialism and the future of Eastern Europe. It was this unique circumstance which opened up the possibility of a reversal of Stalinist policies; the tragedy for those communists who espoused such a reformist vision was that, deep down, Tito was as committed as Khrushchev to the Leninist concept of the leading role of the Communist Party and, therefore, to a system which allowed power to be concentrated in the hands of an unelected bureaucratic caste.

THE NEW COURSE IN THE GDR AND HUNGARY

Although Stalin's crimes would not be fully denounced until the Twentieth Congress of the Soviet Communist Party in February 1956, the Soviet leadership began the process of reassessment as soon as the dictator had died. In spring 1953 it was Stalin's Security Chief Lavrentii Beria and the Prime Minister Georgii Malenkov who took the lead in pushing for reform. While Stalin was only criticised obliquely, many of the policies associated with him, particularly in the field of foreign policy, were quietly abandoned. Thus by the end of May the Soviet Union had re-established diplomatic relations with Yugoslavia and Israel and pushed the North Koreans to adopt a softer negotiating stance, thus preparing the way for the armistice of July. It was in this context that the future of Stalin's other act of anti-Western confrontation, East Germany, was discussed.

On 22 April the Soviet Political adviser Vladimir Semenov was recalled from Berlin for consultations and discussion of a detailed review of the state of East Germany recently undertaken. On 27 May the Soviet Communist Party's ruling Presidium discussed the situation, and debated the proposal of Beria that the Soviet Union should cut its losses and abandon East Germany. The proposal was rejected, but the same meeting decided that a radical overhaul of the SED and its policies was needed, possibly even a leader other than Ulbricht. Semenov returned to Berlin on 28 May and informed Ulbricht he was needed in Moscow. Both Ulbricht and Semenov had talks in Moscow on 2–4 June, and on 5 June both returned to inform the SED what was expected of it.[1]

The message was that the pace of socialist construction should be dramatically slowed, collectivisation put on hold and an effort made to woo the middle class. It therefore completely contradicted the policy pursued by the GDR throughout the previous year. Since summer 1952, at the Second Party Conference, Ulbricht had committed the Party to 'building socialism'. This involved increased exports to the Soviet Union, higher taxes and cuts in consumption. At the same time, the ongoing campaign to collectivise agriculture was accelerated. As a result the number of people leaving the GDR doubled in autumn 1952 and doubled again in spring 1953. However, far from abandoning the policy as these problems mounted, Ulbricht determined to press ahead and in May announced that production norms would be raised by 10 per cent at the end of June.

The dramatic volte-face insisted on by Moscow would not be popular with many party workers, and Semenov insisted that there should be no preliminary plenum of the SED Central Committee to prepare the ground. The 'New Course' was launched at once with a communiqué from the Politburo on 9 June which spoke openly of the mistakes of the past, cancelled price rises and restored ration cards to those deprived of them on class grounds. A fuller statement came in *Neues Deutschland* on 11 June, but the lack of adequate preparation for such a momentous change soon made itself felt. The most contentious issue was that of the increase in labour norms. On 14 June 4000 political prisoners were released and an editorial in *Neues Deutschland* suggested that these revised norms were part of the old hard line which should be abandoned; but the same issue of the paper carried articles praising workers ready to meet the new norms. On 16 June the matter seemed to be clarified when the trade union paper *Tribune* made clear that there was to be no change of policy as far as the norms were concerned.[2]

On 15 June the first building workers in Berlin went on strike, and it was waving copies of the *Tribune* article that the next day they marched first to the trade union headquarters and then to government offices where they received only vague words of reassurance. They resolved to reassemble on the 17th and march through the city once again. As more and more workers joined them, the authorities began to panic. When at midday the demonstrations were so great that traffic was blocked, warning shots were fired. At 12.30 Soviet tanks appeared on the streets. At 1.00 p.m. a state of emergency was declared by the Soviet occupying authorities. By the evening, the Soviet troops had regained control in Berlin, following the total failure of the GDR's own police force to maintain order. And Berlin was not the only town affected. Violent clashes with Soviet forces also took place in Magdeburg, Halle and Leipzig. In Görlitz an alternative democratic government was formed, while in Bitterfeld the government offices were seized. Elsewhere, the demonstrators appeared to have milled aimlessly on the streets, unsure how to put their power of numbers into effect. All over the GDR, however, the situation was totally out of the control of local functionaries, with most demonstrators acting without any strategic plan or sense of purpose; power rested only on the presence of Soviet tanks. Some 21 demonstrators died, seven were later sentenced to death as ringleaders, and over 6000 were arrested. The economic demands of the strikers were immediately conceded; the political demand for free elections was not.[3]

In the initial aftermath of the strikes, the Party leadership prepared a report which would have radically changed the way the Party operated by removing the post of Party general secretary, then held by Ulbricht.[4] This threat to Ulbricht's position was removed when, at precisely the same time as the report critical of Ulbricht was being drawn up in Berlin, in Moscow Khrushchev rallied support for the ouster of Beria. Arrested on 26 June, he was formally disgraced at the Soviet Communist Party's Central Committee Plenum on 2 July on the charge of having plotted the surrender to the imperialists of the German Democratic Republic. In this climate Ulbricht could hardly be disgraced. Instead it was those pressing for reform who were expelled from the leadership at the end of July on the charge of being secret supporters of Beria.

Although the strikes in East Germany were the most dramatic evidence of the strain Stalin's policies had put on those East European countries so rapidly incorporated into the Soviet bloc, the workers of East Germany did not act in isolation. At the end of May 1953 the Czechoslovak government introduced a currency reform and the workers' response was immediate; by the first week in June there were strikes in many towns. Disturbances in Prague, Pilsen and Ostrava were even reported in the censored Czechoslovak press. The trouble began on 1 June, when Pilsen workers aware that the currency reform meant a 20 per cent cut in real earnings tore down portraits of Stalin and Gottwald. Reports sent by the Czechoslovak leaders to the Soviet ambassador reveal that the disturbances reached a peak on the night of 3–4 June and on the morning of the 4th, when activists from Czechoslovakia's former political parties started organising petitions. By tapping phone calls and arresting labour activists the authorities prevented the movement spreading to politically sensitive areas; plans had been drawn up for a strike on the Prague tram network. As well as the stick of arrests, there was the carrot of concessions; the government agreed to drop plans for even more punitive laws restricting labour mobility.[5]

Strikes also occurred that June in Hungary where real wages had fallen 18 per cent since 1949. The Hungarian Party leaders, like those of the GDR, were summoned to Moscow. At talks held on 12–16 June, Beria took the lead in criticising the way Hungary was being run; the economy was in crisis, peasants were resisting collectivisation and 15 per cent of the population were in prison. Breaking a private understanding given to Rákosi on the eve of the visit that he would retain the post of prime minister, Beria proposed that, while Rákosi could stay on a Party leader, the new prime minister should be Imre Nagy, the former minister of Agriculture who had been expelled from the Politburo in 1949 for opposing the pace of Hungary's collectivisation campaign. Although this division of responsibilities would ultimately weaken Nagy's position, it was a clear element of the Beria–Malenkov strategy that the powers of the Party over the economy should be restricted and that government agencies should have precedence of Party agencies. When Nagy suggested that Rákosi might resist reform, Beria threatened to 'break his back' if he did.

After the return of the delegation from Moscow the Party held a Central Committee Plenum on 27–8 June and over the summer of 1953 and for the next 18 months, all major initiatives were taken by the new Prime Minster, Imre Nagy. On 4 July he addressed parliament to propose a radical New Course for Hungary: in line with Malenkov he stressed the need for consumer goods, telling the plenum 'we failed to realise the basic economic law of socialism – the constant raising of the standard of living of the population'. Dissatisfaction amongst the working-class, he believed, was increasing and the link between the working-class and the Communist Party was in danger of being broken.[6]

By far the most radical element of Nagy's programme, only hinted at in his June speech, was his desire to revive the popular front as a new focus for democracy within the country. Only at the end of 1948 had the Hungarian Party leadership got around to creating the sort of popular front 'from below' prefigured at the Cominform Founding Conference of September 1947. The Hungarian People's Independence Front, as it was renamed on 1 February 1949, comprised members of the Hungarian Workers' Party (the name adopted by the communists and socialists after their merger), the Smallholders' Party, and the National Peasant Party, plus the trade union organisation, women's organisation and youth organisation. Since only 13 members of the 43 member National Council represented groups not controlled by the communists, it rapidly became a rubber stamp and by 1951 it had almost ceased to operate. When elections were held in May 1953, only the communists were referred to in literature produced by the People's Independence Front.[7]

Nagy proposed scrapping the People's Independence Front and replacing it with a new Patriotic People's Front. Consciously or not, Nagy found himself raising the very same issues that had exercised Kardelj and Djilas when they decided to rename the Yugoslav People's Front the Socialist Alliance of Working People. Nagy's interest in breathing new life into the old popular front organisation was part of a broader concern for the role of democracy in a socialist society. Nagy described the function of the Patriotic People's Front as being to create a federation supported by the masses, with a base far wider and more extensive than the alliance of workers and peasants; this, he suggested, could only be done by making patriotism respectable, fusing the ideas of democracy and socialism with patriotism, and thus involving all in democratic life. This was not to be another propaganda machine for the Party, but a genuine attempt to democratise the government.[8]

Nagy envisaged a completely new organisation, made up of individual members free to set up their own independent branches as they thought fit. Such an organisation would clearly allow non-party members a significant influence over the political life of the country, and it is hardly surprising that party hard-liners such as Rákosi asked Nagy what he understood by the leading role of the Communist Party if such a scheme were ever introduced. Nagy always insisted, at this time at least, that he accepted the leading role of the Party. Indeed, on more than one occasion, as the Patriotic People's Front was gradually established, Nagy acted to slow the process to prevent the Party being bypassed; but his vision of how the Party's leading role might be exercised was quite unlike that of Rákosi and Stalin. He accepted that initiatives within the Patriotic People's Front could come from outside the Party, and the Party would have to respond to them: the Party would not simply use the Patriotic People's Front to tell other groups what to do as had happened in the past.

Rákosi had never reconciled himself to defeat. He started a whispering campaign that Nagy was 'Beria's man' and therefore needed to be removed from power to bring Hungary back into line with the Soviet Union. When the Hungarian leadership was summoned to Moscow on 7 July 1953 to be told of Beria's arrest, Rákosi at once asked for the New Course to be revoked; even though it was not, he was quick to tell a meeting of Party activists in Budapest on 9 July that Beria's arrest made it clear that it had been a mistake to issue the New Course in the name of the government and not the Party. He was doubly determined to resist any changes to his simplistic view of what was meant by the leading role of the Party. To him, Nagy was risking 'national danger' by allowing any sort of political activity outside the Party; it simply 'revived the activity of the enemy'. He fought tooth and nail to restrict the influence of the Patriotic People's Front and was successful in persuading the Politburo to limit the way in which individuals could participate in it.[9] These and other issues connected to the economic aspects of Nagy's reforms, were debated at length by the Central Committee in October 1954. So bitter had the quarrel between Rákosi and Nagy become that Rákosi tried to prevent Nagy's speech

to the plenum from being published in the Party ne
too brief moment of triumph Nagy got his speech pu
days later, on 23 October 1954, attended the opening c
First Congress of the Patriotic People's Front where he w
received.[10]

There then followed the first tentative experiment in a new democracy. In November 1954 local elections were held. This time, although there remained only one electoral list, it had been drawn up by the Patriotic People's Front not the Party, and people had the option to vote against those selected. The experiment was not welcomed by Rákosi who had spent November in the Soviet Union and returned to talk about 'counter-revolutionary' developments in the Patriotic People's Front. And in a way he was right, for Nagy had no qualms about making Géza Losonczy, imprisoned for political offences between 1951 and 1954, the deputy editor of the daily paper published by the Patriotic People's Front.[11]

It was Nagy's great tragedy that the economic reforms introduced by Malenkov in the Soviet Union in the summer of 1953 had been ill thought out. The problems they provoked were used by Khrushchev to further his own career and marginalise Malenkov. In this new Moscow climate the Hungarian Politburo passed a resolution in December 1954 warning of the danger of 'Right opportunism'; on 8 January 1955 the Soviet leadership received both Rákosi and Nagy and agreed that a 'Right deviation existed'; and in February 1955 Malenkov was sacked as Soviet prime minister. Malenkov's sacking was seized on by Rákosi who used it to justify a vicious attack on Nagy and all his political and economic reforms. At a Central Committee Plenum on 4 March, Nagy was condemned as the leader of the 'Right deviation'; he was expelled from the Politburo and Central Committee in April when he refused to issue a self-critical statement, and excluded from the Party itself in December 1955.[12]

TITO, KHRUSHCHEV AND DE-STALINISATION

For all the negative consequences the fall of Malenkov had on Hungarian reform politics, it greatly strengthened the position of Khrushchev who at once re-addressed the twin problems of Stalin's political legacy and relations with Yugoslavia. A year after the Soviet Union's proposal that diplomatic relations be restored, Khrushchev ad written to Tito suggesting that the time had come to bury the hatchet. In this letter of June 1954 Khrushchev had suggested that since the Soviet Union had executed Beria, the man responsible for engineering the East European purge of 'Titoites', and the Yugoslavs had expelled Djilas, the man responsible for the most trenchant Yugoslav attacks on the Soviet Union, a basis now existed for restored relations. Tito replied that the cases of Beria and Djilas simply could not be linked in this way, and that the prerequisite for reconciliation was a public statement from the Soviet side.[13]

After the demotion of Malenkov, Khrushchev overcame any objections he and the Soviet Politburo might have had about eating humble pie and on 14 May Moscow and Belgrade announced that Khrushchev, Prime Minister Nikolai Bulganin and Foreign Trade Minister Anastasii Mikoyan would arrive in Belgrade on 26 May. There, at Belgrade airport, Khrushchev read out a statement expressing the Soviet Government's 'sincere regret' for the accusations and insults of the Stalin years, and expressing the hope that they could 'sweep away the bitterness of that period'. Those responsible for fabricating the materials on which these allegations had been made had been dealt with.[14] The statement was carefully drafted: it condemned the Cominform resolution passed in Budapest in November 1949, and thus all the charges of murder, espionage and fascism heaped on the Yugoslav regime during Stalin's last years; but it did not condemn the July 1948 decision to expel the Yugoslavs from the Cominform for ideological errors. Equally ambivalent was the Declaration signed at the end of the talks on 2 June 1955: this spoke of 'mutual respect and non-interference in one another's internal affairs', and of 'co-operation between public organisations of the two countries to exchange socialist experience'; but it was not an agreement on inter-party cooperation.[15] Yet this, it seems, was precisely what Khrushchev, if not his fellow Politburo members, wanted.

At the talks Khrushchev bent over backwards to win Tito over. The first day simply showed the gulf between the two sides: Khrushchev tried to skate over the affair as a misunderstanding brought about by Beria's misinformation, while Tito insisted that the root cause had been Greece and Stalin's percentages agreement with Churchill. On the next day, to move things forward, Khrushchev appealed openly to Tito's anti-Stalin sentiments, and began a long monologue about Stalin's crimes, the role of Beria, Stalin's attacks on Khrushchev himself, the details of the plot hatched by Khrushchev and Bulganin to depose Beria, and the details of the charges against Beria. Confiding such domestic secrets to the leader of a once hostile 'fascist' power could only be justified in terms of fellow communists facing up to a common problem, something which must have flattered Tito, creating the impression that the two men might play a common role in reforming communism.[16]

If Khrushchev seemed to be looking for help from Tito in his campaign against Stalinism, Tito was also glad to have Khrushchev's support. The cost of the break with Stalin had been phenomenal, not only had there been industrial losses in the order of 429 million dollars, but between 1948 and 1950 defence expenditure had tripled. As a result, after the deals with a US bank in September 1949 and the International Monetary Fund (IMF) in October 1949, Yugoslavia had been increasingly involved in borrowing from the West. This dependence on Western loans began to worry Tito in the spring of 1953, and was another of the issues raised at the time of the Brioni Plenum in June 1953.[17]

During 1953 and 1954 Tito was impatient at the slow pace at which the Soviet–Yugoslav rapprochement was developing.[18] Once the 1955 Declaration had been signed, Tito spoke enthusiastically about his new partner: the Soviet Union had agreed to cancel debts and aid Yugoslavia, without demanding the crippling interest charges insisted on by the West; a common language with the Soviet Union had been found. 'We shall not, for the sake of anyone's pleasure, wage a war – not even a propaganda war – against the Soviet Union and other East European countries', he said. The current Soviet leadership, he went on, were 'new men: men who do not wish the delusions, false moves, and actions of the past to be repeated; men who wish to start along another road for the benefit of themselves and of the whole world; men who wish to prove that they are not what they are rebuked as being by the West, but are just leaders of a socialist country'.[19]

Rapprochement with Tito was bitterly resisted by conservative circles within the Soviet leadership, especially by Molotov. While at the July 1955 Plenum of the Soviet Communist Party Khrushchev and Bulganin bubbled with enthusiasm for 'these real fighters, people who had spent their whole lives fighting for Bolshevik principles', Molotov stuck to the line that the Yugoslavs had initially been guilty of a nationalist deviation, and since then had drifted away from Marxism–Leninism to a point where they were indistinguishable from 'right socialists'. Molotov insisted that while Beria had made things worse after Molotov's dismissal as foreign minister in 1949, the logic of blaming it all on Beria was to accuse Stalin himself 'which could not be allowed'. However, it was precisely Stalin whom Khrushchev proposed to blame. In these acrimonious exchanges Khrushchev told Molotov bluntly and repeatedly that the full Politburo had never discussed the break with Yugoslavia, it had simply been agreed between Stalin and Molotov without other Politburo members being consulted.

Early in 1956 Khrushchev had overcome Molotov and the conservatives and in February 1956 summoned the Twentieth Congress of the Soviet Party at which he read his 'secret speech' denouncing Stalin's crimes since the early 1930s. Then, on 18 April 1956, the Cominform, the organisation originally set up with Tito's blessing but then used to vilify him, was formally dissolved.[20] On 2 June 1956 Tito arrived in Moscow for a three-week visit and was fulsome in his praise for Khrushchev: 'we believed that the time would come when everything that kept us apart would be transformed and that our friendship would acquire new and firm foundations. That time had now come, thanks to the Leninist policy of the government and the Soviet Party [and] the courageous and far-sighted policy of the collective leadership of the USSR.' On 20 June the Moscow Declaration was signed restoring relations between the Yugoslav and Soviet Parties.[21]

There was, however, a stumbling block in the process of rapprochement between the Soviet Union and Yugoslavia. Stalin had been replaced by Khrushchev, but elsewhere in Eastern Europe the Stalinist leadership remained largely intact. Tito's concerns were limited to those leaders of surrounding countries. He quickly came to terms with Gheorghiu-Dej in Bucharest (indeed it has been suggested they were actually secretly in contact with each other even during the height of the Cominform's attacks on Yugoslavia), and he took particular pleasure in seeing the former Bulgarian Party leader Vulko Chervenkov forced to announce his resignation as the country's premier in the presence of a visiting Yugoslav parliamentary delegation.[22] The problem was Hungary.

There had, of course, been a change of leadership under Nagy, but that had been negated by the neo-Stalinist counter-revolution staged by Rákosi in March 1955. Rákosi was a particular thorn in Tito's side. It was not just that the Rajk trial had been aimed at Yugoslavia, but that Rákosi had played such an active role in the Rajk purge process. He told a Soviet security adviser early in 1950 that for more than a year he had spent the greater part of every day dealing with the trials. Tito felt personally affronted by the Rajk trial; after the verdict had been announced he went in person to the Hungarian Embassy to hand in a protest note. Yet Rákosi's sins in Yugoslav eyes went beyond the Rajk trial. From spring 1949 onwards the terrorist groups of Yugoslav émigrés preparing to overthrow Tito were based in Hungary; in July 1949 Rákosi urged the Cominform to agree to launch an armed struggle, for 'with propaganda alone we will not remove the Tito clique'; while in January 1950 he moaned to a Soviet security official that not enough was being done to support the Yugoslav émigrés. When signing the Moscow Declaration in June 1956, as well as praising Khrushchev, Tito denounced the Hungarian leadership: 'these men have their hands soaked in blood; they have staged trials, given false information, sentenced innocent men to death. They have dragged Yugoslavia into all these trials, as in the case of the Rajk trial, and they now find it difficult to admit their mistakes before their own people.'[23]

Khrushchev promised Tito he would act against Rákosi, but then his conservative opponents staged a comeback. Although a Soviet emissary visited Hungary around the end of June, Rákosi was not removed. The reason was this: at the end of June all Eastern Europe was shaken by the riots which broke out in the Polish town of Poznan, and hardliners in the Soviet leadership turned on Khrushchev, alleging his anti-Stalin policy and his reconciliation with Tito were responsible and risked the break up of the whole system. For a while Khrushchev was unable to assert his authority and the Soviet Politburo agreed to 'ease things for Rákosi'.[24] Far from quietly disappearing from the scene, he chaired a meeting of East European leaders in Moscow which resulted in a letter being sent to all East European Parties on 13 July questioning the ideological basis for a reconciliation with Tito. Less than a week later, Khrushchev was in a position to assert himself once again, although not as radically as he had at first hoped. In a trade off with the conservatives, he persuaded them that Rákosi had to go, but did not push his original proposal to appoint János Kádár, Tito's favoured candidate who had been imprisoned by Rákosi in 1951. Instead, Khrushchev agreed to Molotov's proposal that Rákosi should be replaced by Ernő Gerő, one of Rákosi's closest associates; Kádár was made a Central Committee secretary. On 18 July 1956 Khrushchev sent Mikoyan to Hungary to tell the Party Plenum then in session that Rákosi must be sacked. To rub in the significance of the message, Mikoyan went straight from Budapest to Belgrade to report on what had taken place. Three weeks later, on 9 August 1956, Tito invited Khrushchev to pay a private visit to Yugoslavia in September.[25]

Together, Khrushchev and Tito seemed to be planning the renewal of communism.

THE HUNGARIAN REVOLUTION OF 1956

After his removal from power, Nagy began to reformulate his ideas in a document called 'On Communism', which he hoped would eventually form the basis for his rehabilitation by the Party. Like the Yugoslav communists had done when they began to reconsider the meaning of communism, Nagy went back to Marx's own writings. There, in some of Marx's writings about the First International, he found guidance on how socialists and socialist states should relate to each other. In particular he was struck by Marx's ideas about the need to defend 'the most simple basic laws of morals and justice, which must rule the relations between private individuals, and which must also be the chief laws governing the contacts between nations'.

This simple message of morality and justice was, Nagy added, the basis for the 1955 Belgrade accord between Khrushchev and Tito, which recognised that all nations would find their own roads to socialism. By being forced into the strait-jacket of the Soviet model, Hungary and the other peoples' democracies had steadily lost the popular, democratic attributes they had once had, and become increasingly dependent on the use of force. The only way forward, Nagy continued, was to 'develop towards socialism by systematically decreasing the use of force [and] utilising democratic forms and methods in the interest of close co-operation on the widest possible scale with the masses of working people'. On the international level, it meant working for the international recognition of Hungary's neutrality, on the Austrian pattern.

Nagy's description of the behaviour of the communist bureaucracy was reminiscent of that of Djilas. 'Power is increasingly being torn away from the people and turned sharply against them ... the people's democracy in which power is exercised by the working class ... is obviously being replaced by a Party dictatorship ... [in which] power is not permeated by the spirit of socialism and democratisation but by a Bonapartist spirit of minority dictatorship.' The origins of this 'Bonapartism' Nagy considered to have been 'when the clique headed by Rákosi ... crushed the basis of Hungary's young democracy and liquidated our people's democratic forces and the democratic partnerships of socialism'. Decoded, this meant returning to the situation of

1948 or earlier when non-communist parties had played a meaningful role in Hungarian politics.[26]

After his dismissal Nagy became the focal point for an intellectual circle of political dissidents. The most active of these groups was the Petőfi Circle, formed in 1954 as a discussion group within the Communist Youth League. While active throughout 1955, the Circle really began to develop after Khrushchev's secret speech in February 1956 and Rákosi's reluctant admission at the end of March that the Rajk trial had been 'based on provocation and was a miscarriage of justice'. The Circle's most spectacular event was related to this admission: on 18 June it organised a public meeting addressed by Rajk's widow. Then, on 27 June, a second mass meeting was organised which demanded the restoration of Nagy's government. That these were no longer isolated acts by individual intellectuals was clear from the strike wave that hit Budapest in the wake of the Poznan riots.[27]

Rákosi tried to respond to this growing opposition to his regime with repression. He banned the Petőfi Circle and summoned a Plenum of the Central Committee at which he presented a list of some 400 opposition activists whom he believed should be arrested, with Imre Nagy at its head. But it was at this Plenum that Mikoyan arrived from Moscow and dismissed Rákosi, paying a call on Nagy before flying on to Belgrade.[28] The new leadership, headed by Gerő, began by reviving some of the spirit of Nagy's economic programme and proposing the reactivation of the Patriotic People's Front; it also called for improved relations with the Yugoslav League of Communists. However, the rehabilitation of Nagy himself, rather than the piecemeal selection of bits of his programme, was not yet considered.[29] It took Khrushchev and Tito to get the question of Nagy back onto the agenda.

On 19 September Khrushchev paid his private visit to Yugoslavia, and Tito returned with him to the Crimea on 27 September, where he stayed until 5 October. In the course of these two holidays Tito and Khrushchev had ten days of talks, without any intermediary, interspersed with swimming, hunting and similar delights. Hungary was high on the agenda of topics covered, and Khrushchev summoned Gerő to join them in the Crimea on 2 October. Tito was cautious about endorsing the new leadership, but after Nagy had been invited to reapply for Party membership an invitation was extended to Gerő and Kádár to visit Yugoslavia in the middle of the month. Nagy was accepted back into the Party on 13 October, the eve of Gerő and Kádár's departure for Belgrade on the 15th.[30]

Another of the terms put down by Tito for reconciliation with the Hungarian communists was the reinterment of Rajk's body. This rather macabre ceremony was held on 6 October and was rapidly transformed into a massive demonstration by the opposition. In spite of the decision to ban the Petőfi Circle in July, it had, by the autumn, blossomed to become a nationwide opposition network, and seized on the opportunity presented by the reburial. Over 200 000 people took part in that demonstration, with a small group of 200–300 breaking away from the mass of demonstrators and gathering outside the Yugoslav Embassy to cheer Tito and praise Yugoslav socialism. The Yugoslav press had consistently taken up the cause of the Petőfi Circle.

The fact that the police took no serious action against the demonstrators emboldened the government's opponents. A fortnight later, on 22 October, students at the Budapest Technical University, supported a little reluctantly on this occasion by the Petőfi Circle, called a demonstration for the 23rd which would demand the withdrawal of Soviet troops and the formation of a Nagy government. That demonstration, at first banned by the government and then permitted after it had started, marked the start of the Hungarian Revolution. As it progressed through the city more and more people joined it. Tens of thousands marched to the Radio Station to demand that it broadcast their demands. Frustrated when this was refused, most demonstrators moved to gather in Parliament Square. The Politburo began to lose its nerve and called on Nagy to address the crowd and appeal for calm.

This placed Nagy in a dilemma: by turning to him, the communist apparatus he knew so well had brought him back into the fold and would restore him to the post of prime minister; yet as someone who believed that communism could be renewed only if it turned to the people, he had to win popular support, not just the support of the Party apparatus. When he addressed the crowd on 23 October he got the balance between these two pressures wrong. He did not realise that the Hungarian flags with the communist emblem torn out which the demonstrators were carrying meant what they symbolised; his appeal 'comrades' was met with the reply 'we are no longer comrades'.[31]

This was a rude shock for Nagy, although he had anticipated as much. Writing on the eve of the October events Nagy had stressed: 'today probably a return to the policy of the New Course and the application of the June [1953] principles ... could still check the growing crisis and avert catastrophe. But it is doubtful whether a return to the June principles would suffice as a solution tomorrow. ... Before long there is a danger that the masses, having lost their faith, will reject both the June way and the Communist Party, and it will become necessary to make a much greater retreat in order to keep the situation under control.'

And that is precisely what proved to be the case. Any chance that Nagy's appointment alone could restore the situation was destroyed when Gerő, who arrived back from Belgrade on the 23rd, used a radio broadcast to denounce the demonstrators in precisely the same terms that Rákosi would have used. Furious demonstrators returned to the Radio Station to demand the right to reply to Gerő's abuse, and as the authorities tried to defend the Radio Station the first bloody clashes occurred. Gerő then appealed for the intervention of Soviet troops. The Soviet politburo heard the request on the evening of the 23rd and, despite Mikoyan's pleas not to do so, decided to send in the requested troops; Molotov endorsed the move with the prediction 'in Nagy's hands Hungary will shake lose'. Thus as victorious Budapest workers established control over the Radio Station on the morning of 24 October, Soviet tanks began to pour into the city, starting four days of bitter fighting.

As a communist brought up on Party procedures, Nagy was powerless to influence the events of that night. Although he had been called on to form a government, he was at that stage a simple Party member; to be a prime minister he would have to be a member of the Politburo. So while Gerő took the fateful decision to call on Soviet troops to support the government, Nagy waited for the Central Committee to gather and co-opt him to the Politburo. Thus Nagy had no say in the decision to call in Soviet troops, nor in the hysterical radio broadcasts referring to 'hostile elements and a small number of counter-revolutionaries' who were fomenting unrest. Nagy had to await the arrival of Mikoyan, on the evening of the 24th before any progress could be made. Then on 25 October, with Mikoyan's agreement, Kádár replaced Gerő as Party Secretary. Only then was Nagy in a position to execute the 'great retreat' about which he had so recently written, and which would now be far more difficult to implement given the involvement of Soviet forces.[32]

On 26 October, with the support of Losonczy, who became the editor of the Patriotic People's Front daily, the only paper to keep appearing regularly through the crisis, Nagy called on the Patriotic People's Front, not the Party, to recommend the composition of a new government which included the former leader of the Smallholders'

Party Zoltán Tildy. Nagy was at first supported by his Politburo and by Mikoyan. When it met over the night of 27–28 October, in the presence of Mikoyan, the lead was taken by Kádár who had been appointed to head the Party's emergency directorate, tasked to oversee affairs until proper Party elections could be held. Kádár and Mikoyan backed Nagy's proposal for a ceasefire followed by negotiations on the withdrawal of Soviet troops. It even accepted Nagy's wording, which referred to those opposing the Soviet troops not as counter-revolutionaries but 'a democratic movement which swept our whole nation in order to secure our independence, which is the only basis of a socialist democracy'. But Mikoyan made clear that this was to be the extent of the concessions; the Party should now show resolution for 'if they make a new set of concessions tomorrow then it will not be possible to stop it'.

Although Nagy told the Politburo that he intended to 'head the huge powerful people's force' in order to control it, it rapidly became apparent to the Kremlin that concession was following concession. The ceasefire, ordered on the afternoon of 28 October, did not end the fighting. As Mikoyan reported on 30 October, many 'rebels' were refusing to comply and were insisting that they would only hand in their weapons when all Soviet troops had left the country; Nagy refused to allow force to be used against those unwilling to comply. In Moscow the conservatives were increasingly alarmed, but despite making critical noises about Mikoyan's concessions the Soviet Politburo accepted that there was no alternative. That remained the case even after Mikoyan's report on the 30th that Nagy seemed to be losing control. Thus, despite its qualms, it decided to go ahead and issue the Declaration on Friendship and Cooperation between the Soviet Union and other Socialist States. This document sought to regularise the stationing of Soviet troops in Eastern Europe by providing a framework in which various anomalies could be cleared up. Soviet troops had withdrawn from Czechoslovakia in 1945 and Bulgaria in 1947, but had remained in Poland, to protect lines of communication with occupied East Germany, and Romania and Hungary, to protect lines of communication with occupied Austria; after Austria's reunification in 1955, the formation of the Warsaw Pact had allowed Soviet troops to stay in Hungary and Romania, ostensibly by mutual agreement.[33]

The Declaration offered Nagy legitimate grounds on which to discuss the future of Soviet troops in Hungary and was an important part of implementing the agreement reached on 28 October. However, later on the 30th, after the decision had been taken to issue the Declaration, the Soviet Politburo received the news that Nagy had decided to restore multiparty democracy and had established a so-called narrow cabinet which, while it included Kádár, also included Béla Kovács, imprisoned in the Soviet Union from 1947–55 for his counter-revolutionary activities; Molotov commented bluntly that a counter-revolutionary government had been formed. The next day, on 31 October, the Soviet Politburo decided to intervene militarily and appoint a new provisional government headed by Ferenc Münnich, a former Hungarian ambassador to Moscow, who had already been lobbying for just such a government to be formed. When Mikoyan arrived in person on 1 November and tried to reopen the decision to intervene, he met with no support; his plea for a further three days to pursue negotiations was turned down.

Nagy and his government at once sensed a change of mood. On 1 November, at Tildy's suggestion, they declared Hungary neutral and later in the day demanded to know from the Soviet ambassador why Soviet troops were still in active operations. Nagy threatened to pull Hungary out of the Warsaw Pact. Kádár, who also attended this meeting with the Soviet ambassador, was unhappy with this threat and later that night accepted Münnich's proposal that they should fly to Moscow. When the two of them attended a meeting of the Soviet Politburo on 2 November, it was Kádár who made the greater impact.

SOVIET–YUGOSLAV INTERVENTION

On 4 November, less than a week after its publication, the Soviet Union tore up its own Declaration and its invasion of Hungary began; Nagy's 'great retreat' was at an end. However, the chances of its success were not as remote as hindsight might suggest. While Stalin's system of communism was rejected by the mass of workers, socialist ownership was not: the leaders of the Socialist Party and Smallholders' Party in Nagy's coalition government rejected the idea of capitalist restoration, as did the most powerful organisations thrown up by the Hungarian Revolution, the workers' councils.

Before the start of the revolt Tito had urged Gerő and Kádár to establish workers' councils and the government first approved their formation on 26 October. Originally it was hoped that they might operate through the intermediary of the existing trade union structure, but working-class pressure prevented this from happening. By 27 October spontaneous working-class action had put many enterprises in the hands of their workers, and on 30 October the coalition government recognised the workers' councils, and other revolutionary committees, as local sources of power.[34] In the course of their desperate struggle against Soviet tanks, workers' councils always insisted the 'collective ownership of the means of production' should be exercised through them.[35]

Clearly the desire to form workers' councils in Hungary was partly influenced by developments in Yugoslavia. What Hungarian workers knew of the Yugoslav system of workers' self-management was inevitably distorted, since it had mostly been described to them by a hostile Stalinist press. However, by the simple device of believing the opposite of what the press told them, workers would have a clear, if rather idealised understanding of what was happening in Yugoslavia. If it was evident that in the Stalin–Tito dispute Tito had been right and Stalin wrong, it was easy to jump to the conclusion that the Yugoslav system of socialism might, in fact, be better than the Soviet one. Then, as Yugoslav–Soviet relations improved, some direct contacts between Hungarian and Yugoslav trade unions were established, and the role of the workers' councils in Yugoslavia was given some coverage by the Petőfi Circle. Participants in such meetings noted much later that all who wanted a reformed socialism in Hungary in 1956 saw Yugoslavia as the model state.[36]

Unfortunately, the reality of workers' self-management in Yugoslavia and the degree of Party control over workers' councils that Tito had enforced after the Brioni Plenum of 1953 was only dimly appreciated in Hungary, as everywhere else. Tito personified anti-Stalinism and the possibility of a renewed communism; but deep down, Tito was a true Leninist when it came to the question of the leading role of the Party. Just what this meant for the future of communism in Eastern Europe would be shown in the role played by Tito during the Hungarian Revolution and subsequent Soviet invasion of Hungary.

From the moment the Hungarian crisis began, Khrushchev was determined to involve Yugoslavia in its resolution. On 25 October he received the Yugoslav ambassador and told him that the Soviet Union was ready 'to answer force with force'. The Soviet Government was unanimous: it would try to work for a political solution, but if that were not possible force would be used; the ambassador had the clear impression that Khrushchev was very pessimistic about the chances of a political solution. Then, on the evening of 2 November, Khrushchev arrived at Tito's holiday island of Brioni and from seven that evening until five the next morning briefed Tito about the plan to invade Hungary, which had already been endorsed by the other East European leaders. While the essence of the plan was military, Khrushchev had been informed *en route* that Kádár and Münnich had arrived in the Soviet Union, and so some sort of political accompaniment to the invasion might be possible.

Tito and his comrades endorsed the decision. For some time the Yugoslav press had been noting with concern that 'counter-revolutionary' elements seemed to be getting the upper hand over Nagy, and this was the line they took at the meeting. They had welcomed Nagy's government of 26 October, and while they never made this public, had been in contact with Losonczy. However, they too had felt that events were swinging to the Right and counter-revolution was on the cards; after all, Tito had never had much time for coalition governments. The Yugoslavs accepted that counter-revolution would have to be confronted by intervention: their only proposal was that this would be more acceptable if it was not carried out by the Soviet Army alone, and that it should be preceded by as much political preparation as possible. A 'revolutionary' Hungarian government would have to be formed to give a political lead and that government should then appeal to the working-class and in particular the workers' councils for support. Khrushchev suggested Münnich should head the government: the Yugoslav side said it would prefer Kádár, a former victim of Stalinism. Although Kádár's candidacy had been discussed by the Soviet Politburo at its crucial meeting on 31 October, it had been rejected. Now Khrushchev was happy to revive it.[37]

And so, with Soviet and Yugoslav backing, Kádár tried vainly to form some sort of popular government with the Soviet Army at his side. In so doing he did for a while stick to the terms of the bargain reached between Khrushchev and Tito. On 14 November a Central Workers' Council of Greater Budapest was formed and agreed to negotiate a resolution to the crisis: Kádár was at first conciliatory and even suggested that workers' councils might elect a National Council of Producers, something very reminiscent of a similarly named organisation in Yugoslavia. At the same time there were clear indications in the Soviet press that workers' councils might be the one element of the Yugoslav experiment that could have more general lessons for Eastern Europe.

Yugoslav–Soviet cooperation in 'saving socialism' in Hungary fell apart when Khrushchev decided that it was no longer possible to negotiate with the workers' councils. As he told the Yugoslav ambassador, while Yugoslavia had workers' councils at factory level, there was no equivalent to the Central Workers' Council of Greater Budapest advancing what was essentially a political programme, that of the restoration of Nagy's government. Kádár dropped his offer to talk to the Central Workers' Council and on 22 November factory councils were banned from discussing political issues; on 26 November the Central Workers' Council of Budapest was denounced as counter-revolutionary. In the meantime, on 23 November, Kádár's government ceased to receive Yugoslav aid.[38]

THE 1956 REFORMS IN POLAND

When Tito tried to make sense of the decision he had taken to support the Soviet invasion of Hungary, he expressed the hope that the Yugoslav Party could struggle against any vestiges of Stalinism arm in arm with their Polish comrades.[39] On the surface this appeal to the Poles appeared to make some sense, given that Poland, too, experienced a profound political crisis in October 1956 and stood firm against Soviet intervention; in practice, however, it was fundamentally misplaced. Both Nagy, with his 'great retreat' and Djilas, with his attack on the Party, had advanced radical proposals for renewing communism; the Gomułka reforms in Poland made no serious challenge to the Stalinist system. They did not do so because Gomułka was all too well aware that since 1944 Poland had been irretrievably in the Soviet orbit, and it was this issue that he sought to address, not the future of communism.

Gomułka's reform movement in Poland during 1956 was always simply that: a movement for the reform of the system, not for its radical overhaul. The reform movement began after the Twentieth Party Congress in February 1956. The Polish Party was at first very uncertain how to respond, and at initial meetings of the Central Committee in the first week of March little was decided, partly because of the ill-health of Party leader Bierut. His death on 12 March, and the subsequent presence of Khrushchev at his funeral in Warsaw, enabled the Party to elect a new leader, Edward Ochab. Ochab had been one of the first to condemn Stalin's personality cult, but the limits of his reformism became clear on the very day of his election; he and his

Politburo colleagues refused point-blank to appoint known radicals to the Party Secretariat. Thus he always appeared to be chasing events, rather than setting the pace. As Party reformers launched a propaganda campaign to acquaint party members with the contents of Khrushchev's speech, held discussions about the relevance to Poland of Yugoslav workers' councils, and encouraged the development of a lively and radical press, the leadership acted hesitantly and with indecision. On 6 April Gomułka was released from prison, but quite what was to be done with him no one knew. On the 19th, he had talks with delegates from the Politburo; on 2 May the former security chief Jakub Berman, the man responsible for his arrest, was expelled from the leadership; but Gomułka's ultimate fate remained uncertain.

On issues of less immediate concern to the personalities on the Politburo, the leadership was more decisive. Thousands of political prisoners were released, and when parliament met in April the prime minister could talk of the prospects for the 'new democratisation of our political and economic life'; but the practical measures adopted only addressed a restricted range of measures already defined in Khrushchev's speech and the population at large expected more. Ever since March 1956 Party reports had noted how workers tended to make links between what Khrushchev had said to the Twentieth Party Congress and their own factory lives. Each factory had its little Stalin with his own personality cult: there were endless numbers of section chiefs and directors who acted dictatorially.[40] The size of the gap between Ochab's abstract phrases about reform and the reality of working-class life was made clear when, towards the end of June, workers at the ZISPO works in Poznan were told to increase productivity by 25 per cent for virtually no increase in pay. For all the new talk of democracy, when the workers' delegates travelled to Warsaw to seek redress, no one was interested. Their comrades in Poznan, having heard nothing, assumed the delegates had been arrested and had never made it to the capital. So on 28 June they marched to the local jail, freed the prisoners and seized weapons from the guards. Then things turned into a riot as the crowd physically attacked obvious symbols of the communist regime, such as the headquarters of the Party and the security police. In the fighting which followed as the army restored order, 53 died and over 300 were wounded; as unrest spread to other cities, the death toll rose to one hundred.[41]

Responsibility for the Poznan events was the major issue debated by the Party's Central Committee when it held its Seventh Plenum on

18–28 July 1956. However, Soviet intervention in Poland was the very opposite of that in Hungary: in Budapest on 18 July Mikoyan deposed Rákosi; in Warsaw, at precisely the same time, Soviet Prime Minister Bulganin reinforced the position of the hard-liners. While Ochab spoke about 'the loss of contact with the masses', 'bureaucratic distortions', and the Plenum passed a resolution making clear that henceforth the Party should be 'guide and educator' rather than 'director and manager', Bulganin blamed the Stalinist litany of imperialist agents and a lack of vigilance for the Poznan events. In a scarcely veiled reference to Yugoslavia he added: 'we cannot close our eyes to the attempts at weakening the international bonds of the socialist camp under the label of so-called "national peculiarity", or to the attempts at undermining the power of people's democratic countries under the label of an alleged "broadening of democracy" '.[42] He could hardly state more clearly that what was happening between the Soviet Union, Hungary and Yugoslavia was not the concern of the Poles.

As a result, the reformists always had to make clear they were working within the system. The plenum was a triumph for the reformist leadership since it was agreed that Gomułka would be admitted to the Party and a series of resolutions called for the revival of Parliament and the local councils. As part of this democratisation programme, the plenum called for the reactivation of works councils: however, these had nothing to do with workers' self-management in the Yugoslav sense – they had always existed, on paper, and in their revived form would continue to be firmly under the control of the trade unions, which in turn would be under the control of the Party; their participation in agreeing wages and conditions was supposed to lessen the likelihood of a repeat of the Poznan events.[43]

The reformers' orthodox opposition to the idea of workers' self-management was seen even more clearly during the dramatic events that restored Gomułka to the Party leadership. The power base of the democrats was the Party's Warsaw City Committee, and in particular the works committee at the Zeran car factory: those conservatives opposed to reform, known as the 'Natolin group', remained strong in the regional Party bureaucracy. It was workers who organised the pressure to bring Gomułka back into the leadership, and the Natolin group, with its links to Moscow, which sought to prevent it.[44]

The Eighth Plenum of the Party's Central Committee was due on 19 October. On the 15th the Politburo met, with Gomułka present, and decided that he should be made the first secretary of a new slimmed-down Politburo. The Natolin group contacted the Soviet ambassador, who informed Ochab that he, the other members of the Politburo, plus Gomułka, should all go to Moscow for talks. Ochab persuaded the Politburo to turn down this invitation and go ahead with the plenum without delay, prompting the Natolin group, with Soviet support, to begin a series of troop movements that suggested preparations for a military coup. These plans were frustrated by the mass mobilisation of workers, whom anti-Stalinist elements in the security services were preparing to arm. A series of non-stop mass rallies began, aimed at preventing any military action. The plenum opened on 19 October and Gomułka was immediately elected first secretary; it then adjourned, since Khrushchev and other Soviet leaders had arrived unannounced for talks. Although Khrushchev threatened armed intervention, the Poles insisted on their personnel changes and made clear that the working-class was mobilised.

As the hours passed, the tension gradually eased as Gomułka explained to Khrushchev that he was loyal both to the Soviet Union and the Warsaw Pact; by 1 a.m. on the 20th Khrushchev had been persuaded that the plenum could go ahead. Yet at first Moscow seems to have assumed military intervention would still be the most likely outcome. The Soviet delegation was furious that Gomułka had not allowed its members to address the plenum, so as the Soviet Politburo reconvened in Moscow on 20 October the talk was still of military preparations. The next day, however, as news came through that the plenum had concluded its work with nothing worse than the election of a new Central Committee by secret ballot, the Soviet Politburo resolved unanimously to 'abandon military intervention and display patience'.[45]

While the plenum was underway there was a constant round of meetings and rallies; on 20 October some twenty workers' delegations were received at the Central Committee building. These continued into the 21st, which although a Sunday, saw continued factory rallies staged by the workers. And yet, despite the crucial role played by working-class action in securing Gomułka's return to power, he took no initiatives on their behalf. In his speech to the Eighth Plenum he was very cautious on the question of workers' councils, and the subsequent resolution made that clear. While it recognised that the decision of the Seventh Plenum simply to extend the rights of existing works councils 'no longer corresponded to the strivings of the most active part of the working class', workers' self-government would be restricted purely to factory concerns such as raising productivity and would not contradict the policy of one-man management. Yet in many factories the rallies surrounding the plenum had been the occasion for the formation of factory committees, which in some instances had proceeded to sack the management.[46] The cause of workers' councils was taken up by the secretary of the Warsaw Party Committee, but when he tried to persuade Gomułka that the workers had not simply wanted his recall, but freely elected workers' councils, Gomułka had made his opposition clear: such councils risked anarchy, he said, the demand was simply outrageous. Less than a month after his return to power, Gomułka had removed from factory councils any political rights they had assumed.[47]

Gomułka's main aim was not the renewal of communism, but a relaxation in the stranglehold the Soviet Union had held on Polish life since 1944: in this he was very successful. During the Eighth Plenum Soviet troops had been involved in the machinations of the Natolin group, something Khrushchev had barely sought to conceal during his surprise visit to Warsaw. After Gomułka's triumph, Soviet dominance of the Polish Army was brought to an end and Marshal Rokossowski removed from the post of defence minister; Rokossowski, who had been born in the Polish provinces of the Tsarist Russian Empire, spoke Polish but had been a Soviet citizen for many years. Gomułka also secured the return of thousands of Soviet officers serving in the Polish Army, an arrangement dating back to the autumn of 1944.

After the Soviet Union published its Declaration on Friendship and Cooperation between the Soviet Union and Socialist States, which raised the possibility of the withdrawal of Soviet troops, Gomułka raised with Khrushchev the future role of the Soviet Army, and insisted that no Soviet troop movements, even relating to communications with Soviet occupation forces in Germany, could occur without the consent of the Poles. This was endorsed in talks held in Moscow on 15–17 November, when the Soviet side added that 'the temporary presence of Soviet troops in Poland [to protect communication lines with occupied East Germany] can in no way affect the sovereignty of the Polish state and cannot lead to their interference in the internal affairs of Poland'.[48]

THE IMPACT OF 1956 ON THE REST OF EASTERN EUROPE

East Germany

For Eastern Europe as a whole, the impact of 1956 was to cast it in the mould it would have for the next thirty years and more. In particular, after 1956, there was to be no doubt that the GDR, East Germany, would be a permanent member of the Soviet Bloc. Despite the Soviet leadership's firm rejection of Beria's 1953 proposal to liquidate socialism in East Germany, such a move was implicit in their 1954 proposal for a united but neutral Germany, an idea which met with considerable sympathy among West German social democrats and church leaders, and which was only rejected by the West during the course of 1955: a similar proposal was successfully negotiated in the summer of 1955 concerning the withdrawal of occupation forces from Austria. It was only in May 1955 that Khrushchev decided to back the GDR fully: when Khrushchev met Tito in June 1955, one of the confidences he shared with the Yugoslav leader was the major doubts he had about the GDR leader Walter Ulbricht; the chances of such a man building socialism were slim, he said, but the decision had been taken to back him. In September 1955 the Soviet Union restored full sovereignty to the GDR and recognised West Germany.[49]

But even then, the Soviet Union's commitment to the GDR could be considered as part of its negotiating posture to secure the convening of a conference to 'safeguard peace and collective security in Europe'. When this had first been proposed, in December 1954, the West had refused to attend, and part of the Soviet thinking behind the creation of the Warsaw Pact in May 1955 was to put pressure on the West to take this proposal seriously; the final clause of the Warsaw Pact stated that 'in the event of the organisation of a system of collective security in Europe, and the conclusion of a general European treaty of collective security to that end, the present treaty shall cease to be effective on the date on which a general European treaty comes into force'.

GDR membership of the Warsaw Pact and the Pact itself was part of the Soviet Union's negotiating strategy for the Four Power Conference in July 1955. By January 1956, when the GDR joined the military wing of the Warsaw Pact, it was clear this strategy had failed, and after the Soviet invasion of Hungary, East–West tension reached such intensity that all talk of a European conference on collective security was shelved indefinitely. Soviet commitment to the GDR thereafter was absolute, as the successive Berlin crises and the construction of the Berlin Wall in 1961 were to show.[50]

As to the stormy events of 1956 in Hungary and neighbouring Poland, the Ulbricht leadership determined to sit tight. Criticisms of Stalin were slight, and much made of the rather inept decision of the West German authorities in September 1956 to ban its German Communist Party.

This was used to justify the arrest of anyone sympathetic to the notion of reform communism: thus Wolfgang Harich a 36-year-old academic at the Humboldt University, who had been arguing for Yugoslav style industrial democracy and an end to collective farms, as well as multi-candidate if not multiparty elections, was arrested on 29 November 1956 and in March 1957 sentenced to 10 years; arrests of other 'revisionists' followed. Thus, although the country was not immune from unrest – there were disturbances in Magdeburg in September and October and sporadic strikes elsewhere in October – protesters were deprived of any political leadership.[51]

Romania, Bulgaria and Czechoslovakia

As to Romania, the impact of 1956 was to start it on the road towards an independent, or semi-independent foreign policy, something Western politicians would find beguiling in the 1970s. Romania, like Poland, had been closely linked to the Soviet Union since the Red Army arrived in August 1944. Like Poland it sought to use the 1956 crisis to reassert its national independence rather than renew the communist system. At first, it is true, it looked as if the Romanian leader Gheorghiu-Dej might throw in his lot with Tito and the Hungarians. Whether there was any substance to the suggestion that Tito and Gheorghiu-Dej had been in secret contact throughout the Cominform years, Tito was quick to sing Gheorghiu-Dej's praises in 1956, stressing to foreign journalists that Romania was not a Soviet satellite. During the height of the Polish crisis, and the first days of the Hungarian Revolution, Gheorghiu-Dej was in Belgrade and the final communiqué on his visit noted the 'inadvisability of foreign intervention in the affairs of other countries', echoing the Yugoslav view which condemned the first use of Soviet troops, but endorsed the second. In another act of independence, Romania gave temporary refuge to Imre Nagy after he had been removed from his initial sanctuary in the Yugoslav embassy in Budapest.[52]

However, realpolitik soon got the upper hand. The Romanians used the Soviet military agreement with the Poles as a basis for requesting the removal of Soviet troops from Romania. Originally stationed there after the 1947 Peace Treaty simply to defend communication lines with Soviet occupation forces in Austria, they had stayed on after Austrian independence under the terms of the Warsaw Pact. The logic was inescapable, if Soviet troops stayed on in Poland merely to defend Soviet communication lines with occupied Germany, there was no longer any justification for them remaining in Romania. Regularly, after first raising it in December 1956, Romania repeated its request that Soviet troops withdraw. Agreement came in May 1958, but cynical observers could not help noticing the price that was paid for this new independence; in June Imre Nagy was put on trial for his life in Budapest.[53]

Whatever he might have said to Tito, Gheorghiu-Dej was never serious about the reform of communism. Romania faced serious disturbances in 1956, the most serious after Hungary and Poland, yet some of the Soviet troops *en route* for Hungary would have to travel via Romania. Gheorghiu-Dej therefore responded with essentially populist concessions. Railway workers organised sympathy strikes and disturbances towards the end of October, so the government literally bought them off with increased pay and improved holidays, something only agreed after senior government figures had addressed the protestors in person. A week later, in another populist gesture, students were promised better grants and an end to the compulsory study of Russian. When it came to bringing reformers into the government, Gheorghiu-Dej made only temporary concessions; those that liberals brought in were all removed in 1957.[54]

The events of 1956 had some limited impact in Bulgaria. Apart from the retirement of Prime Minister Chervenkov, the man most responsible for the Kostov trial and who had already surrendered his post as Party leader in 1954, some new ministers with a partisan career during the war were appointed; yet it was former partisans who were again removed from the leadership in 1957. The Party believed its firm control over the intelligentsia had prevented the Hungarian infection spreading to Bulgaria. The events of 1956 had virtually no impact in Czechoslovakia where the existing Party leadership remained firmly in control.[55]

1956 AND INTERNATIONAL COMMUNISM

Writing in November 1956, Milovan Djilas commented that 'the wound which the Hungarian Revolution inflicted on communism can never be completely healed'.[56] While it would take another 30 years for the system to collapse, after 1956 communism did indeed cease to operate as an international political system. Both the Communist International and the Communist Information Bureau had come and gone, and Khrushchev's attempt to keep some sort of international body alive failed dismally. In January 1957 he proposed a conference of all ruling Communist Parties, to be held in Moscow in November 1957. However, whether the Yugoslavs could be persuaded to attend was debatable, as indeed was the participation of Poland given Gomułka's opposition to the Cominform in 1947. To smooth these fears Tito and Gomułka were invited to pay private visits to Moscow in May 1957, and then in August 1957 Tito and Khrushchev held formal inter-party talks in Bucharest. However, the Yugoslavs refused to sign the November 1957 Declaration and in April 1958 the Yugoslav League of Communists abandoned all attempts at reconciliation with Moscow, adopting a programme setting out its own idiosyncratic version of the one party communist state.[57]

The failure of the November conference and the permanent defection of the Yugoslavs meant the only organisation through which the communist parties of Eastern Europe could be coordinated was the Political Committee of the Warsaw Pact. This had not met since January 1956 and, rather like the Pact itself, its original purpose had not been very clear.[58] After May 1958 the Political Committee of the Warsaw Pact began to meet regularly: it was through this military rather than a political body that Soviet control over Eastern Europe was to be exercised. Djilas' predictions about the death of communism had proved true enough. What held East European communists together was not a commitment to a shared ideology, or joint membership of an international organisation, but common membership of a military alliance to preserve Soviet dominance and the *status quo.*

After 1956, political reform originating from within Eastern Europe was impossible. The events in Hungary had been unique because of the tripartite relationship which had grown up between reformers in Hungary, the Soviet Union and Yugoslavia; with Khrushchev ready to make major concessions if Tito could be brought back into the fold and Tito apparently determined to reform the world communist movement by exporting the concept of workers' self-management, a radical new vista seemed to open up. The Yugoslavs' desertion of Nagy meant the possibilities offered by such a unique conjuncture were never exploited. No similar external pressure for reform existed after 1956, and the Warsaw Pact provided Soviet leaders with a powerful instrument with which to crush any reforms that threatened their vision of socialism. Successful political reform in Eastern Europe would have to await political reform within the Soviet Union. In the meantime, those prepared to continue supporting the notion of undemocratic socialism took comfort from Khrushchev's prediction in 1961 that the socialist states, whose economies were based on rational economic planning, would soon be outstripping the economies of the West.

5

Actually Existing Socialism in Operation

The preceding chapters have documented how communist regimes came to power in Eastern Europe with varying degrees of domestic and Soviet support: motivations had been mixed. For the Soviet Union, despite a notional commitment to the long-term goal of world revolution, the primary concern had been geopolitical. For the local communists who engineered the revolutions there had been an ideological commitment to the socialist ideal nurtured during years of struggle against fascism. By 1958 this ideological commitment was all but moribund. Henceforth the nations of Eastern Europe were bound together not by a shared commitment to communism but by a military alliance and an international economic order, both dominated by the Soviet Union. Communism was no longer a liberation ideology, yet it continued profoundly to structure political, social and economic life, what gradually became known as 'actually existing socialism'.

During the next 30 years 'actually existing socialism' would prove its non-viability. Economic, social, and finally political forces engendered within it ultimately destroyed both the ideology and its military and economic structures. And the pattern of its decline and the nature of what replaced it are linked inextricably to the nature of 'actually existing socialism'. 'Actually existing socialism' was not just another totalitarian regime. It was Marxist–Leninist. Its ideological underpinning was neither nationalist nor racist; indeed, in many ways, it was socially progressive. This too is important for understanding its demise. 'Actually existing socialism' collapsed because of a loss of legitimation resulting from the disjuncture that had developed between the radical promise still present in its ideology and an economic inability to meet it. As promises of equality, solidarity and communal well-being proved hollow, more traditional ideologies such as nationalism and religion took their place.

THE LABOUR THEORY OF VALUE AND THE LENINIST PARTY

When interviewing one of Hungary's new entrepreneurs in 1991, one of the authors was informed that the problems with Eastern European economies could be reduced to two things: Marx's labour theory of value and Lenin's concept of the Party and its leading role. The entrepreneur was not a political theorist nor a social scientist, but his remarks were apposite. Communist parties did try to implement the Marxist classics, and these classics were ultimately flawed. In Eastern Europe, the socialist planners were not starting from scratch, as had been the case in the Soviet Union in the 1920s and 1930s. When they arrived, Soviet advisors brought with them a 'working' model; but it was nevertheless a model derived from Marxism, and Marx's classic *Das Kapital*.[1]

The Labour Theory of Value

The 'labour theory of value' is central to Marx's works. Without it, the concept of 'surplus value' and the manner in which, under capitalism, the working class is exploited, make no sense; and, without this, the critical force of Marxism is lost. Marx asserts that it is not the market that creates value, but labour. The notion derives from his philosophical materialism and his anthropological conception of mankind as a social being. Value must come from the material world and from some kind of social interaction. Labour, the transformation of ideas into concrete products, is the defining characteristic of mankind: it is what separates humans from the animal kingdom. Labour must be the source of value, and the true value of a commodity is not the price that is allocated by the market, but the amount of labour embodied in its creation; to be more precise, since society and technology are constantly changing, it is the amount of 'socially necessary labour time' at any point in history necessary for its creation.

Armed with this philosophically inspired concept, Marx analysed the production relations of capitalist society and discovered its injustices. Because, under capitalism, the working class does not own the factories in which it works, does not own the 'means of production', it is obliged to sell itself to the owners of the factories, the capitalists, in order to make a living. But workers do not sell their labour to the capitalists, rather they sell their ability to labour, their 'labour power'. In a capitalist market economy, goods are not produced for any intrinsic notion of their worth or any socially defined need, but simply to provide additional value – profits – for those who happened to own the means of production. 'Labour power' is a commodity like any other. If it were sold at its true value it would be sold at a rate equal to the socially necessary labour time required to produce it, that is to say to reproduce itself as a social being. But this is not what happens under capitalism. The 'means of production' are owned by the capitalists alone: the workers own nothing but their 'labour power'. Workers are obliged, for fear of starvation, to sell their 'labour power' to the capitalists; and capitalists can force the workers to work for longer than necessary to create sufficient value for self-reproduction. That is to say, the capitalists can force workers to produce 'surplus value', which the capitalists then keep for themselves.

Marx, on numerous occasions, stressed that the critical thrust of his theory was directed at understanding capitalism rather than providing a blueprint for a future socialist society. Nevertheless, since the new socialist society was to transcend capitalist exploitation, it follows from Marx's premises that, under socialism, labour, and of necessity all other commodities, including labour power, should be exchanged at their true value, that is to say in terms of units measuring the amount of socially necessary labour time embodied in their creation. It also follows implicitly from the concept of man's social being that in a society where the 'means of production' are socially owned and a calculus based on 'socially necessary labour time' has been evolved, this will take over from the market as the 'invisible hand' that guides the economy. Conflicting hierarchies of needs will disappear when all needs are quantified in terms of the true calculus: units of 'socially necessary labour time'.

Thus when Eastern European socialists confronted issues of economic organisation, they were informed by two overriding, theoretically inspired principles: first, the market did not define value and some other measure was required for estimating social needs; second, the true calculus for quantifying and comparing value in a socialist economy was units of socially necessary labour time.

Unfortunately, as serious attempts to implement such an economy in the Soviet Union revealed, measuring value in terms of socially necessary labour time proved impossible to put into practice. No workable solution was found to two fundamental problems: how to compare manual and mental labour, and how to account for the labour embodied in capital equipment and the research and development processes necessary to produce that equipment. The theoretical solution was simple enough: the value of commodities produced by mental labour includes the labour required to attain the required level of training; that of commodities produced by complex machinery the value of the labour that went into training the research scientists and the time they spent researching for the particular product. But converting this theoretical solution into a practical calculus for quantifying and comparing value proved impossible.

Marxist economists faced with the task of actually implementing a socialist economy focused on the easier of the Marxist premises: excluding the market from the estimation and comparison of values. If the market was unacceptable and the labour theory of value unoperational as a universally acceptable measure of value, planning for social need could be achieved by democratic planning, the creation of an economic planning board constantly appraised of the needs of society. Here again, operational problems intervened. How could society – everyone in society equally – express preferences on every possible choice society might have to make during a fixed period of, say, a five-year plan? The answer was the Party.

The Leninist Party

When faced with creating a socialist economic system in practice, if the market could not act as an arbiter of value, and a consistent hierarchy of values and needs did not simply emerge from society, what better replacement than the Party? The Party had brought about the revolution and, in theory, embodied the real historical interests of the working class; what is more, because the interests of the working class were, in the final analysis, also the interests of humanity, it embodied everyone's real interests. This economic requirement for the Party to continue to play a guiding, leading role in East European societies was to have enormous importance. It identified the economic managers, the 'bureaucrats', with the interests of the centrally planned economy, making them and the Party antipathetic to any idea of structural economic reform.

Irrespective of Marx's or Marxists' personal preference for democracy and democratic socialism, the problems associated with operating the labour theory of value, of transforming it from a parable describing the genesis of economic surplus and growth into a viable economic calculus, necessarily resulted in the development of 'actually existing socialism' into an economic system structured around central planning in non-market units and informed by an estimation of social need dictated by the Party as surrogate for society as a whole. Marxism in practice required central planning and one party rule, for the good of humanity.

The Leninist input was more conjunctural, but it, too, played a crucial role in the everyday operation of 'actually existing socialism'. The Marxist model was, as we have seen, necessarily centralist. Information flows were vertical rather than horizontal, both within the Party and within the planning apparatus. But if the Marxist model defined the direction of information flows, it was the Leninist concept of the Party that determined the quantity of information transmitted. For a Marxist party operating in conditions of illegality, information could be a liability rather than an asset. Not only did the Party need clear, hierarchical chains of command, it could only divulge information on a 'need to know' basis. And lessons learned in illegality were not forgotten. Once the regimes came to power, the Party might determine need, and party members might be privy to more information than the general populace; but there was no reason for local party units to be privy to the secrets of the centre. Local party activists could exhort fulfilment of the five-year plan with all the more conviction, because only a few people at the centre had access to figures which showed that it was unrealisable and suggested that there might be flaws in the planning model itself. Caught up in the rush of their work and committed to the overall goals, grass roots activists had no reason to question the truth of their propaganda. Leninism strengthened the omniscience of the Party by ensuring the ignorance of those not privileged in its structure.

MARXISM–LENINISM AND THE ECONOMY

By the time the communists had come to power in Eastern Europe, these issues had already been addressed in the Soviet Union, and a workable solution of sorts had emerged: the Stalinist model of central planning. By adopting this model Eastern European economists hoped to ensure for themselves an economic system driven by need rather than the vagaries and injustices of the market. Realistically the regimes had little alternative but to implement the Stalinist model; but it was a model that was not entirely unattractive in the aftermath of the 1930s and the upheavals of the Second World War. Unlike Western Europe, the Soviet economy had experienced rapid growth (albeit at horrendous social cost) in the 1930s, and even Western European governments had introduced planning during the war. Faced with the daunting task of creating a socialist economy from scratch, Eastern European communists were relieved to be in a position to acquire the Soviet model off the peg, even if some of its institutions and priorities did not seem entirely appropriate.

Implementing Central Planning

Throughout Eastern Europe, as the Cominform reorganised the postwar popular fronts, planning offices, which had existed to handle postwar reconstruction, were transformed to conform to the Soviet Gosplan model, and nationalisations were extended beyond those occasioned by the confiscation of enemy property or postwar nationalisation of economic 'commanding heights' such as mines and banks. Enterprises were brought under the direct control of industrial ministries and their subordinate directorates or 'chief administrations' issued with compulsory targets in simple global output terms. Targets were determined on the basis of several iterations of 'material balances' coordinating known demand and known resources in order to find an optimum. Competing commercial banks were abolished and replaced by Soviet-style 'single channel' banking, where each bank had a single predefined function such as savings, investment, foreign trade and so on. Stock exchanges were closed, and auditing practices amended to reflect the requirements demands of the single pyramidic hierarchy of central planning rather than external shareholders. Foreign trade was placed in the hands of enterprises subordinate to the Ministry of Foreign Trade and external trade was wholly isolated from internal trade by the 'price equalisation system' (*Preisausgleich*), by means of which domestic enterprises encountered only the domestic price of their exports or imports, leaving specialist foreign trade enterprises to deal with foreign currency and world prices.

The creation of the central planning system in 1948–9 is summarised in Table 5.1, and Table 5.2 summarises the progression from Land Reform in the immediate postwar years to Cominform-initiated collectivisation in 1948.

It was in 1948–9, too, that the beginnings of the new international context for socialist trade were established. Ideas of autonomous

Table 5.1 *The creation of the Soviet-type planning system in Eastern Europe*

Country	*'Nationalisations'*		*Gosplan-type planning office*		*Soviet-style foreign trade cos.*
	Postwar[a]	*Mass*			
Albania	1944–5	1946–7	1947	Planning Commission	1956
Bulgaria	1944	1947 (Dec.)	1947	State Planning Commission	1948–9
Czechoslovakia	1945	1948	1949	State Planning Office	1948–53
GDR	1945–8	1972[b]	1950	State Planning Commission	1954
Hungary	1946–7	1948–9	1949	National Planning Office	1949
Poland	1945	1946–8[c]	1949	State Comm. for Economic Planning	1947–52
Romania	1946	1948 (Nov.)	1948	State Planning Commission	1948
Yugoslavia	1944–5	1946–8	1946	Federal Planning Commission	1946

[a] Postwar nationalisation includes both the confiscation of the property of wartime collaborators and the taking into public ownership of the 'commanding heights' of the postwar economies.

[b] See Chapter 7 for further discussion of the GDR private sector. Most large-scale industry was nationalised postwar since it could be claimed to have been part of the Nazi war machine.

[c] New company formations were encouraged in 1946, although the private sector came under attack in 1947. Banks were nationalised in 1948–9.

Sources W. Brus, 'Postwar Reconstruction and Socio-economic Transformation', in M. C. Kaser and E. A. Radice (eds), *The Economic History of Eastern Europe, 1919–1975*, vol. 11 (Oxford, 1986), pp. 598–621; H. Matejka, 'The Foreign Trade System', in M. C. Kaser (ed.), *The Economic History of Eastern Europe, 1919–1975*, vol. III (Oxford, 1986), pp. 250–2; A. Åslund, *Private Enterprise in Eastern Europe* (London, 1985), pp. 118–204: M. McCauley, *Marxism–Leninism in the GDR* (London, 1978), p. 94.

Table 5.2 *Land reform and collectivisation in postwar Eastern Europe*

Country	*Land reform*	*Begins*	*Collectivisation halted/slowed*	*Completed*
Albania	August 1945	1948	1953–7	1966[a]
Bulgaria	March 1946[b]	1945[c] 1948	1953–5	1958
Czechoslovakia	June 1945; 1947–8[d]	1948	1953–5	1960
GDR	Autumn 1945	1952	–[e]	1960
Hungary	March 1945	1948	1953–4; 1956–8	1961
Poland	September 1944	1948	1956	n.a.
Romania	March 1945; 1948–9[f]	1948	–[g]	1962
Yugoslavia	August 1945	1945[h] 1948	1953	n.a.

[a] By 1960, 85 per cent of land was in the socialist sector.
[b] Pre-war land ownership in Bulgaria had long been the most equitable in Eastern Europe and this measure had little effect.
[c] In 1945 these were of the 'lower type' where land continued to be owned by individuals and only certain tasks (sowing but not necessarily harvesting) were performed collectively.
[d] 1945 applied to enemy-owned land only. 1947 and 1948 were domestic reforms with an ever-lower upper limit on holdings. State and pioneer collectives also profited from the 1948 reform.
[e] Growth in farm numbers was not steady. By 1958 only 36 per cent of land was in the socialist sector. Collectivisation came in a rush in February 1960.
[f] Extended to royal lands and intensive capitalist farms. Land was used for State Farms or to promote collective agriculture.
[g] Collectivisation in Romania was slow and, until 1955, almost entirely in the form of looser cooperatives rather than collectives proper.
[h] Not very vigorously pursued in the early years.

Sources Brus, 'Postwar…', pp. 588–93; M. McCauley (ed.), *Communist Power in Europe, 1944–9*, pp. 18, 74; W. Brus, '1950 to 1953: The Peak of Stalinism', in M. C. Kaser (ed.), *The Economic History of Eastern Europe 1919–1975*, vol. III (Oxford, 1986), pp. 9, 51, 79–80.

regional associations such as Polish–Czechoslovakian cooperation or the ill-fated Balkan Federation (see Chapter 3) were criticised by the Soviet Union in 1948 when the Yugoslavs were expelled from the Cominform;[2] and in 1949 Comecon was created.[3] Partly at Soviet instigation and partly because the Marxist economic model presupposes a single national economy and leaves foreign trade untheorised, the regimes all pursued the same economic goal of autarchy. Although this aim was arguably justifiable for a continent-wide economy as backward as was Russia in 1917, or 1929, it was less clearly so for the more developed and trade-dependent countries of Central and Eastern Europe. At the end of the Second World War, the level of economic development of the eight Eastern European nations was higher than the level in the Soviet Union prior to industrialisation (and below that of Western Europe), but levels varied. Czechoslovakia and the future GDR were the only industrial countries; Poland and Hungary could be classified as 'agricultural with significant processing facilities', and Romania, Bulgaria, Yugoslavia and Albania as 'agricultural raw material producing countries'.[4] By the time of Stalin's death, the share of the socialised sector in industry and commerce approached 90 per cent, as illustrated in Table 5.3.

One of the ironies of Eastern European history since 1945 is that these structures, which were so hastily installed and which in most countries only operated in their unmodified form for five years, nevertheless exercised a determining effect on economic and social life for the next forty years. Identical models produced identical problems, and these should be considered briefly.

Table 5.3 *Socialised share of industrial output and retail turnover, 1952*

Country	*Industry*	*Trade*
Albania[a]	98	88
Bulgaria	100	98
Czechoslovakia	98	97
GDR	77	54
Hungary	97	82
Poland	99	93
Romania	97	76

[a] 1950.

Source Brus, '1950 to 1953: The Peak of Stalinism', in M. C. Kaser (ed.), *The Economic History of Eastern Europe, 1919–1975*, vol. III (Oxford 1986), p. 8.

Problems of Central Planning

Centrally planned economies are distorted, unbalanced, out of equilibrium. There is nothing surprising in this. Although balanced growth might conceivably be the ambition of a centrally planned economy, historically, and in any realistic context for their emergence, the goal has been the opposite, to overcome the 'natural' course of events, to defy the 'law of value': to overcome economic backwardness by means of rapid industrialisation. Prioritising rapid industrial development necessarily distorts the economy, leaving shortages in non-prioritised spheres such as the services (education, healthcare), the infrastructure (the road system, the telephone system, mains drainage, piped water), and agriculture.

But the economic problems associated with centrally planned economies did not stem simply from the priorities, however misguided, that have informed their implementation throughout the socialist world. Centrally planned economies operating in physical (natural, volume) indicators also suffer from intrinsic problems. They necessarily require an omniscient centre that must know, in the fullest detail, what quantities of any commodity are required throughout the area of the planned economy. Not only this, and in itself this is difficult enough, the centre must also be informed instantly if requirements change, and recalculate the effects of that change on all elements in the plan immediately. Such omniscience is impossible. Some degree of aggregation is unavoidable; but therein lie the problems. Aggregation leads to imprecision. It is not all the same to the customer whether shoes are boots, brogues or trainers; but if the plan specifies only 'shoes', planners cannot be choosy about what shoes are produced. Further, the interests of the enterprise will not necessarily coincide with those of the planners.

Marx's concept of social man in the post-capitalist era assumed that all spontaneously recognise the greater social interest and work towards it. But it is not necessary to adhere to pessimistic views of mankind's inherent individualism or self-serving nature to agree that social structures that share the same polity (usually the nation state) are made up of smaller groupings that are all equally social. Mankind may be a social animal, may be prone to altruistic rather than self-serving activity, yet individual social groups of producers need not automatically identify with the centre. In the situation of perfect knowledge that central planning supposes, agreement would be easier; but even with perfect knowledge, socially concerned individuals can disagree over bution of resources. It follows, therefore, that even if ɛre democratically organised, reflecting the true interests lace collective, they might have interests different from those of the planning centre. Thus, if the planning mechanism only specifies ten pairs of shoes, rather than three boots, three trainers and four brogues, enterprises might be acting in their best interest when they produce the ten shoes that it is easiest (not necessarily cheapest) to manufacture. The planning centre's response is to disaggregate and specify more precisely; but, by thus increasing the targets, planning becomes more cumbersome and time-consuming. Plan targets are aggregated again, and the search for a new type of target that combines simplicity with universality begins.

The example is trivial, but multiplied by thousands of commodities these were the issues the newly formed planning offices of Eastern Europe were struggling with for much of the forty years of socialism, and the search for the most appropriate degree of aggregation and the most powerful synthetic success indicator dominated the second of the four stages of economic reform discussed in Chapter 6.

One of the outcomes of traditional central planning is an absolute shortage of the goods that, for whatever reason, it is not in the interests of enterprises to produce. But there is also relative shortage. Central planning targets specify gross output, the production of so many pairs of shoes. They do not specify that they should be produced at the lowest cost. Indeed, because of planners' Marxist rejection of the market and their failure to develop an alternative socially necessary labour time calculus, pricing quickly became arbitrary in any case. The question of ascertaining the most cost-effective means of producing a commodity was downgraded because the key question was to produce the quantities required by the plan, and there was no realistic basis on which to carry out such a calculation in any case.

To summarise, the centrally planned economies of Eastern Europe were characterised by shortage from four logically separable aspects of Soviet-style central planning: shortage due to the Soviet-inspired emphasis on investment rather than consumption that was required by rapid economic growth; shortage due to the equally Soviet-inspired pro-heavy industry model of industrialisation which derived from the Marxist emphasis on industries producing capital goods; shortage due to the fact that in any centrally planned economy it was in the interests of enterprises to produce only a limited selection of easily manufactured goods; and, finally, the relative shortage of wasted potential because goods were being produced with minimal attention to the most cost-effective means of manufacture. The point is almost trivial, nevertheless central: Eastern European economies were characterised by high degrees of nationalisation and endemic shortage. Overdetermined shortage made queuing a way of life. It also bred corruption and, when the political climate was more relaxed, the growth of a 'second economy' in order to plug the gaps.

Table 5.4 reflects pro-investment shortage, the high rates of national income devoted to accumulation and correspondingly low shares devoted to personal consumption revealed as more balanced policies were adopted following Stalin's death.

Table 5.5 indicates the pro-industry bias of investment outlays and the relaxation of such priorities during the New Course in the Comecon countries and the beginnings of self-management in Yugoslavia.

The narrow range of choice of goods under 'actually existing socialism' can be illustrated by a single example. Before the Second World War Hungary produced 80 different types of shoe. By the first half of 1950, this figure had dropped to sixteen.[5] The fourth dimension of shortage, relative shortage due to wasted potential, cannot be shown directly. Nevertheless, energy consumption can be used as a proxy.

Table 5.4 *Share of net material product devoted to accumulation (net investment in fixed capital plus increases in inventories) and personal consumption (%)*

Country	*Accumulation*		*Personal consumption*	
	1953	*1955*	*1953*	*1955*
Bulgaria	n.a.	n.a.	66	77
Czechoslovakia	25	20	57	61
GDR	n.a.	n.a.	82	81
Hungary	25	15	46	58[a]
Poland	28	22	54	60
Romania	32	24	n.a.	n.a.
Yugoslavia	n.a.	n.a.	53	54

[a] 1954.

Source Brus, '1953 to 1956: "The Thaw" and "The New Course"', in M. C. Kaser (ed.), *The Economic History of Eastern Europe, 1919–1975*, vol. III (Oxford, 1986), pp. 45–6.

5.5 *Share of investment by branch, 1953–5 (Comecon countries gross investment, Yugoslavia net investment in fixed assets)*

y	*Industry*[a]		*Agriculture*	
	1953	*1955*	*1953*	*1955*
Albania[b]	50	41	10	18
Bulgaria	40	39	14	20
Czechoslovakia	42	39	14	20
GDR	50	52	17	15
Hungary	48	41	6	11
Poland	52	43	10	15
Romania	57	57	7	14
Yugoslavia	45	34	5	9

[a] In Yugoslavia, 'manufacturing and mining'.
[b] 1950.

Source Brus, '1953 to 1956: "The Thaw" and "The New Course"', in M. C. Kaser (ed.), *The Economic History of Eastern Europe, 1919–1975*, vol. III (Oxford, 1986), pp. 47, 49.

Table 5.6 compares per capita gross domestic product (GDP) and per capita energy consumption relative to United States levels in 1973. It reveals that while the GDP of the Warsaw Pact countries was between 33 per cent and 50 per cent of that in the United States, per capita energy consumption was almost twice as high, at between 64 per cent and 98 per cent of the United States levels. In a less wasteful economy, that energy could have been used to produce something else.

Despite the reforms to this model (which are the subject of the following chapter), the hierarchical principle informed the behaviour of economic agents throughout the period. Enterprise managers looked not to the market, to customers, to suppliers, to external auditors or shareholders, but to their superiors. They received orders from them, were provided with customers and suppliers by them, and were responsible to them. In most cases, their tasks were defined not as achieving a specific profit, or rate of growth, but simply a physical quantity of goods. The underlying principle was of hierarchical subordination, minimal autonomy, and minimal personal responsibility.

Table 5.6 *Index of GDP and energy intensity of GDP, 1973 (United States = 100)*

Country	*GDP*	*Energy intensity of GDP*
Bulgaria	38.8	97.2
Czechoslovakia	55.8	90.0
GDR	58.4	93.2
Hungary	42.5	64.9
Poland	42.3	81.1
Romania	33.1	90.0

Source V. Sobell, *The Red Market* (Aldershot, 1984) p. 41.

That is to say, it was the very antithesis of the market system – and it was supposed to be.

MARXISM–LENINISM AND POLITICS

It was noted above that the logic of implementing Marx's post-capitalist society required that the Party be the arbiter of value. This economic imperative necessitated the development of a political system in which, whatever guarantees for pluralism were written into the constitution, the Party had to remain *de facto* the leading political force.

Constitutions

The constitutional arrangements of 'actually existing socialism' in Eastern Europe were not identical, but they were remarkably similar, as illustrated in Table 5.7. First, by 1950, all countries had passed a constitution modelled more or less on the Soviet one, and in most there was some kind of reference to the leading role of the Party and unbreakable friendship with the USSR. Where such statements did not figure, they were added later in constitutional amendments, with the exception of Romania, where all mention of the Soviet Union disappeared. Second, the legislature was unicameral except in countries with a federal structure such as Yugoslavia, and Czechoslovakia after 1969. Third, parliament sat only rarely, for a few days only, from two to seven times a year. This required the creation of some sort of body to deal with matters that might arise between sessions. This was the

Table 5.7 *Constitutional arrangements in Eastern Europe*[6]

Country	*Communist constitutions*	*National Front*	*Legislature*	*Sessions per year*	*Inter-session body*	*Head of State*	*Executive*	*Choice of candidate*
Albania	Mar. 1946 Dec. 1976	Democratic Front	People's Assembly	2	Presidium	President of Presidium	Council of Ministers, appointed by Legislature	–
Bulgaria	Dec. 1947 May 1971	Fatherland Front	National Assembly	3	Presidium From 1971 State Council	President of Presidium. From 1971 Chairman of State Council	Council of Ministers, elected by Legislature	–
Czechoslovakia	May 1948 Jul. 1960	National Front	Federal Assembly	2	Presidium	President elected by Assembly	Federal Government, appointed by president	–
GDR	Oct. 1949 Apr. 1968	National Front	People's Chamber	5–7	Presidium. From 1960 State Council	President. From 1960 Chairman of State Council	Council of Ministers, appointed by Legislature	1965
Hungary	Aug. 1949 Apr. 1972	People's Patriotic Front	National Assembly	3–4	Presidential Council	Chairman of Presidential Council	Council of Ministers, appointed by Legislature	1967

Poland	Jul. 1952 Feb. 1976	National Unity Front PRON after martial law	National Assembly	2	Council of State	Chairman of Council of State	Council of Ministers, appointed by Legislature	1957[a]
Romania	Apr. 1948 Sep. 1952 Aug. 1965	Democratic Front. From 1968 Socialist Unity Front	Grand National Assembly	2	Presidium From 1961 State Council	President of Presidium. From 1961 Chairman of State Council. From 1974 President elected by Legislature	Council of Ministers, elected by Unity Front Legislature	1975
Yugoslavia	1946 Apr. 1963 Feb. 1974	People's Front. From 1953 Socialist Alliance	Federal People's Assembly	2	Presidium	President of Presidium. From 1953–80 President of Republic–Tito. From 1971 collectiverotating Presidency from republican assemblies	Federal Executive Council	

[a] From 1957 to 1984 the 'choice' consisted of the right to delete candidates. A choice between candidates was introduced in local elections in June 1984 and national elections in October 1985.

area of greatest divergence in the region. The norm in the early years was for this task to be undertaken by a Presidium or Presidential Council appointed by parliament. In later years in Bulgaria, the GDR, Poland and Romania, the task was taken over by a Council of State, also appointed by parliament, which was usually granted greater powers than the Presidium, such as the ability to issue decrees with the force of law. The significance of this can be overestimated, however. Presidential Councils, such as that in Hungary, could issue decrees with the force of law which were automatically ratified by subsequent parliamentary sessions.

Fourth, the president and head of state was everywhere appointed by parliament. Normally the presidency was collective, embodied in the Presidium (Presidential Council) or, where applicable, the Council of State, and represented in person by the president of that body. The exceptions were Czechoslovakia, where a president proper was appointed directly by parliament, Romania after 1974, where a special post of President of the Republic was created for Nicolae Ceauşescu, Yugoslavia from 1953 until Tito's death, where special arrangements ensured that Tito was President of the Republic, and the GDR prior to 1960.

Fifth, except in the federal republics of Yugoslavia and Czechoslovakia after 1969, the government took the form of the Council of Ministers, appointed by parliament, with the chairman or president of the Council of Ministers acting as Prime Minister. In Yugoslavia, the Federal People's Assembly appointed a Federal Executive Council. Czechoslovakia was unique in that the federal government was appointed by the President.

Sixth, both the Supreme Courts (the highest courts of appeal) and the Prosecutors General (the Attorney General) were appointed by parliament or, where applicable, the State Council. Again Czechoslovakia was an exception and the Prosecutor was appointed by the President. Generally speaking, the interpretation of the constitution was left to parliament or the State Council. However, in 1963 Yugoslavia created a Constitutional Court, whose primary function in practice was to ensure that republican laws were in line with the federal constitution, and in 1983 Hungary created a Constitutional Law Council, elected by parliament, whose primary purpose was to monitor conformity with the constitution.

In theory, then, throughout Eastern Europe parliaments were sovereign, although they were subject to few checks and balances. But they were elected undemocratically, and real power resided in the Party.

Front Organisations and Parties

If the new regimes of Eastern Europe took over the Soviet model of economic planning unamended, they could not simply shake off the heritage of the wartime resistance fronts from which they developed. The Party was the leading force, and its leadership the leadership of the nation, but the regimes had come to power in a different political context from the Soviet Union. The moment when popular front coalitions had become Popular Fronts 'from below', that is under communist control, had occurred at different times in the different countries, with non-communist parties continuing to operate in most of them. These fronts, which we shall rechristen National Fronts to distinguish them from their predecessors in the revolutionary period, were present in all Eastern European regimes (see Table 5.7) and served two important purposes. They were umbrella groups for the party political and electoral systems; and they were umbrella groups for all social organisations acceptable to the regime, as will be discussed more fully below. The National Fronts never acted as anything other than executors of party policy; nevertheless they were a central component of the way in which *de facto* party rule in Eastern Europe was articulated.

Their primary constitutional role was to select parliamentary candidates and organise elections, their *de facto* role was to ensure party dominance within parliament, despite the fact that (as Table 5.8 indicates) only Albania, Hungary, Romania and Yugoslavia emerged from the 1940s as single-party states. In single-party states with single-list elections ensuring party dominance was straightforward. In multiparty systems, the share of seats between the loyal parties had to be determined in advance. With electoral reform later in the period that introduced measures allowing multicandidate elections, the Fronts

Table 5.8 *Minor political parties in Eastern Europe*

Bulgaria	Bulgarian Agrarian Union
Czechoslovakia	People's Party; Czech Socialist Party; Slovak Freedom Party; Slovak Revival Party
GDR	Christian Democratic Party; Liberal Democratic Party; National Democratic Party; Democratic Farmers' Party
Poland	United Peasant Party; Democratic Party

Source See Note 5.

had to ensure that the choice was always between equally loyal candidates.

Internal communist party organisation was unexceptional. Local organisations elected intermediate organisations that elected government organisations, which appointed an executive (the Central Committee), a supreme policy-determining committee (the Politburo) and a permanent Secretariat responsible for party organisation and discipline. That this followed the pattern of regional organisation and thus constituted a parallel structure was neither surprising or remarkable. It only constituted a parallel power structure, a feature frequently stressed in textbooks, because it had *de facto* power and had no rivals. Similarly, the doctrine of democratic centralism and the prohibition on the creation of party factions was not unique to communist parties. All parties prefer to have a united front and evolve informal measures for controlling the behaviour of malcontents and influencing the behaviour of local organisations. What was unusual was the imposition of party discipline by terror in the 1950s, and the impossibility of establishing an alternative party. Nor was the fact that top government figures were also party members (see Table 5.9) particularly remarkable, given the fact that the party-controlled National Fronts organised elections to parliament.

What was specific about party organisation under 'actually existing socialism', however, and what distinguished it from all other totalitarian systems, was the extent to which grass roots organisations were located within the workplace, and the fact that party organisation was inextricably tied up with the running of the economy – because it determined value. The Party in the Marxist–Leninist political system was omnipresent: it had to be. The party machine did not spread its tentacles into every area of life simply because it wanted to control every component of the socio-economic system. It did so because, with the market suppressed, in a fundamental sense it was the system. Every production unit had a party organisation, and neither workers nor managers could take any action without consideration of how the Party might respond. Politics was not a spare-time activity. It structured directly the activities of the majority of the population (the working population) for the majority of their time (their working time).

Marxism–Leninism in Culture and Everyday Life

If, in Marxist–Leninist inspired 'actually existing socialism', the Party rather than the market determined value, and the political system was

Table 5.9 *Full name of Communist Party and Party leader's non-Party post, 1980–1*

Country	*Party name*	*Party leader*	*Leader's title*	*Non-Party post*
Albania	Albania Party of Labour	Enver Hoxha	First Secretary	Chairman of Democratic Front
Bulgaria	Bulgarian Communist Party	Todor Zhivkov	General Secretary	Chairman of State Council
Czechoslovakia	Communist Party of Czechoslovakia	Gustáv Husák	General Secretary	President of the Republic
GDR	Socialist Unity Party	Erich Honecker	General Secretary	Chairman of State Council
Hungary	Hungarian Workers' Party (to 1956), Hungarian Socialist Workers' Party	János Kádár	First Secretary	Member of Presidential Council
Poland	Polish United Workers' Party	Wojciech Jaruzelski	First Secretary	Prime Minister
Romania	Romanian Workers' Party (to 1965), Romanian Communist Party	Nicolae Ceauşescu	General Secretary of State Council	President Chairman
Yugoslavia	League of Communists of Yugoslavia	Lazar Mojsov	President of Presidency	Member of State Presidency (*ex officio*)

Source Compiled from R. F. Staar, *Communist Regimes in Eastern Europe* (fourth edn, Stanford, Cal., 1982).

at no non-party values contaminated the political
prising that the need was felt to extend control
ues, from market worth to the ideological sphere
The socialist values which communist parties
strove to pursue were internationalism and a materialism that was not just hostile to idealism and religious expression, but also reduced all social relations, not so much to an economic base, as to a notion that the relationships which structured the production of social wealth also determined the distribution of social wealth and welfare. Equality in terms of the common ownership of the means of production would automatically bring behind it social equality for all.

Eastern European socialists first destroyed the bulk of the social organisations that had existed prior to socialism. In Hungary, for example, the number of clubs and associations in the country reached a peak of between 13 000 and 14 000 in the late 1930s, and dropped to around 1000 in 1950 after all mass organisations, political, social, lay and church were banned in 1948, despite the fact that the right to association was reaffirmed in the 1949 constitution.[7] They then encouraged people to join associations carefully vetted by the National Fronts. Common amongst these were party youth organisations, women's organisations, and a trade union structure organised on industrial rather than craft lines. Other organisations frequently found were a partisans' movement or veterans' association. Poland was unique in sanctioning a scout movement in addition to the standard young communist organisation. By herding all social organisations under the National Front umbrella, almost all social activity took place in the context of bodies that ultimately came under the supervision of the Party.

Socialist ideology's internationalism manifested itself in an emphasis on peace, on friendship with the Soviet Union, on social harmony and in a downplaying of nationalism. In addition to the 'mass organisations' noted above, most countries also included an official peace movement, a society for friendship with the Soviet Union, and organisations representing the interests of ethnic minorities. It would be wrong to say that all vestiges of national identity were suppressed under 'actually existing socialism'. National public holidays were replaced by socialist and Soviet ones. National coats of arms were amended to include socialist symbols. Cultural policy included quotas of Soviet films and books. But, except for the high point of Stalinism when, for example, România had to be spelled Romînia to disguise its Latin associations, or Kódaly's *Háry János* was banned because it was 'chauvinist', national and ethnic identities were not suppressed (although they were limited, except in Romania, if they manifested themselves as anti-Soviet). Folk-dance troupes and folk-dancing as a pass-time, for example, were actively encouraged. Even the GDR's tiny Sorb minority was defended by the 1952 constitution.

But national identity was kept in its place, and this was the reason for the widespread feeling that it was suppressed. Marxism saw nationalism as a false ideology, but it was willing to put up with it if it kept a subordinate profile. It could be a component in social identity, but it could not constitute a social identity in itself. Even in Romania where, as will become clear, the regime began actively to use nationalism for its own ends, it was a nationalist version of 'actually existing socialism' that was being propounded, not Romanian nationalism. It was a reaction against the tendency, ever present, but strongest in the 1950s, for 'socialist internationalism' to translate itself into Soviet culture and the foreign policy interests of the Soviet Union; but the tenets of a very Stalinist version of 'actually existing socialism' were unquestioned. What 'actually existing socialism' specifically excluded was the definition of the nation state primarily in terms of a particular ethnic identity. Yet, for the new nation states of Europe created at the end of the nineteenth century such as Germany, this was the norm. Germans invented the untranslatable concept *Deutschtum* (Germanness) to describe the common characteristics of citizens of the German state, and similar neologisms found their ways into East European languages. Aspirations to nationhood of this kind were a nonsense in the ethnic patchwork that was Eastern Europe; but they were aspirations none the less. They had remained unsatisfied between the wars. They had been only a little diminished by the immediate postwar population transfers and the bodily westward shift of Poland. Under 'actually existing socialism' they were ruled out of bounds.

Marxism's materialism revealed itself in two ways. First, as an ideological child of the enlightenment, it was atheistic and hostile to religion. Religion was, in Marx's well-known phrase, 'the opiate of the people', a false ideology encouraged by the ruling class to prevent workers seeing their true class position. Regime hostility was directed primarily at the institutional basis of churches, since it was assumed, mistakenly as it turned out, that religious beliefs would die away once the class system which they served had disappeared and the educational curriculum had been amended to remove all religious content. The religious policy of the communist regimes was to 'nationalise' the churches, controlling them by variously named Departments for Religious Affairs; and to depoliticise them. Religion was to become a personal affair, albeit one officially disapproved of. By and large churches were not banned, except in Albania in its Maoist phase and in Romania and Czechoslovakia which slavishly implemented Stalin's proscription of the Uniate church. The regimes indicated displeasure by breaking diplomatic relations with the Vatican, or failing to appoint bishops; and there was also bureaucratic impatience with small or new churches such as Baptists and Methodists which were institutionally too weak to fight back. But churches were prevented from political activities and, with the exception of Poland, from engaging in religious instruction in the state school system. Of course, the dividing line between moral and political issues is a fine one in the West as much as in the East, and in the early postwar years it was exacerbated by a Vatican decree excommunicating those who supported communism. Whenever the political line hardened, there were plenty of pretexts for tightening the screw on the church. Nevertheless, as with national identity, religion was not totally repressed under 'actually existing socialism'. It was simply subordinate and more or less actively discouraged. Those who believed strongly could find a church, sometimes with difficulty; but they were prevented from extending that personal belief to the desire to proselytise or to mobilise in favour or against 'political' decisions. Yet, it is in the nature of deeply held conviction that this is what believers want to do.

The second dimension of Marxist materialism was more diffuse. It was the belief that all inequalities are class inequalities, that creating the material basis for socialism by rectifying the perceived injustices of the private ownership of the means of production via their nationalisation and introducing a system of more or less universal health and social welfare benefits would necessarily bring with it the end of all inequality. Following nationalisation, the communist regimes of Eastern Europe introduced, or rather further developed, extensive, mainly insurance-based health and social welfare schemes. The general right to health (as well as work) was incorporated into all the Stalinist constitutions.[8] Such schemes, administered partly or fully by the trade unions, presupposed an employment relationship. But, since there was an obligation to work, only the non-collectivised peasantry and the small handicrafts sectors were significant losers. Benefits on collective farms often remained lower than for industrial employees, and in Romania this meant having to pay, although at reduced rates.

Poland took measures in the 1970s to extend cover to its still private peasantry. By the mid-1970s Bulgaria, Czechoslovakia and Hungary operated systems which covered the whole population.[9] Although this much was common, the details of operation and finance in each system differed greatly, an absence of uniformity which reflected perhaps the relatively low profile given to these areas of social life in comparison with the creation of political and economic orthodoxy. The regimes also introduced free, universal education systems that included extensive provision in the form of nurseries for the under-three-year-olds and kindergartens for three- to seven-year-olds in the pre-school years. The curriculum was substantially amended to reflect both the Soviet Marxist view of history and to introduce the new science of dialectical materialism. (Even in market-reformed Hungary, Western-style macro- and microeconomics courses were only introduced in the very last years of communist rule.)

But, having established the structures, it was assumed that social problems would solve themselves automatically. No need was perceived for social policy. In Hungary the Ministry of Popular Welfare was abolished in the 1940s because it was superfluous.[10] The first party decree on matters of social policy in Hungary which did not suppose that welfare would automatically follow from economic growth was passed in April 1980.[11] Problems associated with ethnic minorities or the rights of women would be solved by their incorporation into the labour force. The mass organisations created to represent them did not involve themselves in social policy. In reality, no automatic solution of social problems occurred. The citizens of 'actually existing socialism' experienced continued social inequalities of all kinds;[12] but they also took for granted extensive social provision in education, health and welfare, even if their everyday experience was that the systems did not work very well.

To sum up, citizens of Eastern European 'actually existing socialism' experienced in varying degrees chronic shortage as the attempt to build an economic system based around the Party's estimation of value failed. In their working environment they were located in a structure dominated by hierarchical rather than horizontal ties and reporting relationships. They were unable to escape the influence of an omnipresent Party that dominated political institutions and restricted the right of association to those organisations it approved of. Although Party presence became generally less intrusive from the 1960s on, it was always there. The reaction of the Party was always a factor that had to be taken into consideration, even when displeasing the Party resulted only in an admonition or prohibition on publication rather than arrest by the secret police. Citizens of 'actually existing socialism' found their rights to express national, ethnic or religious identity curtailed rather than suppressed; but rights were curtailed in just that area where those who feel strongly about something want to be able to express it: the political arena. They continued to experience social inequalities of many types, despite the expectation that they would disappear, and, with economic failure, education, health and welfare systems operated less well than promised. Despite this, a high level of education, health and welfare provision free of charge was accepted as the norm.

Chapter 5 performs a pivotal role in the structure of this book both literally and figuratively. Chapters 1–4 have described how Eastern European socialist regimes were established. Chapters 6–8 will document their partial reform and eventual demise. Neither the contours of reform nor the pattern of demise make sense in isolation from an understanding of how the societies that revolutionary socialists created actually operated, how 'actually existing socialism' worked. The limits to reform must be understood not only in the context of the Soviet Union's foreign policy interests, but also of a conception of socialism jointly shared by the ruling elites. When the Soviet Union invaded Czechoslovakia only a model of socialism was at stake, there was no threat to the Warsaw Pact, nor even, directly at least, to the single-party system. Even as late as 1985 in radically reformed Hungary, measures were taken to oblige small businesses to adopt the ideologically more acceptable – because less clearly private – Small Cooperative form. The scale of the privatisation task and of post-communist economic disequilibrium are the direct consequences of 40 years of an economy which nationalised everything and deliberately, and enthusiastically, suppressed the market. Outbursts of nationalist fervour and the flexing of muscles of the established church in the post-communist years stem directly from the marginalisation of national and religious identities over 40 years.

Eastern European communists took their ideology seriously, and so too must students of the system they created.

6

Reform Communism or Economic Reform

The 1960s, more precisely the years following 1956 until 1968, witnessed two major developments in the postwar history of Eastern Europe: the birth of economic reform and the beginnings of heterodoxy between the Warsaw Pact countries, as Stalinism was replaced by neo-Stalinism. Even as Khrushchev was promising a rosy future based on the superiority of the planned economy, serious doubts were being raised about how the planning mechanism should operate. As growth rates fell throughout the region (see Table 6.1), the more advanced economies entered, or endeavoured to enter, an era of 'intensive' rather than 'extensive' economic development. They attempted to build economic growth on technological development and improved productivity rather than additional capital stock and pulling labour reserves into the economy.

At the same time, as the rigours of Stalinism were relaxed, Soviet intervention in Warsaw Pact country affairs lessened. The ideologically unacceptable notion of national roads to socialism was not resurrected; and where it was, in Czechoslovakia, it was suppressed. But in the 1960s, the Warsaw Pact countries capitalised on less ideological forms of control, on the absence of the unchallenged personal authority of Stalin, and on the uncertainties that developed with the Sino-Soviet split to win a degree of autonomy for themselves – a neo-Stalinist space – in domestic and, to a more limited extent, in foreign policy. In some cases this was associated with an increase in political freedoms; in others, it was not.

Table 6.1 *National income, 1956–65 (percentage annual rates of growth of net material product)*

Country	*1956–60*	*1961–5*
Albania	70	5.8
Bulgaria	9.6	6.6
Czechoslovakia	7.0	1.9
GDR	7.1	3.4
Hungary	6.0	4.1
Poland	6.5	6.2
Romania	6.6	9.1
Yugoslavia	8.0	6.9

Source W. Brus, '1957 to 1965: In Search of Balanced Development', in M. C. Kaser (ed.), *The Economic History of Eastern Europe, 1919–1975*, vol. III (Oxford, 1986), p. 95.

Economic reform in Eastern Europe is a confusing topic. The rhetoric everywhere was of autonomy and decentralisation; but realities differed greatly. Eastern European economic reforms have gone through four stages (although most countries went no further than stage two). These can be categorised as follows: (1) revising priorities within the existing structure; (2) variations on the three-levelled pyramid theme; (3) using the market to distribute current goods and resources, but planning for the future; and (4) the extension of the market to influence future-oriented decisions. Reforms of the first stage were the essence of the New Course that immediately followed Stalin's death and sought to nullify excessive distortions towards investment and heavy industry and redirect funds towards consumption, agriculture and the service sector. The second stage addressed the issue of the system's inherent tendency, described in Chapter 5, to increase the number of plan targets: it requires some elaboration.

Crude output targets encouraged irrational enterprise behaviour with little concern for the consumer; more specific targets smothered the enterprises in detail. What was needed was a framework of institutions and incentives that allowed autonomy, but nevertheless permitted extensive controls by central planners. The solution generally adopted was to circumvent the problem by granting more autonomy to a smaller number of units. The units would have formal autonomy, but were few enough in number for central planners to be able to supervise them easily. The result was the paradoxical sounding 'decentralisation through concentration'. What this entailed in practice was the removal of the middle layer of the planning pyramid, the directorate or chief administration, and amalgamating production units into larger bodies, 'associations'. The 'associations' were then directly responsible to the ministry; but because they were few in number they could be entrusted with fewer, relatively unspecific planning targets.

Most economies in Eastern Europe did not go beyond these two stages of New Course readjustment of priorities and tinkering with 'associations', even when a new round of economic reform was begun in the 1980s. Successive 'reforms' were simply variations on the 'association' theme, slightly different names, different degrees of freedom, different component enterprises, different target indicators; but the basic structure remained non-market. The exceptions were Yugoslavia, Hungary and Czechoslovakia's short-lived reform. Hungary and Yugoslavia went through both stages three and four; Czechoslovakia was implementing stage three before it was 'normalised'.

With respect to ideological relaxation as the 1950s turned into the 1960s, Eastern Europe faced challenges to its ideological hegemony from two sources. China, which like Yugoslavia had created a revolution without Soviet aid, followed the Yugoslav example of 1948 and challenged Soviet authority. In 1957, at the November Moscow international conference of communist parties, China had taken a leading role in criticising Yugoslavia and supporting the leading role of Moscow. Harmony between Moscow and Peking did not last long, especially following Tito's attempt to improve relations after October 1958. Relations became increasingly tense, Khrushchev favouring coexistence and improved relations with Yugoslavia, Mao favouring expansionism and use of the European socialist states as an auxiliary force in his struggles with the United States. Finally, on 17 October 1961 during the course of the 22nd Congress of the Soviet Party, the die was cast. Khrushchev denounced Albania's support of China (see later) and Chou En-Lai left Moscow before the end of the conference having pointedly placed a huge wreath on Stalin's tomb.[1]

The Sino-Soviet conflict provided a new political context for the region that permitted a certain amount of freedom for national divergence, though never to the extent seen during the Khrushchev–Tito rapprochement. There was no resurrection of radical Nagy-type national communist renewal, with the partial exception of Czechoslovakia, which will be discussed later. But *de facto* questioning of Soviet authority by China and then Albania, taken together with Khrushchev's second round of de-Stalinisation begun at the 22nd Party Congress in 1961 and the Soviet Union's own flirtation with economic reform, allowed the emergence of two new factors challenging Stalinist orthodoxy. First, the conflict between the Soviet Union and China created a space in which Romania and, to a lesser extent, the GDR could pursue independent foreign policy objectives. In Romania these were related to new nationalist policies on the home front; in the GDR they were occasioned by its own unique situation in relation to its sister Germany.

The second challenge to Stalinist orthodoxy, then, was the acceptance of a degree of ideological pluralism. With the exceptions of Czechoslovakia, where the threads came together to cause an explosion, Albania (where there was no relaxation) and Hungary (where it continued), the relaxation of strictures in the ideological sphere took its cue from Moscow. It began in the wake of Khrushchev's second denunciation of Stalin in 1961 and ended, after Khrushchev's replacement by Brezhnev in 1964, with the trial in 1966 of the dissident Soviet authors Sinyavsky and Daniel. However, the exacting standards of the 1950s were not reimposed.

ECONOMIC REFORMS OF THE 1960s

Precursors

Although the New Course constituted simply a readjustment of priorities, economists in Poland, Hungary and the GDR had begun drafting models for more radical reform. In Poland, as early as the end of 1953, taking Stalin's *Economic Problems of Socialism in the USSR* and its discussion of the law of value as their starting point, economists criticised hyper-centralisation. In Hungary in December 1954, György Péter of the Central Statistical Office published a draft of a model of market socialism that included many of the features subsequently introduced in 1968; and János Kornai completed his seminal book *Overcentralisation in the Economic Administration* in September 1956. Neither was without its impact on economic reform theories. In the short period before the summer of 1957, radical market socialist proposals were developed in Hungary that called for an end to the method of central plan disaggregation and the introduction of indirect controls on enterprise behaviour by price, tax and credit policies. In early 1957, the Varga Commission was established to elaborate a reformist economic strategy for the Kádár government, although its proposals were ignored by the political authorities and, by the second half of 1957, a new attack on economic revisionism had started. Similar reform proposals by Fritz Behrens and Arne Benary in the GDR (published in 1957 but first elaborated in 1956) met with similar government rejection.[2]

The economic reform theorists in Poland were somewhat more successful. In September 1956 a joint Party–Government commission – the Economic Council, chaired by Oskar Lange – was appointed, that drafted three measures central to the 1956 reform attempt: a reduction in the number of centrally fixed targets; the creation of a clear link between bonuses and the financial results of the enterprises; and the Workers' Councils Law, which gave freely elected workers' councils status and powers of veto in the system of enterprise management, if not in politics. The Economic Council produced the 'Theses on Certain Directions of Change in the Economic Model', published in April 1957, which, although cautiously worded, clearly indicated the need for a shift away from an administrative system of plan implementation to the use of economic instruments. Yet the Economic Council was gradually expelled from the Polish body politic. By 1958–9 it had lost most of its importance, and in 1962 it ceased formally to exist. Poland's workers' councils were similarly emasculated. As early as May 1957 they were placed under the direct control of the enterprise trade union, and in December 1958 a new organ was created, the 'conference of workers' self-management', made up of the factory council, the workers' council, the factory party committee and the factory young communist organisation.[3]

Despite his threat to the West over Berlin in 1958, Khrushchev had determined by the end of the 1950s that relations with the West posed no military threat and that the focus should switch to catching up with the West economically. Abandoning the Soviet sixth five-year plan, he adopted a seven-year plan in 1959 at the 21st Party Congress informed by this new economic goal. The Comecon partners (with the exception of Poland) responded by completing collectivisation; restructuring towards growth (implementing Chinese-style Great Leaps Forward in Bulgaria and Albania); and embarking on stage-two type economic restructuring. At this stage, the word 'reform' was not mentioned.[4]

In some countries, the development of 'associations' went in parallel with this return to forced growth, in others it followed on as growth without reform faltered. The process can be seen to have started in Poland in 1958 as a complement to the attack on workers' councils of that year. Industrial directorates were transformed into 'industrial associations', an economic rather than administrative form of horizontal organisation. Yet, despite formally greater autonomy and a planned reduction in targets, the number of obligatory targets had risen again by 1959. The Czechoslovak reform of 1958 followed similar lines: 1417 industrial enterprises were transformed into 383 'productive economic units' (VHJ). The number of obligatory targets given to these associations was reduced, and they were granted more autonomy in investment decisions. This radical aspect of the reform was short-lived, although the associations remained. By 1961–2 the number of obligatory targets had been increased again and investment recentralised. In the GDR the actual creation of associations (the VVB) in 1958 was an element of a larger organisational change modelled on the Soviet *sovnarkhoz* move towards territorial organisation. Some 40 per cent of industry was transferred from national to regional responsibility, and the associations were introduced to replace the chief administrations of the abolished ministries. The changes were essentially administrative since no significantly greater autonomy devolved to the associations.

Hungary was slow to develop its 'associations' or 'trusts'. A number of enterprise mergers took place in 1958 and 1959, but little of substance was done until a Central Committee meeting of 2 February 1962 determined to abolish the directorates and increase industrial concentration, setting a deadline of the end of 1963. In the event, many directorates were not abolished and only 17 new trusts were created; yet there was a considerable increase in industrial concentration. Bulgaria created its 'associations' (DSOs) in 1963 in the context of the need to reform and undo the territorial structure it too had introduced in 1958–9 in deference to the Soviet *sovnarkhoz* experiment. Albania and Romania hesitated, since they were already committed to policies that disapproved of copying things Soviet.[5]

Economic Reform in East Germany

The need to face foursquare the issue of economic reform was forced on the leaderships by a slowdown in the rates of economic growth that was common throughout the region, including Yugoslavia.

In December 1959 the GDR was criticised in a Comecon meeting at Sofia because it had not developed a long-term plan to 1974 in line with changed Soviet policy. It already had a seven-year plan for 1959–65 in place (the *Plan des Wohlstands*, which envisaged catching up with the West in terms of per capita consumption by 1961 as a means of stemming the exodus of workers via Berlin) and did not want to be concerned with longer-term planning. Following this criticism and Soviet advice that the target date should be put back to 1980, the Planning Commission issued in July a draft long-term plan for the period 1965–80 known as the General Perspective. Neither plan lasted long. In September 1960 the economy faltered as the Federal Republic cancelled a ten-year-old trade agreement. Pressing short-term problems jeopardised both the General Perspective and the *Plan des Wohlstands*, not to mention lesser measures such as a price reform planned for 1960. With the possibility in the revised agreement with the West of supplies being cancelled without warning, the March session of the Central Committee cancelled the *Plan des Wohlstands* and sanctioned a new 'freedom from interference' approach. Enterprises were instructed to switch from West German to domestic and Soviet sources of supply, at the expense of hugely increased production costs.[6]

But cancellation of the ambition of catching up with the West had political consequences. The exodus of workers via Berlin had begun to slow towards the end of the 1950s. It had increased again with the completion of agricultural collectivisation in 1960; and now there was no prospect of equal living standards diminishing the attractiveness of the West. The only solution to this costly drain on human resources was to strengthen the border, to erect a physical barrier, to build the Berlin Wall, which was done on 13 August 1961.

Having created a breathing space, planners quietly forgot about the General Perspective plan. In the spring of 1962 the Party set up working parties to discuss possibilities of changes to the economic mechanism. These were given extra impetus by the publication in *Pravda* in September 1962 of the famous Liberman article entitled 'Plan, Profit, Premium'. Assuming that publication of the article presaged a commitment by Khrushchev to economic reform, the Party opted at the very end of 1962 for what it was to call its 'New Economic System' (NES), which was announced at the Party Congress in January 1963. Experiments were begun immediately and their results analysed by the Council of Ministers in July. The decision finally to introduce economy-wide reform from the beginning of January 1964 came in September 1963.

The novel feature of the NES was that the new 'association' body (the VVB) was to act not simply as a semi-administrative unit, but as a fully fledged socialist corporation. Research and development facilities were transferred to the VVBs, which were expected to respond to financial indicators such as profit, sales and costs, although no single indicator was isolated as the major economic target. The centre continued to impose obligatory plan indicators and maintained the physical allocation of resources; but the use of both was substantially reduced, as was the number of obligatory targets, particularly those related to total output. Net profit was taxed at a differential rate depending on the type of enterprise, and retained profits were distributed amongst bonus, fixed capital, circulating capital and reserve funds according to a prescribed ratio.[7]

The NES did not have total faith in 'economic levers' however. All profit-based incentives operated within the constraints of fulfilling the state output plan, and the plan also contained a series of norms that enterprises were obliged to follow. This retention of directives and planned norms threatened to reintroduce elements of the old system and, ultimately, with a certain degree of oversimplification, this is what happened. At the 8th Party Congress in 1967 the NES was renamed the 'Economic System of Socialism', foreshadowing the elimination of its more radical elements. One of the key aspects in this was the introduction of 'planning according to structure-determining tasks', which were to be defined by the centre. By emphasising certain sectors at the expense of others, this policy resulted in disequilibria and the introduction of a new concept of 'object planning' in 1969. Despite the publication in the spring of 1970 of guidelines for 1971–5 still more or less in line with NES, the June Central Committee session decided on recentralisation, and the necessary measures were summarised in a decree published in December 1970 entitled 'Implementing the Economic System of Socialism in 1971'. The 'planned proportional development of the national economy' became dependent on enlarging the role of 'state planning and balancing' and the 1971 plan included a decisive increase in the number of obligatory targets and prescribed planning norms for VVBs and enterprises. Lower-level plans again took the form of disaggregations of higher-level ones, limited autonomy with pricing was withdrawn, and bonuses were increasingly tied to specific tasks rather than overall performance.[8]

Economic Reform in Hungary

In Hungary,[9] renewed discussion of economic reform began after the 8th Party Congress in November 1962 when Kádár had confirmed his personal authority, having, in 1961, got rid of hard-liners and expelled Rákosi from the Party and, immediately before the Congress, expelled György Marosán and 'the unparty group'. The spirit of reform was personified by the appointment to the Politburo, with immediate responsibility for economic affairs, of former socialist Rezső Nyers, who had been Minister of Finance since January 1960. Towards the end of 1963 Nyers put together an informal 'brains trust' to consider economic reform, and formal recognition of the need for reform followed on 21 July 1964 when the State Economy Committee attached to the Central Committee drafted a decree, subsequently passed at the Central Committee session of 10 December, requiring the elaboration of a comprehensive conception for modernising the economic mechanism within two years. The first draft of the reform was prepared in the summer of 1965 and passed at the Central Committee session of 18–20 November 1965. The formulation of detailed directives was completed in the spring of 1966, and the final decision to implement taken by the Central Committee at its session on 25–27 May 1966.

The New Economic Mechanism (NEM) was introduced as a package on 1 January 1968, although it was originally expected that a second stage would follow in the early 1970s. It was by far the most radical reform of the Warsaw Pact countries. The cornerstones of the Stalinist system – central planning in quantitative units and the centralised allocation of resources – were abandoned entirely. Enterprises were instructed to make profits, and the planning process was reduced to setting tax rates and adjusting other financial instruments, which guided the behaviour of these profit-oriented enterprises. The idea underpinning the reform was that the state should withdraw in favour of the market for present-oriented decisions relating to resource and commodity distribution, but should retain a role in planning long-term, future-oriented issues such as the allocation of investment funds. The reform had two further characteristics. First, enterprises were initially to operate in an environment shielded from movements in world prices; second, the structure of economic administration and the size and degree of concentration of enterprises remained intact.

Accounts of Hungary's NEM usually continue with long catalogues of the components of the system: three types of price (fixed, those free to move between levels fixed by the state in various ways and those that were entirely free), numerous types of enterprise fund (the Development Fund, the Sharing Fund and the Reserve Fund), various taxes applicable before the funds were formed (the Production Tax, the charge on assets) and to the funds (the Development Fund tax, the 'wage development payment'), and so on. Many of these funds and taxes had parallels in the less radically reformed economies of Eastern Europe, however. What distinguished Hungary was that the reform was taken seriously. There was no back-up structure of resource allocation or quantitative planning as there had been in the GDR. Central bodies exercised informal influence, of course, but annual plans consisted of no more than modifications to tax rates or the technicalities of, say, the system of wage regulation taxation. The most important consequence of the NEM was the creation of much greater 'consumer sovereignty'. Hungary became much less of a shortage economy than it had been. Unlike the rest of Eastern Europe, which suffered from 'not lack of money but lack of goods', for Hungarians, after the introduction of the NEM, the problem was more 'not lack of goods, but lack of money'.[10] Shortage was less endemic; and, because agriculture was one of the main beneficiaries of the reform (because there were no *de facto* monopoly producers in agriculture), queuing for basic foodstuffs became a thing of the past.[11]

Economic Reform in Yugoslavia

Yugoslavia's 1960s economic reform requires special comment because it was the first, and the only long-lived, stage-four reform. Economic changes introduced in the early 1950s had created the third stage of economic reform in Yugoslavia, almost eighteen years before Hungary's NEM. Industrial directorates were transformed into associations of enterprises, and then abolished in 1952. Command planning and the physical allocation of resources gradually disappeared over the course of 1951. Most prices were freed in 1952, when enterprises also acquired the right to engage in foreign trade and a sixfold devaluation of the dinar was implemented. Plans lost their directive character and were backed up by a comprehensive set of economic instruments. The state retained control of the banking system, however, and, because a very high proportion of enterprise revenue was transferred to territorial and federal authorities, the main investment funds and decisions remained in the hands of state agencies. By 1953 investment self-financed by enterprises represented only a quarter of the total. The state also exercised controls over foreign trade by tariffs, licences, multiple exchange rates and the allocation of foreign currency.[12]

Surprisingly, perhaps, the Yugoslav economy slowed down in the 1960s like its economically orthodox neighbours. Worse, unemployment and inflation began to rise, as did the trade deficit. In the reform climate of the mid-1960s, the leadership responded not by retreating, but by moving further. Preparations in 1963 and 1965 resulted in a reform package passed in July 1965, a fourth stage of economic reform.

The main differences between the pre- and post-1965 systems lay in the decentralisation of future-oriented decisions and investment. The reforms increased the share of gross income remaining within the enterprises by first cutting and then abolishing taxes used to source state investment funds. They also restructured the banking system, transforming banks into commercial institutions entitled to offer investment and current credit operations without restrictions as to territorial zone. The Yugoslav National Bank lost all the features of the Soviet-type single channel bank and assumed the functions of a central bank within a market economy. (In 1971 eight national banks and a Federal National Bank were introduced in the spirit of the constitutional amendments of that time.)

At the same time, the workers' council gained the right to appoint managers, although from a list drawn up by a committee on which the communal authorities had parity representation. In addition, taxation was revised in favour of a retail sales tax, prices were further liberalised, tariffs reduced and import restrictions lifted (only to be intermittently reimposed). Workers' councils also gained full independence in setting wage rates.[13] The reform 'enhanced the independence of the Yugoslav self-managed enterprise, putting into its hands not only decisions concerning current production and the distribution of its own revenue, but also a major share of decisions concerning the future'.[14] Although self-managed enterprises did not formally become the owners of their assets, they enjoyed most of the real powers ownership brings with it.

Economic Reform in Poland, Romania, Albania and Bulgaria

The remaining countries of the region (except for Czechoslovakia, which is discussed separately later) were less concerned with economic reform. In Poland, a second wave of reform discussion began with Party Congress resolutions in 1964 and a Central Committee Plenum in 1965. Measures were taken in 1966 to transform the industrial associations of the late-1950s into units of a more economic character, and a resolution of the Council of Ministers in December 1966 reduced the number of direct orders to the associations. The number of associations was also reduced from 163 to 121, and there were attempts to link enterprise revenue more directly to actual foreign sales. Such measures were at the less radical end of the reform spectrum, and the 5th Party Congress in February 1969 proclaimed the need for further change to be implemented in 1971–5, beginning with a reform of the price and incentive systems. Both fell victim to the workers' revolts of the 1970s.[15]

Bulgaria talked a lot about reform, but did little, primarily because the growth rate only really began to decline in the 1970s. As Włodzimierz Brus has noted:

> Although the rate of growth of national income was substantially lower during the years 1961–5 than in the preceding quinquennium (6.6 annually compared with 9.6), it was still high and never showed the catastrophic falls seen in Czechoslovakia and the GDR. The country's economic structure (by 1965 more than 45 per cent of the active population was still in agriculture and forestry, which contributed almost a third of national income) could hardly warrant a contention that 'extensive sources' of growth had been exhausted.[16]

Nevertheless, there were real causes for concern in the economy. Bulgaria was one of the first countries to extend pensions and welfare provisions to collective farm workers (in 1957). Yet agriculture was in crisis in 1962, causing unrest in some towns and the need to import wheat from Canada.[17]

Between 1963 and 1966 the Bulgarian economic literature was peppered with reform proposals, and a number of practical experiments were carried out in selected enterprises, beginning in June 1964. In as much as the chosen major success indicator was gross income, the proposals were closest to the Czechoslovak model; but in all other respects they were closer to the later variants of the GDR's NES: binding targets and material balances were reduced, but not abolished. In December 1965 the Politburo passed its 'Theses' on economic reform, approved by the Central Committee in April 1966, and in 1967 the system 'based on "Theses"' was claimed to be a success, covering 70 per cent of industry and all of agriculture. But at the July 1968 Plenum of the Central Committee the general direction of the reform was reversed. Three-tier pricing, wage flexibility and greater enterprise input into the planning process were all withdrawn; and the list of directive indicators was expanded.[18] Retreat from reform, as in the GDR, but unlike Hungary, pre-dated the intervention in Czechoslovakia.

Romania did not get around to economic reform in the 1960s. Until 1965 it followed the classic Stalinist model, and frequent modifications thereafter only changed the way in which central control was exercised. The beginning of so-called reforms was the October 1967 directive 'On the Improvement of the Management of the National Economy', which was passed by the Party's National Conference in December 1967. These explicitly rejected any move from direct to parametric planning and were, in effect, the basis for economic policy changes in 1978. A system of 'workers' participation' was introduced in 1968 (which was remodelled in 1971), but it never became more than purely formal. In addition, a second-stage 'association' reform was initiated in October 1969, a move that was accompanied by the standard initial reduction (to 170) in the number of categories of centrally allocated consumer goods.[19]

In Albania changes to the economic model did take place, but in the context of cultural revolution rather than 'revisionist' economic reform. By 1967–8 two fundamental points about the Albanian economy were becoming clear: first, China was unable to provide all the aid Albania wanted; second the economy was not performing well. Although 97 per cent plan fulfilment was claimed for the third five-year plan (1961–5), agricultural output was only half the planned figure, industrial output registered only 75 per cent, and national income only 57 per cent. Decision No. 15 of the Council of Ministers in February 1966, 'On the Fundamental Principles of the Methodology of Planning', marked something of a change in economic policy; but it was in the Maoist rather than the 'revisionist' mould. It emphasised the elaboration and fulfilment of plans by propaganda and mass mobilisation, with much reference to 'workers' control', but little substance. In line with the East European norm, however, the number of targets was reduced, as was the size of the state administration, including, most tellingly, the statistical service. By April 1967, in a second phase of the cultural revolution, all remaining private farms (11 per cent of the total in 1966) were collectivised, the size of collective farm members' private plots was cut, and there was agitation for their complete abolition.[20]

THE SINO-SOVIET SPLIT AND AUTONOMY FROM THE SOVIET UNION

If economic reform did not figure strongly in the countries of the Balkans (or in Poland), anti-Soviet politics did. During the 1960s both Albania and Romania publicly distanced themselves from the Soviet Union, Romania drawing on a tradition already established with the withdrawal of Soviet troops in 1958, but Albania taking an anti-Soviet stance for the first time.

Albania

Albania, the smallest and the most backward country in the region, played a role disproportionate to its size in the first years of the 1960s. Albania had been central to Stalin's plan for a Balkan Federation formed in such a way as to keep Tito in check. After the Tito–Stalin break, faced with the alternative of absorption into Yugoslavia, Albania had been Stalin's most loyal ally. Khrushchev's flirtation with Tito had appeared to put all this in jeopardy, and while by 1958 it was clear that there were limits to the Soviet–Yugoslav rapprochement, Albania's leader Enver Hoxha had lost faith in Khrushchev and was looking for an alternative ally. By siding with the Chinese in the Sino-Soviet split and, more importantly, by getting away with it, Albania's actions increased the dimensions of the neo-Stalinist room for manoeuvre.

Albania's relationship with China, then, was conditioned by its deep-rooted antipathy towards Yugoslavia. Both countries viewed Khrushchev's moves towards reconciliation with concern. Albania was also critical of Comecon plans that relegated Albania to the status of agricultural and raw materials supplier to the rest of the bloc. Tension between China and the Soviet Union became visible in April 1960; by May–June it was clear that Albania was siding with China, and the rift entered the world arena at the Moscow World Conference of Communist Parties in November 1960 when Hoxha criticised the Soviet Union for lack of consultation over Yugoslavia, and openly sided with China. The Soviet Union reacted by stalling the negotiations for aid for Albania's third five-year plan (1961–5); Albania responded by signing a trade deal with China on 2 February. The 4th Congress of the Albanian Party of Labour later in February confirmed the anti-Soviet, pro-China line and, some two months later, on 26 April, the day after the details of Albania's trade agreement with China had been made public, the Soviet Union notified Albania that economic aid programmes would be discontinued. By the end of May all Soviet naval bases had been dismantled. Albania was not invited to the 22nd Congress of the Soviet Communist Party and, on 3 December 1961, the Soviet Union took the unprecedented step of breaking diplomatic relations. Albania was unambiguously in the Chinese camp.

In the spring of 1962 relations between China and the Soviet Union improved somewhat but when, in the summer of 1962, Khrushchev renewed overtures to Yugoslavia, Albanian criticisms strengthened again. Relations between the Soviet Union and both China and Albania failed to improve thereafter, despite Sino-Soviet discussions in July 1963. In December 1963–January 1964 Chou En-Lai visited Albania, and at the end of February 1964 the abandoned Soviet embassy in Tiranë was seized. Relations got no better after Khrushchev's fall in October 1964.

Chou En-Lai made a second visit in March 1965 and, despite rumours in 1966 of a rift with China, Albania's own 'cultural revolution' was launched in February, which by mid-July was in full swing. A second round began in February 1967, peaking in the spring and summer with Red Guards criticising teachers, intellectuals and workers, and the implementation of an anti-religious campaign. The following year Albania underlined its disaffection with the Soviet version of socialism by leaving the Warsaw Pact after the Soviet invasion of Czechoslovakia. It had, in any case, never participated in Warsaw Pact exercises. Albania remained a nominal member of Comecon, although it never participated actively in the organisation. The importance of Albania's lead was not so much that it created a space in which it could develop its own Maoism as that, by successfully disobeying Moscow, it increased the space in which others could act.[21]

Romania

Romania, first under Gheorghiu-Dej and then under his successor Nicolae Ceauşescu, made use of the ideological uncertainty occasioned by the Sino-Soviet split to develop its own brand of nationalist, rather than national, communism. The political system and social and economic structure remained the same, that is Stalinist (there was no Romanian model of socialism); but a new nationalist ideology was grafted on top to replace pro-Soviet socialist internationalism, and an independent, nationalist but still avowedly socialist, foreign policy was pursued.

Romania's break with the Soviet Union took place gradually. In 1958 Soviet troops were withdrawn from Romania (see Chapter 4) and, towards the end of the decade, it began to reorient trade away from the Soviet Union, the share of Soviet trade falling from 51.5 per cent of total trade in 1958 to 40.1 per cent in 1960. At the same time, a process of re-Romanianisation began as Russian names were removed from streets and replaced by Romanian ones. Romania's reorientation of trade was in the context of its refusal to conform to the model of international comparative advantage that Comecon evolved in the late 1950s and early 1960s. Khrushchev was keen to convert Comecon, which had lain more or less dormant since its formation in 1949, into a functioning organisation based on national specialisations. The Stalinist presumption of economic autarchy for each country was abandoned. Romanian economists feared that acceptance of the integration plans would lock Romania in a position of dependence in relation to its more industrialised partners. At successive Comecon meetings in November and December 1962, Romanians resisted Soviet pressure, and at the July 1963 summit of Comecon leaders plans for developing Comecon integration to the point of supranational planning were shelved.

The Hungarian historian of Eastern Europe, resident in France, Ferenc Fejtő exaggerates when he describes this as signalling 'the disintegration of Soviet dominance in Eastern Europe',[22] but it was a clear indication of Romania's successful disassociation from Soviet policy and the decline in Soviet authority in the neo-Stalinist years. In furtherance of asserting national independence, in October 1964 the Romanians published Marx's *Notes on the Romanians*, which were critical of Imperial Russian encroachment on Romanian independence. In the same year Romania refused to permit Warsaw Pact exercises on its territory or to allow Romanian troops to take part in Pact exercises abroad.

Ceauşescu continued the move away from Moscow, but first he wanted to establish a clear break with his predecessor. On his accession he implemented two measures to reinforce the divide between himself and Gheorghiu-Dej. In July 1965, at its 4th Congress the Party (which had been formed in 1948 from the merger of the Romanian Communist Party and the Social Democratic Party) was rechristened the Romanian Communist Party, and future congresses were numbered from its precursors' foundation in 1921, so depriving Gheorghiu-Dej of the kudos of being founder of the Party. In August, a new constitution was passed in which Romania's official classification was changed from People's Republic to Socialist Republic. Meanwhile, July saw the first reintroduction of the term Secretary General (rather than First Secretary) for the party leader (later Brezhnev, Husák and Honecker followed suit), and an investigation was initiated to clarify the political situation of certain individuals arrested or sentenced in the 1950s. Ceauşescu used this to confirm his position of personal power and, in December 1967, he changed his own party's rules from 1965 to allow himself to hold a number of positions in both party and state. Finally, in April 1968, a party resolution condemned Gheorghiu-Dej as being personally responsible for the repression of the 1950s.

Gheorghiu-Dej's manipulation of national symbols turned out to have been child's play compared with Ceauşescu's. In 1965 he toasted Bukovina, part of which was in the Soviet Union, and in May 1966 he made a speech castigating Comintern policy and resurrecting the Bessarabian question. The 1965 constitution also had an anti-Soviet dimension in that it described Romania as a 'unitary state', openly contradicting the Comintern line that Romania was a 'multi-national state'. In 1966 and 1967 he staged 'personal encounters' with actors playing parts from Romania's past, and historians were encouraged to rediscover Geto-Dacian civilisation, showing that the ancestors of the Romanian people inhabited Transylvania and Bessarabia long before Magyar or Slavic tribes. Regional reorganisation in 1968 undid the Stalinist system and reintroduced the pre-communist one. Romania roundly criticised the Soviet Union for the invasion of Czechoslovakia, but did not leave the Warsaw Pact, passing instead a new defence law embodying an 'all horizons' defence doctrine that included people's war to resist Soviet invasion. Independence in foreign policy was confirmed by establishing diplomatic relations with Israel and the Federal Republic of Germany in 1967.[23]

East Germany, Poland and Bulgaria

Ulbricht's primary concern between 1955 and 1971 was to get the GDR recognised internationally. In this process, he occasionally antagonised the Soviet Union by overstepping the mark – indeed, it was intransigence over the Berlin Treaty in 1970 that led to his downfall. Throughout the 1960s he goaded the Soviet Union to take actions such as sanctioning the building of the Berlin Wall (which he had wanted since 1958) and acting to prevent a session of the Federal Republic's Bundestag in West Berlin in 1965. His greatest triumph was in 1967 when, following Romania's recognition of the Federal Republic on 31 January, he persuaded the other allies not to establish diplomatic relations with the Federal Republic until it recognised the GDR. In order to aid international recognition of the GDR, a new law of 1967 proclaimed a separate GDR citizenship, and 1968 saw the introduction of a new constitution that formalised Ulbricht's conception of socialism and gave formal recognition to the Council of State and the National Council of Defence, which were created in 1960.[24]

Not all the Balkan countries sought to distance themselves from the Soviet Union. The Bulgarians remained loyal, their friendship with the Russians having a far longer pedigree than the existence of the Soviet Union. Bulgarian political history in the 1960s is unremarkable, consisting primarily of the consolidation of power by Todor Zhivkov. Zhivkov had been appointed First Secretary of the Bulgarian Communist Party in April 1956, following the bloc-wide leadership changes inspired by the 20th Congress of the Soviet Party. In Bulgaria these changes took place at the Central Committee Plenum 2–6 April 1956, subsequently known as the 'April Plenum'.

Zhivkov's authority increased in 1957 with the purge of the 'counter-party' group, although the hard-liners regrouped prior to the period of the 'Great Leap' of 1958–9, which had been Zhivkov's initiative, an attempt to prove his ideological credentials. In November 1961, with Khrushchev's direct support, Chervenkov was finally relieved of his Politburo seat, and at the 8th Party Congress in November 1962 he was expelled from the Party, with Zhivkov adding the prime ministership to his posts. By 1964 Zhivkov was sufficiently well-entrenched to survive the fall of his Soviet protector Khrushchev; and in 1965 arrests followed an alleged army plot against him. Finally, in 1969, Bulgaria came to an agreement with Turkey over the emigration of ethnic Turks. The treaty's non-renewal in the 1980s became an issue in the ethnic disputes of that decade. Bulgaria also exhibited a certain foreign policy initiative in relation to its immediate neighbours by raising again the Macedonian issue in 1969 when it claimed that two-thirds of Yugoslav Macedonians were ethnically Bulgarian.[25]

Poland did not need to participate in the post–Sino-Soviet split endeavour of regimes to distance itself from Moscow; it had achieved its own form of special status after 1956. When the new wave of collectivisations took place in 1958, Khrushchev accepted that Poland would not take part and would remain mainly uncollectivised. He even closed his eyes to the facts that, between 1957 and 1963, Poland was the recipient of US aid for grain purchase, and that, at approximately 30 per cent of total turnover, Polish trade with the West in the 1950s and 1960s was unusually high.[26] Hungary, like Bulgaria, but for reasons of realpolitik rather than genuine loyalty, made no attempt to distance itself politically from the Soviet Union. Economic reform was enough. The 'Kádár compromise', learned from 1956, was to remain loyal on foreign policy and one-party rule, but experiment with economic policy at home. Hungarian troops therefore dutifully took part in the invasion of Czechoslovakia in August 1968.

LOOSENING IDEOLOGICAL ORTHODOXY

Bulgaria

The second wave of de-Stalinisation initiated by the 22nd Congress of the Soviet Communist Party in 1961 resulted in something of a relaxation of cultural controls throughout the region, not least in Bulgaria. Initially, Zhivkov took a paternalistic interest in literature and the arts and slavishly followed the policies of his patron Khrushchev, using the latter's attack on modernism to remind writers in 1963 not to stray from socialist realism. By 1965, however, many previously unpublishable authors appeared in print and works of writers such as Solzhenitsyn, Apollinaire, T. S. Eliot and Kafka were translated. Freedom of expression did not last. In 1967 the Committee for Art and Culture reopened the cultural offensive, which was, however, somewhat relaxed the following year.[27] In religious affairs, Patriarch Kiril had been something of a propagandist for the regime and did not demur when it was announced in 1967 that 'the great majority of the people have already freed themselves from the shackles of religion and religious morality'.[28]

East Germany

Economic reforms in the GDR were accompanied by a political thaw, and for a brief period writers and film directors were able to criticise the Stalinist past, West Berliners were allowed to visit the East and the study of sociology was authorised. There was a significant exception, however: Robert Havemann, professor of Physical Chemistry at East Berlin's Humboldt University, who gave a series of public lectures during the winter of 1963–4 in which he called for a regeneration of dialectical and historical materialism. This resulted in his dismissal from the university in 1964, although he continued writing critically during the 1960s and 1970s, seeing in the Prague Spring the proof that socialism and freedom could be combined.

Havemann's downfall was atypical of the climate in 1964. By 1966, however, the tide had turned and Erich Honecker (already seen as Ulbricht's heir apparent) led a counter-attack, labelling the writer Stefan Heym a traitor, for example, for having published in the West. The 1968 constitution removed from the population of the GDR the rights to strike and emigrate, and introduced a duty as well as a right to work. In church affairs, Ulbricht was able to rely on the compliance of the Bishop of Thüringen in his attempt to form a separate Evangelical Church of the GDR from its Federal Republican sister. This was finally achieved in 1969.[29] As early as 1960, however, Ulbricht had told parliament that 'Christianity and the humanist goals of socialism are not irreconcilable'.[30]

Yugoslavia

In Yugoslavia too, the 1960s were the decade of the rise and partial fall of reform. The decade began with economic reforms in 1961 (reduced price control, greater control by banks over credit policy, the devaluation of the dinar), but in 1962, as Tito sought rapprochement with Moscow and downplayed Yugoslavia's economic unorthodoxy, Minister of the Interior Aleksandar Ranković succeeded in eroding these measures and purging the Party. The balance tipped again towards reform when the 7th Party Congress in 1964 legitimised the reformist principles inherent in the 1963 constitution and the 1965 economic reforms (see earlier). The reformists' political victory came in 1966. At the Central Committee meeting on 1–2 July at Brioni, Ranković was denounced for abuse of his police powers and factional activities and dismissed. (It appears that Tito was only willing to act against his long-standing ally after army intelligence had demonstrated that he had been bugging Tito's own offices and residences.) As decentralisation was implemented in the economy, controls over intellectual life relaxed. But this let the nationalist genie out of the bottle. In the early part of the decade (1961–2) nationalism had expressed itself mainly in economic terms, with the exception of a polemical debate on the nature of Yugoslavism. In 1967 cultural issues came to the fore as Croatian and Serbian intellectuals clashed over the status of Serbo-Croat as a language, fuelling further nationalist sentiment and with it mutual distrust, especially between Belgrade and Zagreb.

But the reformist victory was short-lived. Student demonstrations broke out in Belgrade on 2 June 1968, inspired both by developments in the East and by the 'events of May' in France. The government promised to meet many of the demands, relying on the inability of the student movement to link up with the forces of organised labour. Those dissatisfied with such reforms congregated around the Praxis group, already the butt of government criticism in 1966, which continued to publish articles critical of social and economic reforms into the 1970s. Nationalist unrest in Croatia in 1970–1 finally signalled the need to re-establish discipline. Although liberal reformers had wanted to democratise the League, they did not want to endanger the position of the Party within society; and they were under threat from the old guard, especially those grouped around the Veterans' Association. In the formal political sphere the major development of the 1960s was the new constitution of 1963 (submitted to parliament in September 1961 but only ratified in 1963) and its subsequent amendment in 1968. The constitution was essentially a reformist document, introducing the rotation principle and a maximum term for all elected officials of two four-year periods of office. It also enhanced the powers of the Republics, upgraded Kosovo from the status of region to province and created the Constitutional Court. By 1968 the antagonisms between the republics concerning the levies on richer republics to finance underdeveloped regions and the access of republics to foreign exchange (especially from tourism) had reached a point where a constitutional amendment became necessary, strengthening still further the rights of the republics by enhancing the powers of the Chamber of Nationalities. Relations with the church also generally improved. In June 1966 Tito signed an agreement with the Vatican over the exchange of representatives, followed in January 1968 by support for the Pope's World Peace Day.[31]

Poland

Poland was out of step. In the vanguard of economic and political reform in the mid- and late-1950s, having emerged victorious from 1956, it spent the 1960s re-imposing orthodoxy; and when Gomułka's rule was challenged, he responded by increased repression spiced with anti-Semitism.

Although acting within clearly defined limits, Poland in 1957 was at the forefront of political reform. It was the first country in the region to sanction a form of (negative) electoral choice; in 1957, 750 candidates competed for 459 parliamentary seats. Yet, that same year, press restrictions were re-imposed. In the 1960s further retreats occurred. Agricultural Circles were begun as a substitute for collectivisation (charged with helping the private sector increase production while simultaneously bringing it into closer contact with, and dependence on, the national economy) and the cultural line hardened. Although sociology and economics flourished during the 1960s, their proponents, such as Jan Szczepanski, Oskar Lange and Włodzimierz Brus were constantly coming into conflict with the authorities. More specifically, in 1962 the philosopher Leszek Kołakowski came under attack, in June 1963 two leading literary weeklies were closed down and on the eve of the June Party Congress, the leader of a small Maoist group was obliged to escape to Albania after circulating a critical pamphlet.

In 1964, the Party clamped down further, denouncing a letter signed by 34 intellectuals calling for more freedom of expression and closing the Party-sponsored discussion club at Warsaw University. In November 1964 student leaders Jacek Kuroń and Karol Modzełewski were arrested and expelled from the university. In early 1965 they wrote their famous 'Open Letter' critical of 'actually existing socialism'; and, in July 1965, they were sentenced to three and a half years imprisonment. The Sinyavsky–Daniel trial in the Soviet Union in February 1966 signalled a new ideological freeze. Kołakowski was criticised again in 1966 and expelled from the Party. In March 1967 Adam Michnik was suspended from his university post for a year. But things came to a head in 1968.[32]

Despite the consistent hardening of the political line over the course of the decade, Gomułka's rule was not wholly secure. The Israeli victory in the Arab–Israeli war of 1967 was enthusiastically received by air force officers of Jewish origin. This resulted in a backlash against them and a systematic policy of discrimination was followed between 1967 and 1969. Anti-Semitic sentiment in the Party was supplemented by hostility to students and intellectuals generally in early 1968 when students, excited by developments in Czechoslovakia, demonstrated against the banning of a classic, strongly anti-Russian play in January. On 8 March 1968 student demonstrations took place in Warsaw

University to protest against the arrest of Michnik and others for having led the January demonstrations. Initially peaceful, they were broken up by special militia units under the control of the Chief of Security Police General Mieczysław Moczar.

Moczar was leader of the 'partisans' group in the Party who shared a common background as resistance fighters and a communist orthodoxy tinged with demagogic nationalism laced with anti-Semitism. Solidarity actions followed in Gdańsk, Łodz, Szeczin, Wrocław and Kraków. Gomułka appealed to the nation for calm on 19 March, but students in Kraków and Warsaw responded with a sit-down strike. The regime responded with further arrests: Kuroń and Modzełewski, who had been released in 1967, were rearrested as ringleaders, and on March 25 Kołakowski and five Jewish professors were dismissed from their posts. In April Warsaw University closed eight departments and announced that the 1300 students affected would have to apply for readmission. By this time Moczar was on the point of seizing power; but Gomułka was saved thanks to the support of the future Party leader Edward Gierek and the Soviet Union. The 'partisans' blamed the demonstrations on Zionists. With the aid of Gierek, Gomułka placed himself at the head a movement that made a distinction between Zionist Jews, cosmopolitan Jews and patriotic communist Jews, who deserved to be treated as loyal Poles.[33]

Romania

There was little relaxation of ideological orthodoxy in Romania. A minor relaxation of cultural policy took place after 1965, with the rehabilitation of avant-garde and spiritualistic poets. But tolerance did not extend to ethnic minorities. The policy of Romanianisation was not only directed against the Soviet Union. Romania's Hungarian autonomous region, which had been established in 1952, came under increasing pressure from central authorities from 1958 as Romanianisation strengthened. In 1959 the Hungarian university in Cluj was merged with the Romanian one, and in 1960 the region was renamed the Mureş Magyar province and restructured so that formerly Hungarian districts came under Romanian administration. The opposition this caused within the Hungarian minority was only partially rectified by the creation of two counties in 1968 with large Hungarian majorities but low levels of economic development. Church relations, on the other hand, improved. In January 1968 the prime minister and foreign minister visited the Pope, setting the seal on a process that had begun the previous year.[34]

Hungary

In Hungary the 1960s were characterised by Kádár's famous dictum published in the Party daily paper *Népszabadság* in January 1962: 'Whereas the Rákosiites used to say that those who are not with us are against us, we say, those who are not against us are with us.'[35] In this spirit, a Central Committee decision of August 1962 finally rehabilitated Rajk and 190 other victims of the 1950s, and the 8th Congress took matters further, passing such reformist measures as opening universities to all, irrespective of political and class background, and abandoning the class struggle vocabulary of 'former exploiters', 'working peasants' and 'kulaks'. In March 1963, Kádár passed a general amnesty for most of those involved in 1956, after a partial amnesty in April 1960 had released many of the writers sentenced for participation in the uprising. Following this, censorship was relaxed, publishing houses were permitted to issue translations of Western works and cinema and theatre productions were renewed.

Also in 1963, agreement was reached with the Vatican over the appointment of bishops and the clergy's oath of loyalty to the government, and Kádár was reconciled with Tito following a visit to Yugoslavia in the autumn. Three years later, in 1966, Hungary followed Poland's lead and reformed its electoral system, replacing the single-list system with one based on individual constituencies where more than one candidate was permitted to stand. In the first elections held on this basis, in 1967, only nine seats were contested, although the number increased fivefold in the next elections in 1971. Unlike the rest of the region, there was no significant re-imposition of ideological controls in the late-1960s; indeed, until August 1968, it was assumed that the NEM constituted part of a more general reform package. Protesters against the invasion of Czechoslovakia lost their jobs, Maoist students were dismissed from university; but sociologists, economists and artists generally continued to function with minimal interference.[36]

THE CZECHOSLOVAK SPRING AND THE WARSAW PACT INVASION OF 1968

The three themes discussed so far in this chapter came together in Czechoslovakia.[37] As the 1950s turned into the 1960s, Czechoslovak communism 'still exuded unquestioning self-confidence, and Antonin Novotný, Party leader since the death of Gottwald in 1953, was personally at the height of his power. Czechoslovakia was proclaimed to have reached the stage of "socialism" ... [and] a new constitution was duly introduced in 1960'.[38] Yet, in the early 1960s the Czechoslovak leadership came under pressure from two quarters. First, Khrushchev's renewed anti-Stalinism campaign forced it to come to terms with the early 1950s, something it did not have to do in 1956. Political trials had continued in Czechoslovakia beyond Stalin's death and no serious attempt had been made to come to terms with the Stalinist past. Some victims of 1952–4 were released, but not rehabilitated; and the brief cultural thaw in 1956 ended in 1957. The turning point came only with the 12th Party Congress of December 1962, following Khrushchev's public denunciation of Stalin at the 22nd Congress of the Soviet Communist Party in October 1961. Then liberal, together with Slovak, elements began to increase their influence within the Party.[39]

Second, the economy ran into severe problems. Although a New Course had been adopted, little had changed. For agriculture it resulted in little more than a temporary pause in the collectivisation drive. Overall, the Czechoslovak economy encountered severe growth problems, as reflected in Table 6.1. The immediate cause of the 1962–3 economic crisis was the decision taken in 1962 drastically to reduce investments and focus on a restricted number of key targets, but the underlying problem was a failure to find non-Comecon markets for its machinery exports. The crisis resulted in the dramatic decision, taken in August 1962, to abandon the third five-year plan. The Party set up a commission, under Ota Šik, to consider economic reform, which, from mid-1964 onwards, was influenced by the works of the Polish economist Brus and formulated a stage-three type reform combining plan and market.[40] The main economic differences between the Czechoslovak and Hungarian proposals were the use of gross income (net of labour costs, an indicator used in the Hungarian agricultural sector and one that has been suggested for worker cooperatives in the West) rather than profit as the enterprise maximand,[41] the staggered nature of the reform implementation on a phased basis from 1965 onwards and the greater use of central targets. In 1967, for example, many 'informal indicators' were treated as targets.[42]

But the political context of economic reform was very different. Because the ghosts of the 1950s had not been laid, the Czechoslovak Party was not unified. Economic reform measures were introduced in a context where intellectual and cultural dissent, which had found no voice in the 1950s, made its presence strongly felt, notably at the Fourth Writers' Congress in June 1967 when writers, including the future Czechoslovak president, Václav Havel, attacked all forms of censorship. This process of ideological relaxation had begun four years earlier with the 'revolt of the intellectuals' in the Writers Unions in 1963, the year in which Franz Kafka was rehabilitated.[43] When the political crisis finally broke, another element had been added to the political ferment, Slovak nationalism; Slovak politicians felt that both government and Party were unduly dominated by Czechs.

Over the course of the October 1967 and the December 1967–January 1968 sessions of the Party's Central Committee the tide swung against Antonin Novotný; and, at the January session, he resigned in favour of Alexander Dubček, First Secretary of the Slovak Party. During the first weeks of the new leadership there were few signs of change. But from March onwards, censorship was abolished, the victims of the 1950s were rehabilitated, Novotný was obliged to resign from his remaining post as president (on 21 March, to be replaced by Ludvik Svoboda), and relations with the churches were regularised.

By this time, the reform had taken on an entirely different character and was no longer a party affair.[44] This change of character was confirmed on 10 April when the Party published its Action Programme that declared the objective of building 'a new profoundly democratic model of Czechoslovak socialism conforming to Czechoslovak conditions'. This rekindled the issue of national communist renewal that appeared to have been buried a decade previously with the execution of Nagy. More than that, talk of a Czechoslovak road to socialism revived memories of the years 1945–8.

Dubček's reform movement both looked back to the ideas of Nagy and forward to those of Gorbachev. Like Nagy, the revival of the National Front was a key element in his democratic programme. His Action Programme stated clearly that the 1945 decision to establish a National Front was irrevocable; but the post-1948 practice of using the National Front simply as a rubber stamp for the Party was no longer acceptable. All members of the National Front, parties and mass organisations, such as the trade unions, were to be given equal status. Recognising this led Dubček, like Nagy, to redefine the leading role of the Party. It had to earn its leading role, it could not be a monopolistic concentration of power: 'the Party's goal is not to become a universal "caretaker" of society ... its mission lies primarily in arousing socialist initiative ... in winning over all workers by persuasion and example'. Like all communist reformers, Dubček hoped to revive socialist enterprise through some system of enterprise or workers' council.

In other areas, Dubček looked forward to Gorbachev rather than back to Nagy. It is true that Nagy had denounced the Rákosi clique and the economic policies it had pursued, but he had not clearly linked economic problems to shortcomings in the socio-economic infrastructure. The challenge from the 'new class' of functionaries would disrupt all Gorbachev's attempts at economic reform and, in singling out this problem, Dubček was echoing some of Djilas' concerns. Thus in the Action Programme the maintenance of the old command system of management is derided and clearly linked to the deformations in the political system. 'Socialist democracy was not expanded in time, methods of revolutionary dictatorship deteriorated into bureaucracy and became an impediment to progress in all spheres of life.' Just as Marx had praised the positive role once played by the bourgeoisie while simultaneously calling for its overthrow, so Dubček suggested the historically 'positive' and 'progressive' role played by communist bureaucrats was now over.

Where Dubček clearly looked forward to Gorbachev was in his concern for the law and legality. Although under Novotný none of the purge victims were rehabilitated, the majority – at least those still alive – were quietly released from prison; reviews of their cases discovered that, while guilty as charged, their sentences had been excessive. Such servility on the part of the legal profession highlighted the all-encompassing power of the Ministry of the Interior and the security police. Dubček's Action Programme made clear that these pretensions were to be curbed and all citizens made equal before the law.[45]

As had been the case with Nagy, and would be the case for Gorbachev, Dubček's reformist caution was soon overtaken by popular demands for more radical change. In his report to the Central Committee Plenum held at the end of May, Dubček showed how he hoped to keep the bourgeoning Prague Spring within bounds. His chosen method was a combination of the rule of law and the National

Front. On the one hand, he was determined not to resort to the police methods used in the past, but on the other hand he wanted to restrict the activities of 'various organisations [acting] without a legal basis'. His solution was a Law on Assembly, to define clearly what sorts of public meetings could, or could not, take place, and which organisations could, or could not, publish propaganda material; the clear implication was that only organisations already in the National Front, or prepared to join the National Front, would be recognised by this law.[46]

However, all the time the demand was growing for political pluralism and for an end to any limitations on legitimate forms of political opposition. These culminated in the revival of the Social Democratic Party, outside the National Front, and a document entitled '2000 words', published on 27 June and signed by sixty intellectuals, which called for resistance to any future government retreat from reform. Although among the Czechoslovak reformers there were no serious proposals for the country to declare itself neutral and withdraw from the Warsaw Pact,[47] the echoes of Hungary 1956 created by demands for political pluralism were not lost on the Soviet Union.

Soviet warnings had started as early as a Warsaw Pact meeting in Dresden on 23 March. They were repeated in May, and again in June. Reacting to the '2000 words' and the formation of enterprise councils (due to take place in three stages from the beginning of July), the first secretaries of the sister parties, meeting in Warsaw on 15 July, sent a letter to the Czechoslovak leadership demanding the reassertion of Party control over the media and non-communist organisations. The demands were repeated at a meeting of Soviet and Czechoslovak leaders at Cierna nad Tisou between 29 July and 1 August. The Czechoslovaks repledged loyalty to the Warsaw Pact and Comecon and agreed that organisations outside the National Front, such as the Social Democratic Party, should be suppressed. Consistent with Dubček's National Front policy, that party's right to exist had already been questioned by the statement by the Ministry of the Interior in May to the effect that 'organised activity purporting to be that of a political party' would be considered illegal.[48]

This agreement appeared to solve the crisis. Nevertheless, on the night of 20–21 August, Soviet, Bulgarian, East German, Hungarian and Polish troops invaded. The Soviet leadership had already agreed that 'we will not surrender socialist Czechoslovakia' on 17 July and two days later preparations for 'extreme measures' began. Cierna nad Tisou was for them Dubček's last chance. In a series of phone calls made in the first half of August, Brezhnev kept repeating to Dubček that he was not implementing the agreement they had reached. He showed no signs of bringing the media and non-communist organisations under control, and none of the personnel changes advised by Moscow had been introduced. Dubček's insistence that these things must await the forthcoming 14th Party Congress was precisely what Brezhnev did not want to hear. The Soviet leadership had convinced itself that Dubček, by constantly promising to take measures to restore the authority of the National Front and then failing to deliver the goods, was deliberately deceiving them; the alternative explanation, that he was unable to enforce his will on the Czechoslovak leadership, was equally alarming from the Soviet point of view.

In a final telephone exchange Brezhnev asked Dubček on 13 August to make the requested personnel changes on the CPCz Presidium there and then, or the Soviet side 'would be forced to reassess the situation and take new, independent measures'. When Dubček responded 'Comrade Brezhnev, take those measures which your Politburo considers correct', Brezhnev responded in despair: 'if you answer like that Sasha [the short form of Alexander], I must tell you [the intimate *ty*] that you cannot be serious'. On 17 August the full Soviet Politburo backed Brezhnev's call for the 'extreme measures' to begin. The final choice of date for the invasion was to prevent the Czechoslovak Party holding its extraordinary 14th Congress, which was scheduled to pass new rules concerning party organisation and to endorse the radical reform of the political system envisaged in the Action Programme, institutionalising both internal democracy within the Communist Party and Dubček's vision of a revived National Front. As Brezhnev told fellow Politburo members on 17 August, reporting his final phone conversation, he believed 'there was a genuine danger that at the forthcoming congress the rightist wing would triumph'. Although the Congress took place in defiance in a factory in a workers' district of Prague – it called for a one-hour protest general strike and elected a new Central Committee in which anti-reformers lost their seats – Dubček's reforms were summarily cut short by the arrival of Warsaw Pact tanks.

The Soviets had hoped to be able to form a collaborationist Czechoslovak Revolutionary Workers' and Peasants' Government along Hungarian lines (the name itself echoed the official designation of Kádár's regime), but no such government emerged, and the Soviets were obliged to negotiate (between 23 and 26 August) with President Svoboda, who went to Moscow on his own initiative, and the Czechoslovak leaders they had arrested and removed to Poland and then the Ukraine in humiliation. At the conclusion of these negotiations, Dubček and his colleagues remained in office, but they surrendered to Moscow's demands. The government and Party reshuffle that followed Dubček's return actually favoured reformists; but on 6 September a Soviet emissary arrived to help the Dubček Government implement the Moscow agreements.

On 26 September the phrase 'the Brezhnev doctrine' entered the political vocabulary as Western writers responded to a *Pravda* article entitled 'Sovereignty and the International Obligations of Socialist Countries' calling for a 'class attitude' to the notion of sovereignty and noting that, 'a socialist state that is in a system of other states constituting a socialist commonwealth cannot be free of the common interests of that commonwealth'.[49] Subsequently, in October, Dubček promised in Moscow to replace the Party and state leaderships with people who 'stood firm on the position of Marxism–Leninism' and, on 16 October, in Prague, a treaty was signed 'temporarily' stationing Soviet troops in Czechoslovakia. The fact that Soviet troops had been 'temporarily' in Hungary since 1956 left no uncertainty as to their true purpose, nor the length of time they intended to stay. In November 1968, a new eight-member executive committee of the Party Presidium was appointed with only two reformist members.[50] The long process of 'normalisation' had begun.

The Czechoslovak communist reformers were unfortunate prisoners of history. What had made renewal possible in Hungary in 1956 was the unique international situation created by Khrushchev and Tito's joint interest in de-Stalinisation. There was no similar conjuncture in 1968. A decade earlier Dubček's reform might have succeeded, but Novotný had locked his country into a time warp. Ultimately, Dubček's ideas were more cautious than those of Nagy. While Nagy had spoken of a 'great retreat' and established a coalition government, Dubček's plans for the future envisaged the Communist Party retaining its hegemony within a revived National Front. Dubček's proposal, that the Communist Party should have an institutionalised majority within the National Front to guide the country during the transition from communist dictatorship to the moment when the population would be prepared democratically to vote communist, was remarkably similar to that later advanced by Gorbachev, and equally doomed.[51]

Khrushchev had been unwilling to countenance the revolutionary transformation of communism: Brezhnev would not even countenance the guided transformation of communism. The message of the 1960s was clear: whatever the economic problems, whatever the foreign policy ambitions or ideological trimmings, when it came to reform, only economic reform was possible.

7

NEO-STALINISM TRIUMPHANT

In the 'long decade' of the Brezhnev doctrine, between successful 'normalisation' in Czechoslovakia and the accession to power in the Soviet Union of Mikhail Gorbachev, neo-Stalinism ruled triumphant. The Eastern European regimes were politically stable, secure beneath the Soviet umbrella. International acceptance of the 'actually existing socialism' world system was confirmed by the Helsinki Final Act of 1975: and the economies appeared to be sound and to have staved off the 'oil-shock' from which the rest of the world had suffered. Growth rates in the 1966–70 plan period had been good. Those for 1971–5 were even better, although the considerable trade deficit run-up by the region with the West suggested caution.[1]

But then things started going wrong. An excess of ideological commitment and a failure to realise that acceptance by the Helsinki Final Act did not sanction the extension of 'actually existing socialism', even where it was, arguably, the outcome of domestic political forces, resulted in Soviet intervention in Afghanistan. International relations degenerated quickly into a second Cold War. More tellingly, from the end of the 1970s, the economies entered a period of decline. Growth slowed, living standards stagnated or fell, foreign indebtedness increased, and where it did not, severe administrative measures were taken to curb demand. The first 'oil shock' took its belated toll, and was compounded by the second. Furthermore, the seeds of future destruction began to emerge; the 1970s was the decade in which, to a greater or lesser extent, the opposition became a structural feature of Eastern European social life.[2]

Yet, despite common themes, the era of the Brezhnev doctrine was also one of increasing diversification along fissures begun in the 1960s.

And the trajectory of these fissures began to take on a Balkans–Central Europe dimension. Economic failure, common throughout the region, was openly acknowledged and addressed in Poland and Hungary, where high levels of foreign debt could neither be concealed nor camouflaged behind renewed ideological fervour. Likewise, indeed it was part of the same process of declining ideological commitment, in Central Europe (Czechoslovakia, Poland, Hungary and, to a lesser extent, the GDR), dissident voices became increasingly organised following the events of 1976 in Poland; and they gained further in strength at the end of the decade. As ideological alternatives grew, so the socialist economy declined; and in Hungary and Poland embryonic private sectors emerged offering new models of economic organisation.

THE BALKANS

Romania

Romania continued its combination of foreign policy independence abroad and nationalistic Stalinism at home throughout the long decade of the Brezhnev doctrine. Reformist vocabulary of, for example, workers' control in industry, masked an increase in the formal subjugation of national and local government to the Party. Ceauşescu's reaction to debt crisis at the end of the 1970s was to enforce belt-tightening and pay-off the debts.

Unlike the majority of Eastern Europe, where it is fair to say the Party withdrew to an extent from social and political life in the neo-Stalinist era, in Romania under Ceauşescu, Party involvement increased. Political institutions in Ceauşescu's Romania were subjected to much change and 'innovation', usually in the name of extending democracy. But the Workers' Councils of 1970, the numerous joint Party–State organs created in the early 1970s, the 'blending' of Party and State functions announced at the 1972 Party National Conference and even the introduction of multi-candidate elections to the parliament in 1974, all served to increase the power of the Party. Furthermore, by the second half of the 1970s, the Party was increasingly becoming synonymous with Ceauşescu and his family. Three of those promoted to the Permanent Bureau of the Party's Central Committee in 1977 were Ceauşescu's relatives, joining another brother-in-law already a member.

Such appointments coincided with what in different circumstances might have appeared to be worthy campaigns. The promotion of Elena Ceauşescu (the leader's wife) coincided with 'affirmative action' to recruit women to the Party, while the move to promote younger cadres coincided with the promotion of Nicu Ceauşescu, the couple's son. Ceauşescu's own personality cult was unrivalled. By the end of the 1970s he was secretary general of the Romanian Communist Party, president of the Republic and the Council of State, chairman of the Front of Socialist Unity and Democracy, chairman of the Supreme Council for Economic and Social Development, and much more. In addition, he was regarded as the most important living Marxist thinker and the personal embodiment of the national struggle for independence.

Ceauşescu's leadership continued unchallenged and he was duly re-elected general secretary at the 13th Party Congress in November 1984, although there were press reports in February 1983 (officially denied) of a failed coup attempt. Even in the mid-1980s, the Stalinist nature of his regime did not diminish. Romania lost United States' 'most favoured nation' status in 1983 after introducing a decree obliging all émigrés to repay the costs of their education; abortion was made illegal for women aged under 42 in 1984 in an attempt to stay the population decline; and, despite permitting a group of Catholics to go on a pilgrimage to Rome, attacks on religion increased in 1984. Symbolically, the Brezhnev era closed with the completion of a grandiose Stalinist project. On 26 May 1984, the Danube–Black Sea canal, abandoned in 1953 and begun again in 1973, was finally completed.[3]

Foreign policy was distinguished by two features. First, independence from Moscow was continued by maintaining relations with the Chinese, demurring to support the invasion of Afghanistan and signing a treaty with the Khmer Rouge. Although, after prolonged bargaining, Romania followed Czechoslovakia and signed a treaty of friendship and mutual aid with the Soviet Union on 7 July 1970, this treaty excluded any reference to a mutual obligation to rescue the socialist achievement. Second, the Ceauşescu regime took the somewhat surprising line of extending its growing trade ties with the developing world to the point of declaring itself a developing nation. Trade with the Less Developed Countries had increased over the 1970s as part of Romania's attempt to keep a distance from Comecon. The Less Developed Countries were seen as appropriate partners since their quality requirements were lower than those of the West and they could function as a source of raw materials. Although the policy ultimately backfired (a trade surplus in 1971–5 was replaced by a trade deficit in 1976–80) the declaration, agreed in 1972, that Romania was a 'socialist developing nation' proved a shrewd move, facilitating membership of the General Agreement on Trade and Tariffs (GATT) in 1971 and the International Monetary Fund (IMF) in 1972. From 1974 Romania also benefited from the developing countries' systems of preferences with bodies such as the European Community.[4]

In the economic sphere, recentralisation was followed by minor reform. In 1972 the central reorganisations of the 1960s came to an end and the industrial ministries regained much of the authority they had been forced to surrender. In 1974 foreign trade was recentralised. Following this, the Party endeavoured to reassert its own macroeconomic control via the Congress of Councils of the Working People in Industry, Construction and Transport, the 'workers' control teams' and the Legislative Chamber of People's Councils, all of which held national forums in 1976–7; a criterion of 'own effort' was also developed at the microeconomic level. The latter sought to differentiate, when evaluating bonuses, between targets unmet through circumstances beyond the enterprise's control and those that could be blamed on poor enterprise performance.

In 1978 the 'New Economic and Financial Mechanism' was introduced. Despite echoes of the Hungarian NEM in its name, it was far from radical. Quite the reverse. The emphasis was on conformity, and the number of centrally adopted material balances and physical plan indicators was increased. Enterprises received no greater autonomy; but, in the spirit of 'own effort' they were expected to be more self-reliant. Reflecting the new emphasis on self-financing, 'net output' replaced 'gross output' as the key economic indicator, imposing a genuine imperative on enterprises to reduce costs. At the same time, investment was controlled more centrally, there were moves towards greater enterprise concentration, and notional enterprise freedom to draw up long-term contracts was constrained by the duty to base them on the annual plan.

In agriculture, Romania was unique in retaining, although under a variety of names, the Stalinist institution of the machine and tractor station. Further, when the economic situation was at its worst, regulations concerning the private plots of collective farm members were tightened and the peasantry obliged to sell at state-determined prices. It did, however, adopt the practice of paying members an advance on their collective farm incomes from 1973. The 'systematisation' policy, of razing certain villages and concentrating the rural population in others, was adopted by the Party Conference in 1972 and became law in 1974, although it was not until 1988 that it was implemented seriously.[5]

By the mid-1970s it was becoming clear that economic performance was slowing. Annual growth of 3.9 per cent between 1975 and 1980 was lower than in the previous five-year period, and in 1980 it was negative. In late 1981, Romania followed Poland to become the second Comecon country to request rescheduling of its hard-currency foreign debt. The prospect of becoming dependent on Western financial institutions clearly frightened Ceauşescu. In 1982 he announced the goal of paying-off the foreign debt entirely by 1990, and in order to achieve this, bread rationing was introduced, and the use of refrigerators, vacuum cleaners and other household appliances banned.[6]

In Romania's more Stalinist than neo-Stalinist climate it is not surprising that no serious opposition movement emerged. This can be explained by the degree of political repression and control of everyday life, although traditions of Ottoman dissimulation and the absence in intellectual life of a Marxist tradition have been adduced as additional factors. The only *samizdat* that emerged in the period was ethnic Hungarian, a reaction to the policy of *de facto* Romanianisation that was taking place in the context of, on paper, not illiberal laws on national minorities. The only dissident who gained international renown was Paul Goma who, after expressing solidarity with the Charter 77 movement in Czechoslovakia (see later), was arrested and obliged to emigrate to Paris. Industrial unrest by miners took place in 1977, 1981 and 1983, and at the Braşov tractor works in 1978; a Free Trade Union of Romanian Workers existed briefly in 1979.[7]

Bulgaria

In line with its relatively greater degree of backwardness at the end of the war, the rate of economic growth of the Bulgarian economy only began to decline in the 1970s, and modifications to the economic model continued the spirit of concentration of the previous decade. The number of associations, which at the same time became, in theory, organs of economic management and the basic units of account, was reduced in 1970 from 120 to 64. Wholesale prices were rationalised in 1971 (postponed from 1969). But, in 1973, three new industrial ministries were created, reducing the independence of the associations.

In 1975, the focus switched from associations to 'combines' with an experimental reorganisation of the chemical industry. In 1978 Zhivkov praised the combine as a means of bypassing the intermediary level. But the greater independence enjoyed by the combines was restricted: eight binding directives remained. In agriculture, always a significant sector in the Bulgarian economy, concentration entailed creating Agri-Industrial complexes. Traditional collective farms were abolished by 1977. Yet, despite recentralisation, Bulgaria, unlike Romania, encouraged the household plot production of agricultural workers and introduced 'symbiotic' measures to support it, similar in essence to those employed in Hungary. In 1981 restrictions on household plots were lifted, and in 1982 a decree noted their role in developing marginal land.[8]

Further partial economic reform followed in 1978–9 and 1982. In 1979 the number of success indicators was cut again and ministries were instructed to stay out of the daily affairs of economic management. But no institutional measures were taken to ensure this. A relaxation of controls in the banking system followed in 1981–2, together with the Small and Medium-sized Enterprise Programme. The latter were simply semi-autonomous units within the large associations, not a movement towards private enterprise. The Bulgarian Industrial Association and the Mineral Bank were also formed at this time. The former offered consultancy services to the small and medium businesses, the latter provided funding. Although the phrase 'New Economic Mechanism' had been self-consciously adopted in 1979, actual change associated with it was rather insignificant.[9]

Bulgaria succeeded in avoiding major political crises during its forty or so years of existence as a socialist state, and no really significant dissident movement emerged in the 1970s. Only three or four minor manifestations of open opposition to the Bulgarian Communist Party are recorded: the most significant of these came early in 1978, in the wake of the Charter 77 movement in Czechoslovakia, when an anonymous group entitled ABD published a six-point manifesto 'Declaration 78'; but it did not develop a significant base. Most political developments were entirely orthodox. In 1971 Bulgaria passed a new constitution by which it technically became an advanced socialist state. The Party's role was also strengthened to become 'the leading force in society and the state'. The constitution also introduced a State Council in place of the Presidium of the National Assembly, and Zhivkov immediately took on its presidency, relinquishing the premiership.[10]

Bulgarian foreign policy continued to be the very antithesis of Romania's: continued loyalty to the Soviet Union. In the climate of détente, diplomatic relations with West Germany were established in 1973, and in 1975 Zhivkov visited the Vatican. By 1979 Bulgaria had a full complement of Catholic bishops for the first time since the 1940s. Tensions with Yugoslavia over Macedonia relaxed in the early 1970s, but then increased again, reaching a climax in 1979 when an aged Politburo member claimed in her memoirs that Yugoslavia had reneged on a wartime agreement over the future of Macedonia. The only case of minor divergence from Moscow was Zhivkov's willingness in September 1984 to pay a friendship visit to the Federal Republic of Germany at a time when the Soviet Union disapproved.

Culturally, Bulgaria experienced a renaissance under Liudmila Zhivkova, Zhivkov's daughter, who became an increasingly important figure in cultural affairs during the 1970s, finally becoming Minister of Culture. She died in July 1981 before her fortieth birthday, having successfully introduced a new spirit of adventure and a reassertion of Bulgarian national identity into cultural life, without introducing anti-Soviet elements. When cultural policy stultified again after her death, the ethnic issue re-emerged. In 1981 national identity was removed as an item on identity cards, and in 1984, the government initiated a campaign to complete the assimilation of the Turkish ethnic minority. Both Turkish names and Islamic rituals were attacked in the press.[11]

Albania

Albania continued its splendid isolation. In 1976 a new constitution was passed, which recognised the Party as the 'sole directing political power in state and society'. It further stated that private property had been abolished, that no religion was recognised by the state, that no individuals should pay taxes and, uniquely, that the first secretary of the Party was also Commander in Chief of the Armed Forces. Enver Hoxha remained in command for the entire period, dying in 1985. Politically he was unchallenged, save for a rumoured attempt by Mehmet Shehu and others to murder him in December 1981. Albania was invited to the Conference on Security and Co-operation in Europe in August 1975 but refused to participate. It was thus the only European country not to sign the Helsinki Final Act. Like Romania, its Stalinist cousin, it was not troubled by political dissent.[12]

Exaggerated Maoism informed economic policies in the early 1970s, and anti-peasant measures continued. Following the failed attempt of the late-1960s to abolish agricultural household plots altogether, their maximum size was reduced to 300 square metres in 1971; then, in 1981, the marketing of private produce was forbidden. In a form of decentralisation Maoist-style, the number of plan indicators was reduced in 1970, and numerous enterprises were placed under the jurisdiction of the local authorities rather than ministries. This was accompanied by a notional fostering of workers' control under the leadership of the enterprise Party organisation. But, by 1976, the move was back to centralisation. The chairman of the State Planning Commission was dismissed and executed, accused of striving 'to distort the principles of socialist planning... and set our economy on the road of revisionist self-management'. In the economic sphere, the constitution of 1976 further forbade all types of foreign investment, including the acceptance of foreign credits, and in September 1977 a number of decrees gave ministries rather than local authorities greater control over supply.[13]

In July 1978, following increased tension between China and Albania after the death of Mao in 1976, the downfall of the Gang of Four, and the rehabilitation of Teng Hsia-ping, not to mention the welcoming of Tito to China in 1977, China suspended its foreign aid. The Albanian economy went into decline. Per capita output had grown 4.2 per cent per year in 1971–5, well below the planned levels; but it plummeted to 0.5 per cent per year in 1976–80 and to a negative −0.1 per cent in 1981–5. Trade in the post-China era took place with the West, Yugoslavia and Romania; and was mostly in deficit, funded, despite the theoretical unconstitutionality of such activity, by borrowing in Western capital markets.[14]

Yugoslavia

Unlike the Comecon Balkan countries, Yugoslavia was not in a position to disguise its economic failings. Indeed, its history in the 1970s is that of economic failure that heightened regional tensions culminating in a debt crisis and the declaration of Martial Law in Kosovo. Central to the history of the period is the process by which the most radical economic reform in Eastern Europe – the only fourth-stage reform to function for any length of time – first disintegrated rapidly into inflation, overinvestment and debt; and then became impossibly enmeshed in the regional web of Yugoslav politics.

'Social ownership' Yugoslav-style quickly ran into the problem of a 'lack of clarity about the ownership of capital'.[15] Workers, the nominal owners of self-managed enterprises, demanded higher than justifiable pay rises; and managers, the *de facto* owners, readily agreed: it was not their capital that was at risk, borrowings could cover wage rises as well as investment projects. And capital was not seriously 'at risk' in any case, because the banking system was ultimately underwritten by republican governments, which were dominated by the Party and which would not let 'their' enterprises go bankrupt. The economic system was characterised by 'soft budget constraints', providing political rather than economic guarantees of financial discipline. Between 1965 and 1967, average real personal incomes grew by 24 per cent, while national income grew by just 11 per cent. Enterprise indebtedness meanwhile grew dramatically, and by the late 1960s the bulk of enterprise net income was going on debt service. By the middle of 1969 more than half the enterprises in Yugoslavia were unable to meet their financial commitments. By September 1975 business enterprises held unpaid bills totalling 273 billion dinars, but themselves owed 262 billion dinars to the banks; meanwhile a wave of strikes in 1971–2 was precipitated largely by unpaid wages as management struggled to meet outside commitments.[16]

To make matters worse, the large sums devoted to investment were put into projects of questionable worth. In 1972 the World Bank rejected 85 per cent of projects proposed by the Yugoslavs because of poor costing or grossly over-optimistic assessment of sales prospects on world markets. In the 1980s the Yugoslav Prime Minister admitted that half of Yugoslavia's foreign debt was invested in projects that turned out to be mistakes or was used for consumption, and others estimated that one-third of the total debt had been used to finance mistaken investments. Despite the market reform, investment strategy in Yugoslavia was depressingly similar to that in scarcely reformed Poland. As the British economic historian David Dyker noted:

> The reform had failed to establish the market principle in the sphere of fixed capital formation, and large-scale projects, bad ones and good ones alike, were in the post-reform period decided on by coteries of politicians, bankers and (sometimes) managers. ... Yet in 1969, out of a total number of 8955 enterprises unable to meet their financial obligations, only 109 went into liquidation. The fact is that no procedure had been set up to permit creditors to force firms into receivership.[17]

The 1965 reform had pinned high hopes on monetary policy, but by 1971–2 it had clearly failed. The money supply increased by 28 per cent in 1972 and by 36 per cent in 1973. In addition unemployment was rising – 300 000 in 1971, half a million in 1974 – and inequalities were widening. Furthermore, with the official flotation of the dinar in July 1973 and the greater availability of international credit after 1974, the relationship between importing financial capital and specific investment plans was almost totally lost, only exacerbating the problems cause by poor project assessment.[18]

As the economic situation became more acute, it became overlaid with regional issues. Croat nationalist sentiment, centred around the historic cultural association Matica Hrvatska, was able to latch on to economic issues and pursue a number of economically rather meaningless, yet symbolically very powerful arguments about the contribution of the various republics to the federal economy, more specifically to the Yugoslav balance of payments. The immediate political crisis was solved by a purge of the Croatian Party leadership in December 1971–January 1972 and, in the years that followed, Party discipline was re-established. The liberals (victors in the 1960s) were the chief victims of purges in 1972–3. A more restrictive law on the press was passed in 1972 as university autonomy was overridden in order to dismiss the Praxis philosophers from Belgrade University while at the same time Croatian nationalists were put on trial. In 1975, Praxis was silenced by persuading the printers not to publish it. Yet in both economic and political decentralisation, much of the spirit of the 1960s reforms remained. Constitutional changes hammered out in 1971 prior to the purge, confirmed in the constitution of 1974, continued these trends and, with them, the move towards regionalisation.[19]

The 1974 constitution established the collective Presidency, with its principle of rotation for president and vice president, increased the economic autonomy of workers' councils, further devolved powers from the federal to the republican level and codified a new system of income distribution between republics. It also, to the annoyance of elements in the Serbian leadership, gave the autonomous provinces (Vojvodina and Kosovo) greater independence from Belgrade, including powers of veto. Kardelj's Law on Associated Labour of 1976, which defined the Basic Organisation of Associated Labour and the Complex Organisation of Associated Labour and introduced a system of 'social agreements' between economic and social or political agents, further increased regional power. 'Social agreements' reintroduced political controls, but at a republican or sub-republican level. The powers of 'the centre' increased, but there were eight centres (six republics and two autonomous regions). Although the 1974 constitution enshrined the principle of a single Yugoslav market, regional autarchy increased. By the late 1970s only one-third of total turnover in goods and services in Yugoslavia involved crossing republican or provincial boundaries, and regionalism was further exacerbated by the extension of 'self-determination' to infrastructural and service sectors such as energy and transport, education, health, employment and cultural services.[20]

After the death of the system's principal architects – Kardelj died in 1979, Tito in 1980 – the contradictions not only continued but intensified. In 1981, the ethnic issue boiled over in Kosovo. For Serbian nationalists, Kosovo was 'the holy place of all Serbs' because it had formed the centre of the medieval Serbian Empire destroyed in 1389 by the Ottoman armies. Yet, since becoming an Autonomous Province in 1963, the Kosovo population and its administration had been Albanianised. Student demonstrations over the seemingly trivial issue of hostel living conditions in March escalated into demonstrations for the release of students and full republican status for Kosovo, and then turned into generalised revolt. Martial Law was finally declared in April.

Economic problems followed hard on the heels of these riots. In 1982, economic decline culminated in a debt-service crisis that was finally solved only by means of a massive rescheduling package with the IMF. This was announced in April 1983, and, thereafter, production stagnated and living standards fell steadily; by 1984 a cumulated reduction of 30 per cent in living standards had been absorbed by the Yugoslav people. Initially the self-management system proved capable of absorbing this without too much political dislocation. However, ten years of patience would be exhausted by the end of the decade.[21]

CENTRAL EUROPE

Czechoslovakia

'Normalisation' in Czechoslovakia took two years. It was a painful and dispiriting process, symbolised by the suicide by burning – inspired by the actions of Buddhist monks in Vietnam – of Jan Palach on 16 January 1969 in Wenceslas Square. Between May 1969 and June 1970 all former reformists were removed from the Central Committee and important Party and public office. Dubček's fall began earlier. On 17 April 1969 he was replaced by Gustáv Husák as first secretary of the Party, a move engineered by his former supporters rather than the old hardliners. In December 1969 he was appointed ambassador to Turkey; in January 1970 he was expelled from the Central Committee; in May 1970 he was withdrawn from Turkey; and in June 1970 he was finally expelled from the Party, becoming a lowly official in the State Forestry Administration in Bratislava.

Despite this, he was for many a somewhat compromised figure. As a member of the Presidium until September 1969 and the chairman of Parliament until October 1969, he was directly implicated in the dismissal of Šik from the Central Committee and the expulsion from the Party of the leading reformer František Kriegel; he was also involved in passing the emergency laws of 22 August 1969 that were declared after demonstrations on the first anniversary of the invasion and used as the legal basis for the mass dismissals and persecutions in the country in the following years. Full-scale purges began in January 1970 with an exchange of Party membership cards organised by Miloš Jakeš, then head of the Control and Auditing Commission of the Central Committee. Some 28 per cent of the membership of 1 January 1968 was refused a new card or resigned of their own accord. Some two thousand journalists, every second member of the Union of Czechoslovak Journalists, lost their jobs, as did 900 professors and 1200 scholars in the Academy of Sciences; some 130 000 individuals emigrated.

On 6 May 1970 Czechoslovakia and the Soviet Union signed a friendship treaty confirming that the defence of socialist achievements was a joint international duty of socialist countries and, finally, in December 1970, the Plenum of the Central Committee issued *The Lesson Drawn from the Crisis Development in the Party and Society after the 13th Congress of the CPCz*, which gave, in Brezhnev's words, an 'in-depth Marxist–Leninist analysis' of the events in Czechoslovakia since 1966, fully reflecting the Soviet version of events, including Czechoslovakia's appeal for assistance in the face of possible counter-revolution. Not all the forces behind the Czechoslovak reform movement were losers however. Some of the demands of the Slovak lobby were met on 1 January 1969 when Slovakia became a republic of equal status with the Czech lands within a federal republic.[22]

At first it seemed as if the economic reform would be left untouched, but everything changed after the fall of Dubček. In May 1969 retail prices were increased and then frozen. The proposed Enterprise Law was shelved. In the second half of the year preparations for the 1970 plan reintroduced compulsory indicators, although in 1970 they were only 'agreements', becoming imposed targets in 1971. Physical balances and the central allocation of 450 basic products were reintroduced in 1972. Although certain profit-related incentive funds remained, their size was reduced, with taxation increasingly non-parametric. Direct planning of foreign trade was also reintroduced, although the number of enterprises allowed to engage in foreign trade increased in the 1970s. Recentralisation did not return completely to the *status quo ante*, but, although never officially revoked, the reform of the 1960s was dead by 1972.[23]

As the economy deteriorated at the end of the decade, experiments were started, in 1978, which led to two sets of 'complex provisions' published in 1980 and 1984, which resembled very closely documents published in the Soviet Union in 1979 and 1983. These focused on issues of detail and had a minimal impact. 'Continuous updating' of wholesale prices introduced some flexibility in pricing, but the wage regulation reform proved too complex, and changes in foreign trade too small, to have any effect. Formal institutions of self-management were introduced, but they did not infringe the principle of one-man management. By 1980–1 the economy was again in trouble, with annual growth rates for national income of −0.1 and 0.2 per cent respectively. More important was the decline of the Czechoslovak economy relative to comparable European economies. In 1960 Czechoslovak per capita GNP had been 90 per cent that of Austria; by 1985, it had dropped to 60 per cent of the Austrian level.[24]

Having, like Kádár before him in Hungary, de-politicised the population by harsh repression of the opposition, Husák sought to increase standards of living, although without risking the political uncertainty of introducing radical economic reform. The existing economic order was rejigged to favour private consumption (which increased by 36.5 per cent between 1970 and 1978) at the expense of investment, military expenditure and foreign aid to Vietnam and Cuba. Party activity at a local level ended almost entirely. A confidential report in early 1972 revealed that a third of the membership had not engaged in any Party activity in the preceding year. Membership figures, on the other hand, remained high because of the prerequisite of Party membership for career advancement. At the level of formal politics, Husák added Head of State to his other posts in 1975, and at the end of the period took over the role of supreme defender of the faith for the Soviet Union, leading campaigns within the Warsaw Pact criticising Hungary for joining the IMF in 1982 and being too enthusiastic about détente, and the GDR for pursuing its special interests with the Federal Republic.[25]

Opposition in Czechoslovakia did not begin in 1977, but it was with the formation of Charter 77 that the opposition movement gained worldwide prestige, although it could never claim to be a mass movement. Immediately after the invasion, small groups of disenchanted socialists and communists had formed opposition groups, but their readerships were arrested and sentenced to long prison terms. Between 1972 and 1975 opposition took the form of individual actions, although it was in these years that the publication of *samizdat* literature by Ludvik Vaculík and Václav Havel began. The various strands of the opposition came together over the arrest in March 1976 of the Plastic People of the Universe rock band, and in December 1976 the idea for creating the 'Citizens' Initiative Charter 77' was born. The founding declaration was dated 1 January 1977. The Charter was not a political group, and had no such aspirations. Its limited goal was that of 'resisting the lie', of not remaining silent. The initial 240 signatories to the Charter increased to 1200 by the mid-1980s.[26]

The government's immediate response to the Charter only increased its profile. Rather than simply arresting the leaders, it ran a media campaign against them, culminating in an 'Anti-Charter' that party members and others in authority were pressured to sign. The chartists were never left alone by the regime. Between 1977 and the summer of 1980, 61 chartists were sentenced to imprisonment and at least another 108 were arrested for longer or shorter periods. The strength of the movement was weakened somewhat by the mid-1980s after over 300 chartists, including Zdeněk Mlynář, a leading member of the Dubček team, had been obliged to emigrate. In its first ten years of activity, the Charter published 350 letters, communiqués and analyses on a wide range of subjects.[27]

East Germany

Politics in the GDR in the long decade of the 1970s continued to be defined by its relation to the German Federal Republic; but the nature of the relationship changed. Ulbricht had not been at home with policies of détente and had been disappointed when, in August 1970, the Soviet Union and the Federal Republic signed the Moscow Treaty pledging non-aggression and confirming the Oder–Neisse line as Poland's western border. For him it was the writing on the wall. In May 1971, he was replaced as first secretary by Erich Honecker who was more of a pragmatist. At the 8th Party Congress in June 1971 Honecker presented his reformulation of foreign policy that was altogether more in line with détente: the objective of reuniting Germany under a socialist government was dropped and replaced by *Abgrenzung* – separate development. As under Ulbricht, the GDR was seen as a separate socialist German state, but implicit reference to future unification was dropped. The GDR was not an alternative socialist state for the whole of Germany, but a separate state, which happened to be socialist, with, as ideologists quickly manufactured, a wholly separate historical experience. In 1974 the constitution was duly amended. The GDR became a 'socialist state of workers and peasants' rather than the 'socialist state of the German nation' it had been since the 1968 constitution.

The political fruits of this change in policy were the Four Power Agreement on Berlin (agreed in September 1971, effective June 1972) and the Basic Treaty with the Federal Republic (agreed December 1972, effective June 1973). The first of these regularised the status of Berlin, protecting trade and travel between the former capital and West Germany, while insisting that West Berlin, unlike East Berlin, enjoyed a special status. In the Basic Treaty the two Germanies pledged to recognise one another's sovereignty; and in September 1973 both countries joined the UN, achieving final international recognition for the GDR. Whereas 19 countries had recognised the GDR between 1969 and 1972, 68 nations did so in the year following the signing of the Basic Treaty, and the GDR capped the process by establishing diplomatic relations with the United States in April 1974. This represented a considerable diplomatic success for Honecker, although he did not succeed in establishing diplomatic relations as such with the Federal Republic, and the free flow of traffic from West Germany to West Berlin was guaranteed by the Soviet Union rather the GDR.[28]

Honecker's 1971 programme also specified the main task of domestic policy, namely economic progress through state planning. Economic policy continued with variations on the 'association' theme, with a switch towards the *Kombinat* rather than the VVB, the distinguishing feature being the merger within the *Kombinat* of major suppliers and customers, so achieving an unusual degree of vertical integration. The role of the *Kombinat* was re-emphasised in 1979–80 when, in the face of economic crisis, a new emphasis was placed on 'modernisation' and the bringing of experts into the economic system. The number of *Kombinats* increased from 45 in 1975 to 316 ten years later. The planning methodology remained traditional, however, with around 4540 individual balances in effect in 1982.[29]

The 1970s also witnessed the nationalisation of much of the private and all of the semi-private sectors of the economy, further reducing the significance of the market. Agreed at the Party Central Committee Plenum of December 1970, mass nationalisations followed in the spring of 1972. The GDR had uniquely preserved a large private sector outside agriculture, partly a result of the uncertain future of the country until the mid-1950s. There had been no general nationalisation in the Stalinist period, although the property of those compromised under Nazism had been brought into the state sector. The official view had been that the superiority of national ownership would be revealed through competition. Even the formal foundation of the GDR had only a small effect on the size of the private sector.

The first socialist offensive against the sector began in 1952, but ended six months later with the death of Stalin. Between 1958 and 1960, many private factories had become 'semi-state-owned', which is to say that the state participated in company capital for which it shared a proportion of profits, but the private owner accounted for the residual risk, and remained managing director. In 1971 private and semi-state enterprises employed 1.5 per cent of the industrial work force, and, although they had been performing remarkably well, were regarded in the Brezhnev decade as an anachronism. A further unique feature of the GDR economy was its organisation of agriculture. In the 1970s and 1980s, in two waves, collective farms were reclassified on a product-group basis. The crop producing sides of collective farms were merged with Machine and Tractor Stations to form specialist crop-producing collectives, while separate farms specialising in animal husbandry were developed out of the collective farms' livestock sectors. As elsewhere in Eastern Europe, private plot production was encouraged after 1979.[30]

The East German economy was widely regarded as having been the most successful in Eastern Europe, but, behind the impressive aggregate output figures, the economy was ailing and becoming increasingly dependent on its special relationship with the Federal Republic. From 1975 onwards a trade deficit was recorded with the Soviet Union; and by 1981 net indebtedness to the West had reached $11.66 billion (from $6.6 billion in 1977), second only to Poland among Comecon states.

In 1982, as in other countries in the region, the crisis became particularly acute: retail trade turnover grew by 1 per cent rather than the planned 3.7 per cent, and the turnover of industrial goods fell by 0.1 per cent. Although standards of living in the GDR had been increasing relative to those in the West (from 30 per cent in 1960 to 50 per cent in 1975 and 55 per cent in 1982), by 1985 they had started to decline again, falling to 50 per cent. Furthermore, although in Comecon markets the GDR was known for its industrial and especially engineering products, these scarcely figured in its trade with the West. Capital goods exports declined as a percentage of all exports from 27.5 per cent in 1976–80 to 15.9 per cent in 1983, and mineral oil products became the main hard-currency earner.

The crisis of the early 1980s was alleviated by major credits in 1983 and 1984, worth approximately DM 1 billion each, backed by the West German government. The GDR also gained considerable benefits from 'inner German' trade. First, by virtue of this trade it gained access to the entire European Community and avoided completely all of its tariffs and quotas. Second, the terms of the trade agreement between the two Germanies effectively allowed interest-free credit on its trade deficit until the annual settlement of balances. In addition, the GDR benefited from road and toll charges for transit across its territory, which, together with visa charges and the like, totalled, in 1982, an estimated DM 2.18 billion.

When Poland entered its Solidarity crisis (see later), Honecker responded by tightening the political line generally, renewing demands for recognition by West Germany of East German citizenship, and increasing the amount of compulsory currency conversion for visitors to the GDR. But economic weakness enforced the renewal of inter-German détente, and by the mid-1980s the GDR was displaying an unusual element of foreign policy disloyalty to the Soviet Union. The issue was that of Honecker visiting the Federal Republic: although the GDR finally gave in (the visit took place in the September of 1987 rather than 1984), a more or less open quarrel over the issue persisted between the GDR and the Soviet Union from the spring to the autumn of 1984.

The GDR of the long decade of the Brezhnev doctrine also developed its dissidents. Perhaps the most celebrated of these was the Marxist Rudolf Bahro whose *The Alternative in Eastern Europe*, for which he was sentenced to eight years imprisonment, was published in excerpts in *Der Spiegel* in August 1977. However, the autonomous peace and ecological groups, and the growing voice of the Evangelical Church may have been of longer-term significance. As elsewhere in the region, groups that had been rather isolated in the 1970s had become almost an integral part of social life by the early 1980s. In 1978, church, parents' and autonomous peace groups objected to the introduction of compulsory theoretical and practical pre-military training for 14–16-year-olds. In 1982, a conference of the Evangelical Church Directorates condemned nuclear weapons as a moral evil; the, by then annual, Dresden Peace Forum was particularly well-attended; and a 'Berlin Appeal' was lunched by Havemann and Rainer Eppelmann calling for the withdrawal of all occupation troops from the GDR and the Federal Republic and the conclusion of a peace treaty. By 1986, it was estimated that about 200 peace groups, with a few thousand members, existed in the GDR. Generally the regime adopted 'repressive tolerance' towards its intellectuals in the 1970s and early 1980s. Critical writers were given a limited space – in the form of restricted publication runs in the GDR or permission to publish in the West – the precise terrain of which was forever contested.[31]

Hungary

Hungarian history between 'normalisation' and Gorbachev continued to be dominated by matters economic. In the first half of the period, economic reform and liberalism came increasingly under attack; in the second, it was gradually acknowledged that the search for radical economic reform should be renewed. There was no change in the political leadership, and no radical change in overall policy, although there were periods of greater and lesser tolerance of dissent. The new constitution in 1972 served merely to document belatedly the break with Hungary's Stalinist past and to record officially the transition to the status of socialist state. As economic reform was rediscovered the dissident voice became increasingly an integral part of the political scene.

It had always been intended that there would be a second stage to the New Economic Mechanism, addressing the need to create some sort of capital market, break up monopolies and make enterprises more sensitive to world market prices. But, in the spirit of normalisation, such plans were shelved and the NEM itself came under attack. Recentralisers had gained clear supremacy by the Central Committee session of November 1972, which issued a statement noting that the reform 'in places ... was not operating in the desired direction'. Subsequently, in 1973, 'privileged' enterprises were created (accounting for 64.6 per cent of socialist industry's fixed capital, 50 per cent of total production and 60 per cent of exports), for which the full rigours of market discipline no longer applied.

In the following months all prominent pro-reformers (including Nyers, in 1974) were removed from positions of influence. At the same time, András Hegedűs, Gerő's prime minister in 1956 turned head of the Sociological Research Group, was expelled from the Party, together with members of the 'Budapest school' of philosophy; Miklós Haraszti was put on trial for his book *Worker in a Workers State*; and Iván Szelényi was forced into exile for his manuscript written with György Konrád, which became *Intellectuals on the Road to Class Power.* Although the attack on the NEM was primarily a political one, the Hungarian economy did undergo an investment crisis in 1970–1, and it experienced unprecedented rates of labour mobility. Administrative measures were introduced to address both problems in 1974.

The 11th Party Congress of March 1975, which used the vocabulary of an earlier era, marked the culmination of recentralisation. Three years later, as hardliners fell from the Central Committee, economic policy changed again. A crisis in the small-scale agriculture sector, caused by peasants slaughtering livestock because of reduced purchase prices, threatened to jeopardise Hungary's whole foreign trade policy that, because of successful collectivisation, was by this time predicated on agricultural near self-sufficiency.[32]

Macroeconomic policies initiated in 1978 aimed at reducing domestic consumption, while the economy was restructured prior to renewed growth in 1982–3. In the event, a severe liquidity crisis in 1981–2 (which resulted in Hungary joining the IMF and the World Bank) meant that renewed growth was postponed to the 13th Congress of 1985. The reforms of 1978 and 1982 focused not so much on decentralisation as on the stimulation of restraint and financial realism (price reform in 1980, a single exchange rate in 1981 and the extension of foreign trade rights) and institutional reform (the break up of 'trusts', the creation of a single Ministry of Industry and new forms of small business). Reform discussion centred on the notion of the socialist holding company that would take over property rights, then held by the ministries, and place them on a commercial footing. In this climate, the opposition flourished. Leading dissident János Kis even described 1980–1 as the 'best years of the democratic opposition'. In 1979 the opposition moved from writing and statement signing to practical activities when Ottilia Solt and others established the Poor Support Fund (SZETA). By the end of 1981 it had moved from producing occasional *samizdat* materials, to publishing a regular periodical, *Beszélő*.

Although the 1981 calls for 'holding company' reform fell on deaf ears, measures taken between 1983 and 1985 resulted in the creation of what was effectively a Yugoslav-style fourth stage of economic reform. In 1982–3 enterprises were permitted to issue bonds, creating the beginnings of a capital market. In 1983 enterprise directorships were opened up to competitive tender, in 1984 bankruptcy regulations were applied with somewhat greater rigour and, in 1985, enterprises gained almost total autonomy from the centre. All enterprises, outside a new non-profit sector, were obliged to transform themselves into one of two types: those run by an enterprise council, and those run by an elected leadership. And in both cases, the majority of the rights stemming from ownership of state property passed formally to the enterprise itself rather than its controlling ministry.

Concurrently, radical developments were taking place in the political sphere. Multi-candidate elections had been possible since 1967: in 1983, they were made mandatory. In the 1985 elections, the Patriotic People's Front, unsurprisingly, successfully prevented prominent dissidents such as László Rajk (son of the Rajk executed in 1949) and Gáspár Miklós Tamás from contesting. Nevertheless, some eminent politicians were defeated (such as Jenő Fock, prime minister from 1967 to 1975), and a number of genuinely independent deputies elected, such as Zoltán Király. In 1983 Hungary also created a body unique in the Warsaw Pact countries, a Constitutional Law Council whose primary purpose was to monitor possible violations of the constitution. In addition, Kádár made foreign policy overtures to the West.

Yet, pressure on dissidents increased in 1983. Rajk's *samizdat* 'boutique' was closed down in May 1983, the editor of *Mozgó Világ*, a legitimate journal with a radical tradition, was sacked, and in September a law was passed setting the maximum penalty for illegal publishing at a fine of 10 000 forints. Despite relatively good, short-term economic results in 1984 and the optimistic tone of the 13th Party Congress in 1985, the state sector of the economy was in decline. (It contributed 65.2 per cent of national income in 1985, compared with 73.3 per cent ten years earlier.) In addition, state enterprises were increasingly dependent on subsidies, and the structure of foreign trade (an inability to export manufactured goods to the West) remained constant. Foreign convertible currency debt continued to rise alarmingly, from 33 per cent of GDP in 1975 to 38.7 per cent in 1978 and 42.2 per cent in 1984.

On the other hand, the private, or non-socialist (that is neither state nor traditional cooperative) sector that had been made possible by reforms in 1982 grew rapidly. Some 600 Small Cooperatives and 30 000 Work Partnerships existed by 1985. The most common form (over 20 000) was the Enterprise Economic Work Partnership (EEWP), however, and this illustrates an important feature of Hungary's 'private sector' in the 1980s: its incorporation within the socialist economy. The EEWPs were a schizophrenic creation by which a group of workers undertook, in their normal place of work but outside normal working hours, to do the same jobs they normally did, but on a subcontracting, profit-maximising, work-team basis rather than in fulfilment of an employment contract. Use of EEWPs increased both enterprise output and employee income; but at the expense of institutionalising what was common knowledge: productivity in the socialist sector was risibly low because employees conserved effort for after-hours work. Dynamism was generated on the basis of encouraging private endeavour and condoning cynicism towards socialist sector employment.[33]

POLAND'S CRISIS

Hungary in 1956 represented both the economic crisis of classical Stalinism and the birth of what would later be known as the Brezhnev doctrine. The Czechoslovak crisis of 1968 confirmed the doctrine and saw it formalised; it was less clearly an economic crisis, although it was in part a critique of the economics of neo-Stalinism. The Polish crises of the decade of the Brezhnev doctrine represented the beginnings of the crisis of neo-Stalinism itself.

Poland was the Achilles' heel of neo-Stalinism. Its succession of political crises, each precipitated by economic failure, was the consequence of its atypical reformism in the 1950s. Poland had not collectivised agriculture. Although this certainly protected the peasantry from the injustices experienced by their counterparts in the region, its economic consequences were negative rather than positive. Private agriculture was essentially alien to the neo-Stalinist economic system, so Polish agriculture inevitably remained locked in small-scale peasant production. As British anthropologist Christopher Hann has noted: 'The main problem in Poland in the 1970s was that the emergence of a robust, new, entrepreneurial class [of peasant] remained precluded by the official ideology.'[34]

Polish agriculture was locked in expensive, small-scale production, and peasants could be persuaded to increase production only by increasing the prices they received for agricultural products. This required raising either state subsidies or consumer prices. Economic reform dictated cutting subsidies; but every time this was done, industrial workers went on strike, a political crisis ensued and price increases were withdrawn. If the long-term non-viability of the neo-Stalinist economic system became apparent in Poland first, it was because the system had not been fully implemented in the first place. Yet, only at the third playing were wide-reaching political demands added to economic grievances.

The Baltic Crisis

The 1970 events are usually referred to as the 'Baltic crisis', although they extended beyond the Baltic ports. On Saturday 12 December 1970 the government announced food price increases averaging about 30 per cent. Demonstrations beginning in the Gdańsk Lenin shipyard on Monday were followed by demonstrations and clashes with the police in the other Baltic cities the next day, the use of tanks by Thursday, strikes in Warsaw on Friday and the call for a general strike on the following Monday. Over the weekend of 19–20 December the Central Committee met, removed Gomułka from power and replaced him by Edward Gierek, who announced concessions (new bonus schemes, new allowances for low-income workers) and a promise not to raise prices further for two years. This was not enough. The strikers wanted the increases withdrawn. Strikes in the Baltic, at the Ursus tractor factory in Warsaw and in textile factories in Łodz continued through January and into February, and in Gdańsk and Szczecin the strike committees were transformed into workers' committees, exerting an influence throughout the Baltic region and raising new, more political, demands for press and trade union independence. Finally, on 15 February, after securing a special loan from the Soviet Union, Gierek announced that prices would be frozen for two years and fixed at the old, pre-December levels.[35]

The cornerstone of Gierek's solution was to borrow heavily from the West and gamble on imported Western technology to both stimulate the Polish economy and produce goods that could be sold in the West in order to repay the loans. A Committee for Modernising the Economic System and the State was appointed in 1971; its report was accepted by the 6th Congress of the Party in 1972; and on 1 January 1973 the reform came into effect. Reform was confined to the 'association' level, the so-called WOGs, which were increased in number from 27 in 1973 to 125 in 1975; it was thus a second-stage type reform. Never radical in conception, between 1978–80 the reform faded away. Its half-hearted nature was typified by a producer price revision that was introduced in the WOGs only at first, and even then only applied to new products. Investment decisions for all but replacement and modernisation remained wholly under the control of the central authorities. Foreign trade rights were granted to a number of larger enterprises, however.[36]

Nevertheless, in the early 1970s, developments seemed positive. In agriculture Gierek abolished the system of compulsory purchases that the Gomułka regime had retained despite uncollectivised agriculture. He also introduced measures that singled out for government credits and subsidies 'specialist' farmers who contracted to sell to the state, and granted pensions to peasants who transferred their land to the state to encourage the gradual increase of the state's assets. Other measures to help the peasants followed thereafter; these included a lifting of the ban on the sale of agricultural machinery to private farmers, a lifting of the ban on the sale of state land to private farmers and, ultimately, in 1977 the granting of pension and national insurance rights to all private farmers. At the same time, the Party was substantially reorganised in an attempt to increase the degree of working-class participation within it. And, with the help of foreign loans, Polish factories were modernised and standards of living rose markedly, by a greater degree than elsewhere in Eastern Europe.

However, by 1975, it was becoming clear that the gamble on Western credits was not working. Foreign indebtedness continued to increase, when in theory repayment should have begun, and despite some modernisation, the structure of exports to the West remained the same. In agriculture, despite considerable increases in output as prices to producers were increased, production did not meet consumer demand and agricultural imports increased. Worse, from 1975 onwards the United States rather than the Soviet Union became a major agricultural supplier – for hard currency. By 1976, subsidies on food prices to the consumer amounted to 12 per cent of Poland's GDP.[37]

Meanwhile, Gierek sought to confirm the regime's orthodoxy by amending the constitution in February 1976 to pronounce Poland a socialist state, confirm the leading role of the Party and strengthen 'friendship and cooperation with the USSR and other socialist states'. This wording was on the milder end of the continuum of commitments to obeisance to the Soviet Union in Eastern European constitutions, but formal reference to both the leading role of the Party and friendship to the Soviet Union were new and far from popular. The conflict generated by this constitutional change – an estimated 40 000 took part in protest activities – was sufficient for the demise of the independent Catholic group (Znak) in parliament.

Events in the summer of 1976 followed the same pattern as those in 1970: the same issue, the same working-class response, and the same climbdown by the regime. Price increases were announced on 24 June 1976: by 60 per cent. The leadership had had the sense to warn the population that price increases were imminent, but gave no indication how large they would be. The next day, three days before the twentieth anniversary of the Poznan rising of 1956, mass demonstrations and strikes took place in Radom, the Ursus tractor factory near Warsaw, the Baltic ports and elsewhere throughout the country. Unlike Gomułka, Gierek gave in at once, following up with arrests and dismissals of the militant working class, which lasted into October. These aggressive tactics succeeded in uniting the students and the intelligentsia with the workers and, after a number of uncoordinated protests, the Committee for the Defence of Workers (KOR) was formed in Warsaw in September. The church, too, called for the release of workers who had been arrested. The strength of the opposition was such that initiative passed away from the Party in November–December, and a campaign was underway for a full parliamentary inquiry into police brutality during and after the June events. The circle had still not been squared, indebtedness was increasing, and opposition was taking on a semi-organised structure.[38]

The Solidarity Crisis and Martial Law

In 1980, the government tried to slip in price increases unnoticed. The increase of 1 July 1980 took the form of transferring to 'commercial' (more expensive) status many of the better cuts of meat, and was announced by a minor official. If the government's tactics were new, the reaction of the population was not. Strikes broke out at Ursus and elsewhere, but they were initially settled piecemeal in the form of higher salary awards. The leadership attempted to divide and rule: managers of important plants were flown to Warsaw and instructed by the Central Committee to buy 'social peace', at any price if need be. It might have worked had not KOR, a product of the 1976 crisis, acted as a clearinghouse for information on settlements. On 14 August the workers at the Lenin Shipyards at Gdańsk went on strike under the leadership of Lech Wałęsa, a former worker who had been sacked. Faced with generous concessions by management, Wałęsa all but settled; then, sensing that he had misjudged the workers, he called for a solidarity strike and an occupation of the factory.

Strike committees and inter-factory strike committees were organised and soon the delegates of the Gdańsk committee had produced a twenty-one point charter, the first two points being the right to independent trade unions and the right to strike. By August 19 Szczecin was brought to a standstill, and the next day contact was made with intellectuals such as Tadeusz Mazowiecki and Bronisław Geremek, who offered to act as expert advisors, and a statement of intellectual support had been published. On 24 August Gierek announced a government reshuffle and promised economic reforms. But, in the light of the government's barely legal policy of arresting, releasing and then rearresting prominent KOR leaders such as Kuroń and Michnik every 48 hours, so as to avoid having formally to prosecute them, these seemed very insignificant concessions.

Negotiations began in earnest on 26 August, the central issue being that of free trade unions, although the word 'free' was amended to 'independent and self-governing', hence self-governing trade union Solidarity – *NSZZ Solidarność*. This the government and the workers were ready to accept; but the government insisted on two crucial additional clauses, one recognising collective property and the other recognising both the leading role of the Party and supporting the established system of international alliances. The agreement, signed on Sunday, 31 August 1980, although radical and a challenge to the system, thus fell within the accepted parameters of the Brezhnev doctrine. The touchstone of orthodoxy, the leading role of the Party was still in place.[39]

Less than a week later Gierek was replaced by Stanisław Kania after suffering a genuine, though convenient, heart attack. But the trouble was not over; and it became clear that the government had no intention of relinquishing in fact the authority it had signed away in theory.

First, there was ambiguity in the agreement over whether it applied merely to Gdańsk or the whole country. The government chose the former interpretation – and precipitated three weeks of strikes as region after region acted to gain the rights won in the Gdańsk Charter. Second, there was a struggle to get Solidarity officially recognised, which only ended in November after the threat of a national strike. Next, Solidarity and its advisors were subjected to semi-legal harassment, to which Solidarity responded with threatened or actual strikes. In the emerging climate of distrust, genuine concessions, such as authorising the publishing of the independent weekly paper *Solidarność* went by scarcely noticed, and Solidarity leaders who were willing to compromise such as Wałęsa lost their authority with the rank and file.

By early 1981 the government appeared to have accepted the need for compromise with Solidarity. On 9 February General Wojciech Jaruzelski was appointed prime minister, with the liberal Mieczysław Rakowski as deputy charged with negotiating with the unions. Moves towards compromise were frustrated when the local police broke up a Solidarity meeting in Bydgoszcz in March 1981; this raised the tension once again, and a four hour general warning strike was held on Friday 27 March. However, Solidarity was split over how to respond and Wałęsa cancelled the planned general strike. Moderates within both the Party and Solidarity appeared to have won. The Party's first Extraordinary Congress, held in July 1981 was a milestone in this process. The Central Committee was almost entirely replaced: only four of the fifteen Politburo members remained in office. Further, the congress itself had been preceded by a massive reform by which half the regional heads and more than half the plant secretaries had been replaced.

By the autumn of 1981, compromise was less certain. Solidarity had undergone a complex change by the summer of 1981, and the cautious blue collar, working-class leaders, schooled in the struggles of the 1970s, found themselves supplanted in the process of elections to Solidarity's First Congress by articulate and radicalised white-collar workers who were less attuned to the political consequences of the path they were adopting. Elections among the regional level activists of Solidarity saw a dramatic change of personnel, having an inevitable impact on the composition of delegates to the First Congress held in the autumn. Thus when the First Congress met for six days at the end of September and a further twelve days in October, Solidarity had evolved into a self-proclaimed 'social movement' with a clearly defined political programme calling for the restructuring of the state;

clearly Solidarity was no longer willing to acknowledge the Party's leading role, and to rub home the point it called for a referendum to be held calling for free elections. Solidarity was challenging for state power.

This had two consequences. First, a gap opened up between the regional leadership and the rank and file. The regional leaders wanted large-scale strikes with a clear political agenda, condemning as 'wild cat' factory level disputes called by blue-collar leaders. By the end of November national strike calls were going unheeded. The second consequence of Solidarity's political agenda was that the state responded politically. In October, just a week after the congress, Kania was removed and Jaruzelski took over as Party leader, combining the job with that of prime minister. At first the tactic was compromise. On 4 November, the Catholic primate Archbishop Glemp brought Wałęsa and Jaruzelski together and a pact between the government and Solidarity seemed again a possibility.

However, there were clear ideological limits even for reform-minded communists. Solidarity's congress had shown clearly that the idea of that movement accepting the leading role of the Party was no longer tenable; but Jaruzelski could only propose a new version of the 'national front' tactic. Solidarity would be one, but only one, representative on a new Front for National Cooperation comprising seven public organisations, including existing political parties, Solidarity itself and other 'mass organisations'. The echoes of the immediate postwar years of 1956 and 1968 were all too clear: the Party would cling on to power by incorporating the opposition into a Party-led national front. Wałęsa rejected the government's proposal and called on 12 December for the referendum to go ahead; later the same day Jaruzelski abandoned compromise, proclaiming the following day a 'state of war' or martial law, arresting Solidarity leaders, and establishing a Military Council of National Salvation (WRON). Solidarity leaders did not give up; strikes spread; and the church's view shifted from resignation to resistance.[40]

Jaruzelski had been preparing the martial law option for some time, having rejected the Soviet offer of Warsaw Pact intervention. A Kremlin commission had been monitoring events since August 1980, and by early December plans for military intervention by Warsaw Pact forces were ready to implement. Jaruzelski, then merely Defence Minister, refused to allow the intervention to go ahead. However, as early as October 1980 Jaruzelski had first considered the idea of declaring martial law, and once appointed prime minister in February these plans were elaborated in detail. The Kremlin wanted immediate action, but Jaruzelski insisted that timing was of the essence and the Bydgoszcz affair had greatly strengthened Solidarity; plans to declare martial law in April were abandoned. By autumn, however, when the divisions had opened up between the Solidarity leadership and the rank and file, the chances for success had greatly improved. At the last moment Jaruzelski hesitated. The Kremlin had made clear that, since the vetoing of the Warsaw Pact intervention a year earlier, Jaruzelski was on his own; no Soviet troops would arrive if martial law failed 'even if Poland were to be ruled by Solidarity'. Clear about the consequences, Jaruzelski began his meticulously prepared operation on 13 December 1981.[41]

If martial law did nothing else, it finally provided a context in which prices could be increased, by 76 per cent in 1982, producing a 25 per cent drop in average living standards. A notionally third-stage 'self-government' economic reform – 'self-management under military command' – was passed in February 1982 and came into effect in July. But the government abandoned further price reform, and the organs of self-government were stillborn in conditions of martial law. Indeed, the 1982 Polish reform project was bogged down by the interaction of political and economic disequilibria from the start. An *ad hoc* system of negotiating exemptions emerged, and the centre developed a system of 'operational programmes' and 'government orders or contracts' that effectively limited autonomy. Although the reform intended to remove the middle-level 'associations', they reappeared, now 'voluntary', in almost their original numbers.

This re-emergence of old forms was not unconnected with the fact that the Soviet Union stepped in to aid Poland as Western credits disappeared. This culminated in the agreement signed in May 1984 on 'The Long Term Programme for the Development of the Economic and Technical Co-operation between the USSR and Poland'. The economy was being reintegrated into Comecon rather than Western markets. Economic growth was 6 per cent in 1983 and 1984, but, as in Hungary, this mid-decade improvement proved a false dawn. Growth fell back to 3 per cent in 1985 and was accompanied by disappointments in export performance and the control of inflationary pressures. By 1986 hard-currency debt was $33 500 (compared with $24 800 in 1982), five times the level of annual hard-currency exports.[42]

More promising was the emergence post-1982 of a new generation of entrepreneurially minded, well-qualified young persons in the private sector. A new element in this private sector was the 'Polonia' companies whereby the state encouraged émigré Poles to return and found private companies. By the mid-1980s there were 326 000 individual workshops, 152 000 service or retail outlets, 90 000 taxis, 16 000 heavy transport outfits and 683 Polonia firms making up the private sector, which contributed some 7 per cent of GNP. Unlike Hungary, however, private and socialist sectors remained distinct. At the same time, the Party remained equally ambivalent about private agriculture. In July 1983 a constitutional amendment 'protected' private farming, but still gave no guarantee of continuing private ownership of the land.[43]

Solidarity was forced underground and in the autumn of 1982 was officially abolished. Party membership was also purged. Some 12 000 members were expelled so that Party membership had dropped by 129 000 by the end of February 1982. Martial law was lifted in July 1983, but Jaruzelski and other military personnel remained in key posts, armed with repressive legislation passed under military rule. Attempts to attract people back into the Party after the ending of martial law failed, although membership decline ended in mid-1985. When local elections, originally scheduled for spring 1982, were finally held in June 1984, they were treated by the authorities and opposition alike as a trial of strength, with Solidarity urging non-participation. The official turnout was 75 per cent, significantly less than the normal near 100 per cent figure, and Solidarity claimed it had been only 60 per cent. New elections were necessary in 330 seats because the required 50 per cent of those entitled to vote was not achieved. A similar trial of strength accompanied the national elections in October 1985. In like manner, the new unions that the regime sought to establish, having declared all unions illegal in October 1982, were slow to form. Solidarity had achieved a membership of 9 million in a matter of weeks in 1980. The new unions only had a membership of just over 4 million by the end of 1984 when a new central union organisation (the OPZZ) was established.[44]

If official politics was characterised by apathy, Solidarity survived and became the basis of a dissident movement on a scale unmatched in Eastern Europe. Where the Czechoslovak Charter 77 was issuing individual documents and reacting to individual acts of oppression, and the Hungarians were beginning to produce the occasional underground publication, the Polish underground published 690 books between 1982 and the mid-1980s. In addition to overtly political groups that existed outside the law, the post-Solidarity era saw the emergence of other groups striving for official recognition under the existing law on associations, the beginnings of what came to be called the 'second society'. That 'second society' would move to centre stage in the Gorbachev years.[45]

8

THE FALL OF ACTUALLY EXISTING SOCIALISM

This chapter presents the collapse of the *ancien régime* in Eastern Europe, a process that would not have been possible without the role played by Mikhail Gorbachev. Not long after the Soviet invasion of Czechoslovakia, Ferenc Fejtő wrote:

> One may hope – certainly the people of Eastern Europe hope – that the next Dubček will appear in the nerve centre of the system: Moscow.[1]

In March 1985, the Moscow Dubček arrived.

Almost as soon as he got to power, Gorbachev made clear that the era of imposing solutions on Eastern Europe was over, that the Soviet Union would no longer interfere in the internal affairs of its own satellites. It took time for this reality to dawn on the neo-Stalinist leaders of Eastern Europe, but Gorbachev's decision in September 1988 to wind up the Soviet Communist Party's Central Committee Department for Liaison with Communist and Workers' Parties in Socialist Countries should have left them in no doubt. The channel through which in 1989 the Soviet Party might have intervened to persuade the Hungarian Party to close its borders to East German refugees had simply been abolished. The era of Soviet control over Eastern Europe had gone, and East European communists, too late in the day as it turned out, were being left to their own devices.[2]

Gorbachev's espousal of *glasnost* and *perestroika* legitimised the increased autonomy of civil society pioneered in Poland and the principles of economic reform adopted in 1968 in Hungary. These measures were intended to prevent the collapse of communism. But things had gone too far. Hungary's NEM was no longer sufficient and, as generations changed, increasing dissatisfaction with the regimes was openly expressed. Change of generation was true for both sides. As older members of the Party leaderships retired, they were replaced by a generation that had been brought up under an imperfectly functioning socialism. Its ideological commitment was necessarily less wholehearted than that of the generation that had fought for an ideal. On the other hand, a new opposition generation was emerging for whom the idea of socialism had no positive associations whatsoever. While the 1956 generation had fought for non-Soviet communist renewal, and the 1968 generation for a more humane brand of socialism, all that socialism and communism meant for those in their teens and twenties in the second half of the 1980s was the grey Brezhnev years of cynicism, corruption, shortage and falling living standards. For those in a position to make use of the political space provided by Gorbachev, socialism was a dirty word.

The distinction that had been emerging in the Brezhnev years between Central Europe and the Balkans asserted itself more strongly as the regimes fell. It was in Poland and Hungary with their severe economic crises, strong opposition movements and low levels of regime legitimacy (in Poland because of martial law and the treatment of Solidarity, in Hungary because of increasingly institutionalised cynicism about the operation of the socialist economy) that the collapse began. That the fall of 'actually existing socialism' was the result of its failure as a socio-economic system is reinforced by the fact that the trigger for collapse throughout the region came in Hungary, the most liberal country, with the most radically reformed economy (as radically reformed as Yugoslavia at the end), and a standard of living that was the envy of all except the wealthier republics of Yugoslavia. The end of communism in Poland was in a sense a coda to the Solidarity crisis of 1980 that, as was argued in Chapter 7, was the consequence of the fact that neo-Stalinism had never been fully implemented. Communist failure in Hungary was the failure of 'actually existing socialism' at its most sophisticated.

The bastions of orthodoxy in Central Europe (the GDR and Czechoslovakia) had to be pushed, although only very gently. In the

Balkans, the regimes tried to save themselves by becoming either reform communist (Bulgaria and Albania) or nationalist (Yugoslavia, where the former communist parties had a nationalist ideology and the nationalist parties had former communist leaders) and by attempting to control the creation of political pluralism themselves. Even in Romania, where a violent revolution was necessary to remove Ceauşescu, the National Salvation Front that replaced it behaved as a reform communist party, with a strong nationalistic bent. In Bulgaria, Albania and Romania the reform communist governments that won hastily held elections were subsequently challenged by popular unrest and obliged to share power; and in Bulgaria and Albania they were ultimately defeated in new elections. In Yugoslavia, passions inflamed by perceived national interest meant that people rallied around republican governments of whatever persuasion as the country descended into civil war.

CENTRAL EUROPE

Poland

By the mid-1980s it was becoming clear to the Polish leadership that martial law and its aftermath had failed. Indebtedness to the West rose inexorably: $26.3 billion in 1983, $29.3 billion in 1985 and $39.2 billion in 1987. The hard-currency squeeze had resulted in a dramatic decline in foreign licence purchase, only nine between 1981 and 1986 compared with 452 in the decade to 1980, and their share in exports had always been disappointing at 5.3 per cent in 1980, the same as a decade previously. But by 1986 the share of foreign licenses in exports had fallen to 1.6 per cent.[3] National income declined 0.8 per cent between 1981–5, rose by 4.9 per cent in 1986 and 1988, but by only 1.9 per cent in 1987. Real incomes fluctuated wildly: a 2.7 per cent increase in 1986, a 3.5 per cent decrease in 1987, a 14.4 per cent increase in 1988.[4] But the 1985 figures were 12.4 per cent lower than in 1978, and the target date for restoring living standards to 1978 levels was put back to 1995. By the mid-1980s health indicators were pointing to a breakdown in the quality of life. Some 60 per cent of pensioner households were poor in terms of the social minimum and 40 per cent of families with three or more children and 30 per cent of single-parent families living in poverty in 1987.[5]

With the economy in an increasing debt crisis there were growing signs of dissatisfaction with the Party and a questioning of its competence. By 1987, a party source revealed that only 25 per cent of members played an active role and 60 per cent did no more than pay their dues and attend meetings.[6] In this atmosphere of crisis and distrust, the Jaruzelski government felt the need to gain additional support for the regime, especially since a new 'second' round of economic reform in 1987 (although still cautious since it would create a single Ministry of Industry out of seven branch ministries, but not release 300–400 large-scale enterprises from their long-term agreements within Comecon)[7] was likely to have negative consequences for many groups within the population.

The process had begun with the 10th Party Congress in June–July 1986; this, despite general continuity of membership with previous years,[8] engineered the release from jail of Solidarity activists like Adam Michnik and Zbigniew Bujak. In September, Solidarity responded by agreeing to end underground activities and 'ease the transition to legal and open undertakings', despite the fact that the Temporary Council of Solidarity (its underground organisation) remained illegal. In November 1987, a referendum was held on the second stage of economic reform and limited political liberalisation; but this attempt to win popular support for government measures failed to achieve its goal of winning at least half the support of the electorate. Only 67 per cent of the population participated, of which 60 per cent supported the economic reform and 69 per cent the political reform.

The spring and summer of 1988 witnessed a succession of industrial strikes in protest against price increases that in some cases were 100–200 per cent[9] and, in August 1988, the Party took the momentous decision to work towards an Anti-Crisis Pact with the 'constructive opposition'. After an autumn of fruitless negotiations, in December Wałęsa formed a Civic Committee within Solidarity that marginalised those radicals within his movement opposed to negotiations; shortly afterwards, in January 1989, Jaruzelski, Rakowski and their moderate allies, used the threat of resignation to get the Party to accept the re-legalisation of Solidarity and its entry into Round Table negotiations.

Round Table negotiations for a pluralist, but still communist-dominated, Poland began on 6 February 1989. They ended on 5 April, with an agreement on the re-legalisation of Solidarity and Rural Solidarity, and the holding of elections in which 35 per cent of seats would be open to genuine opposition candidates: at last, all talk of the leading role of the Party and loyalty to a 'national front' had disappeared. However, if Jaruzelski had hoped that the population would rally around his attempt at socialist pluralism, the election results were a great disappointment. The rejection of communism was as convincing as it would have been had the elections taken place in 1947. In the first round (4 June), on a relatively low 62.1 per cent turnout, Wałęsa's team won 92 out of the 100 Senate seats and 160 out of the 161 Sejm seats available to it. Only two of the government coalition's 35 candidates on the National List received the necessary 50 per cent of the votes cast to be elected. Major figures such as Rakowski and General Czesław Kiszczak, Minister of the Interior, failed to get elected. The second round (18 June) confirmed the pattern of the first. Solidarity had gained approximately 65 per cent of the votes cast and 40 per cent of the total electorate.

Even before the second round of the elections had taken place, Jaruzelski invited Solidarity to participate in a Grand Coalition. After being elected to the new post of executive president on 19 July, he repeated the offer on 24 July. But it was refused. The offer of 'socialist pluralism' seemed unconvincing in the light of the experience of 1944–7. As the communist-led government continued with reform measures, Wałęsa announced, on 7 August, that Solidarity should form and lead the new government, an idea first floated by Michnik in July. After much argument within Solidarity and a stormy 14th Plenum of the Party, both sides accepted this idea, and on 20 August, Jaruzelski, as president, asked Tadeusz Mazowiecki of Solidarity to form a government 'based on broad agreement among Poland's political and social forces'.

Between September and the New Year the Mazowiecki government initiated a series of measures removing the pillars of the communist state: the army was depoliticised, the Citizen's Militia was transformed into an ordinary police force, the riot police and secret police were reorganised and the Patriotic Movement for National Rebirth dissolved itself. The leading role of the Party was excised from the constitution in September when Poland once more became a simple republic rather than a People's Republic. In line with this change of mood (and following the example of other parties in the region), the Party dissolved itself and re-emerged as the Social Democratic Party between 27–29 January 1990.

Meanwhile, at the end of December 1989, the Sejm passed a budget drawn up by Finance Minister Leszek Balcerowicz, the nearest thing in political and economic reality to the 'shock therapy' tactics advocated by the Harvard economist Jeffrey Sachs. At a stroke on 1 January 1990 practically all prices were decontrolled as were most imports. Limited currency convertibility was introduced together with an extremely restrictive monetary policy and strict wage controls. This sudden unleashing of market forces resulted in huge price increases in the first months of 1990, but then to a relative stabilisation. By the second half of 1990 'shock therapy' appeared to have worked.

On the political front, Solidarity, which had already split over the issue of entering government, split further. Wałęsa was re-elected chairman of the Solidarity trade union in April 1990, and soon after initiated pressure for Jaruzelski to resign as president and call a presidential election. In the summer of 1990, following local elections in May where the Civic Committee with 43 per cent of the seats on a 40 per cent turnout was the largest party, Solidarity split. Bujak and others formed ROAD (Democratic Action Civic Movement) to support Mazowiecki's candidacy for president, while a new Centre Alliance supported Wałęsa.

The dissipation of the Solidarity movement was reflected in the first round of the presidential election in November. These were surprising in two ways: Wałęsa did not achieve the expected overall majority in the first round, and the unknown Polish-born Canadian Peruvian Stanisław Tymiński received more votes than Mazowiecki, who resigned as prime minister. Wałęsa gained a clear majority in the second round and was sworn in on 22 December, with Jan Krzysztof Bielecki as his prime minister. Poland's political divisions reflected its continuing economic crisis. Despite the initial success of 'shock therapy', the economic situation was precarious. The annualised rate of inflation was creeping up towards 200 per cent by the end of the year compared with the planned 70 per cent; output had fallen 23 per cent rather than the expected 5 per cent and unemployment was rising steeply.

If the Polish constitution with its strong president was based on the French Fifth Republic, the larger part of 1991 was characterised by French-style cohabitation between a democratically elected president and a still communist-dominated parliament. Agreement on electoral law proved elusive. Ideas of an election on 3 May, the two hundredth anniversary of the 1791 constitution, were abandoned and a date finally set in October. By September over one hundred bills were awaiting passage and only 9 of the 44 central reform bills planned since January had been passed. Meanwhile, the process of party formation out of the formerly united Solidarity continued, with overlapping Christian democratic and social democratic constituencies. A total of some 70 parties registered before the election.

In March Poland had received the welcome economic news that the 'Paris Club' of 17 creditor countries had agreed to write off 50 per cent of its debt to foreign governments and the United States promised a 70 per cent reduction of its debt. In April, the IMF approved financing until 1993 on the basis of a programme that would deliver 36 per cent inflation by the end of 1991. Poland nevertheless missed its debt interest repayment in June, and, in late September, the IMF announced that it would await the new Polish government before agreeing to a resumption of lending since Poland had failed to fulfil most of the targets in the agreement.

No clear winner emerged from the elections of 27 October. On a turnout of only 40 per cent, the biggest party was Mazowiecki's Democratic Union with only 12 per cent of the vote. Most of the large parties were critical of 'shock therapy' and advocated anti-recessionary policies. Negotiations over who should form a government continued into December, and, once Jan Olszewski had been endorsed as the new prime minister, two further weeks of negotiations, and the threat of resignation, were necessary before a government could be formed. A new cohabitation emerged in which the president was committed to continued 'shock therapy' and the government wanted to slow it down; Wałęsa, however, had the advantage of IMF support.

'Small privatisation', of properties owned by local authorities, began in Poland in May 1990, and a general privatisation act (which included a 10 per cent ceiling on foreign ownership without special permission) was passed in July. Between August and November 1990 a pilot privatisation of seven enterprises by public offering of shares was organised. Despite enthusiastic public statements, this experiment was scarcely a success. Only one enterprise was sold within the original time limit, while five more were sold after the deadline was extended into December. Privatisation policy subsequently underwent a transformation and, rather than emphasise value for money in a stock market floatation, the new priority (as in Czechoslovakia and belatedly Hungary) became speed of sale. In June 1991 the 'mass privatisation programme' was approved, which was to sell 400 leading enterprises (a quarter of the total) according to the following proportions: 30 per cent state owned, 10 per cent owned by employees, and the remaining 60 per cent in the hands of one or more of the five to twenty new 'National Wealth Funds' in which each citizen would have the right to a number of shares.

Hungary

Kádár's rule was based on a dual compromise with the Soviet Union on the one hand and the Hungarian population on the other. Kádár remained loyal in foreign policy in return for leeway in domestic and especially economic reform; and he provided constantly improving living standards in a relaxed ideological climate in return for acceptance of the legitimacy of the communist regime. With the advent of Gorbachev, however, both compromises broke down. No fine line had to be trod between what was acceptable to the Soviet Union and what was not, and living standards had stopped increasing. From the mid-1980s onwards, public opinion surveys revealed significant increases in the numbers of people who felt that the government was unable to resolve the country's economic problems. The 13th Party Congress promised a return to economic growth, but this was inconsistent with the realities of Hungary's parlous economic situation. Worse, under the stage-four type economic reforms of 1985, Hungarian enterprises lost all financial discipline and foreign convertible currency debt leapt to 56 per cent of GDP in 1986 and 62.2 per cent in 1987, giving Hungary the highest per capita debt in Eastern Europe.

In 1987, dissidents gained in confidence. Radical economists published a document that for the first time brought into the public domain the extent of economic decline, the 'democratic opposition' produced a special issue of its magazine *Beszélő* calling for political pluralism and a free press, and, on 27 September, the Hungarian Democratic Forum (HDF) was founded in the village of Lakitelek. In response, the Party announced a Special Party Conference in May 1988. The pace of political events then accelerated. In the first half of the year a series of dissident meetings was held at the Jurta Theatre, which, as a Small Cooperative, was independent of government control. In March the 'democratic opposition' and other groups established the Network of Free Initiatives, while a younger generation of oppositionists founded the Alliance of Young Democrats (FIDESZ). In April, four prominent reform-minded intellectuals were expelled from the Party for attending the Jurta and similar meetings; but at the Special Communist Party Conference in May, it was the hard-liners who were defeated. Kádár was replaced as First Secretary, and a new generation that had lived its adult lives under 'actually existing socialism' came into the leadership.

After a quiet summer, opposition activity began again. The Democratic Forum held a second meeting in Lakitelek in September and the

Alliance of Free Democrats was established as a party in November out of most of the organisations in the Network of Free Initiatives. The Independent Smallholder Party re-founded itself, also in November, and Hungary's Social Democratic Party followed suit in January 1989. By February 1989, the Party had accepted that Hungary would become a multiparty democracy; in March the opposition groups and parties established an Opposition Round Table and the Christian Democratic People's Party was founded; and in June, as its reformist wing gained in strength, the communists agreed to negotiations with the Opposition Round Table. While these talks were under way, on 11 September, the government made its historic decision to allow East German 'tourists' to cross the border into Austria.

On 18 September 1989, the Round Table talks concluded with an agreement on certain 'cardinal laws' on the transition to democracy; but the Free Democrats and FIDESZ refused to sign it. They rejected the idea of holding direct elections for a new president before parliamentary elections, and they were unhappy that the Party had not committed itself to disbanding the workers' militia, withdrawing from work places and rendering an account of its property. While the Party held an Extraordinary 14th Party Congress in October, at which the reformists won the day and the Party's name was changed to the Hungarian Socialist Party, the Free Democrats and FIDESZ collected sufficient signatures to force a referendum on the disputed elements in the September agreement.

Although many viewed the referendum as a distraction since, in the interim (on 23 October 1989) Hungary had become a Republic (as opposed to a People's Republic) and all reference to the 'leading role' of the Party had been removed from the constitution, it served the purpose of highlighting, at an early date, the differences of opinion within the opposition. While the Free Democrats and FIDESZ opposed the government, the Democratic Forum advised its members to abstain. This was a mistake. Turnout for the referendum on 26 November exceeded 50 per cent, and the anti-government view narrowly won the day. Following the referendum, politics changed radically. The Free Democrats gained mass support and the Democratic Forum momentarily lost prestige and adopted a more consistently anti-communist line. As to the former communists themselves, they went into decline; with the other socialist regimes collapsing around them, their justifiable claim to be truly reformist cut little ice.

Parliamentary elections finally took place in two rounds in March and April, 1990. No party gained an absolute majority, and, after a month of negotiating, the Hungarian Democratic Forum under József Antall formed a coalition government with the two other parties of a nationalist-Christian orientation, the Smallholders' and the Christian Democrats. Jointly these parties won about the same share of the vote as the Smallholders in 1945; the former communists fared rather worse. The largest opposition party was the liberal Alliance of Free Democrats, followed by the former communist Hungarian Socialist Party and FIDESZ. All other parties failed to cross the 4 per cent threshold and enter parliament and promptly disappeared from mainstream politics. Árpád Göncz, a Free Democrat, was finally appointed president of the Republic on 3 August 1990 after much disagreement on whether parliament or the people should appoint the president. Despite commitments to rapid change, the government's first 100 days achieved little, other than establishing a framework for local elections, and causing a furore by appearing to give churches a free hand for religious education in schools. Elections to the new local authorities took place in September and October. Turnout was lower than in the parliamentary elections of the spring and the coalition government was severely punished for its inertia in the summer, losing to the Free Democrats and, especially, FIDESZ.

In October 1990, the strength of the new political institutions was put to the test. After months of postponing petrol price increases, the government announced an average 65 per cent rise from midnight on Thursday 25 October. Spontaneously, throughout the country, communicating by means of short-wave radio, lorry and taxi drivers blockaded towns, bridges and border crossings during the course of Thursday–Friday night. The crisis was defused by Sunday after negotiations between the government and representatives of the strikers had been broadcast live on television. Public opinion surveys taken immediately after the negotiations revealed high levels of support for the drivers and criticism of the government; and a public opinion survey taken in November 1990 revealed that, after only six months in office, the first democratically elected government in forty years inspired rather less confidence than the previous communist one.

After the excitement of 1990, 1991 was a rather quiet year. Politics stabilised and the economy responded ambiguously, but on the whole positively, to the radically changing economic realities. If the government was stable, it was not popular. By April 1991 the most popular party was FIDESZ with 35 per cent support, followed by the Free Democrats with 18.4 per cent. The Hungarian Democratic Forum, the major coalition partner, could only muster 13.6 per cent support. After much debate, and at the insistence of the Smallholders who felt obliged to implement their clearest party political commitment, namely to return land holdings to their pre-collectivisation structure, a Compensation Law was passed in June (after twice being rejected by the Constitutional Court) permitting redress for property, including farm land, appropriated by the state since 1948. In July a law on church property allowed churches to claim back properties, including schools, confiscated by the state. The growing importance of the Catholic Church to the regime was reflected too in the lavish ceremonial reburial of Cardinal Mindszenty in May and the visit of the Pope in August. In October the government adopted a Bill allowing for the suspension of the statute of limitations in the case of prosecuting former communists. It was passed by parliament in November but submitted immediately by the president to the Constitutional Court, which promised a decision at the end of January 1992.

Although political structures since the elections had seemed secure, both the Free Democrats and the Smallholders' Party began a process of political metamorphosis in 1991 in which idealists were replaced by professional politicians. The Smallholders' Party was all but taken over by József Torgyán a right-wing demagogue who saw in this party of elderly pro-peasant romantics a vehicle to pursue his personal ambition. As to the Alliance of Free Democrats, after becoming a mass party suddenly in November 1989, it had experienced a rift between its intellectual leadership and its mass base. This came to a crisis in October–November when the more populist Péter Tölgyessy, who had only entered politics at the time of the Round Table negotiations, was elected leader in place of the former dissident János Kis.

In terms of economic stabilisation, Hungary had something of a headstart over its neighbours. In the final years of communist rule the government had introduced Western-style banking (in 1987), Western-style taxation (in 1988) and generous conditions for foreign investors, including full repatriation of profits (in 1989). Consumer subsidies had always been smaller than elsewhere in the region, and in 1988 it had also begun a programme of liberalising foreign trade and reducing subsidies such that, by the time the Antall government came to power, many of the most painful measures had been taken and the population was well-used to price increases. Nevertheless a new austerity package had to be introduced in July 1990, and the projected budget deficit for 1991 reduced before a three-year agreement with the IMF could finally be signed. By the end of 1991 external economic relations were favourable and the currency sound, but unemployment was above 6 per cent and there were signs that the government was shifting from its free market commitment towards greater intervention in order to counteract and overcome recession.

As in stabilisation so too in privatisation: Hungary had a head start. With the Company Act of 1989 and less significant economic legislation passed in 1984 and 1987, a legal framework had been created for what became know as 'spontaneous privatisation'. State companies restructured themselves into state-owned holding companies with a number of limited liability and partially, privately owned subsidiaries. In one of its last acts the communist government created a State Property Agency to oversee privatisation and ensure that the underselling of state assets, which had been an integral part of 'spontaneous privatisation', did not continue. In the autumn of 1990 the Antall government announced a grand privatisation programme for twenty prime companies.

East Germany

With both Poland and Hungary on some sort of new course in early 1989 (although at this stage the expectation was still of a future in which the communist parties and the Soviet Union played an important role) and Gorbachev refusing to intervene, the orthodox regimes of the region were pushed onto the defensive. The proximate cause of the fall of the Berlin wall, and thus the collapse of the GDR regime and the unification of Germany, was the Hungarian decision in September 1989 to allow German 'tourists' in Hungary to emigrate over the border with Austria. But there was an economic background to the sense of frustration in the GDR that manifested itself most visibly in the desire for foreign travel.

Even the official measures of economic performance revealed a declining trend in growth: 5.2 per cent in 1985, 4.3 per cent in 1986, 3.3 per cent in 1987, 2.8 per cent in 1988, 2.1 per cent in 1989. It was later admitted that gross industrial production fell by 2.5 per cent between November 1988 and November 1989, that 40 per cent of the main plan targets were behind schedule, and that the state budget was in deficit by 5–6 billion marks. It was also revealed that trade with the Federal Republic, 20.6 per cent of total trade, was only slightly less than that with the Soviet Union (22.9 per cent), and that nearly a third of GDR trade was with the European Community. The GDR was not so much the manufacturing powerhouse of Comecon, as a producer of semi-finished goods for the European Community, to which it had privileged access. Even so, convertible currency debt increased sharply in the second half of the 1980s from US$11.6 billion in 1984 to US$19.1 billion in 1987 and US$20.6 billion in 1989.[10]

Hungary's decision radically altered the parameters of the foreign travel issue, which had been slowly building over the course of 1989. Despite minor revisions to travel regulations in January and April 1989, there was a demonstration in Leipzig in March for the right to emigrate. In the local elections in May, the votes against the National Front list slightly increased. Mass action for emigration began in August. On 8 August the West German mission in East Berlin was forced to close under pressure of would-be emigrants, on 13 August the Budapest embassy had to do likewise and on 22 August the Prague embassy followed suit. Even after several hundred GDR citizens had broken through the unfenced Hungarian border with Austria on 19 August, the GDR government took no measures to prevent citizens leaving for Czechoslovakia and Hungary, suggesting a failure of confidence within the regime.

The Hungarian decision not only gave an impetus to the emigration movement, it gave confidence to the small dissident movement that had been gathering its strength in the GDR. On 11 September, *Neues Forum* was founded, followed the next day by Democracy Now. The next significant boost to the opposition was given by Gorbachev who arrived on 6 October to attend the celebrations of the fortieth anniversary of the GDR. At classic Stalinist festivities the following day, Gorbachev pointedly warned: 'he who comes too late is punished by life'.

Meanwhile, demonstrations throughout the GDR against the regime were met with force. By 9 October, the participants at the by then regular Monday anti-government demonstrations at Leipzig numbered about 700 000, and the following weekend Egon Krenz and others made plans to remove Honecker from power. This took place on 18 October when Krenz was elected general secretary. With demonstrations becoming more frequent, declarations of amnesties, the dismissal of the old guard and even a new travel law cut no ice. Mass demonstrations continued. On 8 November a new Politburo was elected; and on 9 November it was announced that borders with West Berlin and West Germany would be opened. The Berlin Wall was breached before midnight that same night.

With hindsight, the unification of Germany after the fall of the wall was inevitable, but at the time it was, at most, a long-term goal. Relations between the two Germanies were improved, and the GDR set about forming a reform communist government. Hans Modrow, former mayor of Dresden became prime minister on 18 November, reference to the Party's leading role was excised from the constitution on 1 December, Krenz resigned from his posts soon after and at the Party Congress on 8–9 December, Gregor Gysi a former critical intellectual within the Party was elected chairman. The Congress resumed on 16–17 December and agreed to change its name to the SED-PDS Party of Democratic Socialism. (On 4 February 1990 it became simply the PDS.)

In January, the date for elections was brought forward from May to 18 March, and in February Modrow brought representatives of opposition parties into his government as ministers without portfolio. Before the elections took place, the Modrow government set up the Trust Agency, a public institution subordinate to government, which became the new legal owner of all former state enterprises. Although the PDS still thought in terms of a future for Germany as a neutral confederation, the bandwagon for rapid unification grew as the right wing of the GDR's political spectrum was filled with ready-made parties from West Germany. Indigenous parties had no time to establish themselves properly by March, but, while the victors of over-hasty elections in the Balkans tended to be the communist parties, in the GDR the victor was the political right of West Germany. Promising rapid unification and a 1:1 conversion of the GDR mark in currency union, the Christian Democrats came out of the March elections as the biggest party, although even with its electoral allies it did not have an overall majority. Meanwhile, the wartime allies (the United States, USSR, the United Kingdom and France), together with the two German foreign ministers had agreed to the 'Two-plus-Four' talks on German unity.

The Christian-Democrat-led coalition government was formed on 9 April and approved by parliament on 12 April. Economic and social union took place on 1 July 1990; and on 31 August a 200-page unification treaty was signed, essentially extending the laws of the Federal

Republic to the East. On 12 September, the 'Two-plus-Four' talks concluded and the allies abandoned all remaining responsibilities for Germany. Finally, at midnight on 2 October, the two Germanies were united, and on 14 October elections were held in the five reconstituted East German Länder. (Four of the five new Land administrations were Christian Democrat-led coalitions or outright Christian Democrat victories; only in Brandenburg was a Social Democrat-led coalition established.) On 14 November Germany and Poland signed a treaty confirming the Oder–Neisse line as their border, and on 2 December all-German elections to the Bundestag were won by the Christian Democrats.

In the course of these political developments, the Trust Agency's remit changed in favour of selling rather than rescuing East German assets. Indeed, rapid unification with the West brought questionable benefits to the East German economy. If East German politics was hijacked by West German parties, the economy was swamped by West German companies. For them, the East was an enormous new market; but, as the slow pace of privatisation via the Trust Agency attests, few contemplated serious investment in East German manufacturing industry. Following currency union, shops in East Germany were flooded with West German products; but short-time working and unemployment increased alarmingly after the GDR disappeared from the history of Eastern Europe.

Czechoslovakia

The Czechoslovak leadership tried its best to ignore the advent of Gorbachev to the Kremlin. The 17th Party Congress in March 1986 brought about no change of policy or personnel. The only straw in the wind was a speech by Prime Minister Lubomír Štrougal calling for a different economic policy, although studiously avoiding phrases such as 'economic reform'.[11] There was some need for this. The rate of growth of the economy was stagnating at around 2 per cent, and foreign debt, although low compared with Hungary and Poland, was growing rapidly from US$3.3 million in 1985 to US$5.1 million in 1987.[12] A government commissioned report completed in November 1988 on the Czechoslovak economy in the year 2010 revealed a country 'struggling to remain in the second league of industrialised states'.[13]

By 1987, however, it was clear that Gorbachev was unassailable and some sort of political accommodation could not be postponed indefinitely. Husák declared himself in favour of Gorbachev's reforms at the March session of the Central Committee, and the entire leadership pronounced itself in favour of Gorbachev's policies on the occasion of his visit in April. Nevertheless, there was little clear evidence to back up such pronouncements. At the December session of the Central Committee, when Husák unexpectedly resigned, he was replaced not by a reformer but by the suitably orthodox Jakeš.

At the beginning of 1989, Czechoslovakia seemed to be as secure from revolutionary change as the GDR; but, as with the GDR, things were beginning to change under the surface. The mood in the country had been changing somewhat since the mid-1980s. The churches, especially the Roman Catholic Church, had become more outspoken and manifestations of religious belief such as pilgrimages were more common. Younger people generally had more of a fighting spirit than the normalised generation of their parents,[14] and thousands demonstrated at the twentieth anniversary of the Soviet invasion in 1988. Demonstrations against the government in 1989 were on a larger scale than before. Those commemorating the twentieth anniversary of Jan Palach's suicide in January lasted a week; 2000 attended a counter-demonstration on 1 May; several thousand took part in a demonstration on the anniversary of the Soviet invasion on 21 August; and 10 000 took part in an unofficial demonstration in Prague's Wenceslas Square on the seventy-first anniversary of the founding of Czechoslovakia. Demonstrators were not put off by the arrest and sentencing of Václav Havel in February, nor mollified by his release in May. A petition entitled *A Few Words* circulated in June had attracted 37 000 signatures by November. There had only been 242 original signatories to Charter 77, a figure that had increased to only around 2000 by the late 1980s.

As soon as the Berlin wall fell, events moved very rapidly. On 17 November an officially sanctioned student demonstration in Prague, marking the anniversary of the murder of a student leader by the Nazis, was attacked by the security police in what is now thought to have been a KGB-approved attempt to provoke a minor crisis and install a reform communist regime. Demonstrations were provoked, but their consequence was far more radical than a pro-Gorbachev reform communist regime. On 19 November Havel and other opposition figures formed Civic Forum to coordinate a pro-democracy campaign, and a few days later a Slovak counterpart – Public Against

Violence – came into existence. In the following week a succession of massive demonstrations took place in Prague's Wenceslas Square demanding the resignation of the communist leaders and an end to one-party rule. A two-hour general strike on 27 November demonstrated that the workers, too, supported the opposition.

Meanwhile, at an extraordinary session of the Communist Party Central Committee the entire leadership resigned. Continuing a belated attempt to transform itself into a reform Communist Party and salvage as much power as possible, on 29 November the Federal Assembly approved the deletion of references to the Party's leading role from the constitution. On 3 December, the newly appointed Communist Federal Prime Minister Ladislav Ademec formed a 21-member government with sixteen communist and five non-communist members; on 7 December, in the face of opposition refusal to accept this government (the historical precedent of the Party's destruction of genuine coalition in 1948 was not encouraging), he resigned.

Three days later, having first sworn in a Government of National Understanding led by Marián Čalfa, in which the majority of the 21 seats were given to candidates nominated by Civic Forum, Public Against Violence and the non-communist political parties, Husák resigned as president. Similarly constituted republican governments were created in the Czech Republic on 5 December and in Slovakia on 12 December. On 19 December the new Federal Government announced its intention to prepare for free elections and begin the transformation towards a market-based economy. A week later, on 28 December, in a gesture rich in symbolism, Dubček was elected Chairman of the Federal Assembly; and the following day the Federal Assembly elected Havel president. The 'Velvet Revolution' was complete.

Elections, in which 23 parties participated, were held on 8–9 June 1990. Civic Forum and Public Against Violence clearly won, gaining a majority in the Federal Assembly and the Czech National Council, and a plurality in the Slovak National Council. The new governments, formed at the end of June, were all coalitions, although this was only necessary in Slovakia; and on 5 July Havel was re-elected president by the Federal Assembly. The government's reform programme was adopted by the Assembly on 17 September. Its key features were the removal of price controls, the establishment of partial currency convertibility by January 1991, and the introduction within the next year of a programme of privatisation of small- and large-scale industry. In recognition of these measures, Czechoslovakia received an IMF loan in January 1991.

In the last months of 1990, the nature of politics subtly changed, as Civic Forum and Public Against Violence fared less well in the local elections of 23–24 November and Slovak nationalists began to emerge as a serious political platform. As 1990 turned into 1991, Civic Forum and Public Against Violence began to break up. Civic Forum finally split formally in February into the Civic Democratic Party (led by Federal Finance Minister Václav Klaus as a right of centre party) and the centrist Civic Movement. Some Civic Forum deputies switched allegiance to other parties, such as the Social Democrats. Public Against Violence followed suit in March, with the populist Vladimír Mečiar, more in favour of Slovak autonomy and state intervention, forming a Platform (in June a Movement) for a Democratic Slovakia. He was dismissed as Slovak prime minister in April and replaced by Ján Čarnogurský of the Christian Democracy Movement. Umbrella groups were slowly evolving into parties with precise political programmes and the political spectrum of the interwar years reasserted itself, although the parties had new names.

Political life in 1991 was dominated by the national question and the desire to punish the communists. The former issue remained unresolved until the national 'divorce' between Slovakia and the Czech lands was announced in 1992. The latter, beginning with the revelation in March that 10 deputies had worked for the secret police, culminated in legislation in November banning from public office former communists and those who had allegedly been police informers.

As to the economy, Czechoslovakia's privatisation strategy was radical. In February 1991, following earlier measures in November 1990, legislation was passed concerning the return of property to former owners; and in May further legislation permitted the return of land (but, pending a law on the transformation of cooperatives, not the confiscated plot of land) to those who had lost land during collectivisation. In June 1991, as a taster, fifty large state enterprises were offered to foreign investors, and in October coupons went on sale for the first round of voucher-based privatisation in November. Enterprises drew up their own privatisation plans, for vetting by their controlling branch ministry, for Czechoslovakia's under-reformed economy had not moved away from the branch ministry concept. Czechoslovakia's voucher system was both competitive and residual. Vouchers, which every citizen had a right to purchase, were to be used to bid for assets not already sold in some other way; and, unlike in Poland, were not distributed free of charge.

Czechoslovakia's privatisation did not work out quite as planned. As soon as vouchers went on sale, some 450 investment funds, not envisaged under the original scheme, entered the market, buying up vouchers from the general public and concentrating ownership in what had been intended to be a highly decentralised process. The experiment in people's capitalism was destined to be short-lived.

THE BALKANS

Bulgaria

Bulgaria began a new round of economic reform rhetoric in 1985–6. The prime minister was replaced and six ministries were closed down; almost immediately, however, five 'voluntary associations' were formed and by July 1987 the ministerial structure had largely been reconstituted. Despite this show of indecision, in 1988 further economic restructuring was announced and enterprises permitted to become 'firms' that could issue stock or bonds.

Reform of the economy was required desperately: the rate of growth fell from 5.3 per cent in 1986 to 2.4 per cent in 1988 and −0.4 per cent in 1989. Foreign debt, beginning at a low level as in Czechoslovakia, snowballed much more quickly. A gross debt of US$3.5 billion in 1985 became US$6.2 million in 1987, US$7.7 million in 1988 and US$9.0 million in 1989.[15] Some 40–45 per cent of production facilities were obsolete, and the economy was aptly described as being 'on the verge of a heart attack'.

As in Czechoslovakia, 1989 began with dissident activity and arrests that, with the benefit of hindsight, were more substantial than in previous years. Zhivkov offered lip service to *perestroika* and some Bulgarians insisted on taking him at his word. Members of the intelligentsia, especially in Sofia, joined Clubs for the Support of *Glasnost* and *Perestroika* and, in February, an independent trade union (*Podkrepa*) was formed, which quickly began to enrol thousands of members. An ecology movement and human rights organisations were also founded. In February 1989 the Politburo met with 'representatives of the intelligentsia' and warned that attacks on socialism would not be tolerated. In March recognition was sought for a newly formed Committee for Religious Rights, Freedom of Conscience and Spiritual Values. In May, prominent dissident Zheliu Zhelev, who had taken a leading role in these discussion clubs, was arrested for circulating an appeal for democratic reforms. Not long afterwards the ethnic Turkish issue flared again, this time resulting in the opening of the border with Turkey and the exodus of 310 000 ethnic Turks, before the border was closed again in August.

The very day after the Berlin Wall fell, Zhivkov was obliged to resign and his replacement, Petur Mladenov, set in motion a rearguard action to preserve power on a reform communist platform. Dissidents were rehabilitated and opposition groups recognised on 13 November; an attack was launched on Zhivkov and his closest associates on 16 November; and on 30 December, the Bulgarisation programme was ended and ethnic Turks who had fled were invited to return. Meanwhile, on 7 December seven dissident organisations formed the Union of Democratic Forces with Zhelev as chairman.

Mladenov's task for 1990 was to ensure victory for reformers in the Party and then hold elections that the Party would win. The first of these goals was achieved by a 'Congress of Renewal', held at the end of January and during the first week of February. At the end of March, Round Table negotiations between Communists, the Union of Democratic Forces and the Agrarian Union produced an agreement on the basics of political reform. These were adopted by the National Assembly on 3 April and instituted some major changes: Mladenov was elected to the new post of president of the Republic; the communists changed their name to the 'Bulgarian Socialist Party' (BSP); and, although the agreement banned the formation of ethnic and religious parties, the Party of Rights and Freedoms emerged as a *de facto* Turkish Party. Elections were agreed for 10–17 June, too soon for the opposition parties to generate strong party machines, even though the BSP no longer operated in the workplace. The results were a disappointment for the UDF, which had been campaigning on an anti-BSP platform and advocating 'shock therapy' in economic policy, but neither did they represent an overwhelming socialist victory. With 47.15 per cent of the votes, the BSP had a small parliamentary majority.

The outcome of the elections was political stalemate. The UDF refused to enter a coalition, and the government refused to take painful economic measures without the agreement of the opposition. It had already been obliged to suspend payments on the principal of its US$10 billion foreign debt in March, and interest payments in June. In July, Mladenov was obliged to resign over a videotape showing him proposing the use of tanks against a demonstration in 1989. Zhelev was appointed president by parliament in his place on 1 August, but this did not resolve the impasse. With domestic production declining 11 per cent in the first three quarters of 1990, and rationing for most staples by the autumn, in October the new prime minister Andrei Lukanov proposed a 'shock therapy' type economic reform.

For its own reasons, the opposition refused to cooperate with the proposed economic reform (even though their own economic programme advocated similar measures), and capitalised on government disarray to precipitate its downfall. The independent trade union *Podkrepa* organised a widely supported general strike and this extra-parliamentary pressure persuaded the communist majority in parliament to vote down the proposals of their own prime minister. On 29 November he resigned and on 7 December Dimitur Popov, a non-party jurist, was invited to form a government until new elections could be held in 1991; an interim cabinet was formed on 19 December with representatives from the three major parties on the basis of an Agreement Guaranteeing a Peaceful Transition to Democratic Society.

In 1991, the interim government set about implementing a policy more or less in line with that of the former socialist regime. On 12 July the new constitution was finally approved, and on 22 August the new electoral law passed. In the economy, the removal of price subsidies in February resulted in 400–1200 per cent price rises; but the government convinced the IMF of Bulgaria's seriousness of intent sufficiently to allow the granting of special drawing rights. (A World Bank loan would follow in August.) Further price liberalisation took place in June, and a 'social peace' agreement was signed between the government and the trade unions; unemployment running at 10 per cent by October put this under immediate strain. Other reforms proposed in the December Agreement were well behind schedule, especially privatisation measures, which, with the exception of agriculture, had made little progress. (In February the Land Reform Law had permitted the return of equivalent land or financial compensation for those who had lost land during collectivisation.)

Elections on the basis of the new constitution took place on 13 October 1991. The UDF, which split into four factions immediately before the elections, emerged victorious, with some 36 per cent of the vote. But the BSP retained the tradition of legitimacy of Bulgarian communism since the 1940s, with 33 per cent of the vote. In November, the new government announced its intention to establish a bourse by Christmas and began pushing ahead with the most noticeable gaps in its economic arsenal – legislation for privatisation, a banking law and a law regulating foreign investment. Presidential elections in January 1992 confirmed the strong residual support for the communists however. Zhelev won, but the candidate supported by the former communists received 45 per cent of the popular vote.

Romania

In the first half of 1989 Romania seemed secure in its illiberalism. Violent demonstrations in Braşov in November 1987, student demonstrations and an arson attack on the offices of the Party daily *Scînteia* the following month were all a year away and had apparently been successfully suppressed without lasting consequences. Relations with neighbouring Hungary were bad (in 1987 the age-old dispute over the history of Transylvania had emerged again), but they often were. Nothing seemed to disturb the regime's triumphs, which that spring were the week-long festivities to celebrate Elena Ceauşescu's birthday, in January, and the government's announcement on 12 April that all foreign debt had been repaid.

Under the surface, however, things were moving. An open letter was written by six members of the Party in March, which charged Ceauşescu with violating the constitution; but this was dealt with by harassment and arrest in the normal way. In September 1989, a document was circulated calling for the removal of Ceauşescu, signed by an anonymous National Salvation Front, but this had no impact on the 14th Party Congress of 20–24 November, which was equally unaffected by the events in the GDR and Czechoslovakia. Political and economic reform, even the creation of small businesses, was condemned, and the achievements of the Ceauşescus fulsomely acknowledged. Little attention was paid to the decline in the rate of growth (an annual rate of 7.3 per cent in 1986 became 4.8 per cent in 1987 and 3.2 per cent in 1988) or to the fact that real wages were stagnating.[16]

In a sense it was the Hungarian dimension to Romania's problems that precipitated the downfall of the regime. By the spring of 1989 Hungary was already committed to political pluralism and the restoration of a market economy, although the details remained unclear. Romania was so worried about the flood of refugees into Hungary (21 000 between mid-1987 and mid-1989, by no means all ethnic Hungarians) that for a period in the summer it reinforced its border with Hungary by a wire fence. Relations worsened further in August when Hungarian television broadcast an interview with King Michael of Romania, followed by an interview with László Tőkés, a Hungarian pastor in Timişoara. Tőkés was briefly held by the police at the time, and in October was expelled from his Reform Church congregation. He refused to move to another part of the country and, on 15 December, was served with a deportation order. Between 16 and 20 December attempts to prevent his removal escalated into street protests, sympathy demonstrations, the occupation of the Communist Party offices in Timişoara, calls for free elections and an end to repression and the deaths of seventy-one at the hands of the *Securitate* security police as a state of emergency was declared in Timişoara.

Ceauşescu nevertheless went on to hold a rally in Bucharest on 21 December. Boos and catcalls at his speech escalated into widespread anti-government demonstrations. The next day it was clear that the army had sided with the people against the *Securitate*, and, with the television and radio stations captured, a National Salvation Front (NSF) was organised in the TV station. The Ceauşescus fled by helicopter, but were detained and finally executed after a summary trial on 25 December. On 27 December the country was renamed simply Romania with Ion Iliescu, NSF Council chairman, as interim president and Petre Roman as prime minister, pending elections in April 1990. Although a comprehensive programme of political and economic reforms was also promised, prominent dissident Doina Cornea voiced suspicions about the real intentions of the new government that same day, and by 29 December the NSF had taken over the structures of communist power, including establishing NSF committees in the workplace.

In the first half of 1990 the NSF initiated numerous reform measures: the partial distribution of collective and state farm land, the abandonment of village systematisation, the issue of passports, an end to the ban on foreign borrowing. Elections, originally promised for April, were put back to May following opposition objections, Round Table talks between 29 opposition parties agreed on 1 February to power-sharing with the NSF within a Council for National Unity. The suspicion that the NSF was merely the communist party under a different guise remained however, and on 18 February five thousand demonstrated against the NSF. The next day several thousand miners arrived in Bucharest to rally in support of Iliescu and the NSF. In March ethnic tension erupted in Transylvania with three deaths.

Perhaps not surprisingly given the years of authoritarianism and the need for violent revolution, Romania did not generate new political parties with mass support. The biggest parties were the 'historical' National Liberals and National Peasants, led by an elder generation, some of whom had returned after years in emigration. Among the seventy five or so smaller political associations, only four had a chance of electoral success and their constituencies were limited: intellectuals, environmentalists, students and ethnic Hungarians. Against this unimpressive opposition, the NSF was the overwhelming winner of the elections on 20 May, gaining two thirds of the vote in both houses of parliament; and Iliescu was elected president with 85 per cent of the vote. Despite many accusations of fraud, international observers concluded that the result was a genuine expression of the wishes of the electorate.

The democratic commitment of the NSF was further questioned by events in June. Anti-communist demonstrators had been occupying University Square in Bucharest since 22 April. On 13 June they were cleared away in a dawn raid by the police. Their return later in the day resulted in three days of violent clashes as they came under attack from miners brought in by special train. Official figures recorded six deaths and 502 hospitalised.

Meanwhile, the new government began to implement its economic policy. On 10 July subsidies were withdrawn from numerous commodities, although the prices of 100 key commodities remained unchanged. On 25 July a Bill on the reorganisation of state enterprises was adopted, and on 31 August the National Privatisation Agency was established. By November, however, popular opposition to price increases resulted in further widespread demonstrations, the largest being on 15 November, timed to coincide with the anniversary of the 1987 Braşov demonstration against the Ceauşescu regime. Price increases continued to be implemented thereafter, both early in 1991 and again in April, but Iliescu, against the wishes of Finance Minister Teodor Stolojan, insisted on there being a 25 per cent ceiling. April also witnessed legislation permitting the 100 per cent foreign ownership of companies, but with the stipulation that only 15 per cent of profits could be repatriated. Despite the government's efforts to limit price rises, the country suffered a succession of strikes that fuelled internal tensions within the NSF between hard-liners and reformers, something that became clear at its March National Convention.

In September, dissatisfaction with price rises came to boiling point. The miners came to the capital once again, but this time they demonstrated against the government and demanded a price freeze. Whether or not this was an attempted 'communist coup', as the NSF maintained, is unclear. Disturbances lasted from 27 to 29 September, after which Roman resigned as prime minister, to be replaced by the reformist former finance minister Stolojan who was asked to form a broad-based government. The miners won the round, in that on 9 October it was announced that the prices of staple foods and goods and services would be frozen for six months, but they lost the bout. The miners' demonstrations were used as a pretext to postpone a US loan of $300 million.

Industrial output had fallen by 17 per cent in the first 9 months of 1991, which was expected to close with a multi-billion-dollar trade deficit. For all the suspicions about the democratic commitment of the NSF, its privatisation strategy, elaborated in the privatisation law of 14 August, was radical. Another voucher-based scheme, it envisaged allowing 30 per cent of capital to be available free to citizens via their holdings in five private ownership funds, and the remaining 70 per cent being held in a state ownership fund to be sold to foreign investors as appropriate; it was warmly applauded in the West.

On 21 November parliament finally produced its constitutional reform proposals, although five opposition groups voted against them because they gave too much power to the president. Modelled on French constitutional practice, a bicameral system was envisaged, with a strong presidency. A referendum on the constitution was held in December, which recorded 80 per cent in favour.

Yugoslavia

Following the 1982 debt crisis the Yugoslav economy continued as before. Labour productivity first fell and then stagnated. By 1985 the social product was 5.5 per cent smaller than in 1979. Inflation reached 88 per cent in 1986, over 100 per cent in 1987, 157 per cent in 1988 and almost 300 per cent in 1989.[17] 'Self-management' plumbed new depths of financial irresponsibility. The interplay between large enterprises, banks, risky loans and political power-broking is perhaps best exemplified by the *Agrokomerc* scandal of 1987 when the Bosnian food and agriculture combine of this name declared itself bankrupt with debts that exceeded its entire capital value.[18] In this situation of economic collapse long-simmering ethnic tensions finally boiled over.

Yugoslavia, or rather the republics making up Yugoslavia, was among the last to embark on pluralist political reform and radical economic restructuring, partly because of the residue of legitimacy, Tito's self-made self-management enjoyed. Yet, the dominant political discourse had already changed from communism to nationalism following the rise of Slobodan Milošević to a position of unchallenged power in the Serbian Party in October 1987. And the context of the new nationalist politics was, initially at least, the traditional one of constitutional amendment and reform, but with minimal endeavour to avoid contradictions between the federal and republican constitutions. Rivalry between republics diminished the strength of demands for multiparty democracy within them.

In the economic arena, the Law on Enterprises of December 1988 authorised the formation of 'firms' (joint stock companies) to operate alongside the existing forms of social ownership, and a foreign investment law in January 1989 relaxed regulations on joint ventures and the repatriation of profits. At the end of December 1988 the federal government resigned because of obstruction to its economic and political reforms and the unwillingness of the republics to ratify its budget proposals (finally passed in March 1989). A Law on Social Capital, facilitating the transformation of socially owned enterprises into joint stock companies, was passed at the federal level in December 1989, but, like the other elements in the federal programme, had not been ratified by the republics by the end of 1990. On 2 January 1990 the introduction of a new dinar worth 10 000 of the old dinars and pegged to the Deutschmark at 7 : 1 temporarily put an end to the inflationary spiral.

The first half of 1989 was dominated by the Kosovo issue and Serbia's constitutional changes that removed Autonomous Province status from Kosovo and Vojvodina. Serious disturbances were put down by 'special measures', involving the use of 'special courts', so restoring order by April. Throughout April and May republican rivalry and ethnic tensions increased, taking on a clear Croat–Serbian dimension in June when Serbs, returning from celebrations to mark the six hundredth anniversary of the Battle of Kosovo[19] to Knin in Croatia, clashed with local Croats. Following this, at a rally in the village of Srb, 100 000 Croatian Serbs declared their autonomy from Croatia and formed a Serbian National Council. Serbian sensitivities were offended when the celebrant of a mass on 8 October to mark the nine hundredth anniversary of the death of King Zvonimir of Croatia denied that Croats had engaged in genocide in the 1941–5 war.

Multiparty politics and elections, in which some 200 parties eventually participated federation-wide, entered the Yugoslav arena officially in 1990, although they only ever operated at a republican level. No federal elections on a multiparty basis were held before the federation disintegrated. The League of Communists committed itself to multiparty politics at its Extraordinary 14th Congress in January 1990, following the piecemeal formation of parties, in Slovenia and Croatia especially, throughout 1989 (the Croatian Democratic Union in June 1989, the Slovene Democratic League in January); and on January 22 the 'leading role of the League of Communists' was removed from the constitution, 36 years after Djilas had first proposed this.

Slovenia began the 1990 round of multiparty elections in April with two-round elections being held on 8 and 22 April. DEMOS, an alliance of six opposition groups, won 55 per cent of the vote, but the Party of Democratic Renewal (the former League of Communists) was the biggest single party and its candidate was elected president. DEMOS was united only on its anti-communism and desire for independence. In the Croatian elections, held on 22 April and 6–7 May, the Croatian Democratic Union, led by Franjo Tudjman and many other former communists, won a clear victory on a highly nationalistic programme. On 30 May Tudjman was elected president of the Croatian presidency.

In Serbia, where opposition parties remained technically illegal and were denied access to the media, demonstrations calling for early elections took place in June. Subsequently, on 2 July, a referendum confirmed, with a vote of 96 per cent in favour, changes to the Serbian constitution, including the abolition of the autonomous provinces and the deletion of 'socialist' from the name of the republic. The same day, the Slovenian Assembly formally declared its full sovereignty, while, on 25 July, the Croatian Assembly also dropped 'socialist' from its constitution.

Elections in Macedonia, Bosnia and Hercegovina, Serbia and Montenegro followed in November and December. In Macedonia, where there were massive irregularities in the first round, a coalition of nationalist parties emerged as the largest grouping; in Bosnia and Hercegovina ethnic and nationalist parties dominated roughly in proportion to the ethnic mix of the republic. In Montenegro the League of Communists emerged clear winners, as it did in Serbia where the Socialist Party of Serbia, the former League of Communists, won 77 per cent of the vote. In all the republics except Slovenia, whether the winners were nationalist parties or nationalistic communist parties, the opposition parties they faced were small and highly fragmented.

Ethnic tension had continued in 1990. In August, the Serbian towns of Knin and Benkovac set up blockades against Croatian police, and in October villages in the Knin area declared an independent Serb enclave. In 1991, tension escalated further and the Yugoslav federation descended into civil war. On 20 February the Slovene Assembly adopted a secession law and, the next day, the Croatian Assembly passed a Bill asserting the primacy of Croatian laws and the Croatian constitution. A week later, Serbs in the self-proclaimed 'Autonomous Region of Krajina' around Knin declared their region's unilateral secession from Croatia. On 11 April the Croatian government announced the formation of a *de facto* republican army in the form of the Croatian National Guard Corps after the Yugoslav army had deployed tanks following slayings of Serbs in the Croatian Plitvice National Park. On 29 April the army occupied a village near Knin.

In May, in a climate of increased tension and bloodshed three critical events took place, culminating in the outbreak of full-scale civil war. On 8 May, Slovenia announced its intention to secede on 26 June; on 12 May, the 'Autonomous Region' voted in its own referendum to remain part of Yugoslavia; and, on 19 May, a referendum in Croatia voted 90 per cent in favour of secession. The subsequent war in Slovenia was brief, effectively over by early July after a failed ceasefire on 28 June and a more successful one on 30 June, which was backed by the threat of European Community sanctions. Slovenia, like Croatia, agreed on 7 July to suspend independence for three months; but *de facto* independence had already been won, and in October it introduced its own currency, the solar.

Fighting between Croatia and Serbia was much more protracted. All chance of a Yugoslav solution disappeared at the end of July, when Tudjman boycotted meetings of the Collective State Presidency, and broke off all relations with Serbia on 4 August. Repeated European Community attempts to negotiate a ceasefire failed, and as the fighting continued throughout the autumn, roughly a third of Croatian territory, mostly inhabited by Serbs, was lost to Serbia, at the hands of an army comprising the Yugoslav National Army (with its Serbian and Montenegrin dominated officer corps) and Serbian irregulars. By the end of the year a lasting ceasefire negotiated by the UN appeared to be in force, but by then Serbia had gone a long way to carving out a new Greater Serb state – a policy that it would pursue with even greater violence in Bosnia throughout 1992. The country that had once signified for many an alternative vision of socialism, a decentralised, self-managed socialism, had to all intents and purposes ceased to exist. When Tito died, so did communism as an inspirational ideology for Yugoslavs. Nationalism took its place as the only emotion politicians could appeal to for popular support; but nationalism spelled more than the simple dismemberment of Yugoslavia into its constituent parts as the new states of Slovenia, Croatia, Bosnia, Macedonia and the Yugoslav Federation (Serbia and Montenegro) – it would lead to a bloody civil war in Bosnia.

Albania

Albania was the last of the dominoes to fall. The economy was in a parlous state. It had scarcely grown since 1975, and performance deteriorated further from 1986. Net material product grew at an annual rate of 1.7 per cent compared with the planned 6.3 per cent, and net material product per capita fell 0.3 per cent.[20] Nevertheless Ramiz Alia, who took over from Hoxha after his death in 1985, proved a loyal disciple, and the leadership paid little heed to the reform movements in neighbouring countries, until Ceauşescu fell.

That said, in February 1989, a limited restructuring of the Party and government was announced; and in November a limited amnesty, which included some political prisoners, was declared on the forty-fifth anniversary of liberation from Nazi occupation. On 19 December, anti-communist unrest and police repression in Shkodër set warning bells ringing, as did demonstrations in Shkodër on 11–14 January 1990, and Tiranë on 26 January. In May a range of supposed reform measures were introduced, including the right for peasants to sell their food at private markets, and in November a new electoral law was passed allowing secret ballots and multi-candidate (not multiparty) elections in February 1991.

But this was too little, too late, and with its appetite whetted the population demanded more democracy. The pattern of political change that followed showed remarkable similarities to that of Bulgaria. Demonstrations in Tiranë on 9 December were followed by the concession of a multiparty system of government, and the authorisation of opposition parties to take part in the February elections. On Christmas

Day the newly formed Democratic Party of Albania held a rally of over 10 000 in Kavaje demanding the postponement of elections and the release of political prisoners. At a special conference of the APL the next day Alia mildly criticised Stalin, but continued to defend Hoxha.

As 1990 turned into 1991, ethnic Greeks started voting with their feet and crossing the border to Greece and the currency was devalued 100 per cent. On 16 January the government acceded to opposition demands to postpone the elections until 31 March, in return for a pledge from the opposition not to boycott them and to support a wage freeze and ban on strikes until 1 May. On 20 February, Alia declared presidential rule following student demonstrations during which Hoxha's statue was pulled down. Four opposition parties participated in the March elections. As might have been expected with such hastily called elections, the APL won 60 per cent of the votes, mainly in the countryside, although Alia himself and other former leaders were personally defeated in their Tiranë constituencies. The APL won 169 of the 250 seats, the Democratic Party (the biggest opposition party) won 75. The Democratic Party refused the offer to form a coalition government, but retracted its threat not even to participate in parliament. On 25 April the word 'people's' was removed from the constitution, and on 30 April, despite his personal electoral failure, Alia was appointed president by parliament.

As in Bulgaria, the opposition was never persuaded of the validity of rapidly held elections and continued with extra-parliamentary struggle. After a general strike (in support of a 50 per cent wage increase and the bringing to justice of those responsible for earlier deaths of demonstrators) backed by the Democratic Party, the government resigned on 6 June, to be replaced by a non-party Government of National Stability on 12 June, in which the Democratic Party, the Republican Party, the Social Democratic Party, the Agrarian Party and nine non-party organisations were represented. The Democratic Party received seven ministries including the Ministry of the Economy. The next day, at the 10th APL Congress, the Party name was changed to Socialist Party of Albania. During this political drama, the economy had come to a standstill and in the first quarter of 1991 agricultural and industrial output had declined by 33 per cent and 50 per cent respectively on the previous year.

In August, the government began measuring out land in readiness for its return to those dispossessed under collectivisation. By mid-October some 20 per cent of land had been privatised, although no system existed for registering the new owners and issuing title deeds, and the average holding resulting from the process was only 0.3 hectares.[21] On 1 September a draft package of economic reforms was forwarded including the creation of a National Agency for Privatisation, which would also encourage the creation of small businesses, a more independent central bank, the right to hard-currency bank accounts and the creation, from 1 October, of a Foreign Investment Agency. But none of these reforms had an immediate social impact; on 14 September, as import and export regulations were lifted, more demonstrations took place.

On 4 December, the Democratic Party withdrew from the coalition government over its failure to bring forward elections to January or prosecute former communists for alleged corruption. The Democrats also accused the former communists of having halted the land reform and frightened off foreign investors by promoting lawlessness. Former food minister Vilson Ahmeti was appointed prime minister of a caretaker government some days later, as thirty-two died in a food riot. By the end of the year public order had all but broken down completely. When the elections were held in March 1992, the Democratic Party won a comfortable victory and Alia resigned as president.

THE CEMENT CRUMBLES

As the communist regimes in Eastern Europe fell apart, and Yugoslavia, the alternative socialist model, consumed itself in strife, the cement that had held the Warsaw Pact countries together disintegrated. The first element to go was Comecon, the rationale for which was vitiated during the course of 1990 when it was decided that Eastern European trade should be conducted in dollars and at world market prices. The decision to dissolve Comecon was taken in principle on 6 January 1991 and, after some hesitation, formally ratified in Budapest on 28 June 1991.

The demise of the Warsaw Pact was equally protracted. On 25 February a meeting of the Political and Consultative Committee of the Warsaw Pact in Budapest unanimously signed a protocol cancelling the military agreements, organs and structures of the Pact from 31 March 1991. The Pact itself was formally dissolved in Prague on 1 July 1991. Soviet troops had already left Hungary and Czechoslovakia by this time, although withdrawal from the former GDR and Poland was a more protracted affair, scheduled to last until 1993 in the case of Poland and, under the Two-plus-Four agreement, until 1994 in the case of the former GDR.

But before troop withdrawals could be completed, the Soviet Union itself disappeared. In a period of accelerated political change in the Soviet Union following the abortive coup of 19–20 August 1991, the facilitator of change in both Eastern Europe and the Soviet Union itself was removed from the world stage. On Christmas Day 1991 President Gorbachev resigned and, on Boxing Day, the rump of the Soviet parliament formally dissolved the Soviet Union. The most powerful influence on the history of Eastern Europe since 1945 ceased to exist, leaving new free regimes striving to build not socialism, as had been the dream in 1945, but capitalism.

9

Adapting to Capitalism: Consensus or Confrontation?

In the first decade or so following the establishment of democratic parliaments throughout Eastern Europe the division between Central Europe (which Slovenia swiftly jointed) and the Balkans became more rather than less pronounced. From the wreck of the socialist experiment that failed, Central Europe retained the element of social reform inherent in communism; the Balkans clung on to the element of authoritarianism, using nationalism rather than Marxism–Leninism as the ideology of inspiration. A year or so into the new millennium, however, there were some indications, firmer in Bulgaria and Romania than in the former Yugoslavia and Albania, that the divide was perhaps beginning to narrow.

A Central Europe–Balkans divide was particularly visible in the economic sphere. By the end of the millennium, Central European countries had developed what the EU recognised as 'functioning market economies' based on private sector companies; and economic output had just about reached or moved slightly beyond 1989 levels. At least they had got back to where they started. The countries of the Balkans did not, or had just begun to, function as market economies, privatisation was less advanced and economic output wallowed way below 1989 levels. In terms of politics, a model developed in Central Europe that was recognisably social democratic, while in the Balkans the pattern was of regimes inspired by populist rhetoric manipulating patronage at the expense of their less relatively reformed economies. Table 9.1 represents an attempt to portray this diverging performance numerically,

Table 9.1 *Economic and political performance in the 1990s*

Country	*Real GDP in 1999 1989 = 100*	*Private sector share of GDP % mid-2000*	*Institutional performance*[a]	*Cumulative liberalisation*[b]	*Cumulative democracy*[c]
Central Europe					
Czech Republic	95	80	3.2	9.0	11.0
Hungary	99	80	3.5	10.0	11.0
Poland	122	70	3.3	8.0	11.0
Slovakia	100	75	2.8	9.0	10.5
Slovenia	109	55	2.8	8.0	11.0
Balkans					
Albania	95	75	1.9	8.0	6.0
Bosnia and Hercegovina	n.a.	35	n.a.	n.a.	n.a.
Bulgaria	67	70	2.4	5.0	8.5
Croatia	78	60	2.7	7.0	3.5
Macedonia	74	55	2.3	7.0	6.0
Romania	76	60	2.3	6.0	8.0
Yugoslavia	n.a.	40	n.a.	n.a.	n.a.

[a] Unweighted average of transition indicators in 2000 for banking sector, non-banking financial institutions, competition policy and enterprise reform and corporate governance. Scales run from 1 to 4+, the latter being the standards of advanced industrial economies.

[b] Number of years in which a country has achieved a score of at least 3− on price liberalisation and at least 4− on trade and foreign exchange liberalisation.

[c] Number of years in which executives and legislatives have been freely and fairly elected.

Source European Bank for Reconstruction and Development, *Transition Report 2000* (London, 2000), pp. 8, 14, 21, 65.

a divide that was reflected in the attitudes of the international community. The Czech Republic, Hungary and Poland jointed NATO in March 1999, and Slovenia, Slovakia, Bulgaria and Romania were officially invited to join at the Prague summit in November 2002. The rest of the Balkans was encouraged to join, but immediate membership seemed unlikely. In terms of the EU, the Czech Republic, Hungary, Poland and Slovenia were invited to join in March 1998, and were on target for 2004 membership. The invitation was extended to Slovakia, Bulgaria and Romania in October 1999, but only Slovakia responded quickly enough for 2004 membership, the others being encouraged to aim for 2007; while the rest of the Balkans had to negotiate Stabilisation and Association Agreements (SAAs) rather than membership.[1]

This Central European–Balkan division of Europe has historical antecedents that predate 1945. The post-1989 social democratic tradition of politics reasserted itself in precisely those countries where reformist socialists had built strong social democratic parties even before the First World War, in the Czech lands and Slovenia within the Austrian Social Democratic Party, in Poland and, to a lesser extent, in Hungary; although weak in the interwar years, post-1945 the communists were always forced to acknowledge this tradition to some degree. The authoritarian–populist style of government has developed in areas where, at the turn of the century, social democracy was either non-existent or revolutionary rather than reformist in nature, and where, during the Second World War, the communists won an authentic position of authority in the resistance popular fronts; here the social democratic alternative never had to be addressed.

Much was made in the early years of the decade of the contrasting approaches of 'gradualism' versus 'shock therapy'; but nowhere did real world development conform to these abstractions. A more recent approach has been to identify 'Type I' and 'Type II' reforms, the former being the relatively easy economic measures such as macroeconomic stabilisation and price liberalisation, the latter being the development and enforcement of laws, regulations and institutions that ensure a functioning market economy. The path from one to the other is seen to be the ability to collect taxes and minimise corruption and rent-seeking behaviour, something that is much easier to achieve in countries wealthy enough to pay government officials a living wage.[2] According to this approach, the Balkans and Central Europe have implemented Type I reforms, but only Central Europe has implemented Type II. Part of the impetus to progress from one to the other is the prospect of EU and NATO membership. Joining these institutions and adopting the rules that membership imposes, such as implementing the EU's body of law (the *acquis communautaire*) and resolving disputes with actual and prospective member countries, has operated as a virtuous circle, spurring the more reformed countries to reform their legal and political systems further, thereby accentuating the Central Europe–Balkan divide.

CENTRAL EUROPE

In suggesting that a social democratic style of politics emerged in Central Europe in the half-decade after the establishment of democratic politics, care must be taken to distinguish social democratic politics from rule by a Social Democratic Party. The crux is the character of politics – balancing a private enterprise economy with a commitment to social welfare – and it is fundamentally similar to that of Western Europe. Despite the neo-liberal agenda of foreign advisors and influential politicians and parties, welfare remained the key issue: social welfare or budget deficits is what stood at the very heart of economics, politics and society in post-socialist Central Europe. Societies used to high levels of provision for decades were required by those holding the international purse strings to accept cuts. Social democratic politics proved able to manage these cuts and their social consequences. The resentment they caused and the consequent support for populist parties remained a constant shadow on the horizon, but after a decade of post-socialism these parties had only restricted constituencies. The politics of Central Europe was familiar, mundane and rather unexciting.

Poland

In Poland's first democratic parliament there were some eighteen parties, and the coalition governments of Jan Olszewski and Hanna Suchocka both proved relatively short-lived. President Lech Wałęsa called early elections in May 1993, but, contrary to his expectations, they resulted in victory for the Democratic Left Alliance, incorporating the former communist party (Social Democracy of the Polish Republic) and the Peasant Party (PSL). With right-wing parties poorly represented in parliament, Wałęsa took it upon himself to be the chief opposition to the government, and, for a time it looked as if Poland was going to develop along the populist–authoritarian road of politics associated with the Balkans, as he stretched to the limits the powers granted to him by Poland's constitution. Throughout 1994 Wałęsa vetoed legislation relating to the budget, and then, when overruled by parliament, delayed signing the laws into effect; equally he delayed endorsing ministerial appointments. Alarmed at Wałęsa's increasingly authoritarian behaviour, in October 1994 parliament almost unanimously urged the President to stop destabilising the constitutional order; but Wałęsa took no notice and launched a guerrilla campaign against proposed government tax changes. Even after his defeat in the November 1995 presidential elections, Wałęsa tried to destabilise the government by publishing evidence that the new prime minister was a former Soviet agent. After the election of Aleksander Kwaśniewski as president, the former communist settled down to manage a capitalist economy with some success. Poland was the lead economy of the region in the early 1990s and was the first to come out of recession, in 1992.[3]

Unlike in 1993, for the September 1997 elections the parties on the Right coalesced into a mere two groupings, the 'Thatcherite' Freedom Union (FU) and the Solidarity Electoral Action (SEA), a coalition of 36 parties grouped around the Solidarity trade union. Despite an increased vote for the Social Democrats, support for their coalition partner, the PSL, ebbed away and the ruling coalition was defeated. The new government of free marketeers and conservative nationalists did not have the 60 per cent majority necessary to overturn the presidential veto, heralding a further period of 'cohabitation'. As early as December it reintroduced the restrictive 1993 abortion law.

Despite its unlikely composition, the coalition survived 'cohabitation' and the inevitable policy disputes between the free marketeers and the interventionist conservative nationalists until the summer of 2000, when, after two renegotiations of the coalition agreement in March and October 1999, the FU left and the SEA continued to rule alone until the September 2001 elections. By this time a group of twenty one SEA deputies had regularly been voting against the government on economic issues, and, in Warsaw politics, the FU had formed a coalition with the Social Democrats. In the intervening years the government had weathered numerous demonstrations by peasants and workers, triggered by the economic restructuring plans of 1998 and culminating in September 1999 in the biggest demonstration in Warsaw since the fall of communism. It had implemented a new health care system, prompting strikes by nurses and anaesthetists in early 1999; introduced a new three-tier system of local government (taking effect in 1999); but failed in the FU-promoted attempt to reform the tax system radically.

The presidential elections of 8 October 2000 represented a dramatic switch back towards social democratic policies. It was not so much the size of Kwaśniewski's victory, 53 per cent in the first round, as the annihilation of the opposition. The next closest candidate polled only 17 per cent, and Wałęsa received only 1.01 per cent of the vote. A year later in the September 2001 parliamentary elections, the surprise again was not the victory of the social democrats, but the scale of the government's defeat: neither the SEA nor the FU crossed the 7 per cent threshold to enter parliament, although both had split prior to the election and some of their successors did, as did the extremist radical peasant party Self-Defence. The social democrats did not have an overall majority, and, again, formed a coalition with the PSL. With radical nationalism apparently not attractive to more than a minority of the electorate, a question mark was raised about the strategy and tactics of right-of-centre politics in Poland.[4]

Hungary

During 1992 and 1993 there were some signs that the immediate post-communist government of conservatives was becoming authoritarian in spirit. Prime Minister József Antall adopted a presidential style, appointing his representatives to each ministry and introducing the equivalent of French style *préfet* in every county. He also engaged in 'media war' with the state radio and television, keeping both under government rather than parliamentary control. Yet for all his readiness to exploit populist nationalism and provoke ethnic unrest amongst Hungarians living in Romania and Slovakia, by June 1993 he had decided to deal with the populist wing of his party and the anti-Semitic István Csurka and his supporters were expelled, subsequently creating the Hungarian Truth and Justice Party (HTJP).

Throughout 1993, the standing of the former communists, the Hungarian Socialist Party (HSP), rose steadily and the party gained outright victory in the May 1994 elections. Nevertheless it established a government in alliance with the liberal Alliance of Free Democrats (AFD) in order to achieve the two-thirds majority necessary to amend the constitution. In the first year of the administration, difficult decisions remained unresolved. Fuel price rises were postponed, the government agreed to a back-dating of proposed pension increases, subsidies to the big steel plants continued and the promised 'social pact' between government, employers and employees remained unsigned. This caution was eventually too much for the HSP's economics expert László Békesi who resigned as minister of Finance in January 1995, to be replaced by Lajos Bokros, who in March succeeded in pushing through parliament what subsequently became known as the 'Bokros package'. It aimed at reducing spending on welfare, triggered widespread demonstrations and prompted two ministers to resign. Further cost-cutting measures in the health service in 1996 were enough to secure an IMF loan in March that year and membership of the Organisation for Economic Cooperation and Development (OECD).[5]

The coalition stayed together for its full term, despite constant bickering. Once areas of key policy difference had been resolved by the Bokros package, the reason for their disagreements was as much personalities and style of government (Horn's tendency to act before consulting his partners, whose assistance he did not actually need) as policy. Meanwhile the political right underwent a radical realignment. The Hungarian Democratic Forum, the party of the first post-socialist prime minister, split and ceased to be a major actor. The new force on the Right was FIDESZ, the Alliance of Young Democrats who shed their liberal image and presented themselves to the May 1998 elections as the conservative FIDESZ-Hungarian Civic Party. The result was close. The socialists got the biggest share of the vote, but FIDESZ got most seats, although not enough to rule alone. In order to guarantee a parliamentary majority, Viktor Orbán, the FIDESZ leader, had to forge an alliance with the Smallholders Party of József Torgyán, the populist party of the conservative, nationalist right.

Orbán's period in office was characterised by 'presidentialism', a certain disregard for legal and constitutional niceties (he cut by two-thirds the frequency with which parliament met) and judicious nationalism: he let out the nationalist genie when he thought it might bring electoral advantage. He vociferously supported the idea of a Hungarian university in Cluj, Transylvania, and in June 2001 passed the so-called Status Law that extended economic, social and cultural rights to Hungarians living in all surrounding nations save Austria where it was deemed to contravene EU rules on discriminatory practices.

The March–April 2002 elections and their aftermath were interesting in three ways. The least important was that the pendulum principle prevailed, and the HSP–AFD coalition emerged the winners, on an exceptionally high turnout. More important was the impact of the revelation that the new prime minister, Péter Medgyessy, had previously worked as an agent for the internal security services. Medgyessy survived the inevitable scandal, and opinion polling suggested that the population did not care: the past was no longer a political issue. Finally there was the behaviour of Orbán in the face of prospective and actual electoral defeat. He rapidly moved politics onto the street, organising demonstrations, orchestrating campaigns to have the election results overturned because of imagined irregularities (the Organisation for Security and Cooperation in Europe (OSCE) had no complaints about the elections), and announcing a new, non-party, citizens' politics. In Hungary too there was uncertainty about the nature of right-of-centre politics once extreme nationalism was revealed as a minority terrain.[6]

The Czech Republic

The Czechoslovak elections of June 1992 marked the end of the politics of transition. The broad-based popular organisations that had brought about the 'Velvet Revolution' disappeared, and a more conventional Left–Right political spectrum emerged, with Klaus's Civic Democratic Party (CDP) as still the largest party and deputies from the Social Democratic Party being elected for the first time. By the time of the Czech local elections in November 1994, both the social democrats and the communists were able to make significant gains, and during 1995 the Czech Social Democratic Party emerged as a force to be reckoned with. In the June 1996 elections the Social Democrats were only 3 per cent behind Klaus, having quadrupled their vote since 1992. Klaus negotiated a coalition government with minor parties amid signs that all was not well in the economy. The collapse in August of the Kreditní Banka was the seventh that year.[7]

In 1997, the economic crisis worsened, shattering the belief that the Czech Republic was the most successful transition economy. The Czech economy could not support its continued high spending: neither its visible subsidies (on housing, public transport, industry and agriculture), nor its invisible support of insolvent companies. 'Voucher privatisation' had ended up creating what some dubbed 'bank socialism'. Ownership remained opaque, and the ultimate owner, the state, was reluctant to impose bankruptcy, indeed there had been no bankruptcy of a single Czech large state-owned industrial firm. Banks lent to insolvent companies, and their debts were covered by the Konsolidační Banka, which did not appear on the nation's balance sheet. There was a black hole in the nation's finances that could not be hidden. In April 1997 Klaus introduced an austerity package and further budget cuts followed as the value of the Czech crown fell.

Economic failure was compounded by corruption. In September an official report listed thousands of cases of 'tunnelling', the Czech term for corrupt privatisation whereby the choicest of state or investment fund-owned assets were simply transferred to the private companies set up by their managers. Worse, in October it was revealed that Klaus's CDP was not above corruption: it had received funding in return for favours related to privatisation and banking. The government fell in November and President Havel asked the National Bank governor to form an interim government, which the Social Democrats agreed to support in return for early elections. The elections, when they took place in June 1998, resulted in a stalemate. The Social Democrats had 32.2 per cent of the vote and the CDP 27.7 per cent. On paper Klaus could have put together a coalition based on right-of-centre parties and the tacit support of the communists. But the Christian Democrats refused to have even a tacit deal with the communists, and the other party of the Right, the FU, was the creation of former CDP politicians who had tried to make Klaus resign, and they refused to work with him. The result was a minority Social Democrat government and an 'opposition agreement' on the part of the CDP not to initiate a vote of no confidence, in return for being considered the official opposition. This unlikely solution survived until the next elections of 2002, although the details were renegotiated in 2000. The CDP ensured that government spending was not 'excessive', and the two parties cooperated, ultimately not very successfully, to amend the electoral system to favour bigger parties. Meanwhile the economy began to recover, particularly foreign investment, which responded positively to a package initiated by the interim government. Economic recovery favoured the Social Democrats and they won a second term in the elections of June 2002, this time in a coalition government with the Christian Democrats and the FU.[8]

Slovakia

Slovakia's first decade or so as an independent country was made up of two slightly unequal halves: the era of Prime Minister Vladimir

Mečiar, leader of the Movement for a Democratic Slovakia (MDS), during which Slovakia developed a more Balkan style of politics, followed by a coalition government that, though constantly fractious, never lost sight of the long-term goals of EU and NATO membership and undid much of the damage that Mečiar had done.

In his first moves after his election, Mečiar tried to assert his control over the broadcast media and limit the independence of the press. His growing authoritarianism led to clashes with President Michal Kováč. In March 1994 Kováč used his first state of the nation speech to attack Mečiar, which resulted in Mečiar losing a vote of no confidence and conceding power for a while to a caretaker coalition government. That government began to undo some of Mečiar's work, but in the subsequent October 1994 elections the MDS increased its vote and dominated the new parliament. Returned to power, Mečiar began to strengthen his position further and determined to force Kováč to resign. In 1995 this ambition developed into a personal vendetta, when the president's son was kidnapped in extraordinary circumstances, and continued throughout 1996, when the president was deprived of the power to appoint the head of the armed services.[9]

Mečiar also attacked the parliamentary system. In December 1996 he deprived a dissident MDS member of parliament of his seat after he had left the party in protest at Mečiar's authoritarian rule. Further, local government reform not only consolidated the MDS at the local level by centring the new structures in locations of MDS support, it also provided a blueprint for new electoral constituencies within which MDS victory was all but guaranteed. Things came to a head in May 1997 when a referendum was held on the questions of how to elect future presidents and NATO membership. After an ambiguous ruling by the country's highest court, many Slovaks found the only question on the referendum ballot related to NATO membership; the question about presidential elections had simply been left out. With anarchic scenes outside polling stations, the referendum was boycotted by most of the population. In June the EU set three conditions for Slovakia remaining in the first round of enlargement talks, one of which was the passing of a minority-language law. The response was a cabinet-approved memorandum in November stating that the current law was sufficient. No attempt was made to meet the other conditions. Slovakia joined the second rank of EU applicants.[10]

But Mečiar was rejected by the Slovak people on an 85 per cent turnout in September 1998, despite his assumption of presidential powers in March, his manipulation of the electoral law in May and his campaigning alongside media stars such as Claudia Schiffer and Gérard Depardieu. A coalition government emerged spanning centre-right parties including the Christian Democrats, a coalition of the ethnic Hungarian parties, the former communists and other smaller parties. This disparate amalgam of parties inevitably disagreed along predictable lines – the Christian Democrats rejected the coalition's stance on the Vatican and state schools, the Hungarians stuck out for ethnic concessions, the former communists resented concessions to the Hungarians (including in the sphere of local government reform) and opposed radical economic measures – but, with the encouragement of President Rudolph Schuster (the victor over Mečiar in presidential elections in May 1999) it did not let these differences of opinion destroy the coalition.

The government quickly reversed some of Mečiar's more questionable moves, including 'crony' privatisation deals, and pushed ahead with reforms, despite trade union demonstrations that peaked in September 1999. The government responded with alacrity to the EU's change of policy regarding enlargement in December 1999, which abolished the distinction between first round and second round candidates for accession. A year later the EU judged it to have a 'functioning market economy', and by the summer of 2002 it had completed more chapters of the *acquis communautaire* than some of the former first round countries. This turnaround could not have been achieved without some pain, and the MDS became again the most popular party in the country. But over the summer of 2002 this popularity began to wane as NATO and the EU made thinly veiled threats about the consequences of an MDS victory and the MDS itself split in June. The electorate heeded these warnings. In the September 2002 elections, although Mečiar polled most votes (just under 20 per cent), a coalition of centre-right and Hungarian parties could put together an absolute majority. Slovakia had regained a social democratic style of politics; but a social democratic party as such was conspicuous by its absence.[11]

Slovenia

The elections held on 6 December 1992 resulted in the collapse of the broad-based anti-communist coalition DEMOS: the Liberal Democratic Party (LDP) won the biggest percentage of the votes,

21 per cent; the Christian Democrats came next with 14 per cent; and the United List of Social Democrats, as the former communists ended up calling themselves after abandoning the title Party of Democratic Renewal, won 12 per cent. These three parties became the core of the governing coalition. The coalition faced vocal criticism from the confusingly named Social Democratic Party, led by Janez Janša, a hero of the independence struggle, who denounced the ruling coalition as a bunch of crypto-communists who kowtowed to the Italians and betrayed Slovenia's national interest. Local elections in December 1994 showed that such populist rhetoric had had an impact and there was a distinct move to the Right. National elections in November 1996 showed a further shift to the Right. Janša's representation in parliament rose to 16 per cent, with the other nationalist party, the Slovene People's Party, polling 19 per cent. Although the Liberal Democrats improved their showing somewhat, the United List of Social Democrats saw their seats fall from fourteen to nine and remained outside government. Nevertheless when coalition negotiations concluded in February 1997, Janez Drnovšek of the LDP was prime minister leading a coalition made up of the People's Party and the Pensioners' Democratic Party. Continuity was reinforced in November when Milan Kučan was re-elected president.[12]

The government assiduously pursued its goals of joining the EU and NATO, achieving the first league in the former but the second in the latter. It asserted its Central European identity forcefully in November 1997 when it rejected an invitation to the Balkan summit in Crete, insisting that it was not a Balkan nation. The following two years were rather quiet politically. Slovenia's sea border with Croatia surfaced as a minor bone of contention in 1998, as did the Krsko nuclear power plant, which they had jointly constructed in the days of Yugoslavia; and in 1999 the parliament debated but did not pass a new electoral law. In April 2000 Drnovšek failed to win a vote of no confidence after parties of the Right regrouped and merged. Slovenia was briefly ruled by a more right-of-centre coalition under the Argentinean Slovene Andrej Bajuk; but in elections in October, following electoral reform in favour of a proportional system, the centre-left won again and Drnovšek came back as prime minister of his fourth government, with a much stronger coalition, in December. The following years were equally uneventful, although the tensions with Croatia over the same two issues rumbled on. The EU was critical of her slow pace of privatisation, but nevertheless Slovenia had completed twenty-six of the *acquis communautaire* by the end of 2001. In Slovenia's mundane social democratic politics, all that was remarkable was the continuity of its leaders. In December 2002 Drnovšek was elected president: the constitution prevented Kučan standing for a third term.[13]

THE BALKANS

In South East Europe, political life developed along very different lines to those of Central Europe, and it was far from mundane. Populist authoritarianism and personal rule, building on nationalism and authoritarian traditions within Marxism, was the norm for fully the first post-socialist decade, although there were signs of a popular weariness with nationalism and doctrinal politics in the early years of the new millennium, which fed through to the political structures. In some countries the driving force was a desire to rejoin the international community, in others the international community itself attempted to impose a more 'moderate' form of politics. Initially there was an unwillingness to break clearly with the past, and when a clear break did occur, the alternative was either as rigid as the regime it supplanted, or weak and as susceptible as other regimes to corruption. In this politics consensus building was an alien concept. Where strong leaders emerged, they refused to recognise the legitimacy of opposing views, and politics became a vehicle for distributing economic rewards in order to maintain political support. Where the electoral outcome enforced a coalition, the parties endlessly bickered over who should get which ministry, partly because of the political patronage that went with them and partly because of dogmatic adherence to the party line.

Albania

Although the Democratic Party (DP) won a clear majority in the 1992 elections, with the former communist Albanian Socialist Party (ASP) retaining strong representation only in the south of the country, it did not have the two-thirds majority required to change the constitution, and this became an obsessive preoccupation for party leader Sali Berisha. Unable to do anything about the constitution in the short term, Berisha launched an anti-communist crusade: throughout 1993 and into 1994 prominent former communists were arrested on various charges and sentenced to prison terms; of these, the most significant was the arrest in July 1993 of the ASP chairman, Fatos Nano, charged with corruption during his spell as prime minister from April to June 1991; and in September 1995 Berisha dismissed the chairman of the Supreme Court when he agreed to review Nano's case. Support for the Berisha regime was already on the wane, as local election results of summer 1992 revealed, and in 1994 Berisha lost a referendum on how the president should be elected.[14]

Despite apparently falling support, Berisha easily won the elections in May–June 1996, with the two-thirds majority necessary to amend the constitution. This was achieved by intimidation. In September 1995 a 'Law on Genocide', relating to the alleged crimes of the communist era, was passed. This was soon being used as an excuse to break up ASP meetings and even sentence, on the eve of the elections, three former communist leaders to death. There were so many irregularities, including cases of violent intimidation in the elections, subsequently documented by the OSCE, that the ASP and other opposition parties pulled out of the first round, boycotted the second round and continued to boycott the new parliament.[15]

What finally brought Berisha's regime to its knees were pyramid investment schemes. In a country with neither a proper private banking system nor a stock exchange until 1996, investors sought alternative channels. First started in 1993, and pledging big returns for small investments, the pyramid schemes blossomed in 1994, when smuggling from crisis-ridden Yugoslavia also reached a peak. Once the Dayton Accord had been signed, the market for smuggled oil and arms dried up, and with it an important source of income for the schemes. Throughout 1996, IMF and World Bank experts had warned that the country's economy would implode if the schemes collapsed. And this is what happened. The schemes collapsed, and Albanians who had lost everything took to the streets in rioting, which began in late January and early February 1997. By the first week in February the southern town of Vlora was outside government control, the south being an ASP stronghold, Berisha's power base being in the north. As the army was sent to restore order, more and more towns declared a sort of semi-independence and elected new committees to run local affairs. In April an Italian-led multinational force was stationed in the country to maintain peace and oversee the elections that Berisha had belatedly conceded should take place. The elections were held in June and the ASP won an overwhelming majority. Nano was appointed prime minister and shortly afterwards Berisha resigned as president.[16]

Berisha boycotted parliament for much of the next term, but intervened to call for an end to the violence that followed the murder of a DP politician in September 1998, which also resulted in Nano's resignation as prime minister. The government had some success returning the economy to consistent high growth and moving ahead with privatisation; but the World Bank, among others, remained critical of the politicisation and corruptibility of state institutions including the judiciary, and the country suffered regular power cuts, the consequence of endemic non-payment of bills to the state power company. The key political events took place within parties rather than between them, the issues being personal ambition and differing approaches to the key national issues: the situation in Kosovo. Nano opposed open support of the Kosovo Liberation Army (UCK); his ASP opponents were more sympathetic to Berisha's line of more active support from his northern power base. In intra-party wrangling, Nano was successful in removing his opponent, but not in regaining the premiership; Berisha overcame his challenger, Genc Pollo, who left to form a new party.

In the June 2001 elections the ASP won an absolute majority. The OSCE judged them acceptable, but Berisha, again, cried foul and threatened not to participate in the second round. The power struggle within the ASP continued, to such an extent that in October it was unable to sign its SAA with the EU because the country was effectively without a government. The SAA was ultimately held out as a carrot to bring the internecine rivalry to an end. Although Nano had said he would stand for president in June 2002, in the end a compromise candidate, Alfred Moisiu, was elected because the EU insisted on a candidate acceptable to both the ASP and the DP if a future SAA was to be signed. Weeks later, Nano achieved a consolation victory in the ASP's internal power struggle and became prime minister for the fourth time.[17]

Romania

Unity within the National Salvation Front (NSF) did not survive the 1992 election campaign. As early as March 1992 a power struggle within the NSF saw the re-election of the reformist Roman as its leader prompt the conservative President Iliescu to engineer a split and establish the rival Democratic National Salvation Front (DNSF); Iliescu's party went on to win the elections in September, and then to change its name to the Social Democratic Party of Romania. After his election defeat Roman merged his NSF with the DP and adopted that party's name.

Iliescu's victory was not clear-cut. His party emerged as the biggest single party, but was forced to look to allies from other parties to secure a majority and turned to both the far Right and far Left: the nationalist Greater Romania Party and the former communist Socialist Labour Party both agreed to support his government, although they only became formal coalition partners in January 1995, while the other nationalist party, the Romanian National Unity Party (RNUP), became a coalition partner during summer 1994. As a result, while ostensibly committed to economic reform, Iliescu stressed the need to limit the social cost of the reform process, and, to appease the nationalists, he turned a blind eye to chauvinistic outbursts. The position of Romania's Hungarian minority was inevitably affected by these developments, and in August 1995 incidents of harassment, such as the attempt by the RNUP mayor of Cluj to ban celebrations of Hungary's national day, resulted in criticism from the OSCE. Iliescu also failed to promote privatisation, despite pressure from the IMF and World Bank, except in the case of former comrades. Newspapers claimed that 1000 of the country's top 1540 private firms were in the hands of former communist officials.[18]

In the run-up to the November 1996 elections, Iliescu broke with his nationalist coalition partners and promised historic reconciliation with Hungary following the signing on 16 September 1996 of a Treaty of Understanding, Cooperation and Good-Neighbourliness. But it was the opposition coalition made up of Roman's DP, which had merged with the Social Democratic Union, the liberal Democratic Convention of Romania and representatives of the Hungarian minority, that won both the national and presidential elections. The presidential contest was won by the liberal Emil Constantinescu.[19]

The 'first democratic year since 1989', 1997, started optimistically with dramatic dismissals of personnel from the army, television, security services and so on, but it was clear by the end of the first year that the government was not capable of implementing painful policies. The 'shock therapy' of January price rises prompted trade union demonstrations in February, and demonstrations continued throughout the year; the demonstrators generally won concessions. The IMF viewed developments with increasing concern: it agreed to loans in April, became anxious about the slow pace of reform in July and concluded that it was not satisfied by the pace of reform, especially privatisation, in October. The one positive measure was a government ordinance allowing for bilingual road signs where an ethnic minority made up 20 per cent of the population.

The following years of the coalition produced much of the same. Following pressure from Roman's DP, a new Prime Minister, Radu Vasile, was appointed in April 1998. He commented that 'there is no other government in the region that would spend so much time criticising steps taken by the government', and also criticised the 'trade union–state managerial alliance' that was hindering reform. Year-long negotiations with the ethnic Hungarian party over a Hungarian–German university got virtually nowhere in 1998 when the Court of Appeals ruled it unconstitutional because it introduced positive discrimination. An education bill the following year opened the way for minority language universities, however, although it denied them government funds. Financial aid from the IMF and the World Bank was forthcoming in the second half of 1999, but this was as much to do with Romania's aid to NATO over Kosovo as it was to a fundamental change in economic policy. In May 2000 the National Investment Fund collapsed, destabilising the whole financial sector, yet the government offered no compensation to those who lost their savings.

The consequence of the coalition's inability to take difficult economic measures, or make any inroads against endemic corruption, which had been one of its pledges, was electoral collapse. Iliescu's party won the November 2000 elections, and he personally won the presidential elections in December. His opponent did not even come from one of the coalition parties, but from the far right Greater Romania Party. Despite his parliamentary majority, however, Iliescu chose to govern in cooperation with the ethnic Hungarian party in an attempt to improve his image in the international community. Domestically the government was less concerned with a liberal image, continuing Romania's interventionist tradition with regard to the media by placing the official news agency under the control of the minister of Public Information. A pact signed with the unions in February 2001 quickly broke down, but the government was less amenable to making concessions when faced by protest. Inflation and the budget deficit were reduced, and key privatisations pushed through. The optimistic verdict was that Iliescu's party had finally shed its communist past and was moving towards a more social democratic style of politics.[20]

Bulgaria

The first post-communist government formed by the Union of Democratic Forces (UDF) did not last long. It was dependent on the Turkish minority party, the Movement of Rights and Freedoms (MRF) for support, yet pursued policies that were unpopular and gave the MRF no particular benefit. In particular, laws liquidating agricultural cooperatives and returning land within 'historic boundaries' were hugely unpopular in many areas; and they benefited the Turks little because they had had less land in the past, and the government refused to compensate them with land from the State Land Fund. By October 1992 the MRF had had enough and was willing to support the Bulgarian Socialist Party (BSP) in a vote of no confidence, forcing the government's resignation.

The fall of the UDF government was followed first by two years of unstable coalition government, made up of members of the BSP, the MRF and dissident members of the UDF. Formed at the very end of 1992, the government finally collapsed in September 1994 with elections being held in December. The BSP won a clear if narrow outright majority and immediately adopted a triumphalist tone. It promised the impossible – economic recovery without deep cuts in the social safety net – and did so in language reminiscent of the communist past. In March 1995 the party published its so-called White Book, outlining its future plans; but much of the text was a sustained attack on the anti-communism of the UDF and the successor coalition government, and an apologia for the communist past. In April and May 1995 the BSP became engaged in a struggle with President Zhelev to amend the Land Act, and replaced the directors of the state television and radio organisations. By June 1996 relations between the BSP prime minister and party leader Zhan Videnov and the rest of his party were at such a low ebb that he succumbed to pressure to reshuffle his government; that government then survived a vote of no confidence, but it still refused to contemplate closing down loss-making state enterprises or press ahead with privatisation. As in Romania, successful privatisations were the work of former communist officials feathering their nest. The result was that in the autumn the IMF refused a second instalment of an anticipated loan and interest rates had to be raised dramatically.[21]

When presidential elections took place in October and November 1996, the UDF candidate Petar Stoyanov was the clear victor, and

Videnov resigned as BSP leader and prime minister in December. Despite its parliamentary majority, as 1996 ended, the BSP was losing the authority to govern. Continuing financial crisis included a dramatic decline in the value of the lev (by a factor of six in as many weeks). In January 1997 the opposition drew up a Declaration for National Salvation. At first the BSP refused even to discuss its proposals, but violent street disturbances followed in which several hundred people were injured outside the parliament building on 10–11 January. Stoyanov brokered an agreement for early elections in April 1997, elections convincingly won by the opposition. The UDF's Ivan Kostov became prime minister. For the second time in half a dozen years popular demonstrations had removed a socialist government unwilling to reform.[22]

One of the UDF government's first measures, in July 1997, was to resolve once and for all the currency crisis by introducing a Currency Board (which automatically ties a country's monetary emissions to the level of hard-currency reserves). As a result, 1998 was quite successful economically and ambitious plans were launched to privatise 80 per cent of the economy by the end of the year, a target it did not quite achieve. Nevertheless major sell-offs took place in 1999, and the IMF agreed to both the 1999 and 2000 budgets. Symbolic of the end of an era, Todor Zhivkov died in hospital in August 1998. Yet in 2000 and 2001 the positive image became tarnished. Privatisation slowed, and pension and health care reform proved unpopular. More important, ever present corruption became a political scandal because government ministers were involved. A deputy minister and the government's spokesman resigned in April 2000, as did a former minister of Industry, dubbed Mr 10 per cent, in June. Nevertheless, Kostov's proved to be the first post-socialist government to serve a full term.

It was in this climate of dissatisfaction with a non-socialist government and a socialist alternative that had twice shown itself unwilling to reform, that Simeon Saxecoburgotski, the former king Simeon II, who had returned to the country but learned that without five years residency could not stand for president, formed his own party, the Simeon the Second National Movement (SSNM). The party was launched on 6 April 2001, and by June it had attracted sufficient support to win 120 of the 240 seats available in the election, subsequently forming a government with the MRF. The government was young, multi-ethnic and contained many talented individuals; but it lacked political experience, and it could only offer bitter medicine to the population. By 1 November, 10 000 people joined a trade union organised demonstration on the streets of Sofia against his social policy, and in the 18 November elections, against most expectations, it was Georgi Parvanov, the BSP candidate, who won the presidential run-off, becoming Bulgaria's first socialist president since the collapse of communism. Parvanov had run an American-style campaign, presenting himself as a 'modern politician'. Perhaps the electorate saw in him a new generation of socialist, a Kwaśniewski or a Medgyessy, who might lead Bulgaria into a more social democratic mould of politics.[23]

Macedonia

The nationalist coalition government, established in 1990, dominated by the Internal Macedonian Revolutionary Organisation–Democratic Party (IMRO–DP), lasted until summer 1992 when it lost a vote of no confidence over its failure to win any international recognition for the republic. It was replaced by a four-party coalition between the Social Democrats, the Liberals, the ethnic Albanian PPD and the Socialists, a government more in tune with the politics of the president, former communist Kiro Gligorov, that ruled until elections in October 1994 when three of the former coalition parties, united as the Alliance for Macedonia – comprising the Social Democratic Union of Macedonia, the Liberal Party and the Socialist Party – headed by President Gligorov emerged well ahead. In the style of Balkans politics, the nationalist opposition DP and IMRO–DP denounced the elections as rigged and boycotted the second round. The Liberals left the coalition in February 1996 protesting at the slow pace of privatisation. Despite sluggish economic performance, trade with Greece grew steadily, following the ending of its boycott in September 1995, and growth became positive again in 1996.[24]

Ever present ethnic tensions increased despite Gligorov's inclusion of representatives of the Albanian minority's Party for Democratic Prosperity in his government. In the autumn of 1994 Albanian activists decided to set up an Albanian-language university in Tetovo. When in July 1996 the 'dean' of the university was arrested, riots broke out. Ethnic tensions boiled over again in 1997, sparked by the arrest in May of two mayors for flying the Albanian flag on public buildings on public holidays, yet in November Gligorov again refused to legalise the Albanian university in Tetovo. In November 1998, with unemployment at 28 per cent and the social welfare system on the point of collapse, the incumbent government was voted out (in elections regarded as fair) in favour of a coalition made up of the new Democratic Alternative (DA), a vehicle for Vasil Tupurkovski, Macedonia's last representative on the collective Yugoslav presidency, the IMRO–DP (which provided the Prime Minister, Ljubco Georgievski) and, perhaps because of international pressure, the Democratic Party of Albanians (DPA). Tupurkovski was hopeful of being elected president the following year, and unbeknown to the president, arranged for Macedonia to establish diplomatic relations with Taiwan in return for $200 million in direct aid over the next four years. But little of the aid materialised, and Tupurkovski was eliminated in the first round of the November 1999 elections, which were won by Boris Trajkovski of the IMRO–DP. The Social Democratic Union refused to accept the legitimacy of the elections or recognise Trajkovski as president. Meanwhile in February a bilateral treaty had finally been signed with Bulgaria once an acceptable form of words had been found to fudge the issue of whether Macedonian and Bulgarian were distinct languages.[25]

The war in Kosovo severely disrupted trade, and Macedonia had had to cope with 335 000 refugees between March and May 1999. On top of this, the government had to cope with opposition demonstrations in early 2000 aimed at forcing its resignation and early elections. The coalition wobbled. The IMRO–DP splintered. The DA began talks with the Social Democratic Union. In November the DA was expelled from the coalition and Georgievski and the leader of the DPA put together a new coalition, with an even more fragile majority. Prior to this, in July, parliament had accepted an OSCE sponsored proposal to establish a private college in Tetovo with tuition in Macedonian, Kosovan and English; and in November, just before the coalition split, an SAA was signed with the EU.

Despite the apparent solution of the university issue, the ethnic issue boiled over in 2001, pushing the country to the brink of civil war. Trouble started in January and intensified in February with fatal clashes between the National Liberation Army (UCK, not coincidentally the same initials as the Kosovo Liberation Army: it had Kosovan support). In May a government of national unity was created, but it functioned poorly because all parties were concerned about the elections of 2002. In June, the rebels were within 20 kilometres of the capital Skopje. The OSCE brokered a deal to allow the safe withdrawal of the Albanian insurgents. This provoked outrage among Slav Macedonians who in

June stormed the parliament building and in July attacked western embassies and the OSCE office. In the midst of all this the government cut its diplomatic ties with Taiwan and re-established them with mainland China.

Tension was brought to an end by the Ohrid agreement of August 2001, brokered by EU and US envoys, which raised Albanian to the status of a second official language and introduced a variety of measures to raise the standing of the Albanian community. It also gave more powers to local government and an amnesty for UCK fighters, whose weapons were to be collected by NATO forces. But the government was slow to implement the provisions of the agreement, which many found unacceptable, especially as doubts were being raised about whether all UCK arms had been recovered. Nevertheless the constitutional measures were passed in November (the required new election law in April 2002), and shortly afterwards the Southeast European University in Tetovo opened providing education in English, Albanian and Macedonian. The former opposition left the government of national unity a few days later and Grigorievski formed a new cabinet, the seventh in three years. The months leading up to the elections on 15 September 2002 were marred by shootings and police brutality, although, thanks to the presence of NATO-led troops, there were only a few incidences of intimidation on election day. Victory for the Social Democrats under Branko Crvenkovski suggested perhaps that the Slav population was losing its attraction to nationalist politics. But the government was rejected as much for the endemic corruption that it condoned and was involved in as for issues of policy; and support for DPA collapsed as the Albanian vote swung to the Union for Democratic Integration of Ali Ahemeti, leader of the 2001 insurrection. Serious nationalist issues appeared to be unresolved in Macedonia.[26]

Croatia, Serbia and Montenegro

In Croatia, prior to 1996, the build up to the Bosnian war (see later) dominated politics. Franjo Tudjman and his Croatian Democratic Community reigned supreme following their decisive victory in the August 1992 elections. In 1994 Croat independent statehood was enhanced by the introduction of Croatia's own currency, the kuna. Military success in 1995 prompted Tudjman to call early elections to exploit his victory, and he hoped to win the two-thirds majority necessary to amend the constitution. He won convincingly, but, despite the votes of Croats from Hercegovina, enfranchised thanks to an amendment to the electoral law, he failed to cross the two-thirds threshold. What is more, the opposition won in Zagreb and Tudjman rejected the candidates proposed for mayor on four occasions before appointing his own protégé as an 'administrator' in order to deprive the opposition of their victory. To stifle the protests this provoked, Tudjman closed Zagreb's Radio 101, prompting mass demonstrations.[27]

Croatian politics carried on in much the same style until Tudjman's death in December 1999. An OSCE report in 1997 found that in one election Tudjman had received 300 times more media coverage than his challengers. Nevertheless, in 1998, there were signs of a more effective opposition to his rule. In August six opposition parties formed an electoral front, and in December the Social Democrats under Ivica Račan headed Tudjman in opinion polls. They focused their attack on the social inequalities of Croatia's 'crony capitalism', and on the year that had seen its fair share of exposes of corrupt privatisation deals, one of which included Tudjman's grandson. This decline in support continued over the summer of 1999, so it was little surprise that the victor in the January 2000 elections was a centre-left coalition that chose Račan as prime minister.

Although the new government ended Croatia's support of Herceg-Bosna, began to cooperate with the war crimes tribunal and arrested the beneficiaries of some of the most scandalous privatisations, in 2000 it progressed only slowly on privatisation, and gave in to strikes by workers in bankrupt enterprises. Similarly in 2001, despite signing an SAA with the EU in October, the government failed to reform the economy radically or cut its budgetary outgoings. Meanwhile the coalition squabbled. The regional Istrian Democratic Assembly left in June, and despite easily surviving a vote of no confidence initiated because of the decision to handover war criminals to the Hague, it finally collapsed in June 2002 over disagreements about the agreement reached with Slovenia concerning the costs over the shutting down of a power plant jointly constructed in the socialist years. Extreme nationalist politics had disappeared from Croatian politics, but consensus building had not arrived, and national rivalries and sensitivities to perceived injustices of the past continued as central elements of the political agenda.[28]

Serbia's pre-1996 history too was dominated by the wars discussed later. Both Serbia and Montenegro were dominated by their presidents, Milošević and Momir Bulatović respectively, although Milošević's party was less popular electorally than Bulatović's, and the December 1992 elections did not give it an overall majority. During the Bosnian war, his popularity increased and the December 1993 elections removed his dependency coalition partners. But this changed in 1996. In the November 1996 local elections his party lost power in Belgrade and other large cities to a new electoral coalition – Zajedno. When the results were announced, Milošević's supporters lodged protests and succeeded in getting the results annulled on the grounds of alleged electoral irregularities. Protests began at once. Like Tudjman, Milošević's first target was the independent radio stations, but throughout December there were daily protest marches, often held in the driving snow, and eventually Zajedno's electoral victories were recognised.[29]

But Zajedno proved to be a weak coalition. Zoran Djindjić of the Democratic Party (DP) found the extreme nationalist demands of Vuk Drašković (such as the integration of Kosovo into Serbia and the restoration of the Karadjordjević dynasty) of the Serbian Renewal Movement hard to live with, while Drašković fell out with Djindjić because he would not support his presidential bid. By the spring of 1997 there was an open split, and by the end of the year the coalition was moribund. The DP boycotted the Serbian elections in September, which Milošević's party won easily and in which the nationalist Serbian Radical Party also did well. Milošević felt strong enough to do what he had failed to do a year earlier and in October he removed Djindjić from his office as mayor of Belgrade.

With the focus turning to Kosovo again in late 1998 and 1999 (see later), events in Serbia proper (other than those relating to the split with Montenegro also discussed later) were unremarkable. Drašković was brought into Milošević's government early in 1999, but was expelled in April when he suggested that Yugoslavia should negotiate itself out of the Kosovo conflict. In January 2000, however, there was a second attempt to put together an opposition coalition. More than a dozen parties joined the Democratic Opposition of Serbia (DOS), including the DP and the small Democratic Party of Serbia (DPS) led by Vojislav Koštunica. The first test of opposition strength came with the 24 September elections for the federal presidency, for, perhaps in order to strengthen his legitimacy, Milošević had unilaterally amended the federal constitution in July to make this office elected by popular vote rather than the federal parliament. The opposition had no access to the state media and their meetings were broken up by supporters. But they did have access to local media and to local transport facilities, thanks to their victories in the local elections in 1996; and even Milošević supporters were dissatisfied with the economic chaos and influx of refugees caused by the Kosovo war. The DOS claimed victory on 26 September, but Milošević pressured the Electoral Commission to claim that Koštunica had not crossed the 50 per cent threshold and a rerun was necessary. DOS called for a general strike; the miners joined it; and the police refused to force the miners back to work. On 5 October hundreds of thousands demonstrated in Belgrade against the regime; on 6 October Milošević concede defeat; on 7 October Koštunica was sworn in as president. In December DOS got 65 per cent of the vote in Serbian parliamentary elections.

Post-Milošević Yugoslavia was rapidly accepted into the international community and DOS quickly repealed Milošević's more illiberal legislation and opened up police files. DOS was less happy to handover the former president to the war crimes tribunal in the Hague, but did so on 28 June 2001 so as not to lose some $1.3 million in aid. But this opened up divisions already present within the coalition. Koštunica opposed the move because there was no domestic legislation that legitimised it. Djindjić saw its political necessity. The coalition seemed on the verge of breaking up all year, but survived, and almost balanced the budget, although it made little progress reducing state influence over the media. It was in the summer of 2002 that the coalition finally collapsed, the DP accusing Koštunica's DPS of trying to distance itself from the responsibilities of government. Although aggressive nationalism had gone, Serbian politics did not find consensus building easy partly because of deep-seated national sensibilities; and presidential elections held first in October and rerun in December 2002 failed partly because nationalist parties called for a boycott.[30]

Whilst for the first half of the 1990s it was legitimate to treat Montenegro, the minor partner in the Yugoslav federation, as a footnote, in the second half of the decade it forced itself onto the political scene, ultimately changing the nature of the union between the two states. One of the first issues to divide Serbia and Montenegro was privatisation, something officially provided for in the federal macroeconomic stabilisation programme, but left to the republican governments to implement. The Serbian government opposed privatisation and in 1995–6 political controls over the economy became more pronounced; Serbian parties introduced into the federal assembly legislation reversing the little privatisation that had taken place to date. Montenegro, on the other hand, began large-scale privatisation in 1995 and adopted policies of socio-economic reform in the run-up to the 1996 elections.

More radical differences emerged in 1997. Presidential elections were due in both republics in any case, but Milošević's decision to have himself elected federal president rather than subvert the Serbian constitution and stand for a third term as Serbian president, was viewed with alarm by some in Montenegro. In the Montenegrin presidential elections in October, Bulatović was beaten by Milo Djukanović, who openly opposed Milošević and wanted to keep the federal presidency an essentially formal post. Despite accusations of ballot rigging and demonstrations in January 1998 to prevent him taking office, Djukanović became president and his coalition gained a thin majority in parliament. Djukanović was critical of Milošević's policy in Kosovo and announced Montenegro would cooperate with the International War Crimes Tribunal. In return, Milošević suspended the payment of pensions in Montenegro, so Montenegro stopped the payment of income tax and excise duty to the federal government. A year later, in October 1999, a citizenship law proclaimed a distinct Montenegrin citizenship and in November Montenegro introduced its own currency, the German mark. But politicians were wary of having a referendum on full independence because the roughly 40 per cent of the population against were all ethnically Serb, while those in favour were a mixture of Muslims from the Sandžak region and Albanians, and there were doubts about how loyal the latter might be to an independent state.

Milošević's unilateral decision to introduce popular elections to the presidency also upset the Montenegrins, because Serbia's much greater size made it unlikely that a Montenegrin could ever be elected federal president. They therefore boycotted the elections. But with the overthrow of Milošević for many the moment for independence had gone, especially as one of Koštunica's first moves was to lift the economic blockade on Montenegro. Djukanović continued to press for secession, but in November 2001 the EU made it clear that it favoured rather a 'democratic Montenegro in a democratic Yugoslavia'. In March 2002 Serbia and Montenegro announced that they had agreed on an EU-sponsored deal for a new, looser structure with the name 'Serbia and Montenegro', a key proviso of which being that they could re-evaluate the arrangement and move to independence every three years. The deal caused the Montenegrin government to fall. The pro-independence parties left the governing coalition in May and early elections were called for October because no alternative coalition could be patched together. The parties then squabbled about the actual date and finally agreed on 10 September, only days after a visit from the US ambassador. The elections of 20 October 2002 were won by Djukanović who immediately renounced the presidency and made himself prime minister. As in Macedonia, agreement required international intervention, but that then created new resentments for nationalists to exploit.[31]

THE BOSNIAN WAR AND ITS AFTERMATH

The Bosnian War would never have started if the dismemberment of Yugoslavia had been considered a matter of concern for Europe as a whole. Instead, it was left to the leaders of Croatia and Serbia to divide up the spoils of Tito's once flourishing state. It was also a fruitless war, for it ended with a settlement that had been on offer before the fighting had hardly begun. It lasted three and a half years and left 200 000 dead and two million homeless.[32]

Independence for Slovenia posed few problems: there the dominant population was ethnically Slovene, with no national minorities to complicate the situation; Slovenia could slip almost untroubled into independence. In Macedonia, while there was a large Albanian minority, its status was not the concern of another former Yugoslav state; Macedonia could acquire its precarious independence without antagonising its one-time fellow countrymen. Montenegro – ethnically Serb – simply did not want independence (at this time) and remained, despite occasional differences, together with Serbia in the rump state of Yugoslavia. However, for Croatia, Serbia and Bosnia-Hercegovina there was no clear correlation between ethnicity and the borders established by Tito in 1945. These borders were not planned to be international. They were intra-national, administrative divisions to help run a multinational state in an area where history had laughed at the notion of a nation state.

In the sixteenth century, fearful of the advancing Ottoman Turks, the Croats had invited Serbs to escape their own subjugation under

Turkish rule and join them in Croatia where, in return for land, they could help guard the border – *krajina* – between Christendom and the infidel. Croatia, therefore, had a substantial number of Krajina Serbs living in its territory. Throughout the nineteenth century, as Turkey, the sick man of Europe, steadily allowed its influence in the Balkans to weaken and an independent Serbia to emerge, it suited the Great Powers of Europe to allow the Turkish Empire to retain control of Bosnia-Hercegovina until its annexation by Austria–Hungary in 1908; the thriving Muslim community in an area where Serbs and Croats had always intermingled was one result. In Tito's Yugoslavia, founded on the notion of multinationalism, there was never any need for the ethnic and administrative boundaries to coincide. After Tito, an ethnic Croat state, within Tito's 1945 boundaries, was just about feasible if the Krajina Serbs were recognised as a national minority; but Bosnia-Hercegovina only made sense as a multinational state for, as became clear at every stage of the war, the intermingling of ethnic communities made the delineation of sensible boundaries impossible. At the start of the fighting, Europe was aware of these self-evident problems; but the decision in 1992 to recognise the internal borders of 1945 as international borders and recognise Croatia and Bosnia as independent states wrecked any hope of a peaceful solution; this ensured that the only solution would be a trial of strength between Croatia and Serbia for the division of Bosnia.

The Croatian–Serbian War

The Bosnian War began as an open war between Croatia and Serbia, and continued as a proxy one. Victory for Tudjman in Croatia's 1990 elections had provoked panic among Krajina Serbs and armed clashes between the Croat authorities and the self-declared Krajina Republic of Serbia took place as early as August 1990. With Yugoslavia clearly breaking up, Tudjman and Milošević met secretly in March 1991 in one of Tito's former hunting lodges to map out how the spoils could be divided. There the two men looked back to 1939 and the long-forgotten Sporazum agreement that had granted limited autonomy to Slovenia and Croatia within the then Kingdom of Yugoslavia. The 1939 map dividing Serb from Croat split Bosnia into two and was remarkably similar to the line dividing the Serb Republic [of Bosnia] and the Croat–Muslim Federation established by the Dayton Accord of 1995, which ended the war. The Sporazum agreement had two peculiarities: to ensure Croatia's access to the sea, the Krajina Serbs were allocated to Croatia; while to ensure there were no isolated pockets of Serb territory, small areas inhabited by Croats and larger areas inhabited by Muslims were allocated to Serbia – in particular a tract of land around Posavina linked the Serbs of Banja Luka in the northwest to the majority of Serbs in the east, further echoes of the Dayton Accord. Of course, if agreement had been reached in 1991 the Muslim communities would have had no constitutional status and their members would have been reduced to second-class citizens; their fate within the Croat–Muslim Federation was only slightly better in 1997.[33]

As would happen repeatedly throughout the conflict, just when a deal seemed to be on offer, it was thrown into chaos by the activities of the Serbs outside Serbia. Immediately after the hunting lodge talks, the Krajina Serbs escalated armed clashes into open rebellion against the Croatian government. This wrecked all hope of a Sporazum style agreement. To Tudjman, the outbreak of fighting was a clear sign that Milošević had reneged on the idea: he was using the Krajina Serbs as clients, and therefore Croatia would have to fight to see just how much territory of the former Yugoslavia it would control. Thus even before the issue of Croatia's independence from Yugoslavia came to the fore at the end of 1991, an undeclared war was taking place within Croatia between Croats and Krajina Serbs, fighting that soon became concentrated in the territory at the far northeast of the sixteenth-century military frontier, in the Serb territory within Croatia known as Slavonia. Here Croatia and Serbia had a common border, and the issues of Croatian independence and the rights of the Serb minority within Croatia inevitably became intertwined.

By November 1991 the fighting had reached such a state of intensity, with Milošević's army clearly supporting the Krajina and Slavonian Serbs in what looked to the outside world as an attempt to prevent by force of arms Croatia achieving its independence, that peacekeeping troops had to be imposed to keep the armies apart. With the peacekeeping troops came Lord Carrington. Astute enough to understand the complexities of the situation, Carrington could see that Croatian independence from Yugoslavia was not the real issue. He therefore argued that before any of the individual Yugoslav states could be recognised as independent, a Yugoslav-wide settlement had to be reached acceptable to all the former republics; the EU agreed, but drew up clear conditions relating to the treatment of national minorities that would have to be met before independence could be granted.

At the end of 1991 a settlement based on these criteria was put forward but failed in the face of Milošević's determination not to change Serbia's policy towards its Albanian minority in Kosovo. Interpreting Milošević's rejection of the Carrington proposals as an attempt to prevent Croatia seceding from Yugoslavia, rather than reflecting his concern that the EU might 'interfere' in Serbia's sovereignty over Kosovo, the German government lost patience with Milošević and insisted on recognising, and forcing the EU to recognise, Croatia's independence in January 1992; this was done even though no progress had been made on the question of the treatment of the Krajina Serb minority in Croatia and Tudjman had no control over the Krajina area, where Serbs and Croats had been separated by UN peacekeepers and the rebel Krajina Serb Republic continued to exist.

Proxy War in Bosnia: The Serb Republic

Once Carrington's Yugoslav-wide scheme had been wrecked by German overreaction and Croatia recognised as an independent state, war in Bosnia was inevitable. Recognition of Croatia implied recognition of Bosnia. But the Serb communities in Bosnia did not want independence but association with Serbia. The Croat communities were lukewarm about independence. Only the Muslim communities were in any way enthusiastic. Granting independence to people who did not want it was a recipe for disaster. The Bosnian Serb leader Radovan Karadžić organised a boycott of the referendum called by the Bosnian government on independence, and then led the rebellion that began the day independence was granted. This Serb insurrection, supported by Milošević from Serbia proper, led by summer 1992 to an attempt to 'ethnically cleanse' an area of contiguous territory that would be worthy of the name 'The Serb Republic [of Bosnia]'. By the end of that bloody summer Serb forces had gained control of roughly two-thirds of Bosnia and, crucially, the Posavina corridor, which linked the Serb communities of northwest Bosnia to the majority of Serb communities directly abutting Serbia and Montenegro. The Serbs had thus achieved their war aims – except for control of the Muslim enclaves of Srebrenica, Zepa and Goražde, which they totally surrounded – and could prepare to wait for a settlement while always increasing their pressure on the Muslim enclaves.

The first attempt at a settlement came from Lord Owen, who had taken over from Lord Carrington as Europe's peacemaker. In April

1993 he proposed dividing Bosnia into ten provinces or cantons constructed along ethnic lines, with central government having minimal powers. Both Croats and Muslims were prepared to go along with it: so too was Milošević, for the bloody fighting around Srebrenica in spring 1993 and its eventual fall had so outraged world opinion that severe UN sanctions had been imposed on Serbia; the Bosnian Serbs, however, refused to accept it despite all Milošević's powers of persuasion and the Owen Plan collapsed. The disagreement on the Serb side was between pragmatism and principle: Milošević was convinced that the implementation of the Owen proposal could be so rigged that the promised Serb cantons might be knitted together into a 'Serb Republic', which one day could associate more openly with Serbia proper; Karadžić wanted to fight on until agreement on a 'Serb Republic' was signed, sealed and delivered. This was a turning point in the war. The Serb side was split, and in May 1993 Milošević announced he was imposing trade restrictions on the 'Serb Republic'. It was clear that he was tiring of the activities of the Serbs outside Serbia.

Proxy War in Bosnia: The Croat–Muslim Federation

The collapse of the Owen plan brought to a head simmering tension between the Croat and Muslim forces in Bosnia. Notionally allies since the fighting had begun, there had always been an undercurrent of tension between the two sides, especially in Hercegovina, that part of Bosnia adjacent to Croatia's Dalmatian coast. Here, Tudjman's view that the Bosnian Muslims were just Croats who had adopted Islam was commonplace, and Tudjman's party ran most aspects of daily life. Tension turned to war after the crisis brought about by the fall of Srebrenica and the consequent arrival in Croat areas of Bosnia of large numbers of Muslim refugees. Sparked by a Croat atrocity against defenceless Muslims in April 1993, fighting continued into November; an unwanted side effect of the abandoned Owen notion of Croat and Muslim cantons was the determination of both sides to secure control in what were now seen as 'their areas'. This fighting dramatically weakened the bargaining position of the Muslims and this was reflected in discussions in July 1993, which culminated in the agreement in principle of all three sides to form a Union of Bosnian Republics. Initial euphoria died away as the Muslims quickly realised they had been outmanoeuvred. In terms of territory the Serbs got 53 per cent in a contiguous block, the Croats 17 per cent split into two blocks; and the Muslims what remained: left with a landlocked statelet of scattered cantons and bereft of support from a neighbouring power, the Muslims realised they would have no future and reneged on the decision to sign.

Muslim rejection of the July 1993 plan engendered moves towards a Croat–Muslim Federation. Neither Lord Carrington nor Lord Owen had wanted to adopt such an approach, for it meant in essence dictating to the Muslims what was in their best interest; but the events of 1993 had shown just how weak the Muslim position really was. It was the American administration who brokered this Croat–Muslim Federation, announced in Washington in March 1994, and the key to its success was the pressure the Americans put on Croatia. Threatening sanctions with one hand, with the other hand America offered to retrain the Croat Army to make it a force capable of confronting Serbia. The agreement eventually reached involved creating a Croat–Muslim Federation in Bosnia, and foreseeing in the future a confederal relationship, including monetary union, between the Federation and Croatia proper. Milošević made no objections when the formation of the Federation was announced, for it meant there were now only two players, Tudjman for the Croats and himself for the Serbs; and if the Serbs outside Serbia could be brought to heel, the old Sporazum division of Bosnia could be revived.

The Dayton Accord: Imposing the Sporazum

In April 1994, when the Bosnian Serb Army attacked Goražde provoking an international outcry, Milošević decided he had had enough and determined that Karadžić should not be allowed to frustrate the new international peace moves launched in summer 1994. These offered the Serbs 49 per cent of Bosnia, and the new Croat–Muslim Federation 51 per cent. Karadžić promptly rejected it; Milošević tried to force Karadžić to back down; but the 'parliament' of the 'Serb Republic' rejected the plan.[34] In response, Milošević decided to ditch Karadžić and deal directly with Tudjman. During the winter of 1994–5 he began to play down his commitment not only to Karadžić but also to the Krajina Serbs. In January 1995 Tudjman prepared to reoccupy the Krajina and destroy the self-declared Krajina Serb Republic and announced that he wanted the UN force keeping the peace between Croats and the Krajina Serbs to be withdrawn. When in February the

Krajina Serb leader went to Belgrade to seek support in the event of a Croat attack, he was snubbed by Milošević. Then, in a lightening raid on 1 May, the Croat Army seized part of the Serb pocket of Slavonia; there was no response from Milošević. In July 1995, after talks brokered by the Americans between Tudjman and the Muslim leader Alija Izetbegović, a military agreement was reached between the two sides, and on 4 August the Croats attacked first the Krajina Serbs and then moved against the Bosnian Serb Army. Demoralised, the Bosnian Serbs retreated steadily until the territory they controlled had shrunk to roughly half the country. Meanwhile throughout 1995 members of Tudjman's party in Bosnia continued to try to build the Croat mini-state of Herceg-Bosna, even though this was supposed to have been abolished when the Croat–Muslim Federation was established.

With the territory under Serb military control now reduced to near the 49 per cent envisaged in the 1994 peace plan, and the Krajina Serbs sacrificed, the stage was set for the belated imposition of the 1939 Sporazum, disguised as the Dayton Accord of December 1995. The Accord did envisage a central authority, the Republic of Bosnia-Hercegovina, controlling foreign policy, foreign trade and monetary policy, but almost everything else would be devolved to the two constituent units, the Croat–Muslim Federation and the Serb Republic, both of which would have their own armies and both of which could form special relationships with neighbouring countries so long as the sovereignty of the Union was not violated. Problems remained: Goražde would be a Muslim enclave within Serb territory; Sarajevo and its Serb suburbs would be in the Croat–Muslim Federation; and the Posavina corridor's fate would not be determined immediately but subjected to international arbitration. But there was to be no veto from the Bosnian Serbs; the changed military position forced Karadžić to allow Milošević to negotiate on his behalf.[35]

Republic of Bosnia-Hercegovina: Protectorate or Nation State

The tone of Bosnian politics was set from the start. In June 1996 the Croats recreated Herceg-Bosna in order to pressure the Muslims to wind-up the old 1992 administration and transfer all authority to the Federation. This was formally agreed in December 1996, but the Croats continued to support the 'para-state' of Herceg-Bosna, and in

Muslim-dominated cantons the old administration lived on in all but name. Progress creating the institutions of a nation state, or rather the sort of liberal, multi-ethnic state that the Dayton Accord envisaged was painfully slow. The Serbs continued to dislike the idea of the Republic at all, preferring union with Serbia; the bulk of the Croats continued to favour a 'third entity', Herceg-Bosna; while the Muslims and Croats located in regions not adjacent to Croatia, who were more enthusiastic about it, did not want to lose their ethnic identity (as they saw it) in a state that treated all ethnic groups equally.[36]

The international community's High Representative in Bosnia and Hercegovina, as he was finally termed, faced an uphill struggle getting domestic politicians to either cooperate with him or agree among themselves, and ultimately had to impose decisions on them, a power he gained in December 1997. Prior to this Bosnia had no common passports, no single currency, no coat of arms, no citizenship law and no common car number plates. Attempts by the High Representative to sponsor more moderate politicians were only partially successful because they were immediately replaced by hard-liners when the population went to the polls (Biljana Plavšic in the Serb Republic, Kresimir Zubak, leader of the Croats in the Federation) or ignored by domestic politicians (Milord Dodik in the Serb Republic). Until the end of 1999, there were, in reality, three entities not two, the Croat–Muslim Federation only really existed in the Federation's two ethnically mixed cantons. Some 22 000 NATO peacekeepers remained in place, and 13 000 international civilian personnel were involved in everything from media reform, reorganising the police, rewriting textbooks and even scheduling meetings for the bickering local politicians.

The situation changed somewhat for the better after the death of Franjo Tudjman in December 1999 and the ending of Croatian financial support for Herceg-Bosna. Nevertheless in March 2000 a self-proclaimed 'Croatian National Council', supported by local politicians and the local Catholic hierarchy, announced that it was forming a 'third entity'. The move petered out, because of lack of support from Croatia and a NATO raid on the Mostar bank where the biggest party behind the move kept its funds. In local elections in April and national elections in November, with some prompting by Western representatives, nationalist parties did worse than more moderate ones, although Dodik was voted out in the Serb Republic. But day-to-day government was still dependent on the High Representative enforcing an average of one hundred executive or legislative decrees a year. The credibility of the moderate government was challenged when, in January 2002, the government handed over six Algerian 'terrorists' with no guarantees for their security, and nationalist parties were victorious in the October general elections. In Bosnia nationalist politics dominated in a state that was scarcely a state at all.[37]

The Kosovan War and the Second Protectorate

What turned the long-standing Kosovo problem into a war was the emergence in late 1997 of the UCK, initially seen by the West as a terrorist organisation, and its launching of attacks on the Serbian police. This radicalised a situation that was already far from usual. Over the course of the 1990s, Ibrahim Rugova, political leader of the Kosovo Albanians, had established a shadow state in Kosovo with its own school, health care and taxation systems. In March 1998 'elections' were held to this 'government' and Rugova was elected 'president', but many in the UCK, still a collection of armed clans rather than a unified fighting force, refused to recognise him. In the same month the Serbian police began an operation to destroy the UCK. The UN condemned the excessive force used by the Serbian police (in the village of Prekaz fifty died, including women and children) and imposed an arms embargo. Violence erupted again over the summer, but the international community did not act until October, when an agreement was brokered between Milošević and the United States. It quickly fell apart however because the UCK had not been consulted and did not feel bound by it. As the Serbian police withdrew, the UCK, supplied from northern Albania which at the time was still effectively outside government control, moved in, and the Yugoslav army felt obliged to retaliate.

As fighting escalated and more massacres occurred, the Western powers agreed to a package on 6 February 1999 at Rambouillet, which was presented to the Yugoslav and Kosovo Albanian delegations. Both rejected it, the Kosovans because it did not give them independence, the Yugoslavs because it gave NATO forces full freedom of movement within the whole of Yugoslavia. Both sides prepared for war. Embassies were evacuated; the Yugoslav army and Serbian police forcibly expelled the Albanian population living along possible invasion routes. NATO's bombing campaign began on 24 March 1999 and lasted 78 days, intentionally hitting the Serbian television offices, killing 12 civilians, and inadvertently hitting the Chinese Embassy. Meanwhile the mass expulsion of Albanians to Albania, Montenegro and Macedonia continued, as the army tried to hunt down the UCK.

The deal that settled the conflict in June 1999, after the intervention of the Finnish president and a personal envoy of the Russian president, had three key elements: Kosovo remained legally part of Yugoslavia; it had a separate, international administration, the UN Mission in Kosovo (UNMIK); and the forces of the Yugoslav army were to withdraw to be replaced by a 50 000 strong UN force, the Kosovo Force (KFOR). The immediate problem with the deal was the power vacuum created as the Yugoslav forces left but the UN had yet to establish its authority. Criminal elements accompanied the returning Albanians who repaid the persecution they had suffered not only on the Kosovo Serbs but also on the Roma, Croats, Turks and Bosniacs. Some 200 000 non-Albanians left Kosovo; those who remained congregated in small 'cantons' protected by KFOR troops.

The longer-term problem for Kosovo, however, as in Bosnia, was that the settlement pleased none of the parties on the ground. The Albanians wanted independence; the non-Albanians wanted government as part of Serbia. Nor were politics stable. Although Rugova's more moderate Democratic League of Kosovo (DLK) won elections in both 2000 and 2001, the UCK successor party remained a powerful force. The DLK suffered violent attacks and assassination attempts. Further, in 2001, successor organisations to the UCK were involved in insurgency in Macedonia and Serbia proper, although this attempt to expand the struggle beyond the borders of Kosovo petered out after the Americans froze the assets of certain ethnic Albanian organisations. As in Bosnia, it was the externally appointed envoy, the head of UNMIK, who had to intervene, both to get government functioning (brokering in March 2002 an agreement between Rugova and the UCK successor party whereby Rugova became president and a member of the other party prime minister) and to veto politically charged legislation. Despite this apparent rejecting of the premises underpinning Kosovo's status, the UN was adamant that status was not the issue of the day: what mattered was improving the standard of government.[38]

Conclusion

The history of Eastern Europe since 1945 is the story of a once inspirational ideology turned concrete, a system of ideals operationalised into a socio-economic system that was successful in mobilising resources for postwar reconstruction and industrialisation in the absence of Marshall Aid, but that proved unequal to the task of creating sufficient wealth to sustain a multifaceted society with diffuse social, economic and political goals. It is a complex story of ideological commitment and struggle against adversity, of Soviet realpolitik, of dizzy economic achievement yet momentous failure, of laudable ideals and cruel suffering.

It is, soberingly for idealists, a story of the victory of mundane economic realism. The ideological commitment that in the 1940s spurred some native communists to revolutionary action, and persuaded others to suppress concern about Soviet intentions, ripened in the 1950s to the belief that the market could be openly defied. Whole new socialist communities were built around industries for which there had never been an economic justification. Following the political crisis of 1956 and the economic reform discussions of the 1960s, ideology was obliged to take a back seat. The victory of realism over voluntarism was conceded, even in those countries where actual economic reform was minimal. As the 1960s turned into the 1970s and then the 1980s it became clear that socio-economic systems could not continue to create wealth in conditions where prices bore no relation to costs and where no institutional framework existed to ensure that powerful vested interests did not consistently ignore costs for their short-term benefit and pass them on to the population at large.

Nagy had made this point in his New Course speech of June 1953, and had argued consistently for the use of democratic forms to prevent the emergence of self-appointed 'Bonapartist' cliques. Ultimately, however, defending the Leninist concept of the leading role of the Party proved too useful an ideological fig leaf for vested interests. Attempts at creating institutional checks on bureaucratic rule in the form of multiparty democracy or workers' councils were generally interpreted as counter-revolution. Even in Yugoslavia where self-management was institutionalised, Party rule was not questioned and its authority could always be adduced to support decisions made by the small groups which in practice ran self-managed organisations. The result was socialism without democracy. For the generation that grew up under 'actually existing socialism', socialism represented a system that did not provide in practice what the ideology claimed. For this generation, the market system, together with the institution of private property, offered both rational pricing and an institutional structure that provided procedures for penalising poor economic decision-making and the waste it engendered.

The history of Eastern Europe between 1945 and 1989 is the history of the long-term failure of a version of socialism premised on the overwhelming national or social ownership of the means of production. Stalinist central planning, and all four stages of its reform, failed. It is this overwhelming public ownership, together with the one-party political system that controlled it, with tentacles extending into all areas of social and cultural life, that constrained the legacy of 'actually existing socialism' and prospects for political pluralism and the market economy. Market forces were being introduced into economies that, with the partial exceptions of Yugoslavia and Hungary, had made political capital out of the fact that prices had been fixed for decades. Private ownership was being re-established in countries where some 90 per cent of the economy was in public hands, where it was unclear what anything was truly worth, where no one knew how or where to sell property and where no one had any money to buy it in any case. Political pluralism was being created in countries that had been one-party states for forty years and where any commitment to workers' self-management was never more than skin deep, countries that, with the exception of Czechoslovakia, had no prior experience of genuine multiparty democracy to fall back on.

Furthermore, the new political structures were immediately confronted with an irredentist nationalism that the communist regimes had sought first to destroy and then to subordinate. The 'successor states' of 1919 and the population shifts of 1947 failed to solve the national question in Eastern Europe. Indeed, the ethnic map of Eastern Europe makes the formation of ethnically homogeneous nation states an impossibility. Yet the nineteenth-century goal of the unitary nation state continued to inspire the nationalisms of the region.

We have stressed throughout that what characterised Eastern European history between 1945 and 1989–90 was its ideology and the practical implementation of that ideology. In this context it is salutary to warn against simplistic analogies with the collapse of dictatorships in Southern Europe in the mid-1970s. In southern Europe, political dictatorships with feudal ties, presiding over fundamentally capitalist economies were swept away by economic and social forces (rapid economic growth, cultural secularisation) engendered by greater integration with the Western European market economy and Western European culture. In Eastern Europe, although increased contact with the West helped fuel the ideological misgivings, the situation was radically different. The economy was not growing too quickly for the political structures that ran it; rather the political structures had subjected the economy to over a decade of stagnation. Collectivist, nationalist, religious and 'patriarchal' ideologies were not being challenged by secularism and individualism, as they were in Southern Europe. The collectivist, internationalist, welfarist ideology of socialism was being challenged, in the main, by the ideologies defeated in southern Europe, by resurgent, equally collectivist, nationalist, religious and 'patriarchal' ideologies. Liberal democratic individualism and social democratic solidarity were in the minority, although their adherents played pivotal roles in the actual overthrows of the communist regimes. In Central Europe, despite ups and downs in the immediate aftermath of the collapse of the socialist regimes, liberal and social democratic values emerged triumphant. This was far less the case in the Balkans.

To an extent, post-communist Eastern Europe decomposed into Central Europe (the Czech Republic, Hungary, Poland, Slovakia and Slovenia) and the Balkans (Albania, Bulgaria, Romania, Croatia, Yugoslavia, Bosnia and Macedonia). In Central Europe, power was first taken by unambiguously opposition parties that annihilated the communists electorally and rapidly embarked on economic stabilisation and privatisation; as the realities of free market economics became clear and the prospects of NATO and EU membership beckoned, the reformed communists adopted a social democratic platform and returned to influence if not power. Post-socialist politics became a pendulum of right-of-centre following left-of-centre governments arguing over welfare reform, with only the occasional nationalist issue to spice things up on the margins. In the Balkan countries, where the communist claim to political legitimacy was far greater, the former communists at first retained significant authority if not power. Balkan economic stabilisation packages were less radical, and privatisation progressed more slowly. Nowhere were communists able to shed their totalitarian pretensions, and they were replaced either by 'democrats' with similar mindsets, or by coalitions too quarrelsome to achieve consensus. Politics remained the vassal of nationalism, from the relatively mild notion that there might be a less painful Bulgarian or Romanian path for transition, to the vitriol that destroyed Yugoslavia. Despite signs that a more constitutional form of politics was beginning to emerge in the first years of the new millennium, nationalist politics remained a virulent force in the Balkans, threatening the very existence of Yugoslavia, Macedonia and Bosnia Hercegovina.

Strangely, the history of Eastern Europe might have been very different if the neo-Stalinists of Brezhnev's 'long decade' had taken more notice of what Stalin himself said about successfully running a socialist economy, before rejecting the notion of fundamental economic reform. In 1951, shortly before his death, Stalin warned Soviet economists that their pricing policies were defective since they did not understand the law of value, an economic law that continued to operate under both capitalism and socialism, if in rather different ways. His words serve as an ironic epitaph to those who tried to construct socialism in Eastern Europe:

> Engels ... does not speak at all in favour of those who think that under socialism existing economic laws can be abolished and new ones created. On the contrary, it demands, not the abolition, but the understanding of economic laws and their intelligent application.

NOTES

Introduction

1. R. Okey, *Eastern Europe 1740–1980* (London, 1982), p. 176.
2. H. Seton-Watson, *Eastern Europe between the Wars* (New York, 1969), p. 129.

1 Revolution in Eastern Europe

1. H. Seton-Watson, *Eastern Europe between the Wars* (New York, 1969), p. 156.
2. On Tito and the Yugoslav Communist Party, see G. R. Swain, 'Tito: The Formation of a Disloyal Bolshevik', in *International Review of Social History*, vol. 34 (1989), pp. 248–71, where full references to non-English language sources will be found.
3. For the Comintern radio transmitter, see G. R. Swain, 'The Comintern and Southern Europe', in T. Judt (ed.), *Resistance and Revolution in Mediterranean Europe* (London, 1989) where full references to non-English language sources will be found.
4. For the impact of the Nazi–Soviet Pact on Eastern Europe, see Swain, 'The Comintern'. The enthusiastic support for the notion of an imperialist war given by Milovan Djilas, the future dissident Yugoslav communist, is worth noting; see M. Djilas, *Memoir of a Revolutionary* (New York, 1973), p. 329. For the number of East Europeans fighting in Spain, see his *International Solidarity with the Spanish Republic, 1936–39* (Moscow, 1975), p. 106.
5. For the lessons of the Spanish Civil War, see Swain, 'The Comintern'.
6. For the prominence of the Yugoslav Communist Party at this time and the revolutionary views of Tito, see Swain, 'Tito'.
7. For a clear summary history of the Yugoslav partisans, see M. C. Wheeler, 'Pariahs to Partisans to Power: The Communist Party of Yugoslavia', in Judt, *Resistance and Revolution*.
8. For communist control over the liberation committees, see G. R. Swain, 'The Cominform, Tito's International?' *Historical Journal*, vol. 35 (1992),

pp. 641–63, where full references to non-English language sources will be found.

9. For Tito's talks with Mihailović, see M. C. Wheeler, *Britain and the War for Yugoslavia, 1940–43* (New York, 1980), p. 88.
10. Some details of the operation are given in London's memoirs, see A. London, *On Trial* (London, 1970).
11. See Swain, 'The Comintern'.
12. The attitude of Communist Parties to resistance front organisations and the whole question of 'parity' versus representation 'from below' are discussed in Swain, 'The Cominform'.
13. Swain, 'The Comintern'.
14. For the response of French and Italian communists to these instructions, see P. Robrieux, *Histoire Intérieure du Parti Communiste*, 3 vols (Paris, 1981), vol. II, pp. 78–81, and J. Urban, *Moscow and the Italian Communist Party* (Ithaca, N.Y., 1986), pp. 198–9.
15. Wheeler, 'Pariahs'.
16. N. Pano, *The People's Republic of Albania* (Baltimore, 1968), pp. 41–57.
17. The role of the Yugoslav Communists in Greece is discussed in Swain, 'Cominform'.
18. N. Oren, *Bulgarian Communism: The Road to Power, 1934–44* (New York, 1971), p. 201.
19. Oren, *Bulgarian Communism*, p. 202ff. and Sh. Atanasov, *Pod znameneto na partiyata* (Sofia, 1962), p. 145ff. For documents putting Yugoslav support before Red Army support, see *V'or'zhenata borba na B'lgarskiya narod protiv fashizma* (Sofia, 1962). For communications with Moscow, see Yelena Valeva, 'The CPSU, the Comintern and the Bulgarians' in N. Naimark and L. Gibianskii, *The Establishment of Communist Regimes in Eastern Europe, 1944–49* (Westview Press, N.Y., 1997), pp. 47–9.
20. Oren, *Bulgarian Communism*, p. 206.
21. Oren, *Bulgarian Communism*, p. 211.
22. Atanasov, *Pod znameneto*, p. 201. According to Bulgarian police reports, the British had promised as early as February 1944 to support underground and partisan operations to the point of insurrection and the creation of a Fatherland Front Government; see O. Vasilev, *V'or'zhenata s'protiva fashizma v B'lgariya* (Sofia, 1946), p. 566.
23. S. G. Tanev, *Internatsionalnata missiya no s'vetskata armiya v B'lgariya, 1944–7* (Sofia, 1971), p. 43.
24. Oren, *Bulgarian Communism*, p. 224ff.
25. Oren, *Bulgarian Communism*, p. 252ff. Incidents of Red Army support for beleaguered partisans are described in Tanev, *Internatsionalnata missiya*, p. 60, and *Istoriya na BKP: kratkii ocherk* (Sofia, 1969), p. 223.
26. J. Tomasevich, 'Yugoslavia during the Second World War', and W. D. McClellan, 'Post-war Political Evolution', in W. S. Vucinich, *Contemporary Yugoslavia* (Berkeley, 1969); Wheeler, 'Pariahs'.
27. McClellan, 'Political Evolution'; G. W. Hoffman and F. W. Neal, *Yugoslavia – The New Communism* (New York, 1962).
28. Hoffman and Neal, *Yugoslavia*; P. Auty, 'The Post-war Period', in H. C. Darby *et al.* (eds), *A Short History of Yugoslavia* (Cambridge, 1966).

29. Hoffman and Neal, *Yugoslavia*; Auty, 'Post-war Period'.
30. Swain, 'The Cominform'; H. Seton-Watson, 'Albania' in A. Toynbee and V. V. Toynbee (eds), *Survey of International Affairs, 1939–46: The Realignment of Europe* (Oxford, 1955).
31. R. J. Crampton, *A Short History of Modern Bulgaria* (Cambridge, 1987), p. 145ff.
32. Crampton, *A Short History of Modern Bulgaria*, p. 151; H. Seton-Watson, *The East European Revolution* (London, 1961), p. 213. For the report to Moscow, see T. V. Volokitina and A. S. Level (eds) *Vostochnaya evropa v dokumentakh rossiiskikh arkhivov, 1944–53* (Moscow – Novosibirsk, 1997), vol. I, pp. 141–7 (hereafter *Documents*).
33. B. Petranovic, 'Tito i Staljin, 1944–6', in *Jugoslovenski Istorijski Casopis* (Belgrade, 1988); C. Strbac, *Jugoslavija i odnosi izmedju socialistickikh zemalja: sukob KPJ i Informbiroa* (Belgrade, 1984), pp. 69, 259; *Documents*, vol. I, pp. 123–36; V. Volkov, 'The Soviet Leadership and South East Europe' in Naimark and Gibianskii, *The Establishment*, pp. 60–9.
34. Seton-Watson, *Revolution*, p. 213ff.; J. Tomaszewski, *The Socialist Regimes of East Central Europe* (London, 1989), pp. 95–100. For Stalin's communication of July 1945, see *Documents*, vol. I, p. 221.
35. Seton-Watson, *Revolution*, p. 216; Tanev, *Internatsionalnata missiya*, p. 92.
36. Crampton, *A Short History of Modern Bulgaria*, p. 155.
37. Strbac, *Jugoslavija*, p. 257.

2 Different Roads to Socialism

1. S. Fischer-Galati, *The New Romania* (Cambridge, Mass., 1967), p. 18ff.; R. R. King, *History of the Romanian Communist Party* (Stanford, Calif., 1980), p. 37ff.
2. King, *Romanian Communist Party*, p. 43ff. For the Soviet reaction, see D. Deletant, 'New Light on Gheorghiu-Dej's Struggle for Dominance in the Romanian Communist Party', *Slavonic and East European Review*, vol. 73, no. 4 (1995), p. 670 (note 30).
3. S. Fischer-Galati, *Twentieth-Century Romania* (Columbia, 1970), p. 82ff.; J. Tomaszewski, *The Socialist Regimes of East Central Europe* (London, 1989), p. 73.
4. G. Ionescu, *Communism in Romania, 1944–62* (Oxford, 1964), p. 81ff.; Fischer-Galati, *New Romania*, p. 27.
5. Fischer-Galati, *Twentieth Century*, p. 83ff.; Ionescu, *Communism in Romania, 1944–62*, p. 81ff.; N. I. Lebedev, *Istoriya Rumynii, 1918–70* (Moscow, 1971), p. 445ff.
6. Ionescu, *Communism*, p. 288; Fischer-Galati, *New Romania*, p. 28; Fischer-Galati, *Twentieth Century*, p. 90.
7. Ionescu, *Communism*, p. 105ff. For Tartarescu, see *Documents*, vol. I, pp. 135, 157, 163 and 168.
8. Ibid.
9. Tomaszewski, *The Socialist Regimes*, p. 91. Fischer-Galati, *Twentieth Century Romania*, p. 104, argues that the election result was not as fraudulent as

once supposed: a contemporary observer, S. Lowery, also argued that, despite abuses before and after the poll, the opposition would not have won; see his 'Romania' in A. Toynbee and V. Toynbee (eds), *Survey of International Affairs, 1939–46: The Realignment of Europe* (Oxford, 1955), p. 300.

10. J. Coutouvidis and J. Reynolds, *Poland, 1939–47* (Leicester, 1986), p. 113ff.
11. Coutouvidis and Reynolds, *Poland*, p. 120; S. Lowery, 'Poland', in Toynbee and Toynbee (eds), *Survey*, p. 135; A. Polonsky and B. Drukier (eds), *The Beginnings of Communist Rule in Poland* (London, 1980), p. 7.
12. Coutouvidis and Reynolds, *Poland*, p. 124ff. An idea of the importance Stalin attached to this body can be seen by the fact that both the Soviet Foreign Minister Vyacheslav Molotov and the former Head of the Comintern, Georgi Dimitrov, served on it; see T. Toranska, *ONI: Stalin's Polish Puppets* (London, 1987), pp. 232–9.
13. Coutouvidis and Reynolds, *Poland*, p. 124ff.; Polonsky and Drukier, *Beginnings*, pp. 16–22. For Bierut's letter to Dimitrov, see *Documents*, vol. I, p. 46.
14. Coutouvidis and Reynolds, *Poland*, p. 142ff.
15. Ibid.; *Documents*, vol. I, pp. 83 and 99.
16. Lowery, 'Poland', p. 190ff.; Coutouvidis and Reynolds, *Poland*, p. 187. For Gomułka's letter to Molotov, see *Documents*, vol. I, p. 189.
17. Lowery, 'Poland', p. 223; Coutouvidis and Reynolds, *Poland*, p. 175; *Documents*, vol. I, p. 215.
18. Coutouvidis and Reynolds, *Poland*, p. 199ff.
19. Toranska, *ONI*, p. 247; *Documents*, vol. I, pp. 425, 450, 553 and 594; J. Micgiel, '"Bandits and Reactionaries": The Suppression of the Opposition in Poland, 1944–6,' in Naimark and Gibianskii, *The Establishment*, pp. 101–2.
20. Toranska, *ONI*, pp. 37, 274; Coutouvidis and Reynolds, *Poland*, p. 278ff.
21. P. Zinner, *Communist Strategy and Tactics in Czechoslovakia, 1918–48* (London, 1963), p. 74ff.
22. G. R. Swain, 'The Cominform: Tito's International?' *Historical Journal*, vol. 35 (1992), p. 645. For the non-recognition of the Czechoslovak Government in London, see *Documents*, vol. I, p. 210.
23. H. Seton-Watson, *The East European Revolution* (London, 1961), p. 181; Zinner, *Communist Strategy*, p. 99ff.
24. M. Myant, *Socialism and Democracy in Czechoslovakia, 1945–8* (Cambridge, 1981), p. 57; J. Rupnik, *Histoire du Parti Communiste Tchéchoslovaque* (Paris, 1981), p. 159.
25. J. Bloomfield, *Passive Revolution: Politics and the Czechoslovak Working Class, 1945–8* (London, 1979), p. 76ff.; Zinner, *Communist Strategy*, p. 118ff.
26. Zinner, *Communist Strategy*, p. 135ff.
27. Myant, *Socialism and Democracy in Czechoslovakia, 1945–8*, pp. 111–12, 138–40.
28. S. Lowery, 'Hungary', in Toynbee and Toynbee (eds), *Survey*, p. 317ff.; H. Seton-Watson, *Revolution*, p. 97ff.
29. J. Tomaszewski, *Socialist Regimes*, p. 52; Seton-Watson, *Revolution*, p. 192; D. Nemesh, *Osvobozhdenie Vengrii* (Moscow, 1957), p. 148.

30. For the February speech of Rákosi, see A. Ross Johnson, *The Transformation of Communist Ideology* (Cambridge, Mass., 1972) citing the doctoral thesis of W. McCagg. See also *History of the Revolutionary Workers' Movement in Hungary, 1944–62* (Budapest, 1972), pp. 39–40, 52, 88, and Nemesh, *Osvobozhdenie*, pp. 185–7.
31. B. Zhelitski, 'Post-war Hungary, 1944–6,' in Naimark and Gibianskii, *The Establishment*, p. 78.
32. Documents, vol. I, pp. 271–4, 276–300 and 621. See also M. Max, *The United States, Great Britain and the Sovietisation of Hungary, 1945–48* (New York, 1985), p. 33.
33. Max, *The Sovietisation of Hungary*, p. 86; Lowery, 'Hungary'; *Documents*, vol. I, p. 347.
34. Max, *The Sovietisation of Hungary*, p. 88; *Documents*, vol. I, p. 464.
35. Max, *The Sovietisation of Hungary*, p. 89; Lowery, 'Hungary'; *Documents*, vol. I, p. 467.
36. Max, *The Sovietisation of Hungary*, p. 90.
37. *Documents*, vol. I, pp. 559 and 605. Although Britain and the United States protested at the arrest of Béla Kovács, the British authorities at least were convinced that he was guilty of the charges brought by the Soviet authorities; see Max, *The Sovietisation of Hungary*, p. 96. There now seems no doubt that the plot existed, but that its extent and seriousness are certainly open to question. Rákosi told Molotov (see note 38): 'it is a pity the plotters did not have a cache of weapons, then we could have made more of it'; this suggests the plot was sketchy in the extreme.
38. Seton-Watson, *Revolution*, p. 199; *Documents*, vol. I, pp. 613–18.
39. Max, *The Sovietisation of Hungary*, p. 111ff.

3 An End to Diversity

1. G. R. Swain, 'Stalin and Spain, 1944–48,' in C. Leitz and D. J. Dunthorn (eds), *Spain in an International Context, 1936–1959* (Berghahn, Oxford, 1999); A. Ulunyan, *Kommunisticheskaya partiya gretsii* (Moscow, 1994), vol. III, p. 180. Stalin's correspondence with Molotov is discussed in V. O. Pechatnov, '"The Allies are pressing on you to break your will ...": Foreign Policy Correspondence between Stalin and Molotov and other Politburo Members, September–December 1945', *Cold War International History Project: Working Paper No. 26*.
2. The role of the British Labour Party is touched on in S. M. Max, *The United States, Great Britain, and the Sovietisation of Hungary, 1945–58* (New York, 1985), p. 119ff. For a more detailed account, see Ullin Jodah, 'The Labour Party and the Hungarian Social Democrats, 1944–48', University of the West of England, PhD Thesis, 2002.
3. For the Djilas-Molotov meeting, see G. R. Swain, 'The Cominform: Tito's International?' *Historical Journal*, vol. 35 (1992), p. 656.
4. J. Rupnik, *Histoire du Parti Communiste Tchéchoslovaque* (Paris, 1981), p. 193. For Stalin's comments, see *Documents*, vol. I, p. 673, in which Stalin confirms that he had at first suggested participation, only to

change his mind on receipt of Molotov's verdict. For the diplomacy surrounding the Marshall Aid proposals, see S. Parrish, 'The Marshall Plan, Soviet–American Relations and the Division of Europe,' in Naimark and Gibianskii, *The Establishment*, pp. 275–85.The preparatory agenda is referred to on *Documents*, vol. I, p. 689.

5. For the Founding Conference of the Cominform and Tito's speech to the Second Congress of the People's Front, see Swain, 'Cominform'.
6. Events in Slovakia during October 1947 and the first half of November suggest Slánský first tried to reorganise the Slovak National Front, only to have Gottwald intervene to reimpose the status quo; see M. Myant, *Socialism and Democracy in Czechoslovakia, 1945–8* (Cambridge, 1981), p. 173; P. Zinner, *Communist Strategy and Tactics in Czechoslovakia, 1918–48* (London, 1963), p. 193.
7. K. Kaplan, *The Short March: The Communist Takeover in Czechoslovakia, 1945–8* (London, 1981), p. 106; Myant, *Socialism and Democracy in Czechoslovakia, 1945–8*, p. 179.
8. Swain, 'Cominform'.
9. Zinner, *Communist Strategy*, p. 197ff. For the civil service pay deal, see J. Bloomfield, *Passive Revolution: Politics and the Czechoslovak Working Class, 1945–8* (London, 1979), p. 211; for the popular support for the coup, see V. F. Kusin, 'Czechoslovakia', in M. McCauley (ed.), *Communist Power in Europe, 1944–9* (London, 1977), p. 92. A report to Moscow 'on the events in Czechoslovakia' stressed both popular support and 'action committee' intimidation, see *Documents*, vol. I, pp. 806–8.
10. These events can be followed in *Keesings Contemporary Archives*, pp. 9466–10 058.
11. D. Childs, *The GDR: Moscow's Ally* (London, 1983), pp. 15–20; G. Schaffer, *Russian Zone* (London, 1947), pp. 10, 72.
12. Childs, *GDR*, p. 21.
13. Childs, *GDR*, p. 23; *Keesings*, pp. 9032, 9715, 10 028, 10 281.
14. Kaplan, *The Short March*, p. 175.
15. Swain, 'Cominform'.
16. Tito's foreign visits at this time are covered extensively in the Yugoslav daily *Borba*. For Tito's reception, see M. Djilas, *Vlast* (London, 1983), p. 109.
17. Swain, 'Cominform'; G. Ionescu, *Communism in Romania, 1944–62* (Oxford, 1964), p. 151; for the shouts of 'Tito', see the reports of both congresses in *Borba*.
18. See the text of a resolution passed at the instigation of Rákosi by the Hungarian Communist Party Politburo on 8 April 1948, reproduced in V. Dedijer, *Novi prilozi za biografiju Josipa Broza Tita*, vol. III (Belgrade, 1984), p. 388.
19. C. Strbac, *Jugoslavija i odnosi izmedju socialistickih zemalja: subob KPJ i Informbiroa* (Belgrade, 1984), p. 83ff.
20. Z. Brzezinski, *The Soviet Bloc: Unity and Conflict* (Cambridge, Mass., 1971), p. 57.
21. Swain, 'Cominform'; E. Barker, 'Yugoslav Policy Towards Greece, 1947–9,' in L. Baerentzen *et al.* (eds), *Studies in the History of the Greek Civil War* (Copenhagen, 1987); *Documents*, vol. I, p. 762.

22. Swain, 'Cominform'; *Documents*, vol. I, p. 777 and vol. II, p. 45.
23. For the text of the letters, see the Royal Institute of International Affairs, *The Soviet–Yugoslav Dispute* (London, 1948).
24. Swain, 'Cominform'. For Molotov's recollections of the affair, see 'Iz dokumentov iyul'skogo plenuma TsK KPSS, 1955 g.', in *Istoricheskii Archiv*, no. 3 (1999), pp. 4 and 36.
25. T. Toranska, *ONI: Stalin's Polish Puppets* (London, 1987), p. 282.
26. J. Coutouvidis and J. Reynolds, *Poland, 1939–47* (Leicester, 1986), p. 306ff.; *Documents*, vol. I, pp. 815–30.
27. Toranska, *ONI*, p. 287; *Documents*, vol. I, pp. 900–2 and 925.
28. *Documents*, vol. I, p. 939; vol. II, pp. 59 and 173. Had Stalin wanted a trial in Poland, there were ample grounds for one. The Jewish chief of the security service Jakub Berman had had direct contact with Noel Field since his personal secretary had got to know him quite well and had urged Berman to receive him in person. A sixth sense told Berman not to do this, see *Documents*, vol. II, p. 228.
29. For a forceful argument that the Gheorghiu-Dej–Pauker conflict was personal rather than ideological, see Deletant, 'New Light', p. 660. Otherwise see G. Ionescu, *Communism in Romania, 1944–62* (Oxford, 1964), p. 151; *Documents* vol. I, pp. 565, 697 and 747–51 and vol. II, pp. 219 and 744. In September 1949 a Cominform representative informed Stalin that Pătrăşcanu, then under house arrest, had become the focus for gatherings of 'communist veterans' opposed to the regime. As a result he was imprisoned and Stalin informed that he would be tried in spring 1953. When the trial was finally being prepared in August 1953, Gheorghiu-Dej told the Soviet ambassador that Pătrăşcanu had confessed to preparing some sort of coup against the government, but refused to confess that he was an American spy, *Documents*, vol. III, pp. 841 and 952.
30. G. H. Hodos, *Show Trials: Stalinist Purges in Eastern Europe, 1948–54* (New York, 1987), p. 10ff.
31. Hodos, *Show Trials*, p. 15ff.; J. D. Bell, *The Bulgarian Communist Party from Blagoev to Zhivkov* (Stanford, Calif., 1986), p. 104; *Documents*, vol. II, p. 69 (note 2). Because of the problems caused by the opposition of Dimitrov to the trial of his former collaborator, opposition removed by the death of Dimitrov on 2 July 1949, the trial took place after that of Rajk.
32. Hodos, *Show Trials*, p. 26ff. This reconstruction is based on scattered memoir references: for the existence of a USC hospital in Toulouse, see A. London, *On Trial* (London, 1970), p. 33; for the operations of the French Communist Party's Migrant Workers' Office in Toulouse, see I. Gosnjak, 'Jugoslaveni, bivsi dobrovljci u Spaniji, u koncentracionim logorima u Francuskoj', in *Cetrdeset godina: zbornik secanja aktivista jugoslovenskog revolucionarnog radnickog pokreta* (Belgrade, 1960), p. 249. For Field's links with soviet intelligence, see *Documents*, vol. II, p. 229.
33. Hodos, *Show Trials*, p. 30; for the 'partisan route' through Southern France, Northern Italy and Yugoslavia, see Swain, 'Cominform'.

34. Hodos, *Show Trials*, p. 33ff.; *Documents*, vol. II, pp. 66, 95–7, 179 and 231; 'Iz vospominanii M. Rakoshi', *Istoricheskii Archiv*, no. 3 (1997), pp. 112 and 131. For the Cominform Resolution, see *For a Lasting Peace, for a People's Democracy*, 29 November 1949. According to Rákosi, Rajk had met Tito in Paris when *en route* to Spain, and had been in the same French internment camp as Aleksandar Ranković, who became Tito's security chief, see *Documents*, p. 181.
35. Hodos, *Show Trials*, p. 76ff.; E. Loebl, *Stalinism in Prague* (New York, 1968), p. 46.
36. London, *On Trial*, p. 33ff.; E. Loebl, *Stalinism*, p. 46 *et seq.*
37. N. Khrushchev, *Khrushchev Remembers* (London, 1971), p. 217; G. D. Ra'anan, *International Policy Formation in the USSR* (New York, 1983), p. 81.
38. Y. A. Gilboa, *The Black Years of Soviet Jewry, 1939–53* (Boston, Mass., 1971), p. 226ff.
39. Hodos, *Show Trials*, p. 79ff. *Documents*, vol. II, pp. 89, 91, 115, 168–71, 182, 219–22, 267, 327, 580–2, 606–9 and 653–4. For tension between Gottwald and Slánský, see E. Taborsky, *Communism in Czechoslovakia, 1948–60* (Princeton, N.J., 1961), p. 102. Slánský tried to commit suicide in prison, see *Documents*, vol. II, p. 680.
40. Childs, *GDR*, p. 26; J. Richter, 'Re-examining Soviet Policy towards Germany in 1953', *Europe Asia Studies*, vol. 45, no. 4 (1993), p. 676; Hodos, *Show Trials*, p. 114.
41. *Documents*, vol. II, p. 194; B. Press, *The Murder of the Jews in Latvia* (Northwestern University Press, 2000), p. 19.
42. These illustrations from life in the Eastern Bloc at this time were taken more or less at random from contemporary press coverage recorded in *Keesings Contemporary Archives*. The workings of the Stalinist economic system are covered in Chapter 5.
43. A. Ross Johnson, *The Transformation of Communist Ideology* (Cambridge, Mass., 1972), pp. 87–8.
44. Ross Johnson, *The Transformation*, pp. 161–3.
45. Ross Johnson, *The Transformation*, pp. 101–6.
46. Ross Johnson, *The Transformation*, pp. 164–6.
47. S. Clissold, *Djilas: The Progress of a Revolutionary* (London, 1983), pp. 223–5; ibid., p. 203.
48. Cited in Ross Johnson, *The Transformation*, p. 204.
49. Ross Johnson, *The Transformation*, pp. 206–7.
50. M. Djilas, *Rise and Fall* (London, 1985), p. 320. For the Soviet offer to resume diplomatic relations, see *Keesings Contemporary Archives*, p. 13 001, citing *The Times*.
51. Djilas, *Rise and Fall*, p. 320; S. Clissold, *Djilas*, p. 226.
52. A. Rothberg (ed.), *Anatomy of a Moral: The Political Essays of Milovan Djilas* (London, 1959), pp. 39–40, 62–3, 106, 124–42.
53. *Keesings Contemporary Archives*, p. 13 409, citing *The Times*.
54. Ross Johnson, *The Transformation*, p. 169.

4 1956: Communism Renewed?

1. J. Richter, 'Re-examining Soviet Policy towards Germany in 1953', *Europe Asia Studies*, vol. 45 (1993), pp. 673–7.
2. M. Fulbrook, *Anatomy of a Dictatorship* (Oxford, 1995), pp. 180–2; D. Childs, *The GDR: Moscow's German Ally* (London, 1983), p. 31.
3. Fulbrook, *Anatomy*, pp. 184–5; Childs, *GDR*, p. 33.
4. Richter, 'Re-examining', p. 678.
5. For summaries of the Czechoslovak strikes gleaned from the contemporary press, see *Keesings Contemporary Archives*, p. 13 040; the report to the ambassador is in *Documents*, vol. II, p. 924.
6. J. Rainer, 'The New Course in Hungary in 1953', *Cold War International History Project: Working Paper 38*, pp. 8, 16, 19 and 22; Hungary's Secret Speech (Report of Comrade Imre Nagy, 27 June 1953 to the HWP Central Committee), *Labour Focus on Eastern Europe*, no. 1 (1985), p. 11.
7. F. Vali, *Rift and Revolt in Hungary* (Cambridge, Mass., 1961), p. 123.
8. Vali, *Rift and Revolt*, p. 123.
9. I. Nagy, *On Communism: In Defence of the New Course* (London, 1957), p. 207ff.; Rainer, 'New Course', pp. 8 and 38–9; *Documents*, vol. II, p. 937.
10. B. Lomax, *Hungary 1956* (London, 1976), p. 24; Vali, *Rift and Revolt*, p. 153.
11. Vali, *Rift and Revolt*, pp. 154, 206.
12. For the limitations of Malenkov's economic reforms, see A. Nove, *An Economic History of the USSR* (London, 1969), p. 322ff. Otherwise, see G. Litván (ed.), *The Hungarian Revolution of 1956: Reform, Revolt and Repression, 1953–63* (Longman, London, 1996), p. 31.
13. V. Dedijer, *Novi prilozi za biografiju Josipa Broza Tita*, vol. III (Belgrade, 1984), p. 550ff.
14. For Khrushchev's Statement, see *Keesings Contemporary Archives*, p. 14 265, citing the Yugoslav news agency Tanjug.
15. Ibid.
16. Dedijer, *Novi Prilozi*, vol. III, pp. 567–89.
17. Dedijer, *Novi Prilozi*, vol. III, p. 461; M. Djilas, *Rise and Fall* (London, 1983), p. 320.
18. Dedijer, *Novi Prilozi*, vol. III, p. 549.
19. For Tito's speech in Karlovac on 18 July 1955, see *Keesings Contemporary Archives*, p. 14 359, citing Tanjug.
20. 'Iz dokumentov iyul'skogo plenuma Ts K KPSS, 1955 g.', *Istoricheskii Arkhiv*, no. 3 (1999) pp. 4, 10 and 29; P. Zinner (ed.), *National Communism and Popular Revolt in Eastern Europe* (New York, 1956), p. 9. Khrushchev confided his problems in overcoming opposition within the Communist Party Presidium to the Yugoslav ambassador Veljko Micunovic; see V. Micunovic, *Moscow Diary* (London, 1980), p. 27.
21. For Tito's speech and the text of the declaration, see *Keesings Contemporary Archives*, p. 14 937, citing Tanjug; for the Yugoslavs' pleasure with the Declaration, see Micunovic, *Diary*, p. 74.
22. For Tito's secret links with Gheorghiu-Dej, see Dedijer, *Novi Prilozi*, p. 546; for the Yugoslav glee at the downfall of Chervenkov, see J. F. Brown, *Bulgaria under Communist Rule* (London, 1970), p. 67.

23. *Documents*, vol. II, pp. 99, 182, 297 and 318; *Keesings Contemporary Archives*, p. 14 937. For Tito and the protest note concerning the Rajk trial, see *Keesings Contemporary Archives*, p. 10 291, citing Tanjug.
24. Micunovic, *Diary*, pp. 75–6, 178; J. Granville, 'Josip Broz Tto's Role in the 1956 "Nagy Affair"', *Slavonic and East European Review*, vol. 76, no. 4 (1998) pp. 685–6; Litván, *Hungarian Revolution*, p. 47.
25. Micunovic, *Diary*, p. 91.
26. Lomax, *1956*, p. 52ff.
27. Lomax, *1956*, p. 32.
28. Lomax, *1956*, pp. 31, 34; *Borba*, 20 July 1956.
29. *Borba*, 23 and 24 July 1956.
30. Vali, *Rift and Revolt*, p. 249; Micunovic, *Diary*, p. 116.
31. Lomax, *1956*, pp. 47–9, 70; Litván, *Hungarian Revolution*, pp. 54–8.
32. Nagy's words are cited in Lomax, *1956*, p. 68. For the events of 23–25 October, see Litván, *Hungarian Revolution*, p. 59ff.; Vali, *Rift and Revolt*, p. 261ff.; M. Molnár, *Budapest, 1956* (London, 1971), p. 122ff.
33. Ibid. For Kádár, see J. Granville, 'Hungarian and Polish Reactions to the Events of 1956: New Archival Evidence', *Europe–Asia Studies*, vol. 53, no. 7 (2001) p. 1061. For the Soviet Politburo, see 'Kak reshalis' "vopros Vengrii": rabochie zapisi zasedanie presidiuma Ts K KPSS, iyul'-noyabr' 1956 g.', *Istoricheskii Arkhiv*, no. 2 (1996), pp. 87–102 and no. 3 (1996), pp. 87–100. For the Hungarian Politburo, see J. Györkei and M. Horváth (eds), *Soviet Military Intervention in Hungary* (Central European University Press, 1999), pp. 64–79.
34. See *Keesings Contemporary Archives*, p. 15 191, citing contemporary press and news agency reports.
35. Lomax, *1956*, p. 148ff.; Molnar, *Budapest*, pp. 174–5; for Tito's message to Gerő and Kádár concerning workers' councils, see G. Ionescu, *The Break-up of the Soviet Empire in Eastern Europe* (London, 1965), p. 76.
36. Vali, *Rift and Revolt*, for the reminiscences of participants, see F. Feher and A. Heller, *Hungary 1956 Revisited* (London, 1983), p. 51. For the Cominform's assessment of Yugoslav self-management, see *For a Lasting Peace, for a Peoples Democracy*, 7 July 1950, 12 October 1951, 20 June 1952, 7 November 1952 and 3 December 1952. While hostile, these accounts are detailed and informative and mostly written by Romanians, adding credence to the suggestion that the Romanian leadership was not as hostile to Tito as its official stance suggested.
37. Micunovic, *Diary*, p. 131ff.; 'Kak reshalis', p. 87.
38. For Kádár's conciliatory stance on workers' councils and the subsequent fate of workers' councils in Hungary, see Lomax, *1956*, p. 164ff.; for the issue of workers' councils in Soviet–Yugoslav relations, and Yugoslavia's support for Kádár, see Micunovic, *Diary*, p. 178; Soviet support for the Yugoslav concept of workers' councils, and their continued criticism of other aspects of the Yugoslav reforms, is hinted at in *Pravda* articles of 23 and 29 November 1956. At the time, the public side of Soviet–Yugoslav disagreements over Hungary was the presence of Nagy in the Yugoslav Embassy. Hindsight suggests that the question of whether Kádár would stick to the agreement to introduce workers' councils seems to have been equally important.

39. Zinner, *National Communism*, p. 535.
40. A. Kemp-Welch, 'Khrushchev's "Secret Speech" and Polish Politics: The Spring of 1956', *Europe Asia Studies*, vol. 48, no. 2 (1996), pp. 181–206.
41. Granville, 'Hungarian and Polish Reactions', p. 1053. For contemporary press coverage of the Poznan riots, see *Keesings Contemporary Archives*, p. 14 967.
42. Cited in K. Syrop, *Spring into October* (London, 1957), p. 61ff.
43. Zinner, *National Communism*, p. 169.
44. Syrop, *Spring*, p. 83.
45. Syrop, *Spring*, p. 85ff.; L. W. Gluchowski, 'The Soviet–Polish Confrontation of October 1956: The Situation in the Polish Internal Security Corps', *Cold War International History Project: Working Paper no. 17*, p. 30ff.
46. Zinner, *National Communism*, p. 244; K. Reyman and H. Singer, 'The Origins and Significance of East European Revisionism', in L. Labedz (ed.), *Revisionism*, p. 217.
47. T. Toranska, *ONI: Stalin's Polish Puppets* (London, 1987), p. 183; J. F. Brown, *The New Eastern Europe: The Khrushchev Era and After* (London, 1966), pp. 53–4; Reyman and Singer, 'Origins', p. 218.
48. Zinner, *National Communism*, p. 312. Rokossowski's appointment had been Stalin's idea. It was not only opposed by Bierut but by Rokossowski himself, see *Documents*, vol. II, p. 311 and Gluchowski, 'Soviet–Polish Confrontation', p. 89.
49. Dedijer, *Novi Prilozi*, p. 568.
50. R. A. Remington, *The Warsaw Pact* (Cambridge, Mass., 1971), p. 18. The text of the Warsaw Pact is given in *Keesings Contemporary Archives*, p. 14 251.
51. Childs, *GDR*, p. 52; Fulbrook, *Anatomy*, p. 188.
52. G. Ionescu, *Communism in Romania: 1944–62* (Oxford, 1964), pp. 268, 272.
53. A. Bromke, 'Poland's Role in the Loosening of the Communist Bloc', and S. Fischer-Galati, 'Romania and the Sino-Soviet Conflict', both in K. London (ed.), *Eastern Europe in Transition*, pp. 81, 91, 266.
54. Ionescu, *Communism in Romania*, p. 269ff.
55. J. D. Bell, *The Bulgarian Communist Party from Blagoev to Zhivkov* (Stanford, Calif., 1986), p. 115ff. A very brief flowering of the liberal press in Czechoslovakia was confined to the spring of 1956; see F. L. Kaplan, *Winter into Spring: The Czechoslovak Press and the Reform Movement, 1963–8* (New York, 1977), p. 28ff.
56. Djilas' article appeared in the New York socialist paper *The New Leader*. Extracts are reproduced in M. Lasky (ed.), *The Hungarian Revolution: A White Book* (London, 1957), p. 270.
57. Micunovic, *Diary*, pp. 75, 237–320.
58. For the Political Consultative Committee of the Warsaw Pact, see R. A. Remington, *The Warsaw Pact*, p. 37.

5 Actually Existing Socialism in Operation

1. For a much fuller account of how Marx's theoretical constructs were converted into a functioning economic system see: N. Swain, *Hungary:*

The Rise and Fall of Feasible Socialism (London and New York, 1992), pp. 61–8.

2. W. Brus, 'Postwar Reconstruction and Socio-Economic Transformation', in M. C. Kaser and E. A. Radice (eds), *The Economic History of Eastern Europe, 1975–1991*, vol. II (Oxford, 1986), p. 570.
3. J. M. Van Brabant, *Socialist Economic Integration* (Cambridge, Mass., 1980), pp. 31–4. The precise date within 1949 is a matter of some dispute.
4. N. Spulber, *The Economics of Communist Europe* (New York and London, 1957), pp. 21–2. Spulber includes neither the GDR nor Albania, but Albania was clearly the poorest nation in Europe, while the future GDR is clearly categorisable as industrial, even though it included the less industrialised parts of pre-war Germany.
5. Swain, *Hungary: The Rise and Fall*, p. 72.
6. Sources: J. F. Triska (ed.), *Constitutions of the Communist Party States* (Stanford, Calif., 1968); B. Szajkowski (ed.), *Marxist Governments: A World Survey*, 3 vols (London, 1981); R. F. Staar, *Communist Regimes in Eastern Europe*, 4th edn. (Stanford, Calif., 1982); R. J. McIntyre, *Bulgaria: Politics, Economics, and Society* (London and New York, 1988); H.-G. Heinrich, *Hungary: Politics, Economics and Society* (London, 1986); G. Kolankiewicz and P. G. Lewis, *Poland: Politics, Economics and Society* (London and New York, 1988); M. Shafir, *Romania: Politics, Economics and Society* (London and New York); *Keesings Contemporary Archives Record of World Events*.
7. E. Hankiss, *East European Alternatives* (Oxford, 1990), pp. 31–4.
8. J. F. Triska (ed.), *Constitutions of the Communist Party States* (Stanford, Calif., 1968).
9. M. C. Kaser, *Health Care in the Soviet Union and Eastern Europe* (London, 1976).
10. Zs. Ferge, *A Society in the Making* (Harmondsworth, 1979), p. 64.
11. Swain, *Hungary: The Rise and Fall*, p. 188.
12. It is beyond the scope of this book to consider social inequalities under 'actually existing socialism' in any greater depth. The reader is referred to the following works: D. Lane, *The End of Inequality?* (Harmondsworth, 1971); I. Szélenyi, *Urban Inequalities under State Socialism* (Oxford, 1983); Ferge, *A Society in the Making*; Swain, *Hungary: The Rise and Fall*.

6 Reform Communism or Economic Reform

1. F. Fejtő, *A History of the People's Democracies* (Harmondsworth, 1974), pp. 138–55.
2. W. Brus, '1953 to 1956: "The Thaw" and "The New Course"', in M. C. Kaser (ed.), *The Economic History of Eastern Europe, 1919–1975*, vol. III (Oxford, 1986), p. 53; Swain, *Hungary: The Rise and Fall*, pp. 85–95; M. McAuley, *Marxism–Leninism in the German Democratic Republic* (London, 1979), pp. 102–5.
3. Brus, '1953 to 1956 ...', pp. 54–5; W. Brus, '1957–65: In Search of Balanced Growth', in M. C. Kaser (ed.), *The Economic History of Eastern Europe, 1919–1975*, vol. III (Oxford, 1986), pp. 97–8.

4. C. A. Linden, *Khrushchev and the Soviet Leadership, 1957–1964* (Baltimore and London, 1966), pp. 80–7; Brus, '1957 to 1965 ...', pp. 95–6.
5. Brus, '1957 to 1965 ...', pp. 103–20.
6. J. Roesler, 'The Rise and Fall of the Planned Economy in the German Democratic Republic, 1945–1989', *German History*, vol. 9, no. 1 (1991), pp. 51–3.
7. Brus, '1957 to 1965 ...', pp. 110–11; W. Brus, '1966 to 1975: Normalisation and Conflict', in M. C. Kaser (ed.), *The Economic History of Eastern Europe, 1919–1975*, vol. III (Oxford, 1986), pp. 186–7.
8. Brus, '1966 to 1975 ...', pp. 191–3.
9. For a full discussion of Hungary's New Economic Mechanism, see Swain, *Hungary: The Rise and Fall*, pp. 84–114.
10. T. Bauer, 'A Note on Money and the Consumer in Eastern Europe', *Soviet Studies*, vol. XXXV (July 1983), p. 381.
11. For a full discussion of developments in agriculture in Hungary, see N. Swain, *Collective Farms Which Work* (Cambridge, 1985). The key findings of this work are summarised in an article with the same title in T. Shanin, *Peasants and Peasant Societies*, 2nd edn., (Harmondsworth, 1988).
12. W. Brus, '1950 to 1953: The Peak of Stalinism', in M. C. Kaser (ed.), *The Economic History of Eastern Europe, 1919–1975*, vol. III (Oxford, 1986), pp. 22–4; F. Singleton and B. Carter, *The Economy of Yugoslavia* (London, 1982), p. 128.
13. Brus, '1966 to 1975 ...', pp. 165–9; B. McFarlane, *Yugoslavia: Politics, Economics and Society* (London and New York, 1988), p. 126.
14. Brus, '1966 to 1975 ...', p. 167.
15. Brus, '1966 to 1975 ...', p. 195.
16. Brus, '1966 to 1975 ...', pp. 216–17.
17. R. J. Crampton, *A Short History of Modern Bulgaria* (Cambridge, 1987), pp. 178–84.
18. Brus, '1966 to 1975 ...', pp. 218–19; R. J. McIntyre, *Bulgaria: Politics, Economics and Society* (London and New York, 1988), p. 112; G. R. Feiwel, 'Economic Development and Planning in Bulgaria in the 1970s', in A. Nove (ed.), *The East European Economies in the 1970s* (London, 1982), p. 233.
19. Brus, '1966 to 1975 ...', pp. 222–3; A. Smith, 'The Romanian Industrial Enterprise', in I. Jeffries (ed.), *The Industrial Enterprise in Eastern Europe* (Eastbourne and New York, 1981), pp. 64–6.
20. N. C. Pano, *The People's Republic of Albania* (Baltimore, 1968), pp. 179–80, M. Kaser and A. Schnytzer, 'The Economic System of Albania in the 1970s: Developments and Problems', in Nove (ed.), *The East European Economies in the 1970s*, pp. 316–21.
21. Pano, *The People's Republic of Albania*, pp. 130–80.
22. Fejtő, *A History of the People's Democracies*, p. 160.
23. Fejtő, *A History of the People's Democracies*, pp. 158–60, 289–90, 447; M. Shafir, *Romania: Politics, Economics and Society* (London, 1985), pp. 50–71, 159–76; van Brabant, *Socialist Economic Integration*, p. 174.
24. McAuley, *Marxism-Leninism in the German Democratic Republic*, pp. 107, 113, 157.

25. Crampton, *A Short History of Modern Bulgaria*, pp. 179–90; McIntyre, *Bulgaria: Politics, Economics and Society*, p. 68; Fejtő, *A History of the People's Democracies*, pp. 449–50.
26. Fejtő, *A History of the People's Democracies*, p. 176; G. Kolankiewicz and P. G. Lewis, *Poland: Politics, Economics and Society* (London and New York, 1988), p. 180.
27. Fejtő, *A History of the People's Democracies*, pp. 449–50; Crampton, *A Short History of Modern Bulgaria*, p. 183.
28. Cited in Fejtő, *A History of the People's Democracies*, p. 443.
29. M. Dennis, *The German Democratic Republic: Politics, Economics and Society* (Pinter, London, 1988), pp. 47, 91, 118–19; Fejtő, *A History of the People's Democracies*, p. 443; McAuley, *Marxism–Leninism in the German Democratic Republic*, p. 133.
30. Dennis, *The German Democratic Republic*, p. 177.
31. Brus, '1957 to 1965 ...', pp. 118–21; A. Carter, *Democratic Reform in Yugoslavia* (London, 1982), pp. 4–24; McFarlane, *Yugoslavia: Politics, Economics and Society*, pp. 26 and 71; Fejtő, *A History of the People's Democracies*, p. 444.
32. G. L. Weissman (ed.), *Revolutionary Marxist Students Speak Out, 1964–68* (New York, 1972), p. 3; Fejtő, *A History of the People's Democracies*, pp. 179–80, 195; C. M. Hann, *A Village without Solidarity: Polish Peasants in Years of Crisis* (New Haven and London, 1985), pp. 40–1; Kolankiewicz and Lewis, *Poland: Politics, Economics and Society*, pp. 139, 180.
33. Fejtő, *A History of the People's Democracies*, pp. 178, 228, 493; Weissman, *Revolutionary Marxist Students Speak Out, 1964–68*, pp. 5–7; Kolankiewicz and Lewis, *Poland: Politics, Economics and Society*, p. 142.
34. Fejtő, *A History of the People's Democracies*, pp. 289–90, 447–50; Shafir, *Romania: Politics, Economics and Society*, pp. 160–1.
35. *Népszabadság*, 21 January 1962.
36. Fejtő, *A History of the People's Democracies*, pp. 168–9; H-G. Heinrich, *Hungary: Politics, Economics and Society* (London, 1986), pp. 65–6.
37. Good brief accounts of the Czechoslovak events of 1968 can be found in A. Pravda, 'Czechoslovak Socialist Republic', in B. Szajkowski (ed.), *Marxist Governments: A World Survey*, vol. II (London, 1981), pp. 261–92; H. Renner, *A History of Czechoslovakia since 1945* (London and New York, 1989), pp. 49–85.
38. J. Batt, *Economic Reform and Political Change in Eastern Europe* (London, 1988), p. 77.
39. G. Golan, *The Czechoslovak Reform Movement* (Cambridge, 1971), pp. 1–8.
40. M. Myant, *The Czechoslovak Economy 1948–88* (Cambridge, 1989), pp. 95–106, 113.
41. J. Adam, *Economic Reforms in the Soviet Union and Eastern Europe since the 1960s* (London, 1989), p. 58ff.
42. Brus, '1966 to 1975 ...', p. 210.
43. Golan, *The Czechoslovak Reform Movement*, pp. 22–31.
44. Fejtő, *A History of the People's Democracies*, pp. 447–8; Golan, *The Czechoslovak Reform Movement*, p. 278.

45. Dubček's *Blueprint for Freedom* (London, 1968), pp. 132, 144, 152, 165–7.
46. Dubček, *Blueprint*, p. 228.
47. Golan, *The Czechoslovak Reform Movement*, p. 314
48. Golan, *The Czechoslovak Reform Movement*, p. 307.
49. Cited in K. Dawisha, *The Kremlin and the Prague Spring* (Berkeley, Calif., 1984), p. 376; for Brezhnev's belief in Dubček's deceit, the telephone calls and the danger posed by the 14th Congress, see K. Williams, 'New Sources on Soviet Decision-Making during the 1968 Czechoslovak Crisis', *Europe Asia Studies*, vol. 48 (1996), p. 467 and P. G. Pikhoya, 'Chekhoslovakiya, 1968 g.: vzglyad iz Moskvy', *Novaya i noveishaya istoriya*, no. 1 (1995), pp. 39–42.
50. Renner, *A History of Czechoslovakia since 1945*, pp. 75–88.
51. The documents prepared for the 14th Congress of the Czechoslovak Communist Party make clear that the next stage of the Czechoslovak reform was to pass legislation enshrining the revived National Front as the new organisation to which all legal political parties and mass organisations would belong. Once established, political pluralism would take place within the umbrella of the front. However, the documents make equally clear that, for the foreseeable future, and certainly for the next two years, 'it will be necessary to ensure by a complex of well thought out measures that relations with the National Front, and the system of elections, continues to guarantee the hegemony and privileges of the Communist Party'; see J. Pelikan, *The Secret Vysocany Congress* (London, 1971), p. 231.

7 Neo-Stalinism Triumphant

1. Brus, ' 1966 to 1975 …', pp. 142, 150–3.
2. A. Heller and F. Feher, *From Yalta to Glasnost* (Oxford, 1990), p. 163.
3. Shafir, *Romania: Politics, Economics and Society*, pp. 38–94, 178–82, 187; *Keesings Record of World Events.*
4. Shafir, *Romania: Politics, Economics and Society*, pp. 111–14, 178–82, 187.
5. Shafir, *Romania: Politics, Economics and Society*, pp. 117, 142–3; Smith, 'The Romanian Industrial Enterprise', in I. Jeffries (ed.), *The Industrial Enterprise in Eastern Europe*, pp. 75–82; M. Kaser and I. Spigler, 'Economic Reform in Romania in the 1970s', in Nove (ed.), *The East European Economies in the 1970s*, pp. 274–5.
6. Shafir, *Romania. Politics, Economics and Society*, pp. 107–9, 117–18.
7. Shafir, *Romania: Politics, Economics and Society*, pp. 146, 150, 163, 170–3.
8. Brus, '1966 to 1975 …', pp. 220–1; Feiwel, 'Economic Development and Planning in Bulgaria in the 1970s', in A. Nove (ed.), *The East European Economies in the 1970s*, pp. 233–5; Crampton, *A Short History of Modern Bulgaria*, p. 197; McIntyre, *Bulgaria: Politics, Economics and Society*, pp. 99, 101–5. *For a discussion of Hungary's 'symbiotic' policies in agriculture see Swain, Collective Farms*, pp. 51–79.
9. McIntyre, *Bulgaria: Politics, Economics and Society*, pp. 120–1.

10. McIntyre, *Bulgaria: Politics, Economics and Society*, pp. 68, 80–1; L. Holmes, 'People's Republic of Bulgaria', in B. Szajkowski (ed.), *Marxist Governments: A World Survey*, vol. I (London, 1981), pp. 116–44; H. W. Degenhardt (ed.), *Political Dissent* (Harrow, 1983), p. 3.
11. Crampton, *A Short History of Modern Bulgaria*, pp. 191, 201, 205.
12. B. Szajkowski, 'Socialist People's Republic of Albania', in B. Szajkowski (ed.), *Marxist Governments: A World Survey*, vol. I (London, 1981), pp. 34–61.
13. Kaser and Schnytzer, 'The Economic System of Albania in the 1970s; Developments and Problems', in Nove (ed.), *The East European Economies in the 1970s*, pp. 321–4; Brus, '1966 to 1975 ...', p. 299 (includes the quotation cited); M. Milivojevic, 'Albania', in S. White (ed.), *Handbook of Reconstruction in Eastern Europe and the Soviet Union* (Harrow, 1991), pp. 7, 10–11.
14. Milivojevic, 'Albania', in S. White (ed.), *Handbook of Reconstruction in Eastern Europe and the Soviet Union*, pp. 7, 10–11; Szajkowski, Albania ...', p. 42; Kaser and Schnytzer, 'The Economic System of Albania in the 1970s; Developments and Problems', in Nove (ed.), *The East European Economies in the 1970s*, p. 329; P. Sanström and O. Sjöberg, Albanian Economic Performance: Stagnation in the 1980s', *Soviet Studies*, vol. 43, no. 5 (1991), p. 943.
15. H. Lydall, *Yugoslavia in Crisis* (Oxford, 1989), p. 9.
16. D. A. Dyker, *Yugoslavia: Socialism, Development and Debt* (London and New York, 1990), pp. 66–7.
17. Dyker, *Yugoslavia: Socialism, Development and Debt*, pp. 69–70.
18. Dyker, *Yugoslavia: Socialism, Development and Debt*, pp. 69, 72–3, 80–1, 114–15; Lydall, *Yugoslavia in Crisis*, p. 82.
19. A. Carter, *Democratic Reform in Yugoslavia*, pp. 25, 251–4; Dyker, *Yugoslavia: Socialism, Development and Debt*, pp. 77–9.
20. F. Singleton, 'Socialist Federative Republic of Yugoslavia', in B. Szajkowski (ed.), *Marxist Governments: A World Survey*, vol. III (London 1981), p. 796; Dyker, *Yugoslavia: Socialism, Development and Debt*, pp. 87–8, McFarlane, *Yugoslavia: Politics, Economics and Society*, p. 38; B. Magas, 'Yugoslavia: the Spectre of Balkanization', *New Left Review*, no. 174 (March/April, 1989), pp. 9–11.
21. Dyker, *Yugoslavia: Socialism, Development and Debt*, pp. 123–4; Magas, 'Yugoslavia: The Spectre of Balkanization', *New Left Review*, no. 174 (March/April, 1989), pp. 13–14; M. Lee, 'Kosovo: Between Yugoslavia and Albania', *New Left Review*, no. 140 (July/August 1983), p. 63.
22. Renner, *A History of Czechoslovakia since 1945*, pp. 93–103; Fejtő, *A History of the People's Democracies*, p. 482; Pravda, 'Czechoslovak Socialist Republic', in B. Szajkowski (ed.), *Marxist Governments: A World Survey*, p. 268.
23. Brus, '1966 to 1975 ...', pp. 215–16.
24. Adam, *Economic Reforms in the Soviet Union and Eastern Europe since the 1960s*, pp. 190–1, 205–7; Renner, *A History of Czechoslovakia since 1945*, p. 114; G. Wightman and P. Rutland, 'Czechoslovakia', in S. White (ed.), *Handbook of Reconstruction in Eastern Europe and the Soviet Union*, p. 42.
25. Renner, *A History of Czechoslovakia since 1945*, pp. 110–11, 179–80.
26. Renner, *A History of Czechoslovakia*, pp. 121–33.

27. Renner, *A History of Czechoslovakia*, pp. 140–4.
28. Dennis, *The German Democratic Republic*, pp. 35–8.
29. M. Melzer, 'Combine Formation and the Role of the Enterprise in East German Industry', in Jeffries (ed.), *The Industrial Enterprise in Eastern Europe*, pp. 98–105; Dennis, *The German Democratic Republic*, pp. 112, 131–3.
30. A. Åslund, *Private Enterprise in Eastern Europe* (London, 1985), pp. 118–204; Dennis, *The German Democratic Republic*, pp. 140–2.
31. Dennis, *The German Democratic Republic*, pp. 39–40, 78, 114–26, 131, 147, 151–2.
32. N. Swain, 'The Evolution of Hungary's Agricultural System since 1967', in P. G. Hare, H. K. Radice and N. Swain (eds), *Hungary: A Decade of Economic Reform* (London, 1981), pp. 244–7.
33. Swain, *Hungary: The Rise and Fall*, pp. 115–52; H.-G. Heinrich, *Hungary, Politics and Society* (London, 1986), pp. 48, 63, 86.
34. Hann, *A Village*, p. 48.
35. P. Green, 'The Third Round in Poland', *New Left Review*, no. 101–2 (February/April, 1977), pp. 71–8; D. Singer, *The Road to Gdansk* (New York and London, 1981), pp. 157–96.
36. Adam, *Economic Reforms in the Soviet Union and Eastern Europe since the 1960s*, pp. 90–9; Green, 'The Third Round in Poland', *New Left Review*, no. 101–2 (February/April, 1977), p. 81.
37. Green, 'The Third Round in Poland', *New Left Review*, no. 101–2 (February/April, 1977), pp. 71–8, 79–80, 87–96; Hann, *A Village*, p. 44.
38. Green, 'The Third Round in Poland', *New Left Review*, no. 101–2 (February/April, 1977), pp. 99–105; Kolankiewicz and Lewis, *Poland: Politics, Economics and Society*, p. 67; G. Sandford, 'Polish People's Republic', in B. Szajkowski (ed.), *Marxist Governments: A World Survey*, vol. III (London, 1981), p. 570.
39. Singer, *The Road to Gdansk*, pp. 212–27.
40. Singer, *The Road to Gdansk*, pp. 255–72; R. Biezenski, 'The Struggle for Solidarity, 1980–81: Two Waves of Leadership in Conflict', *Europe-Asia Studies*, vol. 48, no. 2 (1996), pp. 269–72.
41. V. Mastny, 'The Soviet Non-invasion of Poland in 1980–81', *Europe-Asia Studies*, vol. 51, no. 2 (1999), pp. 191–206.
42. Kolankiewicz and Lewis, *Poland: Politics, Economics and Society*, pp. 109–10, 185; M. Myant, 'Poland – The Permanent Crisis?' in R. A. Clarke (ed.), *Poland: The Economy in the 1980s* (London, 1989), p. 1; W. Brus, 'Evolution of the Communist Economic System: Scope and Limits', in V. Nee and D. Stark (eds), *Remaking the Economic Institutions of Socialism: China and Eastern Europe* (Stanford, Calif., 1989), p. 257.
43. Kolankiewicz and Lewis, *Poland: Politics, Economics and Society*, p. 127; Polish agricultural policy is more fully discussed in K.-E. Waedekin (ed.), *Communist Agriculture* (London, 1990), p. 279.
44. Kolankiewicz and Lewis, *Poland: Politics, Economics and Society*, pp. 87–93, 164–8; G. Sandford, *Military Rule in Poland* (London, 1986).
45. Kolankiewicz and Lewis, *Poland: Politics, Economics and Society*, pp. 54, 62; Hankiss, *East European Alternatives*, pp. 82–111.

8 The Fall of Actually Existing Socialism

Where no other source is cited, this chapter is based on Western press reports of 1989–91, *Keesings Record of World Events* and two useful source materials for the years of change in Eastern Europe: S. White, *Handbook of Reconstruction in Eastern Europe and the Soviet Union* (Harrow, 1991), and B. Szajkowski, *New Political Parties of Eastern Europe and the Soviet Union* (Harrow, 1991).

1. Fejtő, *A History of the Peoples Democracies*, p. 463.
2. J. Batt, *East Central Europe from Reform to Transformation* (London, 1991), p. 25.
3. Myant, 'Poland – The Permanent Crisis?' in R. A. Clarke (ed.), *Poland: The Economy in the 1980s*, p. 3.
4. Economic Commission for Europe, *Economic Survey of Europe in 1989–1990* (New York, 1990), pp. 87, 116.
5. Kolankiewicz and Lewis, *Poland: Politics, Economics and Society*, pp. 31, 58–9, 100.
6. Kolankiewicz and Lewis, *Poland: Politics, Economics and Society*, p. 71.
7. Kolankiewicz and Lewis, *Poland: Politics, Economics and Society*, p. 133.
8. Kolankiewicz and Lewis, *Poland: Politics, Economics and Society*, p. 75.
9. Kolankiewicz and Lewis, *Poland: Politics, Economics and Society*, p. 28.
10. Economic Commission for Europe, *Economic Survey of Europe in 1989–1990*, p. 204.
11. Renner, *A History of Czechoslovakia since 1945*, pp. 152–3.
12. Economic Commission for Europe, *Economic Survey of Europe in 1989–1990*, pp. 116, 204.
13. Z. A. B. Zeman, *The Making and Breaking of Communist Eastern Europe* (Oxford, 1991), pp. 327–8.
14. Renner, *A History of Czechoslovakia since 1945*, p. 158.
15. Economic Commission for Europe, *Economic Survey of Europe in 1989–1990*, pp. 116, 204.
16. Economic Commission for Europe, *Economic Survey of Europe in 1989–1990*, p. 116.
17. Dyker, *Yugoslavia: Socialism, Development and Debt*, p. 140, 143; Magas, 'Yugoslavia: The Spectre of Balkanization', *New Left Review*, no. 174 (March/April, 1989), p. 6.
18. Dyker, *Yugoslavia: Socialism, Development and Debt*, p. 146.
19. See Chapter 7, for the significance of Kosovo in Serbian national mythology.
20. P. Sanström and O. Sjöberg, 'Albanian Economic Performance: Stagnation in the 1980s', *Soviet Studies*, vol. 43, no. 5 (1991), p. 943.
21. C. Mabbs-Zeno, 'Agricultural Policy Reform in Albania', *CPE Agriculture Report*, vol. IV, no. 6 (November/December 1991), p. 7.

9 Adapting to Capitalism: Consensus or Confrontation?

1. Details on EU and NATO enlargement can be found at: http://europa.eu.int/comm/enlargement/index.htm and http://www.nato.int/.

The apparently superior economic performance of Poland and Slovenia requires some comment. As earlier chapters have revealed, the 1980s were a bad decade economically in both Poland and Yugoslavia. It was therefore relatively easy for them to get back to their 1989 levels.

2. Jan Svejnar, 'Transition Economies: Performance and Challenges', *Journal of Economic Perspectives*, vol. 16, no. 1 (Winter 2002), p. 5.
3. There are clear summaries of events in Poland until the end of 1994 in D. S. Mason, 'Poland' in S. White *et al.*, *Developments in East European Politics* (Basingstoke, 1993); in F. Millard, 'Poland', in B. Szajkowski (ed.), *Political Parties of Eastern Europe, Russia and its Successor States* (Harlow, 1994); and L. Vinton, 'Poland' in the journal *Transition: 1994 in Review.* For events in Poland from 1995 to 1996, see regular reports in *Keesings Record of World Events.*
4. For 1997 onwards see annual and weekly reports given by *Transitions on Line* (TOL) (http://www.tol.cz) and daily *Newsline Reports* by Radio Free Europe, Radio Liberty (http://www.rferl.org).
5. There are clear summaries of events in Hungary until the end of 1994 in N. Swain, 'Hungary', in White, *Developments*, in M. Pittaway and N. Swain 'Hungary', in Szajkowski, *Political Parties*, and in E. Oltay, 'Hungary', in *Transition: 1994 in Review.* For events in Hungary from 1995 to 1996, see Z. Barany, 'Socialist-Liberal Government Stumbles through its First Year', *Transition*, no. 13 (1995); Zs. Szilayi, 'Hungary', in *Transition: Year in Review 1996*; and the regular reports in *Keesings.*
6. See note 4.
7. See J. Pehe, 'Czech Republic', in *Transition: 1994 in Review.* For the rise of the Czech Social Democrats, see S. Kettle, 'Straining at the Seams', *Transition*, no. 9 (1995), and his 'The Rise of the Social Democrats', *Transition*, no. 13 (1995). For the elections, see *Keesings*, pp. 41 152, 41 199. For the 1997 crisis, see *Business Central Europe* (July/August 1997) p. 19. Also, Slay, 'Elections' and his 'Banking Scandals Send Political Reverberations', *Transition*, no. 22 (1996); S. Kettle, 'Of Money and Mortality', *Transition*, no. 3 (1995).
8. See note 4.
9. For Slovakia between 1992 and 1994, see G. Wightman, 'The Czech and Slovak Republics', in White, *Developments*, K. Henderson, 'The Slovak Republic', in Szajkowski, *Political Parties*, and S. Fisher, 'Slovakia', in *Transition: 1994 in Review.*
10. The growing tension between Mečiar and Kováč is discussed in S. Fisher, 'Tottering in the Aftermath of Elections', *Transition*, no. 4 (1995). The abduction, and other clashes between Mečiar and Kováč, are also reported in *Keesings*, pp. 40 511, 40 568, 40 734; and summarised in S. Fisher, 'Slovakia', *Transition: Year in Review 1996.* For local government reform, see M. Bútora and P. Huncik, *Global Report on Slovakia* (Bratislava, 1997). For the anti-Mečiar demonstration, see Fisher, 'Slovakia'. The referendum affair is summed up in *Financial Times*, 26 May 1997.
11. See note 4.
12. For Slovenia in 1994, see P. Moore and S. Markotich, 'Slovenia', in *Transition: 1994 in Review.* For Slovenia in 1995–6, see S. Markotich,

'Stable Support for Extremism', *Transition*, no. 4 (1995), his 'Slovenia' in *Transition: 1996 in Review*, and *Keesings*, pp. 40 912, 41 376.

13. See note 4.
14. For events in Albania in 1992–4, see B. Szajkowski, 'Albania', in Szajkowski, *Political Parties*, and F. Schmidt, Albania', in *Transition: 1994 in Review*. For concern about corruption, see L. Zanga, 'Corruption Takes Its Toll on Berisha Government', *Transition*, no. 7 (1995).
15. F. Schmidt, 'The Opposition's Changing Face', *Transition*, no. 11 (1995), and the same author's 'Can the Democrats Win?' *Transition*, no. 12 (1995). For the Nano review and Genocide Law, see *Keesings*, pp. 40 734 and 41 199. For the elections, see F. Schmidt, 'Albania's Democrats Consolidate Power', in *Transition: Year in Review 1996*; and *Keesings*, p. 41 152.
16. F. Schmidt, 'Pyramid Schemes Leave Albania on Shaky Ground', *Transition*, no. 4 (1997) and TOL annual report for 1997.
17. See note 4.
18. For an overview of events in Romania 1992–4, see R. Bing and B. Szajkowski, 'Romania', in Szajkowski, *Political Parties*, and M. Shafir and D. Ionescu, 'Romania', in *Transition: 1994 in Review*. Also M. Shafir, 'Ruling Party Formalises Relations with Extremists', *Transition*, no. 5 (1995). For privatisation, D. Ionescu, 'Birth Pangs of Privatisation', *Transition*, no. 5 (1995); and *Business Central Europe* (July/August 1997), pp. 37–46.
19. For the elections, see M. Shafir and D. Ionescu, 'Radical Change in Romania', in *Transition: Year in Review 1996*, and *Keesings*, p. 41 376.
20. See note 4.
21. For Bulgaria between 1992 and 1994, see J. D. Bell, 'Bulgaria', in White, *Developments*, B. Szajkowski, 'Bulgaria', in Szajkowski, *Political Parties*, and K. Engelbrekt, 'Bulgaria', in *Transition: 1994 in Review*. For the triumphalism of the BSP, see S. Krause, 'The White Book: Pointing the Finger', *Transition*, no. 10 (1995), and the same author's 'The Coat of Arms as a Political Pawn', *Transition*, no. 13 (1995). For the declining electoral support of the BSP, see S. Kause, 'Socialists at the Helm', *Transition*, no. 4 (1995), and the same author's 'Elections Reveal Blue Cities Amid Red Provinces', *Transition*, no. 24 (1995). For divisions in the BSP, see S. Krause, 'Bulgaria Survives a Dire Year', in *Transition: Year in Review 1996*, and *Keesings*, p. 40 782.
22. I. Krastev, 'Back to Basics in Bulgaria', *Transition*, no. 4 (1997); also Krayse, 'Bulgaria Survives', *Keesings*, p. 41 414, and TOL 1997 report for Bulgaria.
23. See note 4.
24. For events in Macedonia in 1992–4, see J. Allcock, 'Macedonia', in Szajkowski, *Political Parties*, R. Mickey, 'Macedonia', in *Transition: 1994 in Review*; and D. Perry, 'On the Road to Stability or Destruction', *Transition*, no. 15 (1995).
25. S. Krause, 'Moving Toward Firmer Ground in Macedonia', in *Transition: Year in Review 1996*, and *Keesings*, p. 40 961. See also TOL report for 1997.
26. See note 4.

27. See 'Topic: Croatia', *Transition*, no. 21 (1995); D. S. Sucic, 'A Groundswell of Dissatisfaction in Croatia', in *Transition: Year in Review 1996*; and *Keesings*, p. 41 376.
28. See note 4.
29. *Keesings*, p. 41 414, also TOL reports to 1997.
30. See note 4.
31. See note 4.
32. *Keesings*, p. 40 889.
33. For the Sporazum, see H. C. Darby *et al.*, *A Short History of Yugoslavia* (Cambridge, 1966), pp. 199–200, 204–5. Maps 1 and 36, if superimposed, show clearly how this agreement left the Krajina Serbs in Croatia and allowed the Serbs to control the Muslim and Croat territory needed to provide a land bridge to Banja Luka. For the Tudjman–Milosevic meeting, see L. Silber and A. Little, *The Death of Yugoslavia* (Harmondsworth, 1995), p. 143.
34. This summary of the war from autumn 1991 until early 1994 is derived from Silber and Little, *The Death of Yugoslavia*. For the Croat–Muslim Federation, see *Keesings*, p. 39 925.
35. For events during 1995 and the Dayton Accord, see *Keesings*, pp. 41 199, 41 376, 41 414; and P. Moore, 'An End Game in Croatia and Bosnia', *Transition*, no. 20 (1995).
36. For problems establishing the Croat–Muslim Federation, see *Keesings*, pp. 40 961, 41 018, 41 086, 41 152, 41 236, 41 414; R. Donia, A Test Case for the Croat–Muslim Federation', *Transition*, no. 20 (1995); and P. Moore, 'United on Paper but not in Deed', in *Transition: Year in Review 1996*. The formation of the Union of Bosnia-Hercegovina is chronicled in *Keesings*, pp. 41 278, 41 330, 41 376, 41 414. See also TOL report 1997.
37. See note 4.
38. See note 4.

INDEX